The English Novel

form and function

The English Novel

form and function

Dorothy Van Ghent

RINEHART & COMPANY, INC. NEW YORK

Acknowledgment and thanks are due to the following for permission to reprint excerpts from writings under their copyright:

to the Columbia University Press for excerpts from the Hatfield edition of THE COMPLETE POEMS OF EMILY BRONTË

to J. M. Dent & Sons Ltd. for excerpts from LORD JIM by Joseph Conrad

to Harcourt, Brace and Company, Inc. for excerpts from MESSAGES by Ramon Fernandez; to Harcourt, Brace and Company, Inc. also for excerpts from THE LIVING NOVEL by V. S. Pritchett

to St. Martin's Press, Incorporated, New York, Macmillan & Co., Ltd., of London, and the Trustees of the Hardy Estate for excerpts from TESS OF THE D'URBERVILLES by Thomas Hardy

to Random House, Inc. for an excerpt from "September 1, 1939" by W. H. Auden; to Random House and The Modern Library for the excerpt from Wilson Follett's Introduction to the Modern Library Edition of THE EGOIST by George Meredith

to Charles Scribner's Sons for excerpts from THE EGOIST by George Meredith

to The Viking Press, publishers of THE PORTABLE JAMES JOYCE for excerpts from A PORTRAIT OF THE ARTIST AS A YOUNG MAN by James Joyce; to The Viking Press also for excerpts from SONS AND LOVERS by D. H. Lawrence

To BEN LEHMAN

*who first illuminated for me
the critical approach
to literature
as a search for the principle
of form in the work
and implicitly as a search
for form in the self*

Preface

The present series of studies is designed for the general reader and the student as an accompaniment to a rereading of eighteen classical novels. Aside from *Don Quixote,* the series is confined to English novels, followed in roughly chronological order.

With a number of these novels the reader will have been familiar since childhood. With some of the others, familiarity will have been limited to the title and a certain warped, dusty, elderly look of the back of the book as it stood in the family library. The studies offered here are exercises in curiosity, curiosity to penetrate behind the aspect of familiarity, curiosity to see what these novels will look like when opened up side by side in a perspective of three centuries, and, above all, curiosity to explore each of them in its assumed character as a work of art.

The curiosity is not, I think, of the kind called "idle." Two convictions motivate it. First, that novels have their primary interest in the illumination they cast upon life, not life somewhere else and at another time, but immediately here, immediately now. And second, that novels are able to cast illumination upon life only insofar as they are coherent works of art.

The reason for the chronological order of the series is chiefly that examples of an art are developments of the history of the art, and understanding and just appraisement of the examples ask for experience of the history. Furthermore, a novel does change to our perception when set in a special environment of other novels. In the environment provided here—that of well-known English novels in their historical sequence—each of these familiar books inevitably acquires an aspect of freshness, of newness, just by the special juxtaposition with its neighbors. By sheer arrangement, they illuminate each other—and us.

As for placing *Don Quixote* first in a list otherwise of English novels,

Lionel Trilling has expressed the point of justification when he says, in his essay on "Manners, Morals, and the Novel,"

> In any genre it may happen that the first great example contains the whole potentiality of the genre. It has been said that all philosophy is a footnote to Plato. It can be said that all prose fiction is a variation on the theme of *Don Quixote*.

Particularly in reading English novels of the eighteenth century, one is aware of the model set by Cervantes. But even in much later works, when that model has been superseded by others, and when technique has undergone many changes, one recognizes certain generic concerns that are shared with Cervantes by, for instance, Conrad and James and Joyce, as they were also by Fielding and Sterne and Jane Austen; and the recognition of these concerns enlarges our understanding of the later work and deepens our pleasure in it.

Since the problem of the studies is to understand each novel as a work of art, the matter of techniques in fiction is essential to discussion. I have tried to concentrate the earlier studies on single dominant procedures. The discussion of *Don Quixote*, for example, asks for special attention to the procedures of parody and paradox; that of *The Pilgrim's Progress*, to the uses of symbolism and allegory; that of *Moll Flanders*, to the methods of documentary realism and of irony; that of *Clarissa Harlowe*, to the behavior of myth; that of *Tom Jones*, to the function of plot; that of *Pride and Prejudice*, to the activities of style; and so on. It is hoped that, in this incremental fashion, a shared terminology will be established that will be lucid and consistent for this particular undertaking.

In trying to ascertain and place in focus the pattern of each novel as an aesthetic whole, I have been deeply indebted to the critical work of others. A number of the novels considered here have not received very much attention from analytical criticism; but many of them have had so much expert scholarship brought to them, and so many fine insights turned on them in recent years, that a survey of the present kind can do no more than accept with gratitude and attempt to use those insights for its own limited purpose. Detailed acknowledgment is made in the course of the work wherever the discussion has had its source in the findings or suggestions of others.

The book has a special indebtedness to the students in my courses in the novel given at Kansas University from 1948 to 1951. Their constant determination that the novel needed to justify itself by a relationship with life, with *their lives,* has given the book its chief assurance of orientation toward reality.

I should like to express personal gratitude to Sidney Schiffer and David Fanger for their critical reading of a number of the sections of the book; to Robert Brown for his help in research problems; to Thomas Bledsoe, College Editor of Rinehart's, for his warm good faith, which has exercised itself in palpable, practical ways, as well as for his excellent critical suggestions; and to my son, Roger Van Ghent, for his loyal endurance, his sustaining trust.

D. V. G.

University of Vermont
June, 1953

Contents

Contents

Essays in Analysis

Introduction

The subject matter of novels is human relationships in which are shown the directions of men's souls. This is the subject matter also of drama and of the great histories. Let us make a few distinctions among these kinds of writing that have the same subject matter. The distinctions are fairly obvious, but for the sake of common points of reference and common consent it is helpful to get the obvious expressed.

Drama is subject to the conventions of the stage; people are conceived as if they were to be seen and heard in person, under the physical restrictions of tangible space and time. The novel is free of these conventions, although it has others. It can use all sorts of discursive methods that the drama cannot use. But it employs dramatic method most liberally, for it represents human beings *as if* in tangible space and time, that is, "scenically" placed and related. Both the novel and the drama are history in a certain sense: they tell of how people lived or live, their manners, what they held important, how they went about getting what they got, their conflicts, their errors, their heroism. Since some novels look very much like "real" history, like a factual social record, we need to be rather careful in defining the characterizing differences between novels and history.

Like a science, or like mathematics, but unlike history, the novel proceeds by hypothesis. It says, implicitly, "Given such and such conditions, then such and such would take place." The hypothesis on which a novel is built is the abstract aspect of its form. It takes from life the conditions for its hypothesis; that is, it starts from the empirical data that are the "given" data of sentient experience. But it selects and organizes them in a way that suggests a purely creative issue—a series of hypothetical events not "given" at all but cogent as cause and effect from the initial selection.

Being a hypothetical structure, the novel is able to give a leverage to the empirically known and push it into the dimension of the unknown, the possible. Its value lies less in confirming and interpreting the known than

3

in forcing us to the supposition that *something else might be the case*. It is for this reason that the novel is a source of insight.

The fictional hypothesis is peculiar in that it has to carry at every moment the full weight of all its concrete experimental data. For the rate at which bodies fall in a vacuum, it is perfectly irrelevant to science whether the bodies might be feathers or men, ostrich feathers or feathers of a Chinese nightingale, politicians or plumbers. In the equation $x + y = 7$, it is perfectly irrelevant to mathematics whether the figures are written in green ink or blue, on paper or in the sand, or even not written at all. But for fiction the particular body that a thing has is of the very greatest importance to the whole fictional structure. Does it squeak, is it scared, is it brown, is it round, is it chilly, does it think, does it smash? Questions of this kind fiction has to be constantly concerned with in order to have any formal existence at all.

The procedure of the novel is to individualize. As with other art forms, what it has to say that is of collective value is said by inference from individual concrete things. History, on the other hand, proceeds by generalization. It treats people as groups; and when individuals appear they appear as catalysts of large collective actions or as representatives of groups, their significance being that of the group forces, the collection, the sum. This is a difference of convention, and on the conventions of an art depends its special expressiveness.

"After the death of Frederic the Second," Gibbon says,

> Germany was left a monster with a hundred heads. A crowd of princes and prelates disputed the ruins of the empire: the lords of innumerable castles were less prone to obey, than to imitate their superiors; and according to the measure of their strength, their incessant hostilities received the names of conquest or robbery. Such anarchy was the inevitable consequence of the laws and manners of Europe; and the kingdoms of France and Italy were shivered into fragments by the violence of the same tempest.

Let us place beside this passage, describing a state of anarchy, one from *Vanity Fair,* also describing a state of anarchy. Jos Sedley has just heard the rumor of British defeat at Waterloo.

> Such is the force of habit, that even in the midst of his terror he began mechanically to twiddle with his hair, and arrange the cock of his hat.

Then he looked amazed at the pale face in the glass before him, and especially at his mustachios, which had attained a rich growth . . . They *will* mistake me for a military man, thought he, remembering Isidor's warning as to the massacre with which all the defeated British army was threatened; and staggering back to his bed-chamber, he began wildly pulling the bell which summoned his valet.

Isidor answered that summons. Jos had sunk in a chair—he had torn off his neck-cloths, and turned down his collars, and was sitting with both his hands lifted to his throat.

"*Coupez-moi, Isidor,*" shouted he: "*vite! coupez-moi!*"

Isidor thought for a moment he had gone mad, and that he wished his valet to cut his throat.

"*Les moustaches,*" gasped Jos; "*les moustaches—coupy, rasy, vite!*"

In the passage from Gibbon all is plural and collective. We need to know nothing specific about any prelate or lord or about any individual act of hostility or violence: the sum of all the individual situations is sufficiently communicative. In the passage from Thackeray, all is singular and particular, from particular gesture and thought down to the gasp of the voice and Jos's individually bad French. Communicated by this passage in its context are more than specific images of gestures and sounds, although it is all made up of the specific. In Jos's anarchy of soul is read with horrifying vividness the anarchy of a city, and still more, the anarchy of a culture. And yet the complex general meaning of the scene is dependent wholly upon particularity, or "embodiment," and would disintegrate without such embodiment.

Human experience is organized in patterns that are in movement, patterns that some philosophers call "events"—emphasizing the temporal or moving aspect of them—and that some psychologists call "fields of perception," or Gestalten—emphasizing the content of them, as if the content were momentarily static. Inhering in the patterns are sensuous traits (temperature, light, color, texture, sound, and so on); inhering in them also are multitudes of traits of memory, emotion, and thought. We tend to think of events in experience as bodiless, because they slide into each other as stones and trees do not. But held quiet by the mind they are seen to have bodies—to have individual form and function. Fiction tries to isolate the principle of coherence in events, the active principle that holds together all the multitude of particular traits that an event has, and the more extensive principle that makes one event slide into another in human lives. Reflected by the mind, the principle that makes the traits in an event cohere, and the principle that controls the relationship between events, are what we call "ideas."

Philosophy and the sciences use certain abstractive languages for the expression of ideas; and, because of the association of ideas with abstractive language, the reader who turns to the novel from other disciplines may not be willing immediately to recognize the novel's ability to express ideas; for he may feel that the novel's reliance on imagery—imagery of speech sounds and physical groupings and all the other kinds of imagery that make for the novel's necessary "embodiment" of its subject—incapacitates this medium for the expression of valuable ideas. Or he may have the impulse to locate the ideas in a novel only in those passages where the language is that of abstract conceptualism—passages in which, it is possible, the novel's ideas may show at their poorest, or in which the author may even clumsily and blindly falsify the ideas actually inherent in his work. The novel is able to express the most profound ideas, but, because of the nature of this medium, these will lie implicitly in the conjunction of the events that are bodied forth. The ideas in a novel are largely for the reader's inference, his inference of the principles by which the happenings in the book are related to each other.

A novel itself is one complex pattern, or Gestalt, made up of component ones. In it inhere such a vast number of traits, all organized in subordinate systems that function under the governance of a single meaningful structure, that the nearest similitude for a novel is a "world." This is a useful similitude because it reflects the rich multiplicity of the novel's elements and, at the same time, the unity of the novel as a self-defining body. The novel's planetary orbit lies through different minds and different generations of minds, each exerting its special pushes and pulls upon the novel's substance, each interpreting it according to the different spiritual constitution of each. How are we to judge a novel? How are we to evaluate it among other novels? Its strenuous orbit through different minds and generations, each observing it and understanding it with some measure of difference, would seem to deny it any final value status for the reader who approaches it with an awakened critical instinct and a desire for objectively valid judgment.

The sound novel, like a sound world, has to hang together as one thing. It has to have integral structure. Part of our evaluative judgment

6

is based on its ability to hang together *for us.* And like a world, a novel has individual character; it has, peculiar to itself, its own tensions, physiognomy, and atmosphere. Part of our judgment is based on the concreteness, distinctness, and richness of that character. Finally, we judge a novel also by the cogency and illuminative quality of the view of life that it affords, the idea embodied in its cosmology. Our only adequate preparation for judging a novel evaluatively is through the analytical testing of its unity, of its characterizing qualities, and of its meaningfulness—its ability to make us more aware of the meaning of our lives. All these tests test the value of the novel only *for us,* and value for us is all the value that matters. But if the particular novel has been integral and characterful and meaningful for other individuals and other generations as well, however different its appearance to them, the book automatically extends our lives in amplitude and variousness.

ON *Don Quixote*

Perhaps the simplest and yet the most adequate idea which will help us to enter understandingly into this book is the idea of a structure based upon a system of contrasts. The reader is struck first of all with the fertilely humorous contrast between the Knight and his Squire—between the formal, ideal nature of things as they appear to Quixote's mind, and the concrete, down-to-earth nature of things as they appear to Sancho's mind. This contrast offers the germ of the whole drama of adventures; but other contrasts, both minute and on an immense scale, block out the architecture of the book. Between the two volumes of *Don Quixote*— that published in 1605 and that published in 1615—there is a major contrast of narrative design: the 1605 volume contains five individual short novels whose content is apparently dissociated from the main narrative concerning Sancho and Quixote; the 1615 volume contains no digressive interludes of this kind. The settings of the 1605 volume are those of the highway, the inn where strangers meet, lonely landscapes stretching beyond the isolated traveler, craggy mountains, dark night when strange sounds are heard and ominous or lovely visions are conjured up; the settings of the 1615 volume are for the greater part domestic and urban, the populous estate of a grandee where Quixote and Sancho are invited to stay for an extended visit, the town houses of bourgeois gentlemen, city streets, the certainties outlined by sunlight.

Other contrasts are so profuse, from those of the largest and most general kind, down to contrasts between individual motifs (details of action) and even to types of nouns coupled in a single sentence, that we are led to fix on this principle as the governing structural principle of the book. Quixote first comes before the reader as a living person (in the sense in which characters "live" in fiction); but quite suddenly, in the middle of a harrowing adventure, he becomes someone invented by

9

a Moorish author whose manuscripts Cervantes says he has discovered. Thereafter he is a walking hybrid of antitheses: both a man and a literary invention, a living character and an imaginary character, a book-man and a man-book. Among the *novelle* (little novels) of the 1605 volume, one story—Marcela's—is an old-fashioned pastoral concerned with an academic love problem; both setting and problem are idealistic, and the handling is philosophical. Another—Cardenio's story—is a modern story of psychological tenebrosities, the intricate webs formed by the conscience of a solitary individual. Another—Dorotea's history—is a study in the social significance of sex. Still another—the story of the "Curious Impertinent"—is a study in a peculiarly modern performance with which we have become acquainted in the novels of André Gide under the name of the "gratuitous act": a man puts his wife's virtue under trial for no reason at all except the desire to experiment. In these *novelle,* as they follow one after the other, we see contrasts of philosophical handling against psychological handling, problems of the individual moral will contrasted against social problems, inward action contrasted with outward action, solitary aberrations set in contrast with public complacencies and conventions. A number of these stories, related as events that had happened in the past, have their action finished, not in past time, but in the immediate and present time of the main narrative of the adventures of Quixote and Sancho, so that another contrast is set up before the reader's mind, between "story" time and "real" time.

Frequently the contrasts take the form of antithetical parallelisms.[1] At the end of the 1605 volume, Quixote is brought home in a cage with all the indignity of a wild brute; at the end of the 1615 volume, he returns home voluntarily under a contract of honor. There are two descents underground: Quixote descends of his own desire and choice into the cave of Montesinos and has there a consummatory vision, peaceful and beautiful; later Sancho stumbles by accident into a deep pit with his donkey, remains for a while there starved and abandoned, and is finally rescued by a compassionate robber. The idealized pastoral episode of the 1605 volume, in which the heroes dine pleasantly with goatherds and listen to the amorous songs of shepherds, is antithetically paralleled in the 1615 volume by the "pastoral" adventure with the bulls and the

---

[1] This aspect of the book is discussed by Joaquin Caselduero in his essay "The Composition of *Don Quixote*," in *Cervantes across the Centuries,* edited by Angel Flores and M. J. Benardete (New York: The Dryden Press, Inc., 1947).

swine, an adventure of the most brutal and disillusioning kind. There are similar parallels among other episodes, that are parallel in the sense that the *form* of the adventure is the same in each (the return home, the descent into a cave, and so forth) but antithetical and offering contrast in the sense that one adventure presents us with one kind of reality, one set of values, one order of being, and the other presents us with a different kind of reality, a different set of values, a different order of being.

One readily perceives that, in so complex a world of contrasts, there must be something more at stake than the "right" and the "wrong" of certain ways of thinking and modes of behavior as exemplified by Quixote and Sancho themselves. The contrasts pile up in too great a multitude for any pragmatic moral theory to keep them rigidly systematized; and the contrasted terms do not always form themselves as an occasion for acts of judgment, on the reader's part, between "right" and "wrong" or "true" and "false," but play freely among hundreds of antithetical relationships. Two critical concepts—the related concepts of paradox and parody—will help us to ascertain the function of contrast in *Don Quixote*.

The word "paradox" is formed out of a prefix meaning "beside" or "contrary to" and a root meaning "opinion." It refers to the phenomenon in which one thought, opinion, or interpretation of a situation is set up "beside," and simultaneously with, another and different, even opposing, interpretation. The word "parody" is formed from the same prefix and a root meaning "song" or "poem" and referred originally to a song or poem placed in sequence with ("beside") another song or poem. The common element between the meanings of the two words is the element of a simultaneous appearance of two different things, but it can easily be seen that the meanings would develop dissimilarly, inasmuch as a poem contains a good many more elements than an opinion, so that a "parody" —as this word has come to be applied—might be a vast arabesque of interlinked perceptions, while a "paradox" would continue to refer to a concentrated opposition of two outlooks or views both of which had to be held in the mind at once without a discarding of either one.

We shall speak of paradox first, using for illustration the episode of Quixote's "rescue" of the peasant boy on his first sally. The boy has been tied to a tree and beaten by his master because he demanded honest wages. According to Quixote's interpretation of the situation, the boy's demand is just, the master had treated him unjustly, and a Righter of Wrongs and Liberator of the Oppressed might act here in the rational name of justice. On the other hand, the boy's interpretation of the situation is determined by the physical eventuality far more decidedly than by the justice or injustice of the affair; he receives a much worse beating after he is "rescued" than before; hence, to him, Quixote's justice is an injustice. Clearly, the two outlooks are incommensurable, and yet, as clearly, the reader cannot eliminate either one from his own view of the situation; he cannot eliminate the ideal of human justice as an absurdity, without diminishing his vision of life to the scope of a brute's eye; nor can he eliminate the actualities of human psychology and practice as shown in the relationships of the boy and his master. The situation, then, is "paradoxical," in that one event shows two opposed aspects which are both "real" but which are antithetical to each other.

We should be fairly careful, among the paradoxes of *Don Quixote*, not to engage too freely in speculative "if's" about a hero and a story that are not *this* hero and *this* story—we should be careful, that is, to confine our attention to the book Cervantes has written and not to read it as a book we ourselves might write about a man-of-the-worldly and commonsensical Quixote who avoids such troublesome things as paradox by never allowing a paradoxical situation to arise. It might be suggested, for instance, that Quixote, though right in principle was wrong in his methods, and that "if" he had been sensible enough to make a preliminary investigation of the farmer's whereabouts and then abducted the boy and taken him home for his aunt to adopt, justice would truly have been accomplished, ideal and practice commensurated. Obviously such a hero would have to have another name than Quixote, since the name Quixote stands only for that maladdressed man who makes paradoxes sprout. Adventure after adventure repeats the formula, whose marvelous fertility lies in a simultaneity of contrasted extremes. We would sterilize the book if we should try to wring from it always a moral example or a preference for one kind of action or one view over another. The living reality which the book offers is that of the paradox embodied in action, the ineluctable mixture that is at once ideal and corporeal, spirit and flesh. Is it not in this kind of truth to existence that Sancho and Quixote themselves go forth, as companions?

Parody covers more extensive ground than paradox. It might be thought of as a vast complicated system of paradoxes. This idea of parody, however, would emphasize too strongly the notion of direct oppositions. It is, as a matter of fact, this particular idea of parody that dominates our usual loose use of the word. Loosely, we tend to mean by parody a burlesque imitation of something, showing the weaknesses or falsehood of the object imitated. In this sense, the main feature of parody would be not unlike the main feature of debate, implying that one view of things was a "wrong" view and another the "right" view, just as debate is postulated on the idea that there must be a right side and a wrong side of a question (for example, prohibition should or should not be repealed, the western European countries should or should not receive food or arms support, and so forth). But it is possible for parody to be much more complex than debate. Instead of confronting two opposing views with each other, in order that a decision between them be arrived at, parody is able to intertwine many feelings and attitudes together in such a way that they do not merely grapple with each other antagonistically but act creatively on each other, establishing new syntheses of feeling and stimulating more comprehensive and more subtle perceptions. Parody—except that of the crudest kind—does not ask for preferential judgments and condemnations. It is a technique of *presentation;* it offers a field for the joyful exercise of perception and not a platform for derision.

A parody of romances of knight-errantry provides the germinal suggestion, the propagative idea, as it were, of all the action in *Don Quixote*. We have already become well enough aware of the complexity of the book so that we shall not be tempted to take this statement narrowly to mean—as it has often meant in casual-minded academic discussions of *Don Quixote*—that the book can be pigeonholed as an attempt to laugh the old-fashioned romances of chivalry out of existence. If the book were to be adequately described only in this way, we would probably not be reading it ourselves but would leave it for scholars; for our interest in the reading habits of the seventeenth century and in the fact that some people at that time acquired unrealistic notions from chivalric romances cannot be very intense. The parody of knight-errantry is the governing schematic shape of the action in *Don Quixote*, as a journey into danger is the governing schematic shape of the action in *The Pilgrim's Progress* and in Conrad's novels, and the criminal investigation in some of Dostoevski's novels and in Kafka's *The Trial*. But the technique of parody operates intensively in the detail of *Don Quixote*, as well as providing the framework of the action. To illustrate its operation, let us consider the Knight's vigil at the horse trough, again an incident from his first sally. In the loose and inadequate sense of parody, in which parody

13

resembles debate by offering two sides of a situation or problem, one of which must be "right" and the other "wrong," the vigil at the horse trough tells us that Quixote's world is not what he thinks it is, that "reality" is much rougher and more prosaic than what appears to his idealizing imagination: that the armor is not armor but pasteboard, that the trough is not an altar, that the inn is not a castle, that nothing "sacred" and no "consecration" has taken place but only a psychotic misinterpretation of the use of objects. This would be the meaning of the scene if the parodistic impulse were as simple as the impulse to debate the practical advisability ("truth" in the running sense) of a course of action. What else does the scene contain? Night, moonlight, a deserted innyard, a man pacing up and down alone. Arising conceptually from this poignant incantation of scene are the urgency of devotion, the conviction of mission, the subjective solitude of the individual mind, resonances of ancient stories in which Love and Beauty and Goodness impelled men to action, a sense of the sacredness and loneliness of aspiration, a sense of the sacredness and loneliness of defeat. What else? The great jest, the wonderful release of laughter. The muleteers blunder up out of the night to water their mules at the "altar." Here, as in each of Quixote's and Sancho's adventures, yearning and pathos and jest flower together: emotion and burlesque, tradition and immediacy, felt time and the atemporal time of images, brute fact and conceptual delicacy, the abstract and the concrete, the disciplined and the accidental—all "real" in the intricate mixture of experience, and here designed in a simultaneity and a spiraling intertwining as one act of perception.

In the incidents we have used for illustration, the contrasted terms are each extreme: in the incident of the rescue of the peasant boy, Quixote appears as an extremist of justice, while the actions of the master and the boy offer the other extreme of domination by physical and practical exigency; in the scene of the vigil at the horse trough, Quixote's devotion to the chivalric ideal is of that extreme which transforms objects the most trivial and gross into the sacramental, while the circumstances of the vigil—the ménage in the inn, the arrival of the muleteers—are described in such a way as to emphasize to an extreme the grossly physical and materialistic. In the juxtaposition of the two companions, Quixote and Sancho, we are kept throughout the book in the presence of extremes; for not only do Knight and Squire offer to each other the foil of extremist characters, but each is himself exaggerated beyond the silhouette of any ordinary man. No one, in life, is so Quixote as Quixote or so Sancho as Sancho. Yet, strangely enough, it is because they are extremes, grotesque beyond life, that they strike the imagination so forcibly as being "true to life." In the creation of each of these characters, certain special qualities have been selected out from the fairly amorphous blend of qualities that make up the ordinary human being, and have been isolated and heightened to extraordinary proportions. The result is a brilliant visibility for these qualities, which are ordinarily so dimmed and blurred by the swarming commonplaces of existence that we have but a very vague sense of their presence and of their significance in our lives. To discover them in *Don Quixote* is to rediscover them in ourselves and our world, and it is for this reason that we feel the exaggerations and grotesqueries of the book to be "true to life."

But it is not only by extreme heightening of certain characteristics that the book allows us this rediscovery. It is by *perspective* that our vision is adjusted. Without being placed in a perspective, any disproportionately exaggerated form would lack all meaning; it would be grotesque without significance. Quixote is significant in the company of Sancho; Sancho, in the company of Quixote; each gives perspective to the other. Visual perspective is a matter of distinction between foreground and background, allowing for the perception of graded depths between them. We can expand the meaning of perspective so that it applies to events in time, to social phenomena, and to psychological and spiritual phenomena. The crowded streets of Barcelona, in the second volume of *Don Quixote*, are given the perspective of those lonely plains of La Mancha and the craggy wilderness of the Sierra Morena in the first volume. The modernism of some of the *novelle,* and the modernism that we feel in Quixote's own intense subjectivity, is given the perspective of those ancient heroic ballads and Gothic romances that have stimulated Quixote to action. Similarly with the enormous multitude of other contrasts that inform the book. Perspective is achieved by consistent organization of extremes of difference, so that, from the point of observation of one extreme, the other term of the contrast is seen significantly. That is, it is given background or it offers background to the other. But since *Don Quixote* is not a manual of moral *exempla,* since it implies no theoretical principle or thesis as to what constitutes the "good life," but is, instead, a vision of life itself, the perspectives that it affords are constantly reversible. In this respect, the situations in the book are like the figure-ground designs with which psychologists experiment; depending upon the mechanics of the eye, and upon obscurely fluctuating anticipations in the beholder, the figure becomes the ground and the ground becomes the figure. Thus the total perspective on man's destiny that the book gives us is not a perspective confined to certain limited cultural conditions—as it is, for instance, in the "naturalistic" novel—but a great backward and forward unfolding, from Gothic times to what we can only recognize as the essentially modern, and from the manifold external circumstances of human action to the lonely privacies of spirit.

This depth and reversibility of perspective is achieved again and again, not only in the more obviously violent displacements of narration (as between the various *novelle,* or between the 1605 and 1615 volumes), but also in scenic and even in linguistic detail.[2] When we are told, after the abortive expedition in the enchanted bark, that "Don Quixote and Sancho returned to their beasts and to their state of beasthood," we have a usual play on contrast between a concretion and an abstraction, between the literal beasts (Rosinante and Dapple) and the virtual beasthood of man; while the "beasthood" itself is resonant with double meanings, and can be interpreted in the medieval Christian sense—man is a spirit coupled with a beast, and now, sadly, with the giving up of the supernatural exploit in the bark, the beast prevails—or in a modern naturalistic sense—man *is* beast, and is grossly mistaken if he fancies himself beyond beasthood. We may take the statement one way or the other, as we may take the figure-ground designs of the psychologists one way or the other; clearly, it is "reversible." But what we wish to emphasize here is the depth of perspective in even so slight a statement: the concrete "beast" becomes more significant in the light of the abstract "beasthood," and the Christian and naturalistic, medieval and modern interpretations each more significant in the light of the other.

Let us take as another illustration the scene of the night entrance into Toboso, where Quixote and Sancho go to find Dulcinea. Here the great experiment of the practical test of the soul's truth is made in a tranquil darkness, a darkness naturally symbolic of the subjective loneliness of Quixote's quest, both of its obscurity to outward view and of its serene starlit clarity within. This setting for an act of faith is given what we have called perspective by the homely, immediate foreground sounds

2 Helmut Hatzfeld analyzes this aspect of Cervantes' style in the essay "The Style of *Don Quixote,*" in *Cervantes across the Centuries,* cited above.

of braying asses, grunting hogs, and mewing cats—that is, by contrast with objective detail grotesquely irrelevant to a spiritual quest. We see the spiritual event from a point of observation in the nonspiritual, and each heightens the significance of the other; or we could reverse our terms here, and say that the homely Tobosan night sounds echo in the perspective of that other night, the creative night of the dedicated soul. Similarly with that palace of Dulcinea's which seems, because of the tensions of Quixote's expectations, to loom so loftily over Toboso: as soon as Sancho speaks, the ghostly structure is riddled with by-lanes and blind alleys, hovels and bawdyhouses, all the commonplaces of a sleeping city; but immediately another displacement of vision occurs, and it rises before us again—only "two hundred paces" away. Both visual and spiritual perspective are phantasmagorically reversible, depending on whether, with Sancho, we see blind alleys and hovels in the foreground, or, with Quixote, see Dulcinea's palace in the foreground. When Quixote rides up to the church and quietly turns from it with the remark, "We are mistaken, Sancho, I find this is a church," his sobriety and rationality before the solid physical evidence offer us a new perspective on the complex life of the spirit; for this man respects what his senses tell him *at the same time* that his inward vision transcends and transforms all the sense evidence of Toboso; and we are persuaded of the transcendency of the vision by virtue, not of Quixote's lack of rationality, but of his rationality. That is, the visionary is placed in the perspective of the rational, the rational in the perspective of the visionary—and both are qualities of the one man. (Perhaps the most striking presentation of this double activity occurs when Quixote tells Sancho that, though no doubt the barber's basin is a barber's basin to Sancho, to Quixote it is Mambrino's helmet, and to another man it may well be something else. In other words, he refuses to falsify either the vision or the sense evidence.)

Finally, in the passage concerning the night entrance into Toboso, we have psychological foregrounds and backgrounds shifting into each other. Sancho has lied as to his having once seen Dulcinea in her palace —this is the foreground fact. But now that he wants to retreat from the chivalrous junket, by confessing his lie, his own known factuality and Quixote's faith in Sancho's factuality turn the lie back on him as a "fact," and to get out of his difficulties he is constrained to enter into Quixote's sphere of idealization and to "enchant" a country wench into Dulcinea. The lie in the psychological foreground is made a background to an imaginative act, a decisive act by which the gross-bellied Sancho commits himself inexorably to Quixote's visionary world—in counter movement to Quixote's own mysterious acceptance of the world of sense and reason. Here again, metaphorically in this psychological realm, we have the reversible perspective of the city of Toboso seen by night, a deep distance linking blind alley and towering palace and transmuting each by the presence of the other.

There are sharp changes, through time, in the ways that a literary work is read. Readers in the eighteenth century, for instance, found in *Don Quixote* a satire on imagination and fancy, and an essay in applause of reason and fact. In the early nineteenth century, the period of Romanticism, the book was read as a celebration of imagination and the ideal, at the expense of prosaic reason and sordid fact. In both the nineteenth century and the twentieth century, *Don Quixote* has been read as a "bitter" and pessimistic book, in which the author sets out to ridicule all faith in ideas and in human ennoblement. In the mid-twentieth century, if we share in a "climate of opinion" common to students in the scientific disciplines, a point of view that is predominantly rationalistic and positivistic, we can again read the book somewhat as eighteenth-century readers read it; or, "conditioned" by certain modern works, we may be inclined to find in it a prophetic projection of the solitude, sterility, and yearning of *The Waste Land,* or of the systematic disenchantment (Cervantes' *desengañado*) and "initiation" of Hemingway's heroes. It would seem that "great books," those in which many generations of readers have been able to find themselves and a clarification of their own worlds, have a very special ambiguity distinguishing them from lesser works. In the case of Cervantes' great novel, this quality seems to lie in the constant reversibility of perspective between deeply distant extremes. To return to the metaphor used in the introduction to this volume, the metaphor of a novel as a "world," we would say that the "world" of *Don Quixote* is marked and characterized by a perspectively organized extremism. This is its structural character, the ground both of its variety and its individuality.

Wishing to place that character decisively in the immediate procedures of the book, we would say that what the reader's attention is directed to is not one aspect (moral or practical) of an action, but the action itself, the adventure itself, as an event with many aspects. It is rather difficult for the rationalizing, moralizing intellect to think in this fashion. We feel the need of singling out some aspect as predominant and as definitive of worth-while values. An eminent critic of Spanish literature, Americo Castro, will help us here. He says that the theme of Spanish literature, and that of *Don Quixote*, "may be summarized as the difficulty of living, when it tries to integrate body, soul, and mind—which is different from giving preference to the latter at the expense of the other two." [3] And he suggests historical backgrounds for this difficult interest in the fact that

> To the Spaniard, ever since the Middle Ages, the supernatural and the natural, the religious and the profane, the spiritual and the physical, the abstract and the concrete, coexisted in one and the same unity of consciousness. There was not the least critical discrimination between actual experience and that which transcends the witness of the senses . . .[4]

George Santayana expresses obliquely the same aspect of Spanish temperament when he says,

> The most miraculous world, if it were real, would subdue the teachable mind to its own habit, and would prove that miracles were—as they are in the Gospels—the most ordinary and most intelligible of events . . . matter [is] the ancient plastic substance of all the gods.[5]

If we look on the adventures of Quixote and Sancho each as total actions, and not designed to emphasize separated aspects of actions, we shall recover what was perhaps the artist's perception, but certainly we shall recover, through insight made body, more of ourselves and of other men —which is to say, more "perspective"—than if we attempt to rigidify *Don Quixote* into a system of preferences. "The scene of so prodigious a spectacle," Americo Castro says,

> is the workshop in which the life of each one is forged, and is not a didactic or logical transcendency superimposed on the process of living. [It is] a question of showing that reality is always an aspect of the experience of the person who is living it.[6]

[3] "Incarnation in *Don Quixote*," in the cited volume, *Cervantes across the Centuries*, p. 147.
[4] *Ibid.*, p. 143.
[5] *Persons and Places* (New York: Charles Scribner's Sons, 1944), pp. 239–240.
[6] Castro, *op. cit.*, p. 144.

ON *The Pilgrim's Progress*

The Pilgrim's Progress is designed, in its broad lines, as an allegory. Let us define allegory here as Coleridge defined it, and then let us illustrate the definition in its simplest application. Coleridge says that allegory is the employment of a certain set of characters, actions, and circumstances in such a way that these convey to the mind, under the disguise of sense objects, certain moral qualities or conceptions, and so that all the parts combine to form a consistent whole.[1] The large action of Bunyan's book is that of a pilgrimage, and we see the pilgrim going his way on a solid, earthy road, through mud, through green fields, over rocks; and conveyed under this earthy disguise is the notion of the complicated moral life of man, his occasions of serenity, his occasions of despair, the challenges of his mortal estate. It is an ancient, universal image that Bunyan has used—the image of life as a journey; he has given it a special inflection—the journey is not a mere wayfaring but a "pilgrimage," that is, a journey to a holy place. But our definition says that each of the parts, as well as the whole, conveys a moral idea. To illustrate the allegorical operation of one of the parts, we may use the first image in the book—that of the "man clothed with rags, standing in a certain place, with his face from his own house, a book in his hand, and a great burden upon his back." Isaiah says (64:6): "all our righteousnesses are as filthy rags"; and the Psalmist says (38:4): "For mine iniquities are gone over mine head: as an heavy burden they are too heavy for me." We put an equal sign, as it were, between the man's previous complacent notions of his own goodness and the worthless rags that clothe him, and another equal sign between his guiltiness and his burden. This activity, of the equating of a sense image with a moral concept, we engage in

[1] *Miscellaneous Criticism,* edited by Thomas Middleton Raysor (Cambridge: Harvard University Press, 1936), p. 30.

spontaneously as we read, for Bunyan's imagery is drawn from the commonest human experiences and his moral conceptions are drawn from the common Christian heritage.

However, not everywhere in the book do we find so perfectly natural a relationship between image and concept as we find in the paragraph about the man in rags. We shall be able to see the rich potentialities of the allegorical method more truly if we become early acquainted with its limitations. The following passage—from the episode, in Part II, where Matthew gets the gripes—is a mixture of allegory and realism. The realism is of the kind we associate with genre painting, in which commonplace domestic scenes are represented with homely accuracy of detail. What we wish to notice here is the fact that the concepts Bunyan wishes to convey through his allegory do not relate themselves spontaneously with the realistic sense imagery; the scene itself is projected most clearly for the imagination, but this is all that is successfully projected (and it is charming and it is "enough"); as to the intellectual conceptions of which it is supposed to be the vehicle, Bunyan has to tack them onto it in an additional explanation, and we feel that they are arbitrarily imposed and that we could easily dispense with them. Matthew is "much pained in his bowels," "pulled as it were both ends together." The doctor, Mr. Skill, is sent for, and says that the boy must have eaten unwholesome food, which "lies in his maw undigested." One of the children recalls that Matthew, when they passed an orchard along the way, had plucked some green plums from the trees overhanging the wall. He must take a purge.

> So he [Mr. Skill] made him a purge, but it was too weak; it was said, it was made of the blood of a goat, the ashes of a heifer, and with some of the juice of hyssop, &c. When Mr. Skill had seen that the purge was too weak, he made him one to the purpose; it was made *ex carne et sanguine Christi*. (You know physicians give strange medicines to their patients.) And it was made up into pills, with a promise or two, and a proportionable quantity of salt. Now he was to take them three at a time fasting, in half a quarter of a pint of the tears of repentance. When this potion was prepared, and brought to the boy, he was loath to take it, though torn with the gripes as if he should be pulled in pieces. Come, come, said the physician, you must take it. It goes against my stomach, said the boy. I must have you take it, said his mother. I shall vomit it up again, said the boy. Pray, Sir, said Christiana, to Mr. Skill, how does it taste? It has no ill taste, said the doctor; and with

that she touched one of his pills with the tip of her tongue. Oh, Matthew, said she, this potion is sweeter than honey.

Matthew is prevailed upon to take the medicine, which "put him into a fine heat and breathing sweat, and did quite rid him of his gripes." Allegorically, the green plums that Matthew ate are fruit from the Devil's orchard, "forbidden fruit" representing the willful indulgence of appetite; the ingredients of Mr. Skill's first purge, that was too weak, are those sacrifices which the Law insists be made for sin, but which do not have the power of the Christian sacraments; the second and effective set of pills are the Eucharist—the body and blood of Christ; the child, himself incapable of right decision, is led to the sacrament by the persuasion of his elders; and the "tears of repentance" in which the sacraments must be taken are boiled down to a child's capacity. The arbitrariness of these allegorical equations is highlighted by Matthew's very real stomach-ache, which he could have had from eating real green plums, but which he could scarcely have felt as a result of a consciousness of guilt—unless he were a very modern and neurotic little boy; and by the gross physical effects of the Lord's Supper upon him, putting him into a sweat and causing him to purge—these effects being scarcely appropriate to the taking of the Eucharist, though wholly appropriate to the curing of an indigestion. On the other hand, Bunyan's homely diction in describing the stomach-ache, the typical querulousness of the sick child, the doctor's rough "Come, come, you must take it," and the delicate psychological acumen of the mother when she asks the doctor how the medicine tastes, then tastes it herself first—these details have the directness and animation of life. We have to admit that there is another kind of charm in the very crudity of the allegory here, a charm something like that of a rough medieval woodcut figuring a moral emblem or Biblical parable in the swift, gross traits of common life. But Bunyan's true greatness does not rest on crudity. We shall turn now to another scene, where the allegorical fusion of sense impression and moral concept is complete.

This scene illustrates Bunyan's symbolic use of physical topography —the heights and valleys which Christian and the other pilgrims travel. At the foot of the Hill Difficulty, Christian meets two travelers, Formalist and Hypocrisy, who are going his way.

There were also in the same place two other ways besides that which came straight from the gate; one turned to the left hand, and the other

to the right, at the bottom of the hill; but the narrow way lay right up
the hill . . .

Christian refreshes himself with a drink at a cool spring, then bounds
on a run up the hill with a song on his lips. As for the other travelers,

> when they saw that the hill was steep and high, and that there were
> two other ways to go; and supposing also that these two ways might
> meet again, with that up which Christian went, on the other side of the
> hill; therefore they were resolved to go in those ways. Now the name
> of one of those ways was Danger, and the name of the other Destruc-
> tion. So the one took the way which is called Danger, which led him
> into a great wood, and the other took directly up the way to Destruc-
> tion, which led him into a wide field, full of dark mountains, where
> he stumbled and fell, and rose no more.

Bunyan's dream then turns back to Christian, who "fell from running
to going, and from going to clambering upon his hands and knees, because of the steepness of the place." The steep hill itself, the great wood
at one side, the wide field at the other side "full of dark mountains,"
make up a rather crowded terrain, naïvely conceived as by a man who,
never having seen mountainous country, imagines it as did those early
painters who painted their mountains from models made of garden rocks
piled up in ungeological heaps. Nevertheless, we both see it and feel it,
for the imagination does not demand that an actual landscape be photographed for it with the mechanical accuracy of commercial photography.
What we see and feel is the difficulty of the way, the darkness of the
wood where one man is lost, the terror and despair in that field full of
dark mountains where the other man is lost, the change in Christian's
tempo and in his muscular effort as he is forced to slow down. The
landscape, then, though we can visualize it as something external, to be
seen with the physical eye, is really internal: it is a complex image of various kinds of feeling, of muscular sensations of physical difficulty, and of
fear and the sense of abandonment in the dark. But what moral conception can we point to that the scene allegorically illustrates? It does not
seem to be one that we can rigidly label, although its presence is powerfully felt. It does not, in fact, need a label, for it is simply the moral exertion that we feel in Christian's physical exertion as he takes the straight
way up the hill; without moral exertion, he could not have made the

physical exertion. This sense of the meaning of his action is enforced by the contrast with the other two travelers, who clearly were lacking in moral will in their refusal of the physical difficulty. How naturally and spontaneously the full moral conception, which makes this scene "allegorical," arises out of the concrete foreground image of the rocky, wooded landscape and the travelers choosing their three ways through it! Formalist and Hypocrisy (their names here could just as easily have been Joe and John), in making their choices of the apparently easier ways around the hill, are separated; each now goes alone—and the meaning of their solitude is clear: when choice is unanchored in discipline, the pilgrim is a real wanderer, separate and alone, eventually to be lost in a confused darkness. Christian is also alone, but his aloneness has a different meaning: it is the aloneness of the most strenuous and courageous spirits; and later, when his circumstances become more trying, and both courage and discipline fail him, he will find companions in Faithful and Hopeful. In Part II, we see the weaker spirits, women and children, traveling in company and with the guide Great-heart to show them the way.

Effective allegory has a triple achievement. The moral conceptions on which it rests must be culturally viable, or it will not find adequate metaphors for its meaning in our common experience; its primary appeal to the understanding of the reader must be through our common physical and psychological experience, for this provides it the image traits out of which its metaphors are constructed; and the images that it offers us must have the power of symbols, spontaneously to evoke feelings and emotions that naturally associate themselves with moral attitudes and specifically with those attitudes that make up the conceptual framework of the allegory.

Bunyan uses physical topography—the muddy Slough, the Hill Difficulty, the highway where travelers jog along together gossiping, the deep benighted valleys, the entrancing mountains approached from a distance—in such a way that this road lies on our familiar earth: we are sensible imaginatively of the stickiness and treacherousness of this bog, of the fearfulness of this dark valley, of the freshness and cheerfulness of "this sunshine morning." And if Bunyan were unable to evoke the physical scene, he would be unable to equate it convincingly with the psychological state of the travelers. As it is, the physical scene and atmosphere spontaneously impress us with moral meaning: we know that the scene is not only outside the travelers, but within them also, as their personal

25

spiritual topography. The Slough scarcely needs to be named Despond, nor are we forced arbitrarily to put an equal sign between the name of the Slough and the sin of spiritual torpor and thus by a clumsy intellectual operation to understand its meaning in the story; nor, in the episode of the Slough, do we even need to have named explicitly to us the two pilgrims, Christian and Pliable; for Bunyan has so provided that our own acts of making allegorical equations between physical circumstances and moral conceptions take place undeliberately, with free and yet true feeling. Here are two men who must get to the other side of an apparently impassable bog:

> they wallowed for a time, being grievously bedaubed with the dirt; and Christian, because of the burden that was on his back, began to sink in the mire.

The one traveler, who has no burden, kicks and complains for a few minutes, accusing his companion of getting him into this mess, then climbs out and goes back home.

> Wherefore Christian was left to tumble in the Slough of Despond alone; but still he endeavoured to struggle to that side of the Slough that was still further from his own home . . but could not get out, because of the burden that was upon his back . . .

At this moment, Help comes. The little episode is related with the greatest economy; a few slight physical traits noted by the verbs "wallowed," "bedaubed," and "tumble," and the simple pictorial concept of a man wearing a burden and struggling to get through a miry place, are sufficient to raise the scene imaginatively before us. And instantly a coil of feelings and judgments spirals in our minds: we know that the man with the burden has been deeply tried in spirit; we know that if he did not have a spirit of a specially complex kind he would not have been subject to such a trial, for he would have been incapable of experiencing it (his friend Faithful, for instance, who is much simpler psychologically, never had to go through the Slough); we know that his companion Pliable was made of poor moral stuff; we easily recognize the mud in which Christian wallows as mud which we too have felt clogging us psychologically, even if only we have felt depressed from wallowing through real mud in bad weather; and we know what is meant by the fact that "Christian was left to tumble in the Slough of Despond alone," for we know that some experiences of struggle are altogether lonely and their content incommunicable. Coleridge said of *The Pilgrim's Progress,* "I read it once as a theologian—and let me assure you, that there is great theological acumen in the work—once with devotional feelings—and once as a poet." [2] Though we may not, at the moment of reading, be able to analyze all the several ways in which we are reading an episode such as that of the Slough of Despond, and though we may lack the training to label our readings as Coleridge did, it is probable that we too read it in several ways at once, and do so spontaneously; for the artistry with which it is designed is of a kind that releases instinct and stored experience in the reader, revealing them to him in the light of a new insight. It is this that we mean when we speak of the "ambiguity" of some of the great literary works: we do not mean by this word that they are equivocal or obscure, but that they are multileveled projections of human experience—and human experience is always itself multileveled.

Before leaving the matter of Bunyan's use of physical topography as a sign of an inward state,[3] let us speak of the two visions of the Delectable Mountains—the one, when Christian sees them from the roof of the house where the sisters arm him; and the other, when Christian and Hopeful see them again after issuing from the prison of Despair. In the first vision,

> he saw a most pleasant mountainous country, beautified with woods, vineyards, fruits of all sorts, flowers also, with springs and fountains, very delectable to behold.

This is all that is said of the mountains in this place. The image remains with us, probably because we have all seen mountains at a distance, verdurous and delicately lighted, and have wished that we might go there. The second vision occurs under very different circumstances. Christian and Hopeful have been through the long and nearly suicidal experience of despair; finally the dungeon door has given way, and with great difficulty they have got through the iron gate; they find themselves safe on the highway. Immediately the Delectable Mountains appear again.

2 *Ibid.,* p. 406.

3 This aspect of the book is discussed acutely and at length by André A. Talon, in *John Bunyan, l'homme et l'oeuvre* (Paris: Editions 'Je Sers,' 1948).

27

. . so they went up to the mountains, to behold the gardens and orchards, the vineyards and fountains of water; where also they drank and washed themselves, and did freely eat of the vineyards. Now there were on the tops of these mountains shepherds feeding their flocks, and they stood by the highway side. The pilgrims therefore went to them, and leaning upon their staves (as is common with weary pilgrims, when they stand to talk with any by the way), they asked, whose Delectable Mountains are these?

The shepherds reply courteously, and give the travelers their directions for the way onward, and "they looked very lovingly upon them, and said, Welcome to the Delectable Mountains." The second scene is fraught with a special charm, a charm founded in psychological truth; for the mountains are now more beautiful than ever because the immediately preceding circumstances have been dark and full of despair. Into the beauty of the mountains, and with that childlike question, "Whose Delectable Mountains are these?" is poured the sense of release from terrible danger. Most clearly here, the outward topography is an objectification of the inward. The physical journey is always what the travelers themselves spiritually make of it.

We turn now to a few of the characters in the story, in order to see the consistency of Bunyan's method as between his description of scene and his description of persons. Let us speak first of some of the minor characters, the false pilgrims. Each betrays what he is by a word, a tone, a turn of syntax. This is Obstinate, speaking always in exclamatory rushes, the man with his mind made up before he has ever begun to think, thumping out short-winded interjections: "What! and leave our friends and our comforts behind us?"—"Tush! away with your book."—"What! more fools still!" And this is Pliable, in a single delightful self-betrayal contrived by a verb: after seeing Obstinate depart, he tells Christian that he has made up his mind to go along on the journey, but instead of saying, "I have decided," he says, "Well, I begin to come to a point." His moral silliness wobbles through the "begin to come," just as we see him later wobbling out of the Slough. As for Mr. Worldly Wiseman, his condescension, his worldly circumspection, his spiritual obtuseness, his amiability hiding actual indifference, are heard in the first words we have from him: "How now, good fellow, whither away after this burdened manner?" To Mr. Worldly Wiseman, the burden is merely a kind of mannerism or eccentricity or foreign custom; he addresses Christian patronizingly as "good

28

fellow," and (in later speeches) uses to him the condescending second person singular pronoun, as if he were addressing a child or a person of low social status. Bunyan's skill in swift characterization is of the very highest; he reproduces, on a person's first entrance into the tale, the precise and inevitable tone of voice, the mood of the verb, the idiom, and the syntactical rhythm which will put the speaker before us in his essential moral life, and which will cast upon the episode the energy and conviction of reality. The essential moral life—but no more. For this is all that Bunyan's design demands. And because he limits himself to this, his people become severally emblematic of several human qualities, each in separation, "personified" as we say. But let us notice that the quality which is personified is not a quality *in the abstract,* but a quality having the concrete texture of living humanity. Bunyan's characters, Coleridge said, are "real persons, who had been nicknamed by their neighbours." Neither Obstinate nor Pliable nor Mr. Worldly Wiseman are truly the abstract personifications of obstinacy, overcompliancy, and worldly cautiousness, but people whom we have often heard speak and will again, people of narrow temperaments in whom a single trait has been comically or cancerously exaggerated. It is only because Bunyan founds his allegory of human qualities in the objective reality of human manners that his allegory "works" at all. Thus, consistently with his treatment of landscape, his treatment of characters is such that they exist objectively as people to the imagination and at the same time are emblematic of moral, "inward" traits.

Foreground characters, such as Christian and Faithful or Hopeful, afford somewhat more complex examples of Bunyan's method. In the first few pages of the book, Christian has no name. He is "the man" or "he." It is only when he has suffered, and taken fear, and entered strenuously upon his difficult pilgrimage, that he emerges from the anonymity of spiritual complacency and obtains a name—Christian. How is he to be made fully known to us now, both as an individual and as a Christian? He talks to certain foolish people, and we see that he is more strong-minded than they; he goes through the Slough of Despond, and we see that he is capable of moral suffering, that he has both physical and moral courage. But this is not all of a man, nor of a Christian. He meets Mr. Worldly Wiseman, and is easily talked into a way of getting rid of his burden "in credit and good fashion," and a way of finding salvation without having to face wearisomeness and painfulness and darkness and—death. Instead of these, he will have "safety, friendship, and content." This Christian has his weakness. Clearly, Mr. Worldly Wiseman is inside Christian himself, a counsel of softness in the soul. While the foolish patter of Obstinate and Pliable could not win him back from the way, a more subtle temptation is able to overcome him. Now he emerges from the pages more recognizably to us, for he has shadows on him, and a man without shadows is not recognizable as a man. Nor to Bunyan, it would seem, is a Christian without shadows typical as a Christian. Therefore he gives him Faithful as a companion, an exceptional man of faith, with no shadows. Faithful has little imagination and a relatively meager sensibility; he carries no burden, he has not gone through the Slough, the lions have not roared at him, his conversion has been sudden and definitive, he voyages without fatigue. Beside the bright firm surface of Faithful, Christian is thrown into relief as a man who has suffered and been afraid and wallowed in mud, a man of complex and difficult temperament, vainglorious at times in his strength, at other times doubtful or despairing.

Later, after the martyrdom at Vanity Fair, Hopeful will take up somewhat the same role as Faithful, and we observe a similar contrast of light and shadow by which Christian is sculptured out for us in the full visible relief of a complex soul. It is Christian who would take the counsel of the Giant Despair and commit suicide; he quite loses his mental balance and deliberately seeks the unconsciousness of hysteria and coma; three several times Hopeful must urge him to have courage. Had Bunyan given Christian no companion of this kind, how would he have been able to sound the full chord of qualities in the strenuous religious mind? Christian would have killed himself, and we would have had only the despairing Christian, the defeated Christian—not the complete Christian. Hopeful—like Mr. Worldly Wiseman—is a projection of the one mind, Christian's mind. Bunyan has split off from the complex main character certain aspects of his temperament that can be personified separately and that can involve Christian in an outward drama which will realize for us, imaginatively, the drama taking place within the alert soul. This is a phase of the allegorical method somewhat different from those we have observed before. It is inaccurate to say of Faithful and Hopeful that they are merely abstract personifications, without vitality and without depth; for they have their concreteness, their vitality and depth, in Christian himself. Allegory of this kind puts a special but a fair demand upon the reader: the reader's own moral imagination must be at work to integrate the separated aspects of the soul into a psychological unity and to perceive the outward drama as inward drama.

The poet Marianne Moore has spoken of poetry as "an imaginary garden with real toads in it." The landscape of *The Pilgrim's Progress* is often a landscape of dream or of nightmare inhabited by our very solid neighbors; and it is often our solid familiar landscape inhabited by creatures of nightmare or dream. Here is a soiled spring muddied by picnickers—we, too, have seen it; and here is St. George's dragon talking like Satan—perhaps we have seen this monster, too, but not by this spring. There are mirage mountains, and now suddenly they come close and we see, as in a primitive painting, minute details of vineyards and fountains and shepherds with their lambs; and here is Madame Bubble, that tall good-looking woman who makes her hard face smile at the end of every sentence, and who has a certain uncontrollable tic—she can't help scrabbling through her purse while she talks. The dream and the solid reality are brought together in a single experience, as a child constantly brings them together; and by this juxtaposition, the dream becomes palpable and the reality becomes mysterious. Bunyan is in touch with ancient sources of feeling, ancient in both childhood and racial lore; he is also in touch with the immediate forms of his own present; around these forms, and through them, he is able to release the atmosphere of the miraculous. It is thus that he makes a new and integral world with its own gravitational law, its own breathing air, its own inhabitants; and it is because he makes a fully independent world that we call him a novelist.

The first lines launch us with great swift strides into that world.

As I walked through the wilderness of this world, I lighted on a certain place where was a Den, and I laid me down in that place to sleep; and, as I slept, I dreamed a dream. I dreamed, and behold I saw a man clothed with rags, standing in a certain place, with his face from his own house, a book in his hand, and a great burden upon his back. I looked, and saw him open the book and read therein; and, as he read, he wept, and trembled; and not being able longer to contain, he brake out with a lamentable cry, saying, "What shall I do?"

It is a world seen in a dream, but the brief past-tense forms of the verbs, with their clear Anglo-Saxon vowels and serried ranks of consonants— "I walked," "I lighted," "I dreamed," "I looked,"—have the energy and hard feel of reality, and hurry us to that cry, "What shall I do?" which must have an immediate answer in drama. Now we are at the center of the dream, carried there by the muscular urgency of the style—and at the center, among these celestial pilgrims with their nude hearts, we no longer remember that it is a dream.

ON *Moll Flanders*

The editorial preface to a popular modern reprint of *Moll Flanders* speaks of the book as "one of the most remarkable examples of true realism in the whole range of fiction." The statement suggests that "true realism" is specifically that kind of realism which *Moll Flanders* exhibits; by implication, other kinds—if there are other kinds—would not be "true." There can be no gainsaying the realism of *Moll Flanders:* Defoe's book describes minutely the local scene, London; it refers circumstantially to contemporary customs (although not to those of the mid-seventeenth century in which Moll supposedly had her career, but to those of the early eighteenth century when Defoe was writing); it employs "documents" (Moll's "memorandums," quoted letters, hospital bills, etc.) in order to increase the illusion of verifiable fact; and, in general, it aims at "objective," "reportorial," "photographic" representation, as if from the standpoint of an artless observer. In other words, the whole book is oriented toward what we call "facts"—specifically toward those "facts" which are events and objects that have spatial-temporal determination. But it is unfortunate that factual orientation in the novel should have come to determine the definition of realism in the novel; for "realism" inevitably implies a doctrine of the "real"; and it implies, when it is used to describe the factually oriented novel, that spatial-temporal facts are the only "real," and therefore that the factually oriented novel is closer to "reality"—a more trustworthy representation of reality—than any other kind of novel. What is suggested by the statement quoted at the beginning of this essay is not an evaluation of *Moll Flanders* as literature, but a certain popular philosophical conviction of the exclusive "reality" of material facts, a conviction that the so-defined "realistic" novel seems to flatter and support; and what is blurred over by the statement is the *hypothetical* structure of even the most "documentary" or "circumstantial" kind of fiction, a hypothetical structure that it shares generically with all fiction.

33

The hypothesis on which *Moll Flanders* is based might be phrased in this way: given a human creature "conditioned" to react only to material facts, then the world where that person lived might cogently assume the shape that Moll's world assumes—a shape astonishingly without spiritual dimension. In a parallel fashion one might phrase the hypothesis on which *The Pilgrim's Progress* is based: given a person for whom relationship with God was the only "reality," then, in his world, material facts would show as misleading appearances, and the shape taken by his adventures would be altogether spiritually dimensioned. If the world of the particular novel is to create itself fully for us, we must waive for the moment our own *a priori* convictions as to whether material fact or relationship with God is the prime reality; we must approach the fictional hypothesis with as much respect for its conditions and as much attention to its logic as we would give to a scientific or mathematical hypothesis. Defoe's "realism" must be looked upon as a consistent use of certain devices for the creation of a special kind of world, just as Bunyan's allegorical method is a consistent use of certain devices (some of them "realistic" in the same sense as Defoe's) for the creation of a special kind of world. Eventually, the trained and sensitized reader finds that novels called "realistic" are as symbolic as Bunyan's allegory.

The questions we must ask of *Moll Flanders* are those we ask of any other novel: what are its elements? how are they made to cohere in a unity? how are its special technical devices (in this case, those of "realism") appropriate to the making of this particular world? We notice, for instance, that Moll's world contains many *things*—tangible things such as watches and wigs and yardage goods and necklaces and dresses and barrels and bales and bottles and trunks. We may make some judgment as to the kind of world presented in a novel simply on the basis of the frequency with which an author uses certain substantives and images, to the exclusion of others. In *Moll*, there is relatively great frequency in the use of words naming that kind of object which constitutes material wealth. This singularity of *Moll Flanders* becomes striking when we try to remember how many dresses Christiana had for her long journey, and whether Mr. Worldly Wiseman wore a wig or carried a watch.

But let us make a further distinction: these tangible, material objects with which Moll is so deeply concerned are not at all vivid in texture. When Moll tells us that she put on a "good pearl necklace," we do not know whether the pearls were large or small or graded or uniform in size, or whether the necklace hung low on her bosom or was wound around her throat three times, nor do we know if the pearls were real or artificial; the word "good" here indicates simply that the pearls looked costly to a sophisticated eye, and were of a kind that a woman of substantial social position might wear; the "good pearl necklace" is mentioned not in a way that will make a sense image for us, but only in a way that will suggest the market value of the necklace and (through the market value) its value as an indicator of social prestige. Similarly, when she tells us that she gave her son a fine gold watch, we have no sense image of the watch; we do not know its size or design or delicacy or heft; we know only that it is a watch which would bring a good price. Therefore, in saying that the world of *Moll Flanders* is made up to a large extent of *things,* we do not mean that it is a world rich in physical, sensuous textures—in images for the eye or for the tactile sense or for the tongue or the ear or for the sense of temperature or the sense of pressure. It is extraordinarily barren of such images. And yet sense images are certainly "real" even in a world exclusively composed of "facts"; they are the constant means by which we are made aware of facts (the scientific observer himself is dependent upon their evidence). Clearly, then, an intense selectivity has limited the facts of Moll Flanders' world to a certain few kinds of facts, and has ignored great masses of other facts that we think of as making up the plenum of factual reality. Such selectivity warns us that this realistic novel is not actually an "objective," "reportorial," "photographic" representation of reality; its selectivity is that of the work of art, whose purpose is not that of an "objective" report.

What is important in Moll's world of things is the counting, measuring, pricing, weighing, and evaluating of the things in terms of the wealth they represent and the social status they imply for the possessor. What is unimportant (and we learn as much by what is unimportant as by what is important) is sensuous life, the concrete experience of things as they have individual texture. The unimportance of sensuous life in Moll's world is fairly astonishing inasmuch as Moll herself is a lusty, full-bodied, lively-sensed creature. Our instrument or medium of knowledge about Moll's world is Moll. The medium is a sensual medium (what woman, weak in sensuality, would remark, as Moll does: "I never was in bed with my husband, but I wished myself in the arms of his brother . . . in short, I committed adultery and incest with him every day in my desires . . ." or would have given us the scenes in the inns at Glouces-

35

ter and Bath?); but communicated through this medium is an assemblage of objects entirely desensualized, inaccessible to sense, abstract—abstract because represented only by name and by market value on the commercial and social markets. We may speak of this contradiction as an irony, and we shall wish to use the word "irony" here as indicating one character-istic *mode of relationship between elements in a novelistic structure.* Irony can imply many kinds of discrepancy, contrast, contradiction; para-dox is a form of irony; there is irony in a statement that appears to say one thing and actually signifies another; and there is irony in a life situation or in a story situation that contrasts with or contradicts what might be expected from certain of the circumstances. We are always aware of Moll's sensuality, even though it often lies subterraneously or at a subverbal level in the novel; a great many of her adventures are sexual; but the life of the flesh is faded completely by the glare of the life of the pocketbook; and the incipience of sensuality, its always latent presence, contrasts ironically with the meagerness and abstractness of a sensibility which frantically converts all sense experience into cash value.

We shall continue to speak of ironies in *Moll Flanders,* and as we shall be speaking of them as aspects of the book's internal structure, let us formulate what we mean by the structural function of irony. We shall do so most easily by analogy. A round arch is made up of a number of wedge-shaped blocks, and each of these blocks is pulled earthward in obedience to gravity, but each also exerts a sideways push against its neighbor because of its wedge shape and the weight of other blocks around and over it. If there were only the one pull, freely earthward, the blocks would fall and there would be no arch; but because of the counterforce, acting in the sideways direction, the structure of the arch is defined and preserved. The contrasting significances of an ironic statement or of an ironic situation may be compared with the counteracting stresses that hold the arch up and hold it together—that give it its structure. In *Moll Flanders,* a complex system of ironies or counterstresses holds the book together as a coherent and significant work of art. We may speak of the ironies, then, as "structural." In the example that we have cited, Moll's latent sensuality acts as a counterstress to her devotion to financial ab-stractions, and the cross-pulls of these two tendencies define Moll and her world meaningfully for us.

To illustrate further, let us follow some of her characteristic mental processes. Here is one chief inflection of her psychology—the reader will find it repeated again and again as he listens to her tale. It appears in her account of her first marriage, her marriage to the younger brother of her seducer. Five years she has been married to him, she has had two children by him, she has known a long and important period (important because she is still very young) of domesticity and marital tenderness and motherhood. How does she tell us of these matters?

> It concerns the story in hand very little to enter into the further particulars . . . only to observe that I had two children by him, and that at the end of the five years he died. He had been really a very good husband to me, and we lived very agreeably together; but as he had not received much from them [the parents], and had in the little time he lived acquired no great matters, so my circumstances were not great, nor was I much mended by the match. Indeed, I had preserved the elder brother's bonds to me to pay me £500, which he offered me for my consent to marry his brother; and this, with what I had saved of the money he formerly gave me, and about as much more by my husband, left me a widow with about £1200 in my pocket.

We know in some degree from this context, and with added conviction from other similar contexts, what Moll means by a "very good husband" and by saying that they lived "very agreeably": the man had enough money to keep Moll from want, he spent money freely enough to maintain her in comfort and in that kind of social respectability which the spending of money guarantees—therefore he was "good" and their life was "agreeable." Any other characterization of this husband or of their marital life we should not be able to guess at; for Moll, simply by her exclusion of any other kind of perception from her story, stringently limits our own imagination of character; and we must judge that Moll has no other perception of character. The phrases "received much," "acquired no great matters," "my circumstances were not great," and "mended by the match," all focus together on one kind of referent: money. And when we find similar phrases in other contexts, we shall expect that "much" and "matters" and "circumstances" and "great" and "mended" (though these words might have immensely different meanings in other books) will have the same common referent again. As Moll uses them, they are very abstract words, colorless little words, words as limited in meaning as a mathematical sign. By their frequency they compose a picture of Moll's mentality and sensibility, so exclusively focused, so narrow and intense, that if (conceivably) we were offered the same description of symptoms in a clinical case history, we should say that it was a picture of a madwoman. But Moll's is not a case history; it is a hypothesis of personality development in an acquisitive world; and in this world Moll is by no means a clinical subject—she is "well adjusted."

What five years of her young womanhood, marriage, domesticity, and motherhood mean to Moll are certain finances, certain bonds amounting to so much, a certain quantity of cash in her pocket. Of her children by this husband, she says,

> My two children were, indeed, taken happily off my hands by my husband's father and mother, and that was all they got by Mrs. Betty.

The statement informs us, with powerful obliquity, that the way to be happy through children is to have them taken off one's hands; it informs us also that children may be useful in settling family debts. With the greatest placidity and aplomb on Moll's part, the children are neatly converted into a shrewd price by which she gets out of a bad bargain with clean skirts. Schematically, what has been happening here is the conversion of all subjective, emotional, and moral experience—implicit in the fact of Moll's five years of marriage and motherhood—into pocket and bank money, into the materially measurable. It is a shocking formula, shocking in its simplicity and abruptness and entireness. It confronts us again with the irony, or system of ironies, that is structural to the book. A great mass of responses that might be expected from the circumstances (marriage, death, birth) is not what is presented; what is presented of that pyramid of human experience, as its only symbol and significance, is a cash sign. And yet another irony is involved: that is the paradox of Moll's superb "sanity," witnessed by her perfect "adjustment" to her world, and her violent abnormality as a representative of the species called human. A person is sane who is socially adapted in his time and his place, in tune with his culture, furnished with the mental and moral means to meet contingencies (to "mend" his circumstances, in Moll's phrase, when they need mending), accepting the values that his society accepts, and collaborating in their preservation. By these tokens, Moll is eminently sane. She is a collector of quantities of things and of cash, for in the world in which she lives, the having of things and of cash is necessary for survival; it is an expression of the will to live. She has one thing to sell, in order to obtain them, and that is her sex. When this commodity fails her, she simply takes the things and the cash—steals them. In either case, she shows her sanity, her "adjustment" to her world, her ability to meet all contingencies. In this sense she is "normal," exhibiting in her activities and attitudes the social norm of her world; in terms of the full emotional variety of what we think of as the "human," she is monstrously abnormal. Her abnormality is her exclusive abstractiveness as a counter of cash; her subjective life is sunken nearly to a zero.

What will Moll do when she is under severe emotional stress; that is, when there is nothing in her situation that she can abstract into numbers, measurements, cash value, and when whatever is left for her perception to work on is the internal or subjective life of feeling and emotion? At the crisis of her career, she is taken for thieving, put into Newgate prison; and Newgate is hell. We have only Moll's own words for this experience, and how are Moll's words—dictated by a perceptive apparatus adapted exclusively for enumerating and calculating—to describe hell for us? Hell, Milton's Satan said, is a place within the self; that is, it is a subjective place, a place defined by horror and suffering and deep distress of spirit. In all her other circumstances, Moll has never failed to describe and define with the utmost precision such experience as she is capable of. But the hell of Newgate is "impossible to describe." The impossible description of this dead end of human suffering she fills up with negatives, words denying any possibility of description, for she has only negatives and blank counters for the subjective.

> . . . indeed, nothing could be filled with more horror . . . nothing was more odious to me than the company that was there . . . indeed no colours can represent that place to the life.

To get over these impossibilities, the hell of Newgate is expressed by generalized reference to noises and smells (Newgate is most painful because it is not "respectable"; there are loud noises and bad smells here as there are in the slums), and by abstract stereotypes of fiendishness.

> . . . the hellish noise, the roaring, swearing, and clamour, the stench and nastiness, and all the dreadful afflicting things that I saw there . . . ; I thought of nothing night or day, but of gibbets and

halters, evil spirits and devils; it is not to be expressed how I was
harassed . . .

With the intervention of the minister, Moll says she is "perfectly changed,"
she becomes "another body." But since her perceptions are limited to
their familiar categories of number and quantity, suitable for inventory-
ing gold watches and bonds and purse change, but scarcely suitable for
the description of grief or guilt or purity, the heaven of her repentance
is as ineffable as the hell of Newgate. "The word eternity," she says,

> represented itself with all its incomprehensible additions, and I had
> such extended notions of it that I know not how to express them.
> Among the rest, how absurd did every pleasant thing look!—I mean,
> that we had counted before—when I reflected that these sordid trifles
> were the things for which we forfeited eternal felicity.

But immediately, after these weightless matters, these incomprehensible
additions and extended notions, Moll and her husband are back at the
reckoning, the formulary conversion of death and birth, heaven and hell,
into cash.

> Our first business was to compare our stock. He was very honest to me,
> and told me his stock was pretty good . . . I gave him an account of
> my stock as faithfully . . . My stock which I had with me was £246
> some odd shillings; so that we had £354 between us . . .

With her heart lifted up in gratitude to Providence, Moll plans an irreproachable life, for an irreproachable life is now truly possible: Christian virtue and "stock" have become metaphysically identified, an eternal
equation in the mysterious plan of things. From now on, God punches
the buttons of this cash-register world, and it is virtue that lies in the
till. Most grotesque of ironies: the "sordid trifles," the "pleasant things"
that now look so "absurd" to Moll, the things for which she now refuses
to forfeit her "eternal felicity," come to her henceforth in greater quantities than ever before, precisely as the sign of grace and redemption, the
temporal guarantee of her eternal felicity.

   In speaking of the structure of *Moll Flanders* in terms of a hierarchy
of ironies—a system of stresses and counterstresses (to return to our figure
of the arch) that "hold the book together" in significant unity—we are

faced with the need, sooner or later, of making some tentative distinction between what the author might have intended ironically and what actually functions ironically in the book. This question, of the author's deliberate intention, arises particularly in connection with irony; for we think of an author as knowing what he is doing better than another person might know what he is doing, and if he is being elaborately ironic, then—one would assume—he must "intend" at least some of the irony. Irony is "double-talk." But if the author is "sincere" and intends no double-talk, would it not be more consistent usage, on our part, to say that the book is "sincere" in the same sense that the author is sincere, that it contains no double-talk, no ironies?

Let us illustrate this difficulty as it suggests itself in the specifically moralizing portions of *Moll Flanders*. Moll robs a child, comes near to murdering the infant, and moralizes the adventure thus:

> . . . as I did the poor child no harm, I only thought I had given the parents a just reproof for their negligence, in leaving the poor lamb to come home by itself, and it would teach them to take more care another time . . .

She rolls a drunk, after a night spent whoring, comes home to count and weigh her loot, and accompanies her highly satisfactory calculations with moving reflections on the sins which fathers visit upon their children by drunkenness and wenching; she is even inspired to quote Solomon on the foul disease. These reflections are followed by a complacent account of how the adventure, into which she had led the gentleman, had brought him to reform his ways, restored him to the bosom of a loving wife, and secured the happiness of an innocent family. It is to these moralizing thoughts of Moll's that Defoe is undoubtedly referring the reader, in his Author's Preface, when he advises us to make "virtuous and religious uses" of the story. He even mentions, in his Preface, the incident of the robbery of the little girl, and the moral message he associates with this incident is precisely that given it by Moll herself—parents who deck their children in finery and allow them to go to dancing school alone are given a "good memento" of what may ensue; and, generally, the moral that he would have us find in Moll's accounts of her criminal practices is that which Moll (now a reformed soul and "honest" woman at the time of writing her memoirs) is herself always anxious to inculcate. But what, objectively, is the relationship of Moll's moralizing thoughts to her adventures? Her adventures are criminal, but she herself is not a criminal type; she is not a woman of the underworld, but a woman of the bourgeois world; her aspirations are thoroughly middle-class—she wants, above all, economic security and middle-class respectability. She thinks middle-class thoughts; her morality is middle-class morality—platitudinous, stereotypic, a morality suited to the human species in its peculiar aspect as cash-calculator, and a morality, therefore, most particularly suitable to the prostitute.

Criminal in action, Moll will have to moralize crime as a social good: and so she does. Her robbery of a child will have prevented many future crimes of this kind; her depredations upon one drunk will have preserved the happiness of many families: all the readers of *Moll Flanders* will have received her benefactions. Moll's moralizing thoughts are the harmonies of the cash-register world in which she lives, for the cash register, like the celestial spheres, has its harmonies too, as the buttons are punched, the mechanism throbs, and the till rolls out. But these harmonies are so divergent from the harmonies of what we know, from our own observations and from the history of ethical ideas, as the spiritually and morally sensitive life, that their meaning in the total context of the book offers itself as ironic meaning: the morality that is preached by Moll is a burlesque of morality.

But if Defoe "intended" Moll's little moral sermons as the message of his book (and he does, in his Author's Preface, so guarantee them for us as his own persuasions), how can they be said to be ironic? We are left with two possibilities. Either *Moll Flanders* is a collection of scandal-sheet anecdotes naïvely patched together with the platitudes that form the morality of an impoverished soul (Defoe's), a "sincere" soul but a confused and degraded one; or *Moll Flanders* is a great novel, coherent in structure, unified and given its shape and significance by a complex system of ironies. The most irreducible fact about the book is that we read it—and reread it—with gusto and marvel. We could not do this if it were the former of our alternatives. That it may be the latter is justified by the analysis it yields itself to, as an ironic structure, and most of all justified by our pleasure in it. Shall we, then, waive the question of Defoe's "intention" and "sincerity"? Speculations as to these apparently can add nothing to the book nor can they take anything from it; the book remains what it is. And we do not have appropriate instruments for analysis of

Defoe's intention and sincerity, in the deepest meaning of intention and sincerity. We might guess that a great book could not be written by an impoverished soul, and that imponderable traits of moral sensitivity and prophetic intuition might lie in an author and realize themselves in his book without his recognition of them: these would be guesses. Not guess, but inescapable assurance from the quality of the book, is Defoe's understanding of his creature, Moll, whatever else he might not have recognized or understood in the work that was going on under his own hand as the product of his observant eye and his faculty for clean selection and coherent arrangement. In understanding his creature without the slightest divarication from her movements and her thoughts, he gave to Moll the immense and seminal reality of an Earth Mother, progenetrix of the wasteland, sower of our harvests of technological skills, bombs, gadgets, and the platitudes and stereotypes and absurdities of a morality suitable to a wasteland world.

ON *Clarissa Harlowe*

Clarissa is the antithesis of Moll Flanders, as heroine. In the earliest episode of importance in *Clarissa Harlowe*—the attempt of the Harlowe family to force the girl into marriage with "rich Solmes"—we see her in revolt against that materialism to which Moll "adjusted" so nicely and with which she so tirelessly collaborated. The central action of Clarissa's story is a rape, an experience which might have assumed a position of minor importance among Moll's adventures in adultery, bigamy, and incest—conceivably an incident that Moll might even have forgotten to make a "memorandum" of. But Clarissa is sent to her grave by it, and not only does it cause her death, but upon it are made to hinge the sanctions of family life, the structure of society, and the power relationships between the orders of the divine and the diabolic. The chief idiosyncrasy of Moll Flanders' world is the tendency to externalize life, to convert all experience into measurable material quantities and cash; the chief idiosyncrasy of Clarissa's is exactly the reverse: it is the tendency to convert the external forms of life—social customs, physical action, material quantities—into subjective quality and spiritual value. This, at least, describes a striking difference between the two heroines and the two books at the literal level; though we must hesitate, at this point, to decide how deep the difference in values lies.

With materials whose tendency is so strongly subjective, the form of this novel will be one that allows a careful sifting of motives and a sensitive representation of emotions. The technical problem with which we are confronted here is that of the "point of view" (or "focus of narration"), a problem which may be phrased thus: given a certain kind of subject matter, how can it be brought into focus for the reader? From what "angle," what point of observation, can the drama best be seen? From the author's own? or from that of the chief character in the novel?

45

or from that of one of the minor characters? or from the points of view of several characters? or from some presumably automatic and mechanical point of view (like that of a camera)? Both of Richardson's protagonists must, for the full evolution of the tragedy, die in its throes, without that calm distance and settled state of health required for the writing of memoirs. Furthermore, the dramatic impact of the material lies in the vital immediacy, not of only one person's motives and emotions, but of those of at least two persons—Clarissa and Lovelace. If either of the protagonists had been allowed to tell the tale from his own point of view alone, neither would have been able to penetrate into the subjective life of the other. Richardson could not, therefore, solve the problem of point of view as Defoe did, by using the "seeing eye" of a single character. Nor could he use the point of view of the "omniscient author," as did Cervantes, which implies a removed standpoint, disinvolvement on the part of the observer, and a godlike sweep of vision and knowledge of the meaning of events. The reader must be as implicated as Clarissa herself, or as Lovelace, in false hopes, disappointments, expectations, torments, with as little foreknowledge of the way out; he must, moreover, be able to follow the drama from day to day, as it takes place within the minds of both protagonists. Thus the event must be recorded as if at the moment of its taking place; it must be recorded from a subjective point of view; and —additional problem—a certain amount of information must also be allowed to come to the reader concerning a number of other people's attitudes and activities. Richardson used the vehicle of a series of letters, written by major and minor characters, and representing a variety of points of view, all subjective.

The epistolary form of the book slows down the pace of the story almost intolerably, for we are dependent for information upon the mechanics of the postal system and the finger-and-elbow mechanics of the pen wielders. Certain significances attach to this slowness of pace. Before the reader can find out "what has happened" at any one point in the action, he must wait until a half dozen people have had time to write letters, receive answers, and reply; for no one in the story himself ever knows precisely and objectively "what has happened," inasmuch as "what happens" lies not in the objective event but in a multitude of subjective reactions. It is only by the mixed evidence of a number of letters that the "action"—being of a subjective character—can receive clarification. A psychological node, or system of interconnections and cross references, dense, complex, and life-resembling, is thus contrived from the operations of a group of minds on a single event, each mind offering its own fractional information or insight as to what the event is and signifies. Illumination is suspended until each of the fragments falls into place in the slowly accreted group, and meanwhile the action is kept under the pressure of doubt, hope, indecision, misconception, and fatality.

The central event of the novel, over which the interminable series of letters hovers so cherishingly, is, considered in the abstract, a singularly thin and unrewarding piece of action—the deflowering of a young lady —and one which scarcely seems to deserve the universal uproar which it provokes in the book. There is very little subplot. The rape is in the offing, it is at hand, it is here, it is over, Clarissa sickens and dies, and that is all. Against this simplicity of event, one thinks of Moll Flanders' "threescore years of continuous variety." And yet *Moll*, with its long roll of statutory crimes and broken taboos, offers a flat fictional landscape, uniform, unaccented, horizontal (though fascinating in its own quality as are some flat physical topographies, such as the southwestern deserts or the Florida Everglades); whereas *Clarissa* is a dramatically vertical world of fabulous heights and rank profundities, with God the Father at the top, and, at the bottom, the lurid gleam and the foul stench of hell. The epistolary form of the novel provides us with a partial explanation for the fact that Richardson has been able to create so dramatic a world with so simple a theme. This slow and hovering form endows the physiological event—the rape—with profound attraction and significance by holding it up slantwise to view in a murk of shadows, turning it mysteriously, allowing it to emerge slightly, withdrawing it, allowing it to emerge again, and so on. It is as tantalizing and evasive as a trout. Only at long length are we permitted to get it into clear focus, while, in the meantime, we have been steadily bombarded, page after page, with an imagery deriving from various submerged but exceedingly powerful impulses and attitudes.

We have spoken of images and symbols to some extent in our previous studies. With *Clarissa*, these become of primary concern. An image, in its technical psychological sense, is a mental representation of a sense impression, visual, tactile, aural, gustatory, olfactory, thermal, or kinesthetic. In life, the image is frequently bound up with the actual sensation; but in speaking of imagery in a poem or a novel, we should be carefully aware that what we are referring to is the mental representation alone, quite divorced from sensation. Furthermore, an image is rarely single; a whole setting, or a moment of drama in which several characters participate, may form "an image," but it will be an image of a very complex kind, actually a construct of images acting as a unity. Again, a relatively simple image, like that of a porcelain teacup, or a green silk purse, or a parasol with the sun shining through it, though we may speak of it as "vivid," does not necessarily derive its vividness from imagined sensory impressions associated with such a teacup, purse, or parasol. It may be "vivid" as an image while the sensory impressions associated with it are extremely thin and vague. Its "vividness" will be a function of the context in which it finds itself, the way it is spoken of by the author, associations of attitude with the object that may not be sensory associations at all. There are many optical images of this kind in *Clarissa:* for instance, Clarissa in white clothes, kneeling in prayer, seen through a keyhole. What makes this image sharp and vivid are associations of purity and piety with whiteness and with prayer (most particularly in the dramatic context of Clarissa's captivity in a sordid house by a man of foul intentions); also the keyhole frame sharpens the image for us, as if we were looking at her through a telescope, for it focuses the eye on the single figure, cutting off any surrounding area, at the same time that it puts her at a distance like a person in a picture, removing her from any approach except the optical approach (this removal contributes, of course, to the "vividness" of our sense of her purity and piety).

By reiteration and accumulation, and by other always specific contextual conditions, an image may act as a symbol. That is, it may automatically begin to stand for a complex structure of feelings and values that are of great significance in the total structure of the book. We have seen this happen in *Moll Flanders.* So insistently does *Moll* bombard us with gold watches, gold necklaces, gold rings plain or fancy, gold guineas, that when the Bath gentleman opens the drawer full of gold guineas and asks Moll to scoop up a handful, we are—even perhaps without framing the thought deliberately—under the strong impression of a symbolic action, an action that focuses the predilections and values of everyone in the *Moll Flanders* world. Let us consider the evolution of a symbol in *Clarissa Harlowe:* that of the "Clarissa-symbol" itself. In the early scene when Clarissa is brought down into the parlor for a family conference, we are given a picture of the girl as she sees herself in the mirror

48

beside her chair—pale, debilitated, and distraught, with heaving bosom, and most interesting and attractive. Cumulatively, many similar images reinforce this picture of attractive, desirable womanhood: Clarissa wilting like a broken lily on its stalk, Clarissa resting her lovely pale head on the motherly breast of Mrs. Lovick, Clarissa lifting her eyes in gratitude to heaven for a simple bowl of gruel or glass of water, Clarissa on her knees in prayer in miraculously dirt-resistant white garments, or Clarissa in torn clothes and with streaming eyes, prostrated at the feet of her demon-lover. The womanly quality which Richardson has made attractive in these images is that of an erotically tinged debility which offers, masochistically, a ripe temptation to violence. Thus the image of Clarissa achieves, under construction in the context, the status of a symbol, a focus of feelings and attitudes, rich, dense, and deep, however strange and even perverse.

In understanding the Clarissa-symbol, we should add to its associations the effect of the optical framing. Naturally, given the point of view that Richardson has adopted, we must always see Clarissa through someone else's eyes or else as she sees herself in a mirror. This would seem merely an exigency of the letter form of the book; but when we consider, along with this natural optical tactic, the fact that special devices (such as mirror or keyhole) are so often employed to emphasize the *seeing* of Clarissa by someone, and usually under conditions where she must be unconscious of being looked at, we begin to feel that the optical tactic must be "working" in a somewhat complex strategic way. The most extreme case in point is, of course, the episode of the rape itself, when the door of the room is left open and "female figures flit" across it, watching. One effect of this strategy is to make of the reader a Peeping Tom, to make him share in the dubious delights of voyeurism. Also, as strategy, it is consistent with that of the letter vehicle: as the letters "tell all" and the letter writer exposes all, turning himself inside out to his confidant, so the handling of the images offers all—not particularly to be experienced (in imagination) at first hand—but to be *seen*. Paradoxically enough, though the material of the novel is so largely subjective, "inner," yet a definitive quality of the *Clarissa* world is its publicity: no one is alone, can ever be alone, in *Clarissa*, not even in the most private performances of prayer, sex, and death. *Clarissa* is not a world of the individual soul, but, in the most extensive sense, a social world, a public world. We shall perhaps see, in a later consideration of this novel as myth, how the publicity tactics of *Clarissa* are technically coherent with its mythical significance, its significance as a projection of a social dream.

An immense number of the Clarissa-images occur in an erotic context; but Clarissa's whiteness, her narrow range of stances and gestures (she kneels, she prostrates herself, she tears her neck ruffles and exposes her bosom, she wields a key or penknife or scissors), and the distancing and framing of the image for the eye, exclude a large number of associations that might operate in an erotic context—as color modulations, tactile impressions, nature sounds, and so forth. In other words, the erotic situations that are dramatized are excessively simple and abstract, limited to suggestions of bodily violence or violence done to clothes (stabbing or tearing) and the converse, suggestions of violence suffered (weeping, fainting, dying). Clarissa herself is offered as the ideal woman in her purity and debility—and these qualities, too, are extraordinarily limited abstractions from the complex of qualities that might be conceived as making up complete womanhood; at the same time, pure and debile as she is, paradoxically she offers an ideal of the sexual woman (in the world of this book), the physically desirable woman. She is a kind of love goddess, a Venus. She is not the Venus of the Renaissance, with an erotic apparatus of Mayflowers, delicately tinted veils, sinuous tresses, zephyrs, lutes, and cupids, suggesting many enjoyments for the senses, suggesting also the aesthetic act of contemplation.[1] She is much more abstract than that. She is the love goddess of the Puritan middle class of the English eighteenth century, of the bourgeois family, and of mercantile society. She is pure (to be paraded for the sight as an expensive chattel—or, in later generations, to show herself voluntarily as "career girl"), and yet to be violated (for in a society that has desexualized its professed mores, sex is a violation), but still to be seen while she is being violated (for sex insists on perpetuating its attractions, but they must be enjoyed by proxy, as in the movies, or *sub rosa*). The lover to whom she deploys her attractions is the lover as narcissist, as voyeur, as sadist—all abstractionists. Her mythical features still appear to us—for it would be a mistake to think that the Clarissa-myth does not still have deep social and psycho-

[1] In one of his erotic fantasies, Lovelace visualizes Clarissa in a situation bearing some pictorial resemblance to that of the Renaissance Venus with her bevy of cupids, but the difference is significant. He sees her "with a twin Lovelace at each charming breast . . . full of wishes for the sake of the pretty varlets, and for her own sake that I would deign to legitimate; that I would condescend to put on the nuptial fetters."

logical roots—in her two chief aspects: they appear on the covers of *Vogue* magazine, in the woman who is a wraith of clothes, debile and expensive, irrelevant to sense-life or affectional life, to be seen only; and they appear on the covers of *True Confessions* and *True Detective Stories,* in the many-breasted woman with torn dishabille and rolling eyeballs, a dagger pointing at her, a Venus as abstract as the *Vogue* Venus in her appeal to the eye and the idea alone, but differing in that she is to be vicariously ripped and murdered. Clarissa is a powerful symbol because she is both.

Similarly, an image of "the man" begins its evolution into a symbol when Clarissa has her private interview with "odious Solmes." She speaks of his splay feet, his posture "asquat" (like a toad), and his "ugly weight" that presses against her hoop. Perhaps no single word with emotional resonance occurs more frequently in this novel than the word "man." Solmes's own function in contributing to the symbol of "the man" is rather quickly over with; all he has to do, as suitor, is to be repellent; his real status is similar to that of the Harlowe males with whom he is hand-in-glove in action—that is, he is economic man, desexualized man. "The man" proper, as this symbol is deployed, is the man as lover, as the sexual threat. Clarissa screams, when she sees Lovelace in the garden, "A man!" "Ah, this man, my dear!" she exclaims to Miss Howe. "The man, my dear, looked quite ugly!" she tells her friend, after a predatory approach on Lovelace's part. She speaks of his "savage kiss" reddening her hand. Miss Howe confirms her notions of men: they are a "vile race of reptiles." Somewhere Joseph Conrad speaks of "the fascination of the abomination," a phrase which applies nicely to the image of "the man" in *Clarissa;* for as the image grows by reiteration and variation into a symbol, attractive elements are fused with the repellent elements, so that the abominable toadlike reptilian "man" becomes demonically fascinating: a creature obsessed with the desire to violate virginal, high-minded, helpless womanhood, and so single-tracked in his passion to destroy this divinity that he, too, assumes divine stature: he is the evil divinity, the devil himself. It is no wonder that even Miss Howe, after being present at a party where Lovelace has fluttered the dovecotes, confesses to Clarissa that she has begun to see him in her dreams.

The modern reader may fail to see at once in Lovelace the Satan, the archfiend, which many generations of readers have found in this character. Magnificently projected as Lovelace is, we may be inclined to see him as a study in psychopathology, or as a portrait of an egotist, or as a portrait (as one critic has said) of an "overgrown schoolboy." All these he may be, but, to read *Clarissa* in its fulness of implication, we should also be aware of the mythical resonances of the character. There can be no doubt that Richardson and the contemporary audience saw him as an embodiment of "splendid sin,"

> of the pride of life (as reproved by medieval theologians), of irresistible and pernicious fascination, the eighteenth century Lucifer, in fact, a worthy antagonist to his paragon of virtue, Clarissa.[2]

Lovelace himself, as he thinks of Clarissa as "divine," certainly considers himself to be one of the damned. In a dream he sees her angelic white-clad figure rising in a company of angels to the abode of the Seraphim, while an abyss opens at his feet and he falls headlong into it. Nor is this notion of the mythological significance of Lovelace, in relation to Clarissa, confined to Lovelace's own idea of himself, or to Richardson's intention, or to what older generations of readers may have found in the book. André Gide puts the matter succinctly when he says that "in the pages of *Clarissa*, heaven is continually being offered cheap to hell."

We have, in the preceding paragraphs, frequently spoken of *Clarissa Harlowe* as myth, and it is through the conception of this novel as myth that we are able to explain more fully to ourselves the strange fact that, though the book reflects an essentially perverse psychology, it is nevertheless a great and powerful piece of fiction. But let us first of all divest ourselves of the idea that a myth is something "untrue." A myth cannot be "proved" logically or by the observation of physical fact. Whatever "truth" a myth may hold is not susceptible of this kind of proof. Myth is a dramatic vision of life, and we never cease making myths, accepting myths, believing in myths; even in our own positivistic age, we see life dramatically through the myths offered us by Hollywood, by the commercial advertisements, by the detective story, by local politics, by international diplomacy, or by the physicists. Myth appears in a novel when the action and the particular set of manners represented in the book are organized in a total symbolic construct of such a kind that it not only reflects the aspirations and ideals, the attitudes and customs, of a large social group, but also seems to give to these attitudes and customs the sanction

2 Brian W. Downs, *Richardson* (London: Routledge & Kegan Paul, Ltd., 1938), p. 116.

of some "higher authority," perhaps the authority of ancient tradition, perhaps supernatural authority, perhaps the authority of some vaguely defined power-and-knowledge concept such as "law" or "government" or "science" or even "society" itself. Finally, this total symbolic construct is, in myth, projected dramatically. We shall need, for greater clarity, to differentiate myth from allegory, as allegory was defined in the essay on *The Pilgrim's Progress*. Allegory, too, is an organized symbolism; but the differentia of allegory is the fact that its elements are, in gross, to be read off in point-to-point equations into an abstract, discursive, intellectual system. Myth does not offer an intellectual system. What it offers is the dramatization of powers that are assumed to have universal authority over the actions of men. The dominion of allegory (as a total system) is the intellect; the dominion of myth is the irrational.

We shall speak of *the* myth of *Clarissa Harlowe*, but we must be prepared to see it in several different aspects, or as several different sets of mythological ideas which have been mingled and fused by Richardson and given coherence in the large, simple dramatic shape of the story, but which can be singled out as sub-systems for examination. An analogy may help us here. It is as if the *Clarissa*-myth, as a whole, were a universe described by a number of different planetary orbits; the different sets of "mythological ideas" are the different orbits, but these orbits have interrelationships in the larger system of the *Clarissa*-universe, and the whole is held together by complex magnetic correspondences. The analogy helps us to visualize both the strong internal unity of the major system and the distinct existence of the subsystems. For convenience, then, we shall be speaking as if of a number of different myths ("the Puritan myth" in *Clarissa*, for instance, or "the myth of class"), but we should continue to think of them as not actually independent or self subsistent, but as operating only by virtue of the magnetic laws binding them in the unit of the whole.

Certain of these we have already touched on, but we must see them now in fuller articulation and in their correspondences with others. The most evident, and one which had Richardson's own conscious deliberation behind it, is the Puritan religious myth, which was alive in Richardson's culture and which he used to give edificatory significance to his materials. His aim, as he expressed it, was to teach the "highest and most important doctrines of Christianity," and his success in this project is witnessed by the comment of a contemporary Dutch Mennonite divine, who said that if *Clarissa* had formed one of the canonical books of the Bible, it would have furnished proof positive of divine inspiration. The Puritan myth, as it is inflected in *Clarissa,* is a daemonic view of life. Deity and the evil spirit are deeply concerned in the affairs of men. Through charm of body and other lures—wit, worldly graces, worldly power, mobility, uninhibited freedom—and with the most cunning deceit, the evil spirit tempts the woman as he tempted Eve. The ultimate obsession of the devil is, of course, sex, for in the Puritan mythology sex is the culmination of all evil, the unmasked face of fear. Like the Satan who tempted Job, this Lucifer is not interested in small fry. Job was "the greatest of all the men of the east," there was "none like him in the earth," he was "a perfect and an upright man." Similarly, Clarissa is a paragon of virtue, a "divinity of a woman," which is the reason why she holds any interest for the prince of evil spirits. She is virtuous in many ways, she is charitable "to the industrious poor," she disciplines herself to deserve 144 merit marks for virtue every week, and if she omits to earn one of them she has to add it onto the next week's budget. But above all she is chaste. As the devil's evil obsession is sex, so the woman's virtuous obsession is her chastity; but it must be observed that chastity is here a physical attribute (quite as it is in *Moll Flanders*), that innocence of spirit is not distinguished from bodily intactness, that the two are identified as one. Therefore, when the devil has succeeded in befouling the woman's body, he will have obtained a victory over her soul—save for the intervention of the Deity. The woman's will for purity makes her subject to an inspiration of Divine Grace. As Job was selected from among all men for the severest trial of faith, so Clarissa has been selected from among all women for unique travail as preparation for sainthood. Potent as the devil is, the universe is well loaded against him, and when the crisis is over, Providence begins distributing rewards and punishments with remarkable accuracy to everyone in the book, thoroughly satisfying poetic justice. Lovelace is, as Richardson puts it, "condignly punished"; the infamous Sinclair dies in incredible torments of a vile disease; Miss Howe, Mr. Hickman, Belford, the worthy Norton, are all made "signally happy"; the Harlowes themselves are so deeply afflicted in conscience that they take the backstairs the rest of their lives to avoid passing the martyred Clarissa's room; James becomes involved in insupportable financial difficulties; Arabella's husband is unfaithful to her and her wedded life horrid; even the servants are paid off with minute attention to their respective deserts. As for Clarissa, she has received the crown of all joys: her bridegroom is Christ. We may observe that, far from being the tragedy which Richardson, as a literary man with some knowledge of the traditional structure of tragedy, worked hard to make it (Clarissa's "tragic flaw," for instance, is designed with high deliberation), the novel is really a comedy—a "divine comedy"—if we use as the generic distinction between comedy and tragedy the happy and the unhappy ending. It has a "happy ending," the good are rewarded, the evil are punished; and it has this ending by virtue of the Puritan world view whose powerful outlines dominate the novel.

We turn now to another mythological aspect of *Clarissa,* and if, for the sake of clarity, we must pin labels on each of these, we shall call this one a myth of social caste or class. We have said that Lovelace, who has the place of the devil in the Puritan myth, offers the lures of wit, worldly graces and power, mobility, uninhibited freedom; but these are qualities and privileges of aristocracy, and Lovelace himself is a member of the aristocratic class and heir to a title. By contrast, the woman he woos is the daughter of middle-class parents. The Harlowes are London tradesmen, representatives of the prosperous bourgeoisie that has been supreme in society and politics since the consolidations of the seventeenth century. It is a class not distinguished by the social refinements and gallantries or by the intellectual graces, a class that has acquired power through hard work, cash calculation, and sobriety, a class therefore by definition unable to afford aristocratic freedoms such as impulsiveness, enthusiasm, idleness, extravagance, debauchery (as these freedoms are conceived in Richardson's middle-class fantasy on the aristocratic theme).[3] Just as Lovelace, the aristocrat, is drawn larger than life, both as to his vices and his charm, so also the Harlowes are drawn larger than life: not only Clarissa—who is the epitome of that virtue of virginity which, besides a fortune, is the best trade commodity of the middle-class woman, determining her price bracket—but the others as well, the mother and the uncles, and particularly Mr. Harlowe and the son James, with their concentration on hard cash and the consequent brutalization of their feelings. Clarissa herself is powerfully attracted to Lovelace. Possible marriage with him is kept constantly in the foreground of the novel; in-

[3] The discussion of this aspect of the book owes much to the essay "From Pamela to Clarissa," by William M. Sale, Jr., in *The Age of Johnson* (New Haven: Yale University Press, 1949).

deed, even after the crisis, when she has excluded that possibility, it is still kept in the foreground by the other characters, by Miss Howe, for instance, who sees the marriage as a sensible way to settle the hullabaloo and make everybody happy yet. Marriage with Lovelace would be a symbolic act, uniting middle class and aristocracy, bringing the middle class within those delightful open ranges of freedom that are the aristocratic privilege, and endowing it with the refined talents and the graces that it lacks. Clearly, in reading *Clarissa* in this way, we are reading the whole action as "larger than life," larger than a private family's adventures. We are reading it as a symbolic construct reflecting the ideals of a whole culture—that is, we are reading it as myth. A modern commentator has said that Richardson realized

> for his generation the emotions engendered by the conditions of life that defined his generation's hopes and that set limitations upon the fulfillment of those hopes. Before his novels appeared, however, eighteenth century Englishmen were sufficiently aware of the fact that their vital social problem was the interpenetration of the emergent middle class and the surviving aristocracy. His contemporaries had read authors who sought to educate the middle class in the manners and decorum of the disappearing aristocracy; they had been amused by authors who pointed up the gaucherie of the new man and woman, the new peer.[4]

Richardson's particular dramatization of this social condition was the exposure of his middle-class heroine to seduction by a nobleman. The significance of the act lies, on the one hand, in the fact that—up to a point—the heroine does seek union with the aristocrat who threatens her integrity, and, on the other hand, in the fact that the marriage does not, after all, take place. If *Clarissa* may be read as a "parable on the antithesis of the aristocratic and middle-class codes," the parable contrives to demonstrate finally the superiority of the latter.[5] The aristocracy is put in its place (Lovelace, we presume, goes to hell) and Clarissa, on her way to heaven, bestows blessings that assuredly have magical virtue (like the blessings bestowed by Isaac and by Jacob) on her mother and father, her sister, her brother, her uncles, Miss Howe, Mrs. Norton, the nurse, the servants. That is, by her death, symbolically she makes great

[4] *Ibid.,* p. 129.
[5] Downs, *op. cit.,* p. 182.

her class, gives supernatural sanction to its code, donates to it her mana, making of it an embodiment of the order of the universe.

Noticeably, the religious myth and the myth of class overlap in a good many places, for, whether by historical accident or inevitability, Puritanism became the moral code and the religious faith of the commercially prosperous middle class. Noticeably also, however, there are places where these two mythological aspects of the book seem to contradict each other. Lovelace's part in the religious myth is to represent evil; he is to be hated; above all, he is to be feared. But in the class myth he has an ambivalent status; he exerts powerful attraction; nevertheless, as the drama evolves, he is seen to be too vicious after all. Fear of what the aristocracy stands for (or what it stands for in Richardson's fantasy) overcomes the attraction of what it stands for. What has been indulged by this myth is the middle-class wish to be aristocratic, to be elegant and idle and uninhibited; for, like dreams, myths indulge the hopes and passions and impulses of men. But, also like dreams, they are subject to a "censor." The indulgence may be sidled up to, but it must not be carried too far. In actual dreams, the "censor" in the psyche acts by disguising the wish either under forms that can be morally approved, or under forms apparently so fantastic and incoherent that they seem morally irrelevant. In myths, on the other hand, where whole dramas are acted out with narrative coherence, the "censor" may offer a dramatic resolution which negates the indulged wish by substituting some other attraction—as, in *Clarissa*, the wish to be aristocratic is negated by a counterwish, the wish to embody in the middle class itself the universal order, both divine and social. The latter wish offers no moral difficulties; one has merely to look upon oneself and one's class as the highest product of the human race, the epitome of what God intended man to be; and, implicitly, what Richardson tells his readers is that the middle class, to see an image of what is socially and morally desirable, need not look beyond itself, but will find that image in what it already is. This is comforting doctrine, most particularly since the myth has already underhandedly indulged the desire for aristocratic pleasures.

Myth has its power and fertility not in singleness of meaning (like allegory) but in multiplicity of meaning—meaning that changes historically with social changes, and that changes at any one glance with the center one chooses to see in it. We shall have to add another center and another contour to the *Clarissa*-myth: namely, a dramatic vision of family

57

life and its sanctions. If *Clarissa* were a "novel of manners" alone, we should find in it a description of how a family lived and sinned and suffered in the eighteenth century, all possibly psychologically fascinating and perhaps with some universal significance. But, being myth, its vision of family life is raised to intimacy with the supernatural. The Harlowes acquire their "bigness" from other equators and other ecliptics than those that would circumscribe family life in a novel of manners. For Richardson, the family was a microcosm of society. Families were, he said, "so many miniatures" of the community of the world. But the family was not only a miniature of the world; it was an expression of divine order. In a later book, *Sir Charles Grandison* (the hero of which is Lovelace's opposite and thus a moral therapy for readers too attracted to the aristocratic rake), Sir Charles expresses himself on the concerns of Deity: "Does He not," he asks, "interest Himself, if I may so express myself, in the performance of filial duty? May it not be justly said, that to obey your parents is to serve God?" The particular family relationship that is eminent in *Clarissa* is that of female child to male parent, and it is brought dramatically to bear on the affair of marriage. We may learn something enlightening about this relationship from eighteenth-century conduct books. A parent "can no more force a Child to marry against her Consent, than a Child is permitted to act contrary to the Parent." [6] This is a situation comparable to a modern highway situation in Florida, where a sign at a railroad crossing decrees that neither vehicle, car or train, can go ahead until the other one has started. Another conduct book (one which the printer Richardson himself probably printed) offers the possibility of reciprocal modulation and of decision of act. "There is one instance," this writer says,

> wherein obedience to parents is of more importance to children than any other in life, and yet where they too often fail to pay it; and that is in the article of marriage: for, as long as children continue a part of their parent's family . . . they are absolutely in their parent's power, and have no more right to dispose of themselves than they have to dispose of the parents' fortune, or inheritance, or any of their goods . . .

[6] This and the two following passages from conduct books are quoted by Alan D. McKillop, in *Samuel Richardson* (Chapel Hill: University of North Carolina Press, 1936), p. 135.

And then he takes up the parents' responsibility.

> Prudent parents well know, that such accomplishments as either arise
> from, or tend to establish true worth, can alone render any pair happy
> in an union that must last for life. This, I say, all prudent parents
> very well know; and therefore are best fitted to make a right choice for
> their children; but still with this caution, that they do not offer vio-
> lence to their inclinations, by forcing them to marry against their will.
> For the rest, it were infinitely better, that perverse children should
> actually die in the disappointment of their inclinations, than that they
> should make both themselves and their parents for ever miserable, by
> an unfortunate and undutiful marriage.

The critical and helplessly ambiguous situation with which Clarissa is
faced is, as one critic has said, a "crisis that affects not merely the future
of any imaginary individual but the social position of the eighteenth century unmarried woman." [7]

"To obey your parents is to serve God." But Clarissa, dangerously
for this code, is economically independent. She could, practically speaking, do whatever her impulse led her to do. She could seek satisfaction
anywhere that she chose. And she does "go off with a man." Richardson
said, in correspondence, "Going off with a Man, is the thing I wanted
most to make inexcusable." The "man," as we have seen, is an outlaw,
a pariah, a threat, a social terror. But for this particular reading of
Clarissa as a myth of family life, he is—in a word—the lover. Clarissa's
"going off with" him is a symbolical alliance of daughter with lover
against family, an alliance with the outlaw and criminal who represents
enjoyments (in this context, enjoyments of love) which the financially
consolidated bourgeois family cannot tolerate inasmuch as enjoyment
of love would mean failure of sobriety, which is the moral pillar of
family unity and financial security. The book begins with this rebellion.
Actually, however, as the story progresses, it is not the daughter's rebellion that is thematically paramount, but the daughter's obedience; for
her father's curse is far more effective emotionally upon her than the
attraction of the lover, or than her desire to escape the sterile and brutal
cash alliance with the suitor approved by the family. Furthermore, the
father's curse is dramatically correlated with and confirmed by Lovelace's
own viciousness; the lover who would take the daughter out of the family

[7] F. C. Green, *Minuet* (London: J. M. Dent & Sons, Ltd., 1935), p. 403.

is exposed as the worst of all evildoers. From this point of view, the lover is indirectly a kind of moral employee of the father: he is the living scourge exercised by the father upon the rebellious daughter. The paramount motif is, then, not rebellion and escape, but acquiescence in parental values and return. Clarissa is the family's consoling symbol of the right-minded daughter. She has a great act to perform: her financial independence is not societally right; she voluntarily gives it up. And she returns to the parental nest. For Clarissa does make a symbolic return "to her Father's house" (her last, punning, highly disingenuous letter to Lovelace tells him that she will meet him there). "Her Father's house" is, in this context, heaven, and here the Puritan myth and the myth of family life coincide. Mr. Harlowe is proxy for God, and Clarissa's return to her Father's house is a supernatural equivalent of the necessary "return" of all daughters to the parental authority. The values that are given final sanction here are the typical values of the right-thinking bourgeois family: the father's authority is supreme; the daughter must not wed for satisfaction of personal impulse, but, if she weds, must do so for the further consolidation and enrichment of the clan; the lover is condemned; there must, in a word, be no love, except insofar as love can serve the family economy.

Clarissa's whiteness, her debility, and her death are correlatives of the sterilization of instinct and the impotence that are suggested as the desirable qualities of family and social life. As we have said previously, Clarissa's death does not provide a tragic ending for the story, but a "happy ending," inasmuch as her death is equated with supernatural joys and rewards. The scene in the death room is an astonishing one. The room is crowded with people, all pressing around the dying woman to obtain her blessing. The mourning is as public as possible; every sigh, every groan, every tear is recorded. One is given to understand that nothing could be a greater social good than Clarissa's death, nothing could be more enjoyable than to watch her in her death throes (she performs them charmingly), nothing a greater privilege than to be present at this festival of death and to weep and sniffle in the common orgy. An instructive grace note to the scene is Mrs. Judith Norton's observation that to have her own eyes closed in death by her young friend Clarissa was a "pleasure" which she had often "promised" herself—a pleasure now, alas, not to be obtained. This macabre satisfaction crowns the value system of *Clarissa,* triumphantly capping a code of Puritanism in morals, parental authoritarianism in the family, and the cash nexus as the only binding tie for society at large—a cult, in short, of death.

Clarissa returns "to her Father's house" as the perfect daughter, the model of all daughters. The novel offers the symbolic formula for such perfection: Clarissa is the sexless daughter, the dead daughter. In reading *Clarissa* finally as a sexual myth, we are reading it as a construct of irrationals similar to a dream (although, in the case of myth, the myth-maker is "dreaming" not only his own dream, but society's dream as well), and, irrationally, the sexless daughter manages to have the most violent of sexual experiences. It has been said of Clarissa that, by setting such a price upon herself, she "represents that extreme of puritanism which desires to be raped. Like Lovelace's her sexuality is really violent, insatiable in its wish for destruction." [8] In a sense, she keeps her cake while eating it—a proverbial paradox that expresses aptly what happens in dreams, where the forbidden wish is indulged under a disguise of nonindulgence. The mythical potency of *Clarissa,* in this respect, is witnessed by the fascination held for generations of readers by the motif of the carnal assault on a virgin. Novel after novel repeated this motif, obviously feeding an immense appetite of the reading public for more of the same. The assault is sometimes frustrated, sometimes carried through (*Clarissa,* of course, allows both: Lovelace accomplishes his vile ends, but the lady, being drugged, is in a sense not there; moreover, her death and sainthood negate the whole affair). Abduction by a handsome nobleman, captivity in a house of ill fame, and the use of drugs on the virtuous heroine, are devices almost obligatory in these books.[9] Richard Chase, writing on the nature of myth, has suggested that "myth is the repository of repressed wishes" and that

> part of the magic power of myth stems from its ability to furnish "recognition scenes," in which we have the thrilling experience of coming face to face with a disinherited part of ourselves.[10]

[8] V. S. Pritchett, *The Living Novel* (New York: Reynal & Hitchcock, 1947), p. 28.

[9] Cf. Mrs. Davys' *The Accomplish'd Rake* (1756), Jane Marishall's *History of Miss Clarinda Cathcart* (3d ed. 1767), Mrs. Sarah Scott's *Cornelia* (1750), Mrs. Woodfin's *Sally Sable* (before 1764), Diderot's *La Réligeuse* (1760). In the romances of Mrs. Radcliffe, as Mario Praz has pointed out, the motif of captivity manages to exploit the same set of sado-masochistic attractions.

[10] *Quest for Myth* (Baton Rouge: Louisiana State University Press, 1949), p. 101.

The modern reader may be disinclined to find, in the captivity-and-assault sequences in *Clarissa,* "recognition scenes" of this kind, and indeed the device used by Lovelace appears extraordinarily crude; but the reader's disinclination may merely reflect the fact that Hollywood has elaborated subtler stratagems of wish fulfillment, under a more refined censorship. Lovelace's own frenzied fantasy was undoubtedly prophetic when he saw himself in the dock on trial for his life, and all the sympathies of the audience with the handsome criminal: "Even the judges, and the whole crowded bench will acquit us in their hearts! and every single man wish he had been me."

As for Clarissa's own perverted sexuality, we read it in the profusion of sexual images that, paradoxically, at the level of professed narrative intention are meant to illustrate her resistance to Lovelace and her protection of her virginity—for surely we must find ambiguous those contexts which illustrate the virtue of chastity and the wickedness of sex by an imagery making defloration attractive and exciting; but more especially we find her sexual violence in the constant identification of sex and death, phallic images and images of assassination. The identification of love and death is one of the oldest puns and one of the oldest of myth motifs; it is found in the great love stories—in the stories of Tristan and Iseult, Phaedra and Hippolytus, Dido and Aeneas, Antony and Cleopatra (it is found also quite literally in the life histories of salmon, ephemerids, and some spiders, a fact which is perhaps of significance in deepening our appreciation of the literary instinct in this matter). The sexual myth in *Clarissa* is founded in the love-death identification, and acquires power from that ancient and universal perception; but as *Clarissa* formulates the love myth, it becomes perverse, inasmuch as "love" here is conceived so strangely and exclusively as physical violation, an act of stabbing or ripping, with no implication of any aspect of sexual passion except a passion to murder and be murdered. Indeed, it is impossible to think of either Clarissa's or Lovelace's attitudes as involving any sensuality; for the word "sensual" pertains to gratification of the senses, and we find it difficult to discover those senses which might be gratified by stabbing. Their passion symbolizes gratification, not of sensual life, but of a submerged portion of the emotional life whose tendency actually opposes gratification of the senses—the death wish, the desire for destruction. And it is here that the mythical representation of sexual relationships in *Clarissa* coincides with and deeply reinforces the mythical representation of social values and the values of family life. From each point of view, the book is a paean to death. Richardson is the great poet of the adolescence of our own acquisitive, aggressive culture—a culture that has elaborated the cognate political myth of a world divided between two powers, one "good," one "bad," each engrossed in the devising of magical weapons for the destruction of the other, each "censoring" the grand death wish with a diplomacy designed to bring about a marriage in all profit and decency.

Dr. Samuel Johnson said of Richardson's heroines that they all had "a kind of obliquity in their moral vision," and, commenting particularly upon the casuistry which he found in Clarissa, he complained, "You may observe there is always something which she prefers to truth." Clarissa's character has been read by certain critics as a study in the divided mind. We must certainly acquiesce in a reading of her story as a psychological study; but our own reading of the novel as myth finds the psychological study to be but one level in a multileveled construct whose depth and richness derive from vast social dreams in which the individual character, however interesting from the point of view of character study, is at the same time more than an individual character—is a fabulous creature of epic stature, clothed with the ideals of a culture and of a race. In this reading, Clarissa's moral "obliquity," her "divided mind," are a function of mysterious indulgences in the forbidden, through which a Puritan-capitalistic culture found its systematic inhibitions gratefully removed, while, at the same time, it had in Lovelace a whipping boy for the same indulgences. But through Clarissa also the systematic inhibitions of this culture must receive their supernatural sanction, their "higher authority"; for the race does demand "higher authority" for its mores, simply in order to face itself with equanimity and to perpetuate itself proudly. Having so much dependent on her, so many and such complex duties to perform for her readers, Clarissa may well appear as a moral casuist and a divided mind.

ON *Tom Jones*

In order to place *Clarissa* in such a light that it may be viewed all round about, in its complexity, we have had to try to lever it up out of unconscious darknesses where it has much of its nourishment and its vitality. With so vast a book, so deeply rooted in subliminal matter, the process of levering it into critical daylight is a struggle; even after we get it out where we can see it, strange, only half-transparent growths still attach to it, like the rubbery growths of the sea bottom. *Tom Jones*, by Richardson's great contemporary Fielding, is all out in mental sunlight. The product of a generously intelligent, tough and yet elegant art, it too is a complex book, but its complexities are within the immediate view of the reason. Structurally, it is characterized, like *Don Quixote*, by a systematic organization of contrasts, a playing off of one attitude and one way of life against another attitude and another way of life, with a constant detail of contrast in the character relationships, scene relation ships, and even verbal relationships; for with this novel, for the first time in English fiction, the full and direct artistic impact of *Don Quixote* is felt (as distinguished from the general direction which Cervantes set for the modern novel). And like Cervantes, Fielding uses the "point of view" of the omniscient author; his world is too populous and too extensive in its spatial design for the survey of any one character within the book; and the author's own humorous irony is itself one of the materials of the novel, providing, in the "head-chapters," one more contrast in the total aesthetic system—the contrast of plane between the author and his book, between criticism and creation, between intelligence focused *on* the human situation he has created and the intelligence of the characters *within* the created situation.

We have been using the term "structure" to mean the arrangement and interrelation of all the elements in a book, as dominated by the general character of the whole. It is a term that is sometimes used to mean "structure of action" alone, that is, the plot. But, certainly at least with *Clarissa,* we have seen that the total architecture of a novel involves a great deal more than plot, and we have to have some word for that architecture. The word "structure" will do, and we shall distinguish structure, then, from the narrative arrangement of episodes, the plot, plot being but one element among the many that constitute a structure. *Tom Jones* has a far more elaborate plot than any we have yet encountered in these studies, elaborate not only in the sense that the book contains an immense number of episodes, but also in the sense that all these episodes are knit, as intimate cause and effect, into a large single action obeying a single impulse from start to finish. One of our objectives in analyzing the book will be to understand why intricate plot should have such importance, as an element of structure, in this particular novel—or, in other words, to understand what significance, what meaningful character, is given to the *Tom Jones* world by its intricacy of action.

The plot movement follows the curve characteristic of comedy plots, taking the protagonist from low fortune to high fortune. Tom comes on the scene as a bastard; his very earliest activities enforce "the universal opinion . . . that he was certainly born to be hanged"; and his reputation and his hopes are progressively blackened until he reaches his nadir in London, "kept" by Lady Bellaston (a circumstance perhaps more reprehensible to a modern reader's eyes than to eighteenth-century eyes), then accused of murder and thrown in jail, and finally—as if anything still could be added in the way of blackening—presumptively guilty of incest with his mother. But the nadir of his fortune also marks its "reversal" or crisis, and with the concurrent exposure of Blifil's malicious machinations and of Tom's true goodness, his fortune sails to the zenith of romantic happiness; he is proved to be of high birth, he marries the girl of his choice, and he inherits wealth. This is the general plot curve, the concave curve of comic drama (as against the convex curve taken by tragic drama—a metaphor of plot design that has its origin in the medieval emblem of the wheel of Fortune, on whose spokes people were represented as clinging in various stages of shabby or resplendent clothing, while the wheel turned round, carrying them from doubtful beginnings to pleasant endings, or from promising beginnings to unpleasant endings).

Tom goes under and up Fortune's wheel from "low" to "high," and in this shape of his career lies one salient set of contrasts as boldly definitive of the design of the action as the "high" beginning and the "low" end of Oedipus in the Sophoclean tragedy. But in order that the action may evolve in its curve, the wicked Blifil is needed—Tom's "opposite," chief cause of his sorrows, and affording the chief character contrast in the book. For while the curve of tragedy is spun, like the spider's thread, from within the tragic protagonist, produced out of his own passions and frailties, the curve of comedy is spun socially and gregariously, as the common product of men in society. The tragic curve leads to the hero's "self-discovery," the comic curve sprouts a various ornament of "self-exposures" on the part of many men. Also in connection with this characteristic difference between tragic action and comic action, we may notice that while the tragic hero "changes" (that is, comes eventually to a new and revolutionary realization of what he is and what he has done), the characters of comedy are laid under no artistic obligation to "change," since the reason for their artistic existence is that they may be exposed, in their "true" natures, to the eyes of other men—to society. The point is rather important for a reader of Fielding, for the development of the modern novel has accustomed us to look for "change" in characters and to feel that the profundity and importance of a book is somehow connected with such change; and we may therefore be inclined to feel that Fielding's conception of his material is comparatively "shallow," however witty and engrossing. It is well for us, then, to bear in mind the generic characteristics of the comic mode, and the fact that the characters in comedy may remain relatively static while the broad social panorama of comedy need not for that reason be lacking in seriousness and depth of significance. We are confronted in *Tom Jones* with a picture of social interaction among souls already formed, already stamped with operative character, and out of this gregarious action the conflict between hero and villain is propelled to a resolution in which the rogue who appeared to be a good man is exposed in his true nature as rogue, and the good man who appeared to be a rogue is revealed in his true good nature, with many similar exposures of other people along the way.

We can thus indicate, in some degree, the aesthetic necessity of elaborate plot in Fielding's novel: the episodes must cumulate functionally toward a final, representative revelation of character; but, because the significance of this revelation is for all men in the given society, the episodes must illustrate subtle varieties of character and interaction, at the same time representing the complexities of human nature and contributing toward the final revelation which will be, although narrowed down to hero and villain, symbolic of all those complexities. The book must, therefore, have both variety of episode and "unity of action." But we must now describe the plot as it signifies a "theme" or "meaning." In *Tom Jones,* life is conceived specifically as a conflict between natural, instinctive feeling, and those appearances with which people disguise, deny, or inhibit natural feeling—intellectual theories, rigid moral dogmas, economic conveniences, doctrines of *chic* or of social "respectability." This is the broad thematic contrast in *Tom Jones.* Form and feeling ("form" as mere outward appearance, formalism, or dogma, and "feeling" as the inner reality) engage in constant eruptive combat, and the battlefield is strewn with a debris of ripped masks, while exposed human nature—shocked to find itself uncovered and naked—runs on shivering shanks and with bloody pate, like the villagers fleeing from Molly Seagrim in the famous churchyard battle.

But let us stop to weigh rather carefully what Fielding means by that "human nature" which he says is his subject matter, and which we see again and again exposed during that conflict we have described above. Its meaning is not univocal. Broadly it refers to that mixture of animal instinct and human intellection which is assumed to obtain in every personality. But, in many of the incidents in the book, its meaning tips to one side: it tends to lean heavily toward "animal instinct," simply for the reason that the animal and instinctive part of man is (in the *Tom Jones* world) so frequently disguised or denied by the adoption of some formal appearance. Instinctive drives must therefore be emphasized as an important constituent of "human nature." Again, the curious, sometimes beneficial, sometimes damaging uses of intelligence are "human nature." We see "human nature" in the wicked Blifil's calculative shrewdness, in Black George's rationalization for keeping Tom's money, in the absurd intellectual formulas elaborated by Thwackum and Square. But we see it also in Allworthy's high-minded ethics, and in Tom's own idealism. In Blifil himself, "nature" seems to be congenitally and helplessly bad, and we may be led to speculate on his inheritance from a tenderly hypocritical mother and a brutally hypocritical father; and then, in Tom, "nature" seems to be, on the whole, congenitally good, though he had the same mother as Blifil and a father on whom we cannot speculate at all, as he is not described. Let us sum up these meanings of "human nature" so far:

human nature is a balanced mixture of instinctive drives and feelings and intellectual predilections; it is (dependent on the emphasis given by the specific incident) instinctive feeling alone; it is the human tendency to pervert instinct by intellection; it may be altogether bad (as in Blifil); it may be altogether good (as in Allworthy). Obviously we must expect trickiness in this term, and not be too quick to pin it down to any one meaning. But let us cite another and most important meaning that it has, an ideal meaning which the book strives to give to "human nature." Ideally, "human nature" is what is seen in the best specimens of the human species—a nature to which all should aspire. Under this ideal, it is assumed that the best specimens of the species exhibit a homogeneous configuration of instinct and intelligence—not a suppression of instinct by intellect, nor a suppression of intellect by instinct, but a happy collaboration of the two in the full and integrated man. In this sense, "human nature" is "good." This adjustment Squire Allworthy exhibits from the beginning: but because Fielding has given so many meanings to "human nature" in his book, we may feel that Allworthy is too crystallized a specimen, not really representative of all the possibilities of "human nature"; hence the hero, Tom, offers himself more aptly as a representative of "human nature" inasmuch as he has to learn, with difficulty, the appropriate balance in the process of the action, rather than having it given to him in crystallized form at the beginning. Tom yields formidably and frequently to instinct, and in so doing he exhibits the "naturalness"- and therefore the "rightness" of instinct as a constituent of the personality, thus correcting the overemphasis on formal appearances which we see in other characters; but at the same time, in these incidents, he shows a remarkable absence of that useful social sense which we call discretion, a lack of which is damaging certainly to himself and a cause of confusion for others. On the other hand, Tom is no fool: he is an admirer of Handel, he philosophizes with dignity in discourse with the Old Man of the Hill—nor could his proposal to Sophia, at the end of the book, be couched in more civilized, more exquisite language. On the whole, "human nature" in Tom, in all its intricacies and difficulties and mistakes, is a splendid thing; and (and this is its real significance) it is fine and splendid because it is undisguised, it is all out in the sunlight of the social air, the air of common intelligence, readily to be understood, without mask, unpretentious. To schematize over-simply the contrasting aspect of "human nature," let us say that "nature" is not fine and splendid, but indecent and embarrassing when a man, either through inherited disposition or through acquired predilection, adopts a mask for appearance's sake, hugs it too closely and too long, and allows it to warp instinct. Then—when we are allowed to look under the mask—"nature" shows itself perverted. It is the incongruity between what a man might "naturally" be (that is, if he did not deform himself by some kind of over-emphasis) and what he makes of himself by adopting a formulary appearance or mask, that gives "human nature" its variety and funniness and treacherousness. The indecency of "nature" when it has been going around in a mask, and the mask is suddenly ripped off, is illustrated grossly by the exposure of the philosopher Square, squatting "among other female utensils" when the curtain in Molly's bedroom accidentally falls. Square's mask of deistic theory has corrupted his instinctive nature into the narrow channel of lust. Uncorrupted by the cult of appearances, "human nature" is nature committed to the intelligence, opened before the intelligence of all men, and therefore "good" in itself—in a world conceived as fundamentally intelligible and tending in all its phenomena toward the general highest good of total intelligibility.

Let us glance now at the disposition of the separate books of the novel, and the contribution of each to the action. In this discussion, we shall confine ourselves to a very rapid glance at the whole, and then turn back to the first book, and to the first scene of the first book, for a more detailed examination. This method has its handicaps, for it would seem to imply that the first book is more important than the others, more worthy of inspection, which is obviously not at all the case. But a close examination of one book, and then of one scene, has the virtue of showing, in very small scope, those contrasts and tensions which govern the whole novel, and of indicating the precision of Fielding's art in the detail as well as in the whole.

In Book I, Tom is found in Allworthy's bed, Jenny Jones is accused of being Tom's mother and is got out of the way for the time being, and Bridget Allworthy marries Captain Blifil. In Book II, Partridge is fixed upon as Tom's father and is, like Jenny, removed from the picture, and Captain Blifil dies. In Book III, Tom's character comes under attack;

> . . . he had been already convicted of three robberies, viz., of robbing an orchard, of stealing a duck out of a farmer's yard, and of picking Master Blifil's pocket of a ball . . .

and concurrently young Blifil's malignity begins to receive attention, while Black George and his family are inauspiciously introduced. In Book IV, the romance begins between Tom and Sophia. Let us stop here for a moment, to see what has been accomplished and how it has been accomplished. The group composed of Squire Allworthy, Bridget Allworthy, and Captain Blifil has been described with a few swiftly drawn traits, and by the end of Book II, Captain Blifil has been disposed of, leaving on the scene his chief contribution—his son, Tom's half-brother and mortal antagonist; while the group composed of Jenny Jones and Partridge has contributed its special complication to the action—the red herring drawn across the trail of Tom's birth—and has been removed, not to appear again until needed for the ultimate complications. By Book III, the stage has been cleared for the confrontation of young hero and young villain, and here, swiftly and with precision, the chief character contrast is sketched; while the apparently incidental appearance of Black George and his family lays the shadow of that critical blackening of Tom's reputation which will drive him from home. Book IV offers the romance complication, a double complication in itself: Black George's daughter is scooped up from Book III, to cast darkness on Tom's sexual morality, and Tom and Sophia are involved in an emotional affair that is socially impossible because of Tom's birth.

It should be of value to the critical reader to follow these spreading complications, with their multiple intricate knottings, through in this fashion from book to book, until the final unraveling—not simply in order to be able to state "what happens," which is a rudimentary critical project, but to trace out the unity of design as the many incidents contribute to that unity. We shall indicate here, as one suggestion of unifying design, only the pursuit motif from Book VI on: Tom is turned out of doors, and Sophia follows him; she catches up with him in the inn at Upton, and for ample and adequate reasons the pursuit then reverses its character, and from Upton it is Tom who pursues Sophia; meanwhile, Squire Western has set out in pursuit of his daughter; and finally Squire Allworthy and Blifil must go to London in pursuit of the Westerns. The scenes at Upton occur at the center of the story (Books IX and X, in a volume of eighteen books), and it is here that we again pick up Partridge and Jenny Jones, Tom's reputed father and mother, both of them implicated in the initial circumstances of the action and both of them necessary for the final complications and the reversal. It is at Upton also that the

71

set of London characters first begins to appear, with Mrs. Fitzpatrick and her husband as its representatives (again under the aspect of pursuit: Fitzpatrick is after his wife), involving both Sophia and Tom in their London destinies. From the central scenes at Upton Inn, the novel pivots around itself. There have been six books of country life, in the center are six books of life on the highways, and the final six books are concerned with life in London—on a smaller and more local scale, much in the manner of Cervantes' multiple contrasts of perspective; and it is at Upton Inn, in the mathematical mid-point of the story, that country and city come together.[1] The initial pursuit motif, beginning at the end of Book VI, finishes its arabesque at the end of Book XII, again with nice mathematical balance, when Tom reaches London and is enabled to meet Sophia. Now it will be Blifil who is in pursuit of Sophia, so that eventually everyone will wind up in London for the denouement. As to the coincidences by means of which Fielding manages to gather so many pursuing and pursued people together, in the proper places and at the proper times for intricate involvement and complicated intrigue, one may say that "it is, after all, a small world": sooner or later, when people pursue each other with assiduity, they are bound to meet. The pursuit motif is, then, not only a provision for comic situation, but, as the immediate dynamics of action, is integral to the plot development.

Fielding was a writer for the theater before he was a novelist, and one of the reader's strongest impressions is that of dramatic handling of scene and act (the chapters may be thought of as "scenes," a single book as an "act"): the sharp silhouetting of characters and their grouping in such a manner as to avoid any confusions even in so populous a drama; the bright lighting of the individual episode; the swift pacing of scenes so that they flash past for the eye and ear at the same time that they maintain a clear system of witty contrast; and above all, the strict *conceptualizing* of the function of each scene, in relation to the larger unit of the "act" (or book) and to the over-all unit of the drama (the novel), as well as the *objectifying* of the individual scene as a subject in itself, a subject clear and significant in its own right.[2] We are using the word "scene" here purely in its dramatic sense: as the smallest full-formed division of an action, during which there is no change of place and no lapse in con-

[1] Aurelien Digeon makes this analysis of the action in his *The Novels of Fielding* (New York: E. P. Dutton & Co., Inc., 1925), pp. 172–175.

[2] V. S. Pritchett emphasizes these aspects in his chapter on Fielding in *The Living Novel* (New York: Reynal & Hitchcock, 1947).

tinuity of time. In Book I, there are three definite shifts of scene (and time and place), correlated with three definite groups of characters, and Fielding prefaces each shift with a brief, sharp delineation of the new character, or characters, who are to contribute a new direction to the action. The first scene is that of the finding of Tom in Mr. Allworthy's bed, and so that we may have the fullest ironic understanding of the scene, we are first given (in the language of the table of contents) "a short description of Squire Allworthy, and a fuller account of Miss Bridget Allworthy," while Mrs. Deborah Wilkins quite adequately introduces herself during the action. The place of action is shifted now to the parish, upon which Mrs. Deborah descends as investigator of morals; and again we are given "a short account of Jenny Jones," before the scene gets under way. We move, then, back to Squire Allworthy's house, with the scene between the Squire and Jenny, after which Jenny is dispatched out of the book for the time being. Now the new group, composed of the Blifils, is introduced into the original group—the Squire and his sister—with, again, "a short sketch of the characters of the two brothers," before the action itself is released, the curtain goes up. This is the method of the theater. As V. S. Pritchett has said, in the theater

> there is an idea before there is a scene; and one of the fascinating things in *Tom Jones* is the use of the summary method to set the scene, explain the types of character, cover the preparatory ground quickly by a few oblique moralizings and antics so that all the realism is reserved for the main action.[3]

But let us notice the precise relationships of a few scenes in this first book. Mr. Allworthy's compassionate and honest-hearted reaction to the discovery of the foundling is set in almost instant contrast with Mrs. Deborah's furious descent upon the village and upon the supposed erring mother, in all Mrs. Deborah's theoretical righteousness; while we who are *rereading* the novel (and in rereading, as we must in a study of this kind, we are first actually *reading*) have meanwhile, even in so short a sequence, been slyly made aware of the multiple ironic significance of this contrast: of the genuinely compassionate and feelingful character of Allworthy's humanity, for though the babe (as we know, but as he does not know) is his own nephew, his compassion is directed toward the child

3 *Ibid.*, p. 21.

as a foundling—that is, any child, any helplessness; while Mrs. Deborah, who would have cast out the child but has been reoriented by her servility (an economic convenience), takes the opportunity for an explosion of vicious passion upon the supposed mother; while the real mother, Miss Bridget, is protected by her position, her deceit, and her exploitation of the humanity of Jenny herself, so that she is able self-righteously to condemn the sexual indulgences of the lower classes, and at the same time preserve (under moral forms and "appearances") the fruit of her own indulgence. Now, immediately, this seething complex of human motive and passion is capped, ironically, by Squire Allworthy's simple, well-meaning sermon on chastity, directed at poor Jenny; and in the next chapter we are moved outside the door, to the keyhole, where Miss Bridget and Mrs. Deborah are listening, ears glued, each picking up from the well-meant sermon her own corrupt nourishment—Mrs. Deborah taking the vicarious satisfaction of sexual innuendo, and the direct satisfaction of another woman's downfall, and Miss Bridget the satisfaction of her own concealment and of an opportunity to exhibit the virtue of charity toward a woman whom she has herself placed under social condemnation. Thus from scene to scene, and in the interplay of scenes, contrast is effected, character is exposed, masks slip, wholly under the impetus of social interaction—or, in aesthetic terms, "plot"; and we see the Squire, in whom "nature" (here as spontaneous human feeling) has been committed fully and openly to the whole personality and made socially intelligible, contrasted with the two women in whom "nature" (again as instinctive feeling, but particularly as biological drive) has been suffocated under the mask of appearance and therefore dwarfed and distorted. The reader's appreciation of the elaborate and yet strictly controlled interrelationships of scene with scene, as each sets up with the other a contrast of human motivation, will be extended by his own objective analysis of such interrelationships in other books of *Tom Jones*.

We return now to the first scene, and to the internal contrasts within the scene itself and their function in realizing the subject matter of the novel ("human nature"), in defining the theme (the contest between instinctive feeling and formulary appearances), and in illustrating the theme in style. This scene takes place in Chapter III of Book I, where the babe is discovered. Mr. Allworthy, we are told, has just returned from London where he has been gone on business for a full quarter of a year (the notation of "a full quarter of a year" is innocent enough on first reading, full

of implication for the plot and for Miss Bridget's conduct on second reading); it is late in the evening, and he has retired much fatigued to his
chamber, where despite his fatigue, he "spends some minutes on his knees";
then

> he was preparing to step into bed, when, upon opening the clothes,
> to his great surprise he beheld an infant, wrapt up in some coarse
> linen, in a sweet and profound sleep, between his sheets. He stood
> some time lost in astonishment at this sight; but, as good-nature had
> always the ascendant in his mind, he soon began to be touched with
> sentiments of compassion for the little wretch before him. He then
> rang his bell, and ordered an elderly woman-servant to rise immedi-
> ately, and come to him; and in the mean time was so eager in con-
> templating the beauty of innocence, appearing in those lively colours
> with which infancy and sleep always display it, that his thoughts were
> too much engaged to reflect that he was in his shirt when the matron
> came in. She had, indeed, given her master sufficient time to dress him-
> self; for out of respect to him, and regard to decency, she had spent
> many minutes in adjusting her hair at the looking-glass, notwithstand-
> ing all the hurry in which she had been summoned by the servant, and
> though her master, for aught she knew, lay expiring in an apoplexy,
> or in some other fit.
>
> It will not be wondered at that a creature who had so strict a
> regard to decency in her own person should be shocked at the least
> deviation from it in another. She therefore no sooner opened the door,
> and saw her master standing by the bedside in his shirt, with a candle
> in his hand, than she started back in a most terrible fright, and might
> perhaps have swooned away, had he not now recollected his being un-
> dressed, and put an end to her terrors by desiring her to stay without
> the door till he had thrown some clothes over his back, and was be-
> come incapable of shocking the pure eyes of Mrs. Deborah Wilkins,
> who, though in the fifty-second year of her age, vowed she had never
> beheld a man without his coat.

The obvious contrast here is in character, as brought out by the reactions
of two people to an unusual event. Mr. Allworthy, though tired, is immediately touched by humane feeling toward an innocent creature (let
us note, in relation to Fielding's stated subject—"human *nature*"—that
it is Mr. Allworthy's "good-*nature*" which is ascendant at this moment),
and his spontaneous feeling makes him so forgetful of social forms and
appearances that he neglects to cover his nightshirt when Mrs. Deborah

75

comes to the door. Mrs. Deborah, on the other hand, called at an extraordinary hour of the night and therefore aware that the need must be great—perhaps her master is expiring in an apoplexy—has, out of respect to him, given him *sufficient time to dress himself* (usually done when one is expiring in an apoplexy), and also, in her regard to decency, has spent some minutes adjusting her hair at the looking glass. The ironic contrast of character is carried, by a few sly words (such as "good-nature" and "respect to him" and "regard to decency"), beyond the individuals and made into an extensive contrast between generous, uncalculating feeling and calculation of appearances and consequences. The second paragraph caps this original contrast with the shock Mrs. Deborah suffers from seeing the squire in his nightshirt; she is so shocked by his *appearance* (which his feeling has made him forget) that she would have swooned away, no matter what might be the "nature" of the circumstances which had caused him so to neglect appearances, if he had not immediately had the good *nature* to clothe himself in order to alleviate her fright. For Mrs. Deborah "vowed," we are told, "she had never beheld a man without his coat," and in the innocent word "vowed" lies another sly play upon nature and appearance, for one may "vow" much in keeping up appearances. More ironically explicit, her "pure eyes" are "pure" as far as appearances go—"pure," for instance, as she adjusts her hair before the looking glass—but with a dubious purity inasmuch as she cannot see the innocent helplessness and human difficulty of the circumstances in front of her.

Let us remain a moment longer with this scene, to see if "nature" defines itself more fully in the context. Mr. Allworthy's "good-nature had always the ascendant *in his mind*." His good nature, then,—his "sentiments of compassion," as the next phrase qualifies it—is neither raw, untrained feeling, nor is it mental calculation divorced from feeling, but it is feeling as a quality of *mind*. It is civilized feeling, social feeling, intelligent feeling, and it takes total possession of the Squire, making him forgetful of forms and appearances; in other words, there is nothing either covert or to be "exposed" about the Squire, since feeling has been committed to the mind and to the total personality, open to view. Against this intelligential feeling is set an abstruse mental calculation on Mrs. Deborah's part (would we be going too far if we suggested that the fact that her master was a wealthy widower had anything to do with Mrs. Deborah's performances before the mirror?); and though the calculation takes place in Mrs. Deborah's mind, we know that it is *unintelligent* (in the world of this book, though possibly not in the world of *Moll Flanders*), for it makes her engage in a stupid reversal of values, makes her—because of her stupidity of feeling—a comic object, an object of laughter. Later in the novel we see many examples of the same calculative shrewdness and the same stupidity of feeling (the Blifil brothers, Thwackum and Square, young Blifil, Mrs. Western, Lady Bellaston, and a host of others), and always such shrewdness is made to appear, not intelligent, but unintelligent, because it is not informed with natural feeling, and because it succeeds in corrupting natural feeling. At the opposite end of the spectrum is Tom himself, all feeling and little calculative shrewdness whatever. Tom's "mind," indeed, does not seem to operate very frequently at all. And yet, as his career progresses, we become aware that—in this particular world of values—natural feeling is itself *intelligent*; for Tom, after all, does the "right" things, in the long run the "intelligent" things, in acting from his heart and his instincts, as compared with the stupidity of the shrewd and calculative persons.

With these correlations between intelligence and feeling, we may return once more to the scene of the finding of the babe in Mr. Allworthy's bed, to discover in the drawing of the picture a style which contrives to make of the subject, "nature," a conceptual subject (just as the dramatic handling of plot has been constantly under the governance of concept or idea), a comprehensible "idea of human nature," a subject intelligible to the mind. And here, for the sake of emphasis and historical comparison, we may suggest the difference between Fielding's outlook or *Weltanschauung* and the modern world view underlying prevalent philosophies of despair: Fielding looks upon humankind and all its proclivities as offering an ideal of intelligent order; whereas two world wars and the prospect of a third, universally disintegrating, offer to the modern view a notion of humankind as governed by irrational motives, self destructive, incognizant of what civilized order might mean. Our own "nature," as representing humanity, we see as incalculable, shadowy, dark, capable of inexplicable explosions. Fielding's "nature" offers itself not as submerged and incalculable profundities, but as wholly accessible to the intelligence, and his style reflects this attitude. The foundling is described thus:

 . . . he [Squire Allworthy] beheld an infant, wrapt up in some coarse linen, in a sweet and profound sleep, between his sheets. . . . He then

> rang his bell . . . and in the mean time was so eager in contemplating
> the beauty of innocence, appearing in those lively colours with which
> infancy and sleep always display it, that his thoughts were too much
> engaged . . .

The description is generalized. This is any sleeping infant. The generalized image of the child immediately equates with a conception of the
meaning of infancy in general—"the beauty of innocence"; while the
qualifying phrase—"appearing in those lively colours with which infancy
and sleep *always* display it"—again accents the general, the inclusive, the
universal, the timeless aspect of infancy, an aspect yielding itself entirely
to conceptualization (as if sleeping infancy would always inspire these
reflections and impulses in men, even in a concentration camp). In other
words, what is illustrated in the style of even so incidental a passage is
the thorough *intelligibility* of "nature," its yielding of itself to a concept
supposed to have universal and timeless applicableness. What can be re-
composed wholly as idea has the implied status of objectivity and universality; for all civilized men can, assumedly, share an idea, as they cannot share their shadowy, indeterminate subjective feelings as individuals.
"Nature," as conceived in *Tom Jones* and as illustrated in the character
of the hero, is that "nature" which all men presumably share, and the
mark of its universality is its intelligibility. Those characters in the book
in whom "nature" has been perverted by the distortion of "appearance"
are in the long run social outcasts, or die bad deaths, or are made to
suffer a violent shaking-up in order to bring their "nature" out into the
open where it can enter into the intelligible universal order.

In *Clarissa Harlowe,* the "plot" appears under the aspect of fatality,
as a movement from one point on a circle, around the circle and back
to its beginning: from Clarissa's passion for purity, through its exaltation as a passion for death, down to the closing of the circle where purity
and death become one. Not fatality but Fortune rules events in *Tom
Jones*—that Chance which throws up event and counterevent in inexhaustible variety. Tom himself is a foundling, a child of chance. In the
end, because he is blessed with good nature, he is blessed with good
fortune as well. Mr. Allworthy, we are told, "might well be called the
favorite of both Nature and Fortune": from Nature "he derived an agreeable person, a sound constitution, a sane understanding, and a benevolent

heart," and from Fortune "the inheritance of one of the largest estates in the county." Good nature "had always the *ascendant* in his mind": a metaphor derived from astrology, the science of the influence of the stars over man's life and fortune. The reader might be interested in tracing other metaphors of this kind in Fielding's diction, and in relating them to his view of human life. By chance or fortune, acting occultly, the curtain falls down in Molly's room, exposing the philosopher Square. An obsolete meaning of the word "square" is that of "rule" or "principle." Significant in Square's situation in this incident is Fortune's or accident's treacherous play with "squared" (straight-edged) principles, philosopher's rules, dogmatic formulas; for nothing that the philosopher Square might say, to "square" his position, would alter the ignominy of his exposure. Fortune, capricious as it is, has some occult, deeply hidden association with Nature (in Fielding); therefore, in the long run, good nature does infallibly lead to good fortune, bad nature to bad fortune.

The signature of Fortune's favor is wealth. Tom's blessings, at the end of the book, are not dissociable from the fact that he is Allworthy's heir: this is the center and fulcrum of all the rest of his good fortune. In *Moll Flanders*, the signature of the favor of Providence was also wealth, but the wealth had to be grubbed for with insect-like persistence and concentration; to obtain wealth, even with the help of Providence, one had to work for it and keep one's mind on it. In *Clarissa Harlowe*, again, wealth was to be worked for and schemed for: the Harlowe males work as hard and concentratedly, after their fashion, to acquire Solmes's wealth and the title it will buy for them, as Moll does for her gold watches, her bales, cargoes, and plantations. But in *Tom Jones*, wealth is not got by work or calculation or accumulation or careful investment. Blifil, who works shrewdly to obtain it, fails of his ends; Tom, who never thinks of it, is richly endowed with it. The benefits of money are as candidly faced by Fielding as they are by Defoe, or as they will later be by Jane Austen: people need money in order to live pleasantly, and though to be good and to be in love and loved are fine things, the truly harmonious and full life is possible only when one is both good and rich. Fielding is a man of the same century as Defoe and Richardson, the same society and culture (in the anthropological sense of "culture"), but his outlook toward the getting of wealth is radically different. V. S. Pritchett has described one eighteenth-century attitude in this matter: "Fortune," he says, the speculator's goddess—not money—pours out its plenty from the South Sea bubbles and the slave trade in the eighteenth century. Sacks of gold descend from heaven by fantastic parachute, and are stored in the gloating caves, and trade is still spacious and piratical.[4]

Obviously these statements have not much applicability to the attitudes of Defoe or Richardson, but they do cast some light on Fielding's. Also, we find in Fielding the more traditional, aristocratic attitude toward wealth: one simply has wealth—say, in landed properties, like Squire Allworthy—and how one got it is Fortune's business, a mysterious donation of free gifts to the worthy. But what we are fundamentally interested in here is the coherence of this attitude with other elements in the book: that is, the aesthetic coherence and integrity of the whole. We have considered the plot under the aspect of the surprise plays of Fortune, occultly working out its game with Nature, and it is clear that Tom's unsought blessing of financial good fortune in the end is consistent with, all-of-a-piece with, the other activities of Fortune that are exhibited in the action.

There is a certain distortion involved in the attempt to represent a book by a visual figure, but sometimes a visual figure, with all its limitations, helps us to grasp a book's structure. We have spoken of *Clarissa* as making the simple figure of a circle, a figure of fatality. We may think of *Tom Jones* as a complex architectural figure, a Palladian palace perhaps: immensely variegated, as Fortune throws out its surprising encounters; elegant and suavely intelligent in its details (many of Fielding's sentences are little complex "plots" in themselves, where the reader must follow a suspended subject through a functional ornament of complications—qualifying dependent clauses and prepositional phrases and eloquent pauses—to the dramatic predication or denouement); but simply, spaciously, generously, firmly grounded in Nature, and domed with an ample magnitude where Fortune shows herself as beneficent artisan. The structure is all out in the light of intelligibility; air circulates around and over it and through it. Since Fielding's time, the world has found itself not quite so intelligible. Though intelligence has been analytically applied to the physical nature of things in our time much more thoroughly than eighteenth-century scientific techniques allowed, our world is tunneled by darkness and invisibility, darknesses of infantile traumata in the

---

4 *Ibid.*, p. 110.

human mind, neurotic incalculabilities in personal and social action, fission in the atom, explosion in the heavens. We may feel, then, that there was much—in the way of doubt and darkness—to which Fielding was insensitive. Nevertheless, our respect is commanded by the integrity and radiance of the building that he did build.

ON *Tristram Shandy*

In Sterne's deceptively frivolous, deceptively ingenuous novel *Tristram Shandy,* a new type of structure makes its appearance, a type that is of singular importance for the development of the modern novel. This is a structure modeled on the operative character of consciousness as such. Sterne conceives the behavior of consciousness in terms not of logical continuities but of the spontaneous association of ideas. The word "structure" implies controlled form and a unity, and it would seem that mere association of one thing with another could issue in nothing but haphazard multiplicity. Sterne's interest, however, is that of a novelist and not that of a theoretical psychologist. That is, his concern is to create a world. The world that he creates has the form of a mind. It may perhaps help us to grasp the notion of a structure of this sort if we think of the mind in the figure of one of Leibnitz's monads, those elemental units of energy that have "mirrors but no windows": the mirroring capacity of the unit makes of it a microcosm of the universe, in that all things are reflected in it; and yet, because it lacks "windows," it is a discrete world in itself, formally defined only by internal relationships; while the reflections in its "mirrors" have a free energetic interplay unique for this monad —this mind—differentiating it from all others at the same time that it is representative of all others.

The novelty of the method employed in *Tristram Shandy* becomes striking as we review the other novels we have read in terms of the importance of action or plot as an organizing factor in each, and as we consider the relative unimportance of plot in *Tristram Shandy. Don Quixote* and *The Pilgrim's Progress* trace the episodes in a hero's quest or mission; the hero goes somewhere to do something or find something, and the manifest concrete substance of these books lies in the actions he engages in along the way. Similarly, *Moll Flanders* is plotted upon a series

83

of episodic actions, the whole held together formally as Moll's biography. With *Clarissa Harlowe* and *Tom Jones,* action takes on a more unitary —as distinguished from episodic—character: the action of the one book (at least as conceived by Richardson) is that of tragic drama, the action of the other that of comic drama, and obviously both books are unthinkable except with reference to plot complication, reversal, and denouement. What is the "action" of *Tristram Shandy?*

Presumably, like that of *Moll Flanders,* it is episodic and biographical: *The Life and Opinions of Tristram Shandy, Gent.* is the full title. But Tristram is not born until a third of the way through the book; not christened until fifty pages later; the story is more than half over when we are told that he has reached the age of five (scarcely yet the age for "opinions"); is two-thirds finished by the time he is put into breeches; suddenly he appears as a gentleman on his travels in France; and the novel ends with an episode that concerns not Tristram but Uncle Toby. Those sporadic flickers of narrative in which Tristram is seen in chronological circumstance as the hero-in-action (if the hero *can* be thought of as "acting" while he is being born, christened, circumcised, etc.) evidently do not serve the same purposes of narrative that we have observed elsewhere; they are, rather, if they are anything, an intentional mockery of "action." Chronological and plot continuity are, then, not definitively organizational to *Tristram Shandy.* The fact appears extraordinary when we stop for a moment to consider how naturally, habitually, almost stubbornly we tend to think of all experience as somehow automatically dished up to us, like a molded pudding, in the form of chronology; and how this tendency to see experience as actions related to each other undisturbedly by the stages of the clock and the calendar leads us to expect of fiction that it will provide a similar unidirectional action, or series of episodes, taking place chronologically. *Tristram Shandy* pays lip service to this expectation—at least by allowing Tristram to be born before he is christened, to be put into breeches before he goes traveling in France —but so mockingly as to make us aware that Sterne is engaged in deliberate demolition of chronological sequences and (inasmuch as our notions of "time" and "action" are inextricably related) deliberate destruction of the common notion of "action."

But this is the negative aspect only, and if this were all there were to Sterne's concern with the relationship of time and human experience, then the squiggly lines he draws in Chapter XL of Book VI, to show the haphazard progress of his novel, could represent just that: its haphazardness, its lack of form. But it is anything but haphazard or formless. Obeying formal laws of its own, it is as skillfully and delicately constructed as *Tom Jones*. Having ruled out plot chronology as a model of the way experience presents itself, Sterne offers another model: that of the operations of consciousness, where time is exploded, where any time-past may be time-present, or several times-past be concurrently present at once, and where clock-time appears only intermittently as a felt factor. As Cervantes' *Don Quixote* offers fiction as many models as it can use, so it offers this one also. In the episode of Quixote's descent into the cave of Montesinos, the time of dream and of poetry, the ancient heroic time of Montesinos and Durandarte, the modern time of coinage and "new dimity petticoats," and the actual hours of the descent and of the Knight's sleep, merge as one time.

But what is to give unity to this model, if we cannot plot the hero's adventures on clock and calendar in order to know when they begin and when they are ended, and if we do not, after all, have a hero to "act" in the ordinary sense—no time, no hero, no action? The unity of any novel may be described on several different levels; we may speak of the unifying function of theme, or of plot, or of symbolism, or of other elements that appear to have superior importance. The total structural unity of a work does not yield itself to a simple description, but only to a quite lengthy analysis of the complex interrelationships of all major elements. At the most conspicuous level, the unity of *Tristram Shandy* is the unity of Tristram's—the narrator's—consciousness.[1] This is a representative kind of unity, psychologically true to the way in which experience appears to all of us to have its most rudimentary unity; for though clock-time may seem to cut experience into units, these are arbitrary units that melt into each other unrecognizably in the individual's self-feeling; and though we may assume that a shared experience has a certain definite, common form and description for those who share it, yet we know that, as the experience is absorbed into and transformed by the individual consciousness, it is something very different for different people, and that its form and "oneness" or unity are felt most concretely only as the experience is stamped by the character of the individual consciousness.

[1] This point of view with regard to the unity of the work is developed by Benjamin H. Lehman in his essay on Sterne, "Of Time, Personality and the Author," in *Studies in Comedy* (Berkeley: University of California Press, 1940).

Sterne's project in *Tristram Shandy* was not to have a parallel, in the work of a major novelist, until Proust wrote *Remembrance of Things Past*. Though each of these books, so far separated in time and in local culture, carries the highly singular and special flavor of its historical circumstances and of the original genius of its author, they have a strong kinship in subject and plan and quality. Each makes of the narrator's consciousness its subject matter; the artistry of each lies in the "objectifying" of this "subjective" material in its own right and for its own sake, so that the "subjective" becomes an object to be manipulated and designed and given aesthetic form according to laws inherent in it; and each creates an Alice-in-Wonderland world that is unique and inimitable because the individual consciousness is itself unique and inimitable. We do not think of Proust's work as the story of Swann, or the story of Charlus or of Albertine or even of Marcel, or as the history of a transmogrification of social classes and manners in the late nineteenth century, although it is these and other stories and histories as well. Nor do we think of *Tristram Shandy* as a series of character sketches of Uncle Toby and Walter Shandy and Corporal Trim and the Widow Wadman, or as a mosaic of sentimental and slapstick anecdotes, some gracefully pathetic, some uproarious, and all peppered with off-color puns and *doubles-entendres,* the indulgences of a neurotic clergyman—although it is these and still other things. We think of *Tristram Shandy,* as we do of Proust's *Remembrance of Things Past,* as a mind in which the local world has been steeped and dissolved and fantastically re-formed, so that it issues brand new. Still more definitive of the potentialities of Sterne's method, as these have been realized in a great modern work, is James Joyce's *Finnegans Wake,* where the hero's dream swallows and recomposes all time in its belly of mirrors, and where the possibilities lying in Sterne's creative play with linguistic associations—his use of language as a dynamic system in itself, a magic system for the "raising" of new perceptions as a magician's formulas "raise" spirits—are enormously developed. Joyce himself points out the parallel. In the second paragraph of *Finnegans Wake,* "Sir Tristram, violer d'amores," arrives from over the sea "to wielderfight his penisolate war" in "Laurens County," and we know—among these puns —that we are not in wholly unfamiliar territory.

Sterne's project, like Proust's, was to analyze and represent in his novel the creative process; and that Sterne should be the first practitioner of what is called the technique of the "stream of consciousness" in fictional writing is consonant with the kind of subject he set himself. Our fictional center of gravity is not a happening or confluence of happenings nor a character or concourse of characters under emotional or moral or social aspects of interest; it consists rather in the endlessly fertile rhythms of a consciousness, as those rhythms explore the comic ironies of a quest for order among the humdrum freaks of birth and paternity and place and time and language. In reading *Tristram Shandy,* we are never allowed to forget that the activity of creation, as an activity of forming perceptions and maneuvering them into an expressive order, *is itself the subject;* the technique does not allow us to forget it—for let alone the harum-scarum tricks with printer's ink, the narrator plunges at us in apostrophes, flirts his addresses at us with "Dear Sir" or "Dear Madam," explodes into the middle of a disquisition or a scene in defiance of time, space, and logic. Uncle Toby, pursuing the theory of projectiles in the pages of half a dozen military authors, becomes involved among parabolas, parameters, semiparameters, conic sections, and angles of incidence, and Tristram suddenly cries out,

> O my uncle;—fly—fly, fly from it as from a serpent . . . Alas! 'twill exasperate thy symptoms,—check thy perspirations—evaporate thy spirits—waste thy animal strength,—dry up thy radical moisture, bring thee into a costive habit of body,—impair thy health,—and hasten all the infirmities of thy old age.—O my uncle! my uncle Toby.

Toby's investigations were conducted some years before Tristram was born. It is as if Tristram were sitting in a moving-picture theater, watching on a most candid and intimate screen the performance of his progenitors. He is struck suddenly with admiration or consternation, stands up, waves his arms, applauds, boos, wrings his hands, sheds tears, sits down and tickles the lady next to him.

We have said that the unity of *Tristram Shandy* is the unity of the narrator's consciousness; but—without the discipline afforded by chronology, or an objective "narrative line," or a moral thesis of some sort—what is the principle of selection by which the contents of that consciousness present themselves? Sterne himself puts the question, in Chapter XXIII, Book III, and as he states it, it is the problem of every novelist. In setting up a certain body of human experience novelistically, what should come first? what last? what should follow or precede what? Should not everything appear at once and in fusion, inasmuch as this is the way the author's consciousness grasps it in its fullest truth? But the novel itself is an artifact subjected to time law; words follow words and pages follow pages in temporal sequence, necessarily imposing temporal sequence upon the material; everything cannot be said at once, although this disability may seem to injure the wholeness and instantaneousness of the material as the author grasps it. Trim announces to Toby that Dr. Slop is in the kitchen making a bridge. " 'Tis very obliging in him," Toby says, mistaking the bridge (meant for Tristram's nose) for a drawbridge. The author must elucidate Toby's error; but when? Right now, at the moment Toby makes the remark? But the goings-on upstairs in Mrs. Shandy's bedchamber are of the greatest consequence now. Later, then, among the anecdotes of Toby's amours with Widow Wadman? Or in the middle of Toby's campaigns on the bowling green? All of these circumstances press upon the author at once, and are, in the atemporal time of consciousness, contemporaneous. By what principle of selection is he to subject them to the time demands of the novel?

> O ye powers! [Sterne cries] . . . which enable mortal man to tell a story worth the hearing—that kindly shew him, where he is to begin it —and where he is to end it—what he is to put into it—and what he is to leave out— . . .
>
> I beg and beseech you . . . that wherever in any part of your dominions it so falls out, that three several roads meet in one point, as they have done just here—that at least you set up a guide-post in the centre of them, in mere charity, to direct an uncertain devil which of the three he is to take.

Sterne's uncertainty is not really uncertainty at all. His cry of authorial distress is one of the many false scents he lays down humoristically in order to give to his work the appearance of artlessness and primitive spontaneity. At the same time it points up the paradox of all novel writing, the paradox of which Sterne is very much aware: the antagonism between the time sequences which the novel imposes, and the instantaneous wholeness of the image of complex human experience which the novel attempts to present. Sterne has his guidepost in the philosopher John Locke, and it is according to Locke's theory of the human understanding that he finds his way down all the several roads that are continuously meeting in one point in *Tristram Shandy,* or, conversely, we might say that it is with the guidance of Locke that he contrives continually to get his roads crossed. To the French Academician, M. Suard, he said in conversation that "those who knew the philosopher (Locke) well enough to recognize his presence and his influence would find them or sense them on every page, in every line." Locke had attempted to explain the genesis of ideas from sensation. Simple sensations produce simple ideas of those sensations; associated sensations produce associated ideas of sensations, a process which becomes immensely complicated with the accretion of other associations of this kind. Besides the capacity of the mind to form ideas from sensations, it has the capacity of reflection. By reflection upon ideas acquired from sensation, it is able to juggle these into new positions and relationships, forming what we call "abstract ideas." Thus the whole body of logical and inferential "knowledge" is built up, through association, from the simple primary base of sensation. There are two aspects of this theory which are of chief importance in Sterne. The one is the Sensational aspect, the other the Associative.[2] From the notion of sensation as the prime source of knowledge and as the primitive character of experience, arises that doctrine of "sensibility" or "sentimentality" which Sterne made famous: the doctrine that value lies in *feeling* as such. With this we shall concern ourselves later. But at this point let us see how the associative aspect of Locke's theory appears structurally in *Tristram Shandy*.

Tristram starts out on the first page with a disquisition on the need of parents to mind what they are about when they are in the act of begetting. Why? Because their associated sensations at that moment have a determining effect upon the nature and destiny of Homunculus. (Note the manner in which, from the beginning, Sterne's imagination *concretizes* an abstraction, here an abstraction of eugenical theory: the "humours and dispositions which were then uppermost" in father and mother suffuse, somewhat like a glandular tincture, the "animal spirits" passed on to the son; and the metaphor hinted by "animal spirits" becomes instantly a picture of unharnessed horses—"Away they go cluttering like hey-go mad." This concreteness of imagination is one of the secrets of Sterne's surprises and of the Alice-in-Wonderland character of his world, for it is with a shock of astonished and delighted recognition that we suddenly see the pedantic abstraction taken literally and transformed into physiology, complete with hooves, feathers, or haberdashery.) What went wrong with Tristram's begetting was that Mrs. Shandy, accustomed to associate

[2] These observations are based on Herbert Read's discussion of Sterne in *The Sense of Glory* (New York: Harcourt, Brace & Company, Inc., 1930).

the winding of the clock with the marital act (like Pavlov's dogs and the dinner bell), missed the association appropriate at the moment, and in speaking of it to Mr. Shandy distracted his attention and prepared for poor Homunculus nine long months of disordered nerves and melancholy dreams (a pre-Freudian comment on the assumed bliss of this period). Mrs. Shandy's remark about the clock leads then, by association of ideas, to a portrait of Uncle Toby, typically "wiping away a tear"; for it was to Uncle Toby that Tristram owed the information as to the circumstances of his begetting. Again, by association with conception, origin, *the egg*, we are led, in Chapter IV, into a discussion of Horace's dictum on the technique of beginning a literary work: "as Horace says, *ab Ovo*"—which Horace did not say but which nevertheless serves as an apology for Sterne's own technique; thence to an explanation of Mrs. Shandy's unfortunate association between the winding of the clock and the marital act—"Which strange combination of ideas," says Sterne,

> the sagacious Locke, who certainly understood the nature of these things better than most men, affirms to have produced more wry actions than all other sources of prejudice whatsoever.

The explanation leads to a determination of the date of Tristram's geniture and the manner of his birth, which involves a digression into the history of the midwife, which in turn involves a digression into the history of the parson Yorick, who was responsible for establishing the midwife in her vocation; and the history of Yorick necessitates first a description of his horse (before we can get back to the midwife), but the parson's horse recalls Rosinante, and that steed, that belonged to a famous gentleman with a hobby, sets Sterne off on the subject of hobbyhorses in general, which leads to . . . (When are we going to learn the circumstances of Tristram's birth?) Sterne's comment on "the sagacious Locke," who understood the "strange combination of ideas" to which men's brains are liable, indicates the method here. It is precisely in the *strangeness* of the combinations or associations that Sterne finds the contour of his subject, the logic of its grotesquerie and the logic of its gaiety. At the same time, he is in perfect control of the "combinations," as we are slyly reminded again and again; for we *do* come back to the midwife.

Nor, in terms of total structure, is Mrs. Shandy's remark about the clock, in the first chapter, quite as irresponsible as it would seem. In this odd world, where the methodical Mr. Shandy winds up the house clock, together with "some other little family concernments," on the first Sunday night of every month, time is of the utmost importance and the utmost unimportance.[3] Let us illustrate. In Chapter IX of Book IV, Toby and Mr. Shandy are conversing as they walk down the stairs, and from Chapter IX to Chapter XIV we are kept, presumably, in the chronological span that covers their descent from the top to the bottom of the staircase. Chapter IX starts out,

> What a chapter of chances, said my father, turning himself about upon the first landing, as he and my uncle Toby were going downstairs—

and there follows a page of conversation between the two. With the beginning of Chapter X, Sterne reminds us that we are still on the staircase and have not got to the bottom yet.

> Is it not a shame to make two chapters of what passed in going down one pair of stairs? for we are got no farther yet than to the first landing, and there are fifteen more steps down to the bottom; and for aught I know, as my father and my uncle Toby are in a talking humour, there may be as many chapters as steps: . . .

a remark which obviously calls for the insertion here of his "chapter upon chapters" (which he has promised us, along with his chapter on noses, his chapter on knots, and his chapter on whiskers). Hence, by Chapter XI, we are not yet to the bottom of the staircase.

> We shall bring all things to rights, said my father, setting his foot upon the first step from the landing.—

With Chapter XII, Susannah appears below.

> —And how does your mistress? cried my father, taking the same step over again from the landing, and calling to Susannah, whom he saw passing by the foot of the stairs with a huge pin-cushion in her hand— how does your mistress? As well, said Susannah, tripping by, but without looking up, as can be expected.—What a fool am I! said my father, drawing his leg back again—let things be as they will, brother Toby, 'tis ever the precise answer—And how is the child, pray?—No answer.

[3] Sterne's treatment of time, as discussed here, is central to the essay by B. H. Lehman, cited above.

> And where is Dr. Slop? added my father, raising his voice aloud, and looking over the ballusters—Susannah was out of hearing.
>
> Of all the riddles of a married life, said my father, crossing the landing in order to set his back against the wall, whilst he propounded it to my uncle Toby—of all the puzzling riddles . . .

In Chapter XIII, Sterne desperately appeals to the critic to step in and get Uncle Toby and Mr. Shandy off the stairs for him. Obviously, what has been presented to us in this bit of fantasy is the incongruity between the clock-time which it will take to get the two conversationalists down the stairs, and the atemporal time—the "timeless time"—of the imagination, where the words of Toby and Mr. Shandy echo in their plenitude, where their stances and gestures are traced in precise images (as a leg is lifted or a foot withdrawn from the step), and where also the resonances of related subjects (such as chance and chapters and critics) intertwine freely with the conversation of Toby and Walter; and we are made aware of the paradox of which Sterne is so actively aware, and which he uses as a selective principle and as a structural control: the paradox of man's existence both in time and out of time—his existence in the time of the clock, and his existence in the apparent timelessness of consciousness (what has been called, by philosophers, "duration," to distinguish it from clock-marked time).

But the time fantasy still piles up, in Chapter XIII, in odder contours. We are reminded, by Walter's interchange with Susannah, that this is the day of Tristram's birth; and the autobiographer Tristram is also suddenly reminded of the passage of time.

> I am this month one whole year older than I was this time twelve-month; and having got, as you perceive, almost into the middle of my fourth volume—and no farther than to my first day's life—'tis demonstrative that I have three hundred and sixty-four days more life to write just now, than when I first set out; so that instead of advancing, as a common writer, in my work with what I have been doing at it—on the contrary, I am just thrown so many volumes back . . . at this rate I should just live 364 times faster than I should write—

—a piece of mathematical calculation which the reader will follow as he is able. Again, what the fantasy suggests is the paradoxical temporal and yet atemporal status of consciousness, whose experience is at once past experience, as marked by the passage of time, and present experience, inasmuch as it is present within the mind. These considerations of time may seem abstract as set down here, but we are simplifying Sterne's performance so that we may see it structurally and schematically. Actually, what his acute time sense provides is never the dullness and ponderousness of abstraction, but the utmost concreteness of visualization—a concreteness which we have seen in the descent of Toby and Mr. Shandy down the stairs. Mr. Shandy turns himself about upon 'the first landing; he sets his foot upon the first step from the landing; he takes the same step over again; he draws his leg back; he looks over the balusters at Susannah; he crosses the landing to set his back against the wall. These are Sterne's typical time markings, showing the procession of stance and gesture, but they are also the delicately observed details of the dramatic picture, which bring it alive and concrete before our eyes, and which make of the characters of *Tristram Shandy* creatures who, once known, remain unfadingly, joyously vivid to our imagination.

It is because of Sterne's acute awareness of time passage and of the conundrums of the time sense, that he is also so acutely aware of the concrete moment; or, conversely, we could say that it is because of his awareness of the preciousness of the concrete moment, that he is so acutely aware of time, which destroys the moment. In the eighth chapter of the final book, he engages in an apostrophe.

> Time wastes too fast: every letter I trace tells me with what rapidity Life follows my pen; the days and hours of it, more precious, my dear Jenny! than the rubies about thy neck, are flying over our heads like light clouds of a windy day, never to return more—everything presses on—whilst thou art twisting that lock,—see! it grows grey; and every time I kiss thy hand to bid adieu, and every absence which follows it, are preludes to that eternal separation which we are shortly to make.—

Which calls for a new "chapter" of a single line—"Now, for what the world thinks of that ejaculation—I would not give a groat." The philosopher, with his head full of time, is never allowed to sail off into abstraction; he keeps his eye on Jenny twisting her lock. For it is not in abstract speculation about time, but precisely in Jenny's gesture as she twists her lock, that the time sense finds profoundest significance; or in Trim's gesture as he drops his hat on the kitchen floor to illustrate to Obadiah and Susannah the catastrophe of mortal passage into oblivion.

Let us stay with Trim's hat for a moment, for it will illustrate for us another and equally important structural irony in *Tristram Shandy.*

> —"Are we not here now;" continued the corporal, "and are we not"—(dropping his hat plump upon the ground—and pausing, before he pronounced the word)—"gone! in a moment?" The descent of the hat was as if a heavy lump of clay had been kneaded into the crown of it.—Nothing could have expressed the sentiment of mortality, of which it was the type and fore-runner, like it,—his hand seemed to vanish from under it,—it fell dead,—the corporal's eye fixed upon it, as upon a corpse,—and Susannah burst into a flood of tears.
>
> Now—ten thousand, and ten thousand times ten thousand (for matter and motion are infinite) are the ways by which a hat may be dropped upon the ground, without any effect.—Had he flung it, or thrown it, or cast it, or skimmed it, or squirted it, or let it slip or fall in any possible direction under heaven, . . . the effect upon the heart had been lost.
>
> Ye who govern this mighty world and its mighty concerns with the engines of eloquence . . . meditate—meditate, I beseech you, upon Trim's hat.

What, of course, gives the scene that incongruity in which humor lies, is the use of Trim's gesture with his hat as a symbol of mortality: that is, the equating of the trivial with the serious, the unimportant with the important. Coleridge, speculating on the "one humorific point common to all that can be called humorous," found that common point to lie in

> a certain reference to the general and the universal, by which the finite great is brought into identity with the little, or the little with the finite great, so as to make both nothing in comparison with the infinite. The little is made great, and the great little, in order to destroy both; because all is equal in contrast with the infinite.[4]

It is indeed Sterne to whom Coleridge immediately refers for illustration of the point. Trim's gesture with his hat is one among innumerable instances in the book. It is the "finite little" brought into identity with the

4 *Miscellaneous Criticism* (Cambridge: Harvard University Press, 1936), p. 444. Herbert Read, in his discussion of Sterne in *The Sense of Glory,* analyzes Sterne's humor in these terms.

"finite great" (and the references to tens of thousands and the "mighty world" domesticate the "finite great" in the Shandy kitchen and in the even smaller quarters under the crown of Trim's hat), making of both "nothing in comparison with the infinite."

If we are accustomed to think of "humor" as the type of the comic strip, we may feel that Coleridge's definition of humor, and its application to *Tristram Shandy,* are much too serious—too "deep"—to have relevance to the funny. How can we laugh, if our minds are supposed to be oriented to the "finite great" and the "infinite"? It has been said, very wisely, that "comedy is a serious matter"; and though we are not speaking of "comedy" here (for we have reserved this term for dramatic writing of the order of *Tom Jones,* which is constructed on traditional principles of comic drama), but of "humor," we may say that humor, too, is a serious matter. Nor would it be improbable that, in analyzing the source of humor in the best comic strips, the observer would find that Coleridge's definition was applicable. (Needless to say, we do not laugh when we are analytically intent on understanding *why* we laugh. The laughter has come first.) It is a definition of humor that is fertile also for an understanding of certain neglected aspects of modern writers, such as Dostoevski and Kafka, who, though deeply "serious" writers, are at the same time great humorists; and our understanding of the "seriousness" of Sterne's humor can prepare us for a larger understanding of those authors nearer our time, who are concerned seriously with the problems of our time, but who are sensitive also to the sources of laughter.

Let us take one more passage to illustrate our meaning. We have said that we would need to consider rather more carefully that influential aspect of Locke's theory of the understanding which is its Sensationalism —its grounding of knowledge in sensation—and of Sterne's indebtedness to Locke for his doctrine of "sensibility" or "sentimentality," which measures the value of experience in terms of its feeling-fulness, the experience that is full of feeling ("sensation," "sensibility," "sentiment") being the valuable experience. We shall not take one of the famous "sentimental" passages—such as that concerning Uncle Toby and the fly, or the death of Le Fever. Tristram's encounter with Maria (Chapter XXIV, Book IX) will do. What we shall look for here is the equating of "great" and trivial, which resonates in humor because of the strange balance contrived between these incommensurables. Tristram is on his way to Moulins, and hears a flute player on the road.

95

—They were the sweetest notes I ever heard; and I instantly let down the fore-glass to hear them more distinctly—'Tis Maria; said the postillion, observing I was listening—Poor Maria, continued he (leaning his body on one side to let me see her, for he was in a line betwixt us), is sitting upon a bank playing her vespers upon her pipe, with her little goat beside her.

The young fellow utter'd this with an accent and a look so perfectly in tune to a feeling heart, that I instantly made a vow, I would give him a four-and-twenty sous piece, when I got to Moulins—

—And who is poor Maria? said I.

The love and piety of all the villages around us; said the postillion —it is but three years ago, that the sun did not shine upon so fair, so quick-witted and amiable a maid; and better fate did Maria deserve, than to have her Banns forbid, by the intrigues of the curate of the parish who published them—

He was going on, when Maria, who had made a short pause, put the pipe to her mouth, and began the air again—they were the same notes;—yet were ten times sweeter: It is the evening service to the Virgin, said the young man—but who has taught her to play it—or how she came by her pipe, no one knows; we think that heaven has assisted her in both; for ever since she has been unsettled in her mind, it seems her only consolation—she has never once had the pipe out of her hand, but plays that service upon it almost night and day . . .

We had got up by this time almost to the bank where Maria was sitting: she was in a thin white jacket, with her hair, all but two tresses, drawn up into a silk-net, with a few olive leaves twisted a little fantastically on one side—she was beautiful; and if ever I felt the full force of an honest heart-ache, it was the moment I saw her—

This is the adumbration of a pathetic, a "sentimental" story, in the manner of Cervantes' pastorals (and Sterne apostrophizes Cervantes at the beginning of the chapter). What comes under the denomination of the "finite great" in it is the pathos, the communicated feeling or sensation of pity (the postillion speaks "in tune to a feeling heart," and Tristram feels "the full force of an honest heart-ache") over Maria's love tragedy and madness, and the inference of Heaven's interest in her sad career. But the sketch ends suddenly on a different note. Under the spell of Maria's melancholy cadences, Tristram has leaped out of the coach and seated himself beside her on the bank, between Maria and her goat.

> Maria look'd wistfully for some time at me, and then at her goat—
> and then at me—and then at her goat again, and so on, alternately—
> —Well, Maria, said I softly—What resemblance do you find?

The typical goatishness here, and the "sportive pattern of alternation" [5] (with Maria looking at Tristram, then at the goat, then at Tristram—a pattern which is one of the distinguishing traits of Sterne's style) illustrate that term of the humorous equation which is the "finite little," the trivial, the whimsical, and which, capping off the full-blowing cumulus of Maria's pathos, asks finite judgment to suspend its intoxicated action for a moment in a healthy smile at its own potency for exaggeration, hysteria, and error.

Sterne wrote to a hesitant admirer, who had objected to his detailed treatment of Dr. Slop's fall in the mud,

> I will reconsider Slops fall & my too Minute Account of it—but in general I am persuaded that the happiness of the Cervantic humour arises from this very thing—of describing silly and trifling Events, with the Circumstantial Pomp of great Ones—perhaps this is Overloaded— & I can soon ease it.

Happily, he did not "ease it," but left Dr. Slop in full benefit of his original tumble, "unwiped, unappointed, unannealed." Sterne's insight into the nature of the humorous situation, as expressed in the letter, is simply the immediate technical version of Coleridge's later and more philosophical analysis of humor that we have cited; for to identify the "finite great" with the "finite little" becomes, in the actual handling of situation, a description of "silly and trifling Events, with the Circumstantial Pomp of Great Ones" or the converse of this, as in the story of Toby and the fly, where the trifling event is treated with the grand diction and gesture and the palpitating feeling of pompous circumstance. Sterne has been taken to task, many times over, for his indulgence in pruriency, his slips into indecency, his tendency—as in the story of Maria—to lapse into goatishness and spoil a softly solemn, tear-jerking story. That he was perfectly capable of writing the tear-jerker is evident, nor was anyone more aware of this than Sterne. Frequently, one feels, he must have been tempted to outsentimentalize the sentimentalists, knowing the delicacy of his hand

[5] The phrase is that of Ernest Nevin Dilworth, in *The Unsentimental Journey of Laurence Sterne* (New York: King's Crown Press, 1948).

at the pathetic (as in the story of Le Fever's death). But his genius was the humorous genius, and he remained faithful to it. What have been considered his indecent lapses must be taken as an essential element in the whole Sterne, one term of a structural irony, and a provision for keeping the sentimental and the emotional and the pathetic in the same human world with the obscene and the trivial and the absurd. His reference, in the letter quoted above, to the "Cervantic humour" reminds us that the high-minded knight, Quixote, could not continue on his travels without his low companion, Sancho.

ON *Pride and Prejudice*

It is the frequent response of readers who are making their first acquaintance with Jane Austen that her subject matter is itself so limited —limited to the manners of a small section of English country gentry who apparently never have been worried about death or sex, hunger or war, guilt or God—that it can offer no contiguity with modern interests. This is a very real difficulty in an approach to an Austen novel, and we should not obscure it; for by taking it initially into consideration, we can begin to come closer to the actual toughness and subtlety of the Austen quality. The greatest novels have been great in range as well as in technical invention; they have explored human experience a good deal more widely and deeply than Jane Austen was able to explore it. It is wronging an Austen novel to expect of it what it makes no pretense to rival—the spiritual profundity of the very greatest novels. But if we expect artistic mastery of limited materials, we shall not be disappointed.

The exclusions and limitations are deliberate; they do not necessarily represent limitations of Jane Austen's personal experience. Though she led the life of a maiden gentlewoman, it was not actually a sheltered life —not sheltered, that is, from the apparition of a number of the harsher human difficulties. She was a member of a large family whose activities ramified in many directions, in a period when a cousin could be guillotined, when an aunt and uncle could be jailed for a year on a shopkeeper's petty falsification, and when the pregnancies and childbed mortalities of relatives and friends were kept up at a barnyard rate. Her letters show in her the ironical mentality and the eighteenth-century gusto that are the reverse of the puritanism and naïveté that might be associated with the maidenly life. What she excludes from her fictional material does not, then, reflect a personal obliviousness, but, rather, a critically developed knowledge of the character of her gift and a restriction of its

99

exercise to the kind of subject matter which she could shape into most significance. When we begin to look upon these limitations, not as having the negative function of showing how much of human life Jane Austen left out, but as having, rather, the positive function of defining the form and meaning of the book, we begin also to understand that kind of value that can lie in artistic mastery over a restricted range. This "two inches of ivory" (the metaphor which she herself used to describe her work), though it may resemble the handle of a lady's fan when looked on scantly, is in substance an elephant's tusk; it is a savagely probing instrument as well as a masterpiece of refinement.

Time and space are small in *Pride and Prejudice*. Time is a few months completely on the surface of the present, with no abysses of past or future, no room for mystery; there is time only for a sufficiently complicated business of getting wived and husbanded and of adapting oneself to civilization and civilization to oneself. Space can be covered in a few hours of coach ride between London and a country village or estate; but this space is a *physical* setting only in the most generalized sense; it is space as defined by a modern positivistic philosopher—"a place for an argument." The concern is rational and social. What is relevant is the way minds operate in certain social circumstances, and the physical particular has only a derived and subordinate relevance, as it serves to stimulate attitudes between persons. Even the social circumstances are severely restricted: they are the circumstances of marriageable young women coming five to a leisure-class family with reduced funds and prospects. What can be done with this time and space and these circumstances? What Jane Austen does is to dissect—with what one critic has called "regulated hatred"[1]—the monster in the skin of the civilized animal, the irrational acting in the costumes and on the stage of the rational; and to illuminate the difficult and delicate reconciliation of the sensitively developed individual with the terms of his social existence.

"It is a truth universally acknowledged, that a single man in possession of a good fortune must be in want of a wife." This is the first sentence of the book. What we read in it is its opposite—a single woman must be in want of a man with a good fortune—and at once we are inducted into the Austen language, the ironical Austen attack, and the energy, peculiar to an Austen novel, that arises from the compression between a barbaric

[1] D. W. Harding, "Regulated Hatred: An Aspect of the Work of Jane Austen," *Scrutiny*, March, 1940,

subsurface marital warfare and a surface of polite manners and civilized conventions. Marriage—that adult initiatory rite that is centrally important in most societies whether barbarous or advanced—is the uppermost concern. As motivation for the story, it is as primitively powerful an urgency as is sex in a novel by D. H. Lawrence. The tale is that of a man hunt, with the female the pursuer and the male a shy and elusive prey. The desperation of the hunt is the desperation of economic survival: girls in a family like that of the Bennets must succeed in running down solvent young men in order to survive. But the marriage motivation is complicated by other needs of a civilized community: the man hunters must observe the most refined behavior and sentiments. The female is a "lady" and the male is a "gentleman"; they must "fall in love." Not only must civilized appearances be preserved before the eyes of the community, but it is even necessary to preserve dignity and fineness of feeling in one's own eyes.

The second sentence outlines the area in which the aforementioned "truth universally acknowledged" is to be investigated—a small settled community, febrile with social and economic rivalry.

> However little known the feelings or views of such a man may be on his first entering a neighborhood, this truth is so well fixed in the minds of the surrounding families, that he is considered as the rightful property of some one or other of their daughters.

Here a high valuation of property is so dominant a culture trait that the word "property" becomes a metaphor for the young man himself; and the phrasing of the sentence, with typical Austen obliquity, adds a further sly emphasis to this trait when it uses an idiom associated with the possession of wealth—"well fixed"—as a qualifier of the standing of "truth." We are told that the young man may have "feelings or views" of his own (it becomes evident, later, that even daughters are capable of a similar willful subjectivity); and we are warned of the embarrassment such "feelings or views" will cause, whether to the individual or to the community, when we read of those "surrounding families" in whom "truth" is "so well fixed"—portentous pressure! And now we are given a light preliminary draft of the esteemed state of marriage, in the little drama of conflicting perceptions and wills that the first chapter presents between the imbecilic Mrs. Bennet and her indifferent, sarcastic husband. "The experience of three and twenty years had been insufficient to make his wife understand his character." The marriage problem is set broadly before us in this uneasy parental background, where an ill-mated couple must come to terms on the finding of mates for their five daughters. A social call must be made, in any case, on the single gentleman of good fortune who has settled in the neighborhood. With the return of the call, and with the daughters set up for view—some of whom are "handsome," some "good-natured"—no doubt he will buy, that is to say, "fall in love" (with such love, perhaps, as we have seen between Mr. and Mrs. Bennet themselves).

[In this first chapter, the fundamental literary unit of the single word—"fortune," "property," "possession," "establishment," "business"—has consistently been setting up the impulsion of economic interest against those non-utilitarian interests implied by the words "feelings" and "love." [2] The implications of the word "marriage" itself are ambivalent; for as these implications are controlled in the book, "marriage" does not mean an act of ungoverned passion (not even in Lydia's and Wickham's rash elopement does it mean this: for Wickham has his eye on a settlement by blackmail, and Lydia's infatuation is rather more with a uniform than with a man); marriage means a complex engagement between the marrying couple and society—that is, it means not only "feelings" but "property" as well. In marrying, the individual marries society as well as his mate, and "property" provides the necessary articles of this other marriage. With marriage, so defined, as the given locus of action, the clash and reconciliation of utility interests with interests that are nonutilitarian will provide a subtle drama of manners; for whatever spiritual creativity may lie in the individual personality, that creativity will be able to operate only within publicly acceptable modes of deportment.] These modes of deportment, however public and traditional, must be made to convey the secret life of the individual spirit, much as a lens conveys a vision of otherwise invisible constellations. Language itself is the lens in this case—the linguistic habits of social man.

Below language we do not descend, except by inference, for, in this definitively social world, language is the index of behavior, the special machine which social man has made to register his attitudes and to organize his dealings with others. We have spoken of Jane Austen's exclu-

2 This point of view is developed by Mark Schorer in the essay "Fiction and the 'Analogical Matrix,'" in *Critiques and Essays on Modern Fiction,* edited by John W. Aldridge (New York: The Ronald Press Company, 1952), pp. 83–98.

sion of the physical particular. One might expect that in her treatment of the central problem of marriage she could not avoid some physical particularity—some consciousness of the part played by the flesh and the fleshly passions in marriage. Curiously and quite wonderfully, out of her restricted concern for the rational and social definition of the human performance there does arise a strong implication of the physical. Can one leave this novel without an acute sense of physical characterizations— even of the smells of cosmetic tinctures and obesity in Mrs. Bennet's boudoir, or of the grampus-like erotic wallowings of the monstrous Mr. Collins? Nothing could be stranger to an Austen novel than such representations of the physical. And yet, from her cool, unencumbered understanding of the linguistic exhibitions of the parlor human, she gives us, by the subtlest of implication, the human down to its "naturals," down to where it is human only by grace of the fact that it talks English and has a set of gestures arbitrarily corresponding to rationality.

Among the "daughters" and the "young men of fortune" there are a few sensitive individuals, civilized in spirit as well as in manner. For these few, "feeling" must either succumb to the paralysis of utility or else must develop special delicacy and strength. The final adjustment with society, with "property" and "establishment," must be made in any case, for in this book the individual is unthinkable without the social environment, and in the Austen world that environment has been given once and forever—it is unchangeable and it contains the only possibilities for individual development. For the protagonists, the marriage rite will signify an "ordeal" in that traditional sense of a moral testing which is the serious meaning of initiation in any of the important ceremonies of life. What will be tested will be their integrity of "feeling" under the crudely threatening social pressures. The moral life, then, will be equated with delicacy and integrity of feeling, and its capacity for growth under adverse conditions. In the person of the chief protagonist, Elizabeth, it really will be equated with intelligence. In this conception of the moral life, Jane Austen shows herself the closest kin to Henry James in the tradition of the English novel; for by James, also, the moral life was located in emotional intelligence, and he too limited himself to observation of its workings in the narrow area of a sophisticated civilization.

The final note of the civilized in *Pride and Prejudice* is, as we have said, reconciliation. The protagonists do not "find themselves" by leaving society, divorcing themselves from its predilections and obsessions.

In the union of Darcy and Elizabeth, Jane and Bingley, the obsessive social formula of marriage-to-property is found again, but now as the happy reward of initiates who have travailed and passed their "ordeal." The incongruities between savage impulses and the civilized conventions in which they are buried, between utility and morality, are reconciled in the symbolic act of a marriage which society itself—bent on useful marriages—has paradoxically done everything to prevent. Rightly, the next to the last word in the book is the word "uniting."

We have so far attempted to indicate both the restrictive discipline which Jane Austen accepted from her material and the moral life which she found in it. The significance of a given body of material is a function of the form which the artist gives to the material. Significance is, then, not actually "found" by the artist in his subject matter, as if it were already and obviously present there for anyone to see, but is created by him in the act of giving form to the material (it was in this sense that poets were once called trouvères, or "finders"). The form of the action of *Pride and Prejudice* is a set of "diverging and converging lines" [3] mathematically balanced in their movements, a form whose diagrammatic neatness might be suggested in such a design as that given below, which shows the relationship of correspondence-with-variation between the Darcy-Elizabeth plot and the Jane-Bingley subplot, the complication of the former and the simplicity of the latter, the successive movements toward splitting apart and toward coming together, and the final resolution of movement in "recognition" and reconciliation between conflicting claims, as the total action composes itself in the shape of the lozenge (see the chart opposite).

But significant form, as we have noted in previous studies, is a far more complex structure of relationships than those merely of plot. An Austen novel offers a particularly luminous illustration of the function of style in determining the major form. Our diagram of the plot movements of *Pride and Prejudice* will serve as visualization of a pattern of antithetical balances found also in the verbal composition of the book. It is here, in style, in the language base itself, that we are able to observe Jane Austen's most deft and subtle exploitation of her material.

The first sentence of the book—"It is a truth universally acknowledged, that a single man in possession of a good fortune must be in want of a wife"—again affords an instance in point. As we have said, the sen-

[3] The phrase and the observation are those of Mary Lascelles, in *Jane Austen and Her Art* (New York: Oxford University Press, 1939), p. 160.

tence ironically turns itself inside out, thus: a single woman must be in want of a man with a good fortune. In this doubling of the inverse meaning over the surface meaning, a very modest-looking statement sums up the chief conflicting forces in the book: a decorous convention of love (which holds the man to be the pursuer) embraces a savage economic compulsion (the compulsion of the insolvent female to run down male "property"), and in the verbal embrace they appear as a unit. The ironic mode here is a mode of simultaneous opposition and union: civilized convention and economic primitivism unite in the sentence as they do in the action, where "feelings" and "fortune," initially in conflict, are reconciled in the socially creative union of marriage.

This is but one type of verbal manipulation with which the book luxuriates. Another we shall illustrate with a sentence from Mr. Collins' proposal to Elizabeth, where "significant form" lies in elaborate rather than in modest phrasing. Mr. Collins manages to wind himself up almost inextricably in syntax.

> "But the fact is, that being as I am, to inherit this estate after the death of your honored father, (who, however, may live many years longer,) I could not satisfy myself without resolving to chuse a wife from among his daughters, that the loss to them might be as little as possible, when the melancholy event takes place—which, however, as I have already said, may not be for several years."

Fancy syntax acts here, not as an expression of moral and intellectual refinement (as Mr. Collins intends it to act), but as an expression of stupidity, the antithesis of that refinement. The elaborate language in which Mr. Collins gets himself fairly *stuck* is a mimesis of an action of the soul, the soul that becomes self dishonest through failure to know itself, and that overrates itself at the expense of the social context, just as it overrates verbalism at the expense of meaning. We have suggested that moral life, in an Austen novel, is identified with emotional intelligence; and it is precisely through failure of intelligence—the wit to know his own limitations—that Mr. Collins appears as a moral monstrosity. Language is the mirror of his degeneracy. Against Mr. Collins' elaborate style of speech we may place the neat and direct phrasing of a sentence such as "It is a truth universally acknowledged . . ." where the balance of overt thesis and buried antithesis acts as a kind of signature of the intelligential life—its syntactical modesty conveying a very deft and energetic mental dance.

Similarly, elaborate epithet ("your honored father," "the melancholy event") is suspect—the sign not of attention but of indifference, of a moldiness of spirit which, far from being innocuous, has the capacity of mold to flourish destructively and to engulf what is clean and sound, as such epithet itself devours sense. Comedy, let us say again, "is a serious matter," and what is serious in this scene of Mr. Collins' proposal is the engulfing capacity of the rapacious Mr. Collins, from whom Elizabeth escapes narrowly. The narrowness of the escape is underlined by the fact that Elizabeth's friend, Charlotte—herself, we assume, intelligent, inasmuch as she is Elizabeth's friend—complacently offers herself as host to this mighty mold. In the civilized community which is our area of observation, emotional intelligence and quickness of moral perception—as we see them, for instance, in Elizabeth—are profoundly threatened by an all-environing imbecility. It is through style that we understand the nature of this threat; for the simplicity and directness of the governing syntax of the book prepares us to find positive values in simplicity and directness, negative values in elaboration and indirection. Even the canny intelligence of Mr. Bennet is not that emotionally informed intelligence—or, shall we say, that intelligence which informs the emotions—that we are led to look upon as desirable; and Mr. Bennet reveals his failure also in "style," a style of speech that shows a little too elaborate consciousness of the pungency of double-talk, of the verbal effect of ironic undercutting. When Elizabeth suggests that it would be imprudent to send the lightheaded Lydia to Brighton, he says,

> Lydia will never be easy till she has exposed herself in some public place or other, and we can never expect her to do it with so little expense or inconvenience to her family as under the present circumstances.

Being intelligent, Mr. Bennet learns regret for his failure, although (and we delight also in Jane Austen's "realism" here, the tenacity of her psychological grip on her characters) not too much regret—not so much that he ceases to be Mr. Bennet.

From still another point of view, the style of the book is significant of total structure; we refer here to a generalized kind of epithet used in descriptive passages. The park at Pemberley, Darcy's estate, "was very large, and contained great variety of ground"; one drove "through a beautiful wood stretching over a wide extent." What we wish to notice, in diction of this kind, is the merely approximate appropriateness of the qualifier: "large," "great variety," "beautiful wood," "wide extent." This type of diction we might again describe as "modest," or we might speak of it as flatly commonplace; but we shall want to investigate its possibilities of function in the total form of the book. The reader will observe the continued use of the same kind of diction in the passage below, describing the house; what should be noted is the use to which the description is put—its use, not to convey any sense of "naturalistic" particularity, but, rather, to reveal Darcy's taste (of which Elizabeth has been suspicious) and a subtle turn in Elizabeth's feelings about him.

> It was a large, handsome, stone building, standing well on rising ground, and backed by a ridge of high woody hills;—and in front, a stream of some natural importance was swelled into greater, but without any artificial appearance. Its banks were neither formal nor falsely adorned. Elizabeth was delighted. She had never seen a place for which nature had done more, or where natural beauty had been so little counteracted by an awkward taste. They were all of them warm in their admiration; and at that moment she felt that to be mistress of Pemberley might be something!

Wealth applied to the happiest and most dignified creation of environment —that is all we need to know about this setting, a need which the description fulfills by virtue of generalizations—"large," "standing well," "natural importance," "natural beauty," and the series of negations of what is generally understood by "artificial appearance," "falsely adorned," and so forth. More particularity of description would deflect from what is significant in the episode, namely, the effect of the scene upon Elizabeth's attitude toward her lover. Darcy himself has had in her eyes a certain artificiality, unpleasant formality, falseness; he has been lacking in that naturalness which delights her in the present scene, which is his home and which speaks intimately of him; and she has felt that his taste in the handling of human relations was very seriously "awkward." The appearance of Pemberley cannot help putting a slight pressure on her judgment of him, and the description is used with deliberate purpose for this effect. And how shrewd psychologically and warmly human is the remark, "and at that moment she felt that to be mistress of Pemberley might be something!" With all her personal integrity and exacerbated delicacy of feeling about the horrors of acquisitiveness, Elizabeth is smitten with an acquisitive temptation. (No wonder Jane Austen could not find Elizabeth's painted portrait in the galleries, though she was able to find Jane Bennet's there. Elizabeth is quite too human to have a duplicate in paint; only language is able to catch her.) In this final clause, the dramatic concern is solely with the social context—the shifting attitudes of one person toward another, as these attitudes are conditioned by the terms of a narrow, but nevertheless complex, social existence; but as the relationships between persons shift, the individual himself (as Elizabeth, here) is reinterpreted, shows a new aspect of his humanity. In this fashion, the Austen style—here a deliberately generalized and commonplace descriptive style —functions again as determination of significant form, significance in this particular case being the *rational* meaning of a physical setting.

Finally we should remark upon what is perhaps the most formative and conclusive activity of style in the book: the effect of a narrowly mercantile and materialistic vocabulary in setting up meanings. Let us go down a few lists of typical words, categorizing them rather crudely and arbitrarily, but in such a manner as to show their direction of reference.[4] The reader will perhaps be interested in adding to these merely suggestive lists, for in watching the Austen language lies the real excitement of the Austen novel. We shall set up such categories as "trade," "arithmetic," "money," "material possessions," simply in order to indicate the kind of language Jane Austen inherited from her culture and to which she was confined—and in order to suggest what she was able to do with her language, how much of the human drama she was able to get into such confines.

TRADE	ARITHMETIC	MONEY	MATERIAL POSSESSIONS	SOCIAL INTEGRATION
employed	equally	pounds	estate	town
due form	added	credit	property	society
collect	proportion	capital	owner	civil
receipt	addition	pay	house	neighborhood
buy	enumerate	fortune	manor	county
sell	figure	valuable	tenant	fashion
business	calculated	principal	substantial	breeding
supply	amount	interest	establishment	genteel
terms	amounting	afford	provided	marriage
means	inconsiderable	indebted	foundation	husband
venture	consideration	undervalue	belongs to	connection

We could add such verbal categories as those referring to "patronage," "law," "skill" (a particularly interesting one, covering such words as "design," "cunning," "arts," "schemes," and so on; a category obviously converging with the "trade" category, but whose vocabulary, as it appears in this book, is used derogatorily—the stupid people, like Mrs. Bennet, Lady Catherine de Bourgh, Wickham, and Mr. Collins, are the ones who "scheme" and have "designs").

[4] Mr. Schorer's essay "Fiction and the 'Analogical Matrix,'" cited above, closely examines this aspect of Jane Austen's style.

In viewing in the abstract the expressive possibilities open to literary creatorship, we might assume that the whole body of the English language, as it is filed in the dictionary, is perfectly free of access to each author— that each author shares equally and at large in the common stuff of the language. In a sense this is true; the whole body of the language *is* there, virtually, in the dictionary, and anyone can consult it and use it if he wants to. But we have observed fairly frequently, if only by-the-way, in these studies, that each author does not consult the whole body of the language in selecting words for his meanings; that he is driven, as if compulsively, to the selection of a highly particular part of the language; and that the individual character of his work, its connotations and special insights, derive largely from the style he has made his own—that is to say, from the vocabulary and verbal arrangements he has adopted out of the whole gamut of words and rhetorical patterns available in the language. In making these selections, he is acting partly under the compulsions of the culture in which he has been bred and whose unconscious assumptions—as to what is interesting or valuable or necessary or convenient in life—are reflected in the verbal and rhetorical selections common in that culture; and he is acting partly also under compulsions that are individual to his own personal background, but that still maintain subtle links with the common cultural assumptions. The general directions of reference taken by Jane Austen's language, as indicated by such lists as those given above (and the lists, with others like them, could be extended for pages), are clearly materialistic. They reflect a culture whose institutions are solidly defined by materialistic interests—property and banking and trade and the law that keeps order in these matters— institutions which determine, in turn, the character of family relations, the amenities of community life, and the whole complex economy of the emotions. By acknowledgment of the fact that the materialistic assumptions of our own culture are even more pervasive than those reflected in this book, and that their governance over our emotions and our speech habits is even more grim, more sterilizing, and more restrictive, we should be somewhat aided in appreciation of the "contemporaneity" of Jane Austen herself.

But where then, we must ask, does originality lie, if an author's very language is dictated in so large a part by something, as it were, "outside" himself—by the culture into which he is accidentally born? How can there be any free play of individual genius, the free and original play with the language by which we recognize the insight and innovations of genius? The question has to be answered separately for the work of each artist, but as for Jane Austen's work we have been finding answers all along—in her exploitation of antithetical structures to convey ambivalent attitudes, in her ironic use of syntactical elaborations that go against the grain of the language and that convey moral aberrations, and finally in her direct and oblique play with an inherited vocabulary that is materialistic in reference and that she forces—or blandishes or intrigues—into spiritual duties.

The language base of the Austen novel gives us the limiting conditions of the culture. Somehow, using this language of acquisitiveness and calculation and materialism, a language common to the most admirable characters as well as to the basest characters in the book, the spiritually creative persons will have to form their destinies. The project would be so much easier if the intelligent people and the stupid people, the people who are morally alive and the people who are morally dead, had each their different language to distinguish and publicize their differences! But unfortunately for that ease, they have only one language. Fortunately for the drama of the Austen novel, there is this difficulty of the single materialistic language; for drama subsists on difficulty. Within the sterile confines of public assumptions, the Austen protagonists find with difficulty the fertility of honest and intelligent individual feeling. On a basis of communication that is drawn always from the public and savage theology of "property," the delicate lines of spiritual adjustment are explored. The final fought-for recognitions of value are recognitions of the unity of experience—a unity between the common culture and the individual development. No one more knowledgeably than this perceptive and witty woman, ambushed by imbecility, could have conducted such an exploration.

ON *The Heart of Mid-Lothian*

Ultimately, as critical readers, we are concerned with an author's conception of life. But, in a work of art, it is only through the intimate activities of aesthetic form that any conception of life is honestly put before us. The very close correlation between aesthetic structure and what we call "value" or "significance" is the chief mystery in the economy of art—a mystery simply because it is an empirical fact that we recognize again and again in our reading just as we recognize empirically the connection between touching a hot stove and getting burned or between exposure in the rain and getting wet. These are homely analogies, chosen because of the impossibility, in these simple cases, of dissociating the one term of the correlation from the other: we cannot dissociate a burn from something hot, nor a soaking from something wet. Similarly, we cannot dissociate an author's conception of life, and its "value" and "significance," from the aesthetic structure of the literary work. It is for this reason that the "world view" to be found in a finely wrought novel is fairly inexhaustible, and we can reread and reread the book with increasing extension of insight. For on first reading such a work, it is impossible to be aware of all elements, all relationships among them, all inflections given the major rhythm as it engages the minor rhythms; but as our alertness to more and more of these is freed by rereading, the view of life which the book contains becomes changed in our apprehension and appears inexhaustible because of the new aspects constantly being given to that view by newly emerging relationships.

Inasmuch as *Pride and Prejudice* has none of the more obvious attractions of fiction—exalted passions, exotic geography, and so forth—it offers itself particularly well for a test of the aesthetic coherence of the novel, and of its "view of life," as that coherence can be felt in the "parts" that are a novel's very smallest parts—the individual words that make it up; the qualities of this book must be sought with a wholly activated intelligence in the word and the phrasing, the partial and delicate exposure of attitude in an ambivalent thought, an idiosyncrasy of diction, a turn of syntax. Read in this way, the book raises in the mind a rich and subtle conception of life that does not appear on first glance at the tidily commonplace surface; but such a reading also illustrates the fact that this conception of life owes its integrity, and its value for us in making discrimination finer, precisely to the aesthetic integrity of the book. To set *The Heart of Mid-Lothian* beside *Pride and Prejudice* is to set a book colored by illicit passions, violence, riot, crowd scenes, gypsy life and the life of bandits, lynching and murder, picturesque manners in low places and high places, and an environment of crags and castles and filthy dens, beside a book whose color is solely mental; it is also to set a poorly structured book beside a finely structured book, and to witness more convincingly in this juxtaposition of two classic English novels the fact that incoherent structure equates with an incoherent world view, essentially valueless for us no matter how attractive certain single elements of the book may be, while coherent aesthetic structure equates with a coherent world view, potentially valuable to us in the degree of the complexity of those elements that are made to cohere.

The Heart of Mid-Lothian has generally been considered the best of Scott's work, for it is a book in which he is not only the fictional historian and the novelist of "local color," but also the moral psychologist, the investigator of matters of conscience. The figure of Jeanie Deans has moved many astute critics to applause. Her story, in short, is this. Jeanie's younger sister, Effie, is accused of child murder; a curious technicality of the law provides that had Effie once admitted her pregnancy to another person, the shadow of the clandestine would be removed, the case would be dismissed through lack of material evidence, and Effie would be saved from the hangman; Jeanie is the likeliest person to whom Effie might have admitted her condition, but Jeanie's conscience forbids her to speak the necessary untruth, and at the trial Effie is condemned; whereupon Jeanie walks from Edinburgh to London to obtain pardon for her sister from the king. This is by no means a complete sketch of the action of the novel, for Scott's contract with the publisher called for a good deal greater length to the book than the matter of Jeanie Deans's heroic action could provide; and as he needed the money, he supplied the length. We must judge a novel as one whole and at its full length; we cannot excerpt a part of it and call this part the novel, or we should have to allow ourselves the privilege of "editing" every novel in the same fashion, and our standards of critical objectivity would become helplessly disorganized and criticism itself ineffectual. We cannot cut short *The Heart of Mid-Lothian* at that point where its older readers found it still so highly praiseworthy—the point where Jeanie obtains the pardon; we must judge the book at its full length without commiseration for Scott's financial needs in building Abbotsford. And, indeed, the "conception of life" which the book holds is not fully recognizable until the end. Though the moral imagination of generations of readers has been most stirred by Jeanie's original problem and her solution of it, yet the further proliferation of Jeanie's destiny and Effie's (as Scott made up his pence) casts back upon the earlier section a comment that lays Scott's own moral imagination under dubiety.

One other preliminary consideration: the portion of the book dealing with the conviction for child murder and the action of the sister in making the trip on foot to London was founded in fact (Scott's preface describes his interview with Helen Walker—the original of Jeanie); and it is possible that the reader's sense that he is reading a "true story" determines in some degree the admiration he may have for the fiction. But since it *is* a fiction that we are reading, we must exorcise from our minds whatever tendency we may have to estimate the book by its partly factual foundation and by the interest and admiration we might feel for a real Helen Walker. (Who knows how much factual "truth" any number of stories may contain, whose authors did not supply the relevant documentary notes!) We must judge Jeanie's problem as the fictional Jeanie's, not as Helen Walker's, and this portion of the novel as we do the rest of it—as fiction, not as fact.

We shall speak chiefly here of Jeanie's first problem—to lie to save a life, or not to lie—for this problem provides the main dynamics of the book. It is a problem of no trivial interest. Even though we have largely lost the objective moral code which gave such a problem its original gravity—lost it with the loss of religious sanctions—or rather, just because of the loss of a common moral code, it is a question of potentially profound interest for the modern reader. In our own time we have been made more conscious of the subtle and terrible operations of the lie than our immediate forebears could have been, for we have seen its use on the most massive scale in propaganda, and we have seen the close relationship between human destiny and the political manipulation of the lie. Through academic studies in semantics, with their concern for what constitutes "meaning" in the word; through fairly popular exposure to psychoanalytical knowledge, with its interpretation of hidden levels of meaning in our actions and speech; and through the last two decades' experience of the strategies of totalitarianism, with its witty and immensely vicious practice of deceit through the word—we have become highly conscious of the implications of "truth" and of the breakdown of truth, even though we have become proportionately more confused as to what constitutes the truth or the lie. The problem, then, of the lie, on which *The Heart of Mid-Lothian* centers, is one on which we can well afford to dwell.

But we shall want to dwell on it, not in the abstract, but in the concrete aesthetic context in which the problem is raised. The book pivots on Jeanie's decision to tell the "truth"; it is what stirs our interest initially in this main character, and what keeps her a figure of any consideration for us as the story proceeds. If the book as a whole is faultily structured, and if the conception of life that it contains seems inadequate to give organic coherence to those parts of life it attempts to interpret, we might expect that the pivotal moral problem itself would be infected by the general fault of confusion. To get Jeanie's situation firmly before us, let us speak of it in the following way. Her sensibility has been trained by the spare and rigorous code of her Cameronian father, in an extraordinarily limited environment of thought and feeling but an environment extraordinarily powerful in its controls on the individual. She is altogether doubtful of Effie's alleged crime of child murder; there is no evidence, except that Effie had been pregnant and now the child cannot be found; Effie herself denies the act movingly and convincingly; but Jeanie cannot tell a lie to save her sister's life because generations of Cameronian ancestors bind her tongue, ancestors who, after the civil war, waged wars of logic and turned a none too logical theology into a strait jacket of scruples. We look, then, upon the invincible restriction Jeanie puts on herself as an act "conditioned" by her intellectual environment and inheritance. But we look on it also as a morally independent act; for we have to look upon it thus—even taking the "conditioning" into consideration —in order to found our own moral judgment somewhere: a wholly "conditioned" action is a helpless action, relating our pity to it perhaps but not our normative judgment, and Jeanie's action is set before us certainly not to win our pity but to stir our moral interest, our awe possibly, assuredly our judgment.

With this view of the problem, let us set beside it an analogous case of conscience in Shakespeare's *Measure for Measure*. (The comparison is not unfair, for Scott's admirers have continuously compared him honorifically with Shakespeare.) *Measure for Measure* is an ambiguous play, with an ambiguity that is morally unpleasant, for it offers a conventional solution for a problem too deeply rooted in emotional and nervous responses to be solved conventionally. We are, therefore, not comparing this play as a whole with Scott's novel as a whole, to the denigration of the latter; we are comparing only the pivotal problems in these two works, for what light of judgment one may throw on the other. In *Measure for Measure*, a man of known austerity and abstinence is deputized temporarily in the main seat of government; Angelo's first act of authority is to revive an obsolete law against lechery and to condemn to death a young man—Claudio—who has got his sweetheart with child. (We may note here that, as the "crime" in this play is sexual indulgence, so the *real* "crime" in Scott's novel is also sexual indulgence—for Effie is guilty of no other.) Claudio appeals to his sister, Isabella, to plead with Angelo for his life; and Isabella's plea is made so effective by the radiance of her own purity (she is about to take orders in a religious sisterhood) that Angelo, the abstinent man, is moved with lust for her and offers her Claudio's freedom on the condition that she will sleep with him. Isabella returns to Claudio's cell to tell him the consequences of her visit to the deputy; she is certain that Claudio will reject a bargain which would save his life so dishonorably. Here (in Act III, scene 1) the greatest ambiguity enters: we see Claudio, honorable in intention but grazed by the horror of death, brooding on the possible moral irrelevance of the sexual act; he reasons—if Angelo, a man of such pure life and so great in authority, can indulge the lecherous motive, is it actually a sin? Or if a sin, is it a sin of such consequence that Isabella should refuse a moment's use of her body for the saving of her brother's life? Isabella does refuse, and Claudio must face the hangman.

In the last two acts of the play, a conventional compromise is effected: Claudio is freed and Isabella keeps her virtue; but the play does not leave us with the feeling that the problem originally set, and articulated in Claudio's brooding thought, has been solved adequately by the structure in which it inheres. Of this much, though, we are certain: that the morality and the spiritual issues involved are vital, profound and intricate and difficult. Behind Isabella's refusal is not the conceit of a prude merely, but the holy orders she is about to take, and behind these the ascetic attitude of mind, an attitude that is neither an individual's aberration nor the neurosis of a culture, but a discipline of devotion almost universal to the developed religious character and even to the developed philosophical character. In the effect of her purity upon Angelo, in awakening lust in him, is a paradox of the spiritual life—the stimulus which innocence offers to the impulse of violation; and from this point of view, her yielding to him would be an active acquiescence in the germination of the demonic. Furthermore, the problem is set in an environment of sexual ugliness—pimps and whores and that frivolity of the physical which speaks of an uglier frivolity of spirit; this on the one hand—and on the other, a profound engagement of the mind with the uncertain horrors awaiting the soul after death. Between these two—the obsession with sexual ugliness and the other obsession with the horrors of death—neither Claudio's plea that Isabella expose herself to Angelo, nor Isabella's refusal, can be lightly taken. Finally, a subtle notion of perversity—the breaking of something more primitive than a religious taboo—attaches to Angelo's proposition and to Claudio's encouragement of it.

> Is't not a kind of incest, to take life
> From thine own sister's shame?

Isabella asks. The sexual act that might save Claudio is more than dishonorable; it has the taint of the "unnatural."

We have been speaking of the *context* given to Isabella's refusal to save her brother's life through prostitution. If the same problem were presented for our contemplation in the abstract, we might give a swift and facile answer to it: we might say, for instance, that Isabella suffered from barrenness of moral imagination, conceit of virginity, egotism of the spirit. But the concrete context offered by the play forces us to think with more complexity of what is meant by abstinence and prostitution, vice and purity, spiritual life and spiritual death—forces us to think so complexly about them that we (like Shakespeare himself in this instance) cannot give an answer that carries authority for our emotions. In other words, the play stretches our own moral imagination, exercises and toughens it, vitalizes it to a greater awareness of the complexity of the moral life. It succeeds in doing this by virtue of the rich and disturbing context it gives to the central dramatic motif.

In the abstract, also, we might pass a ready judgment on Jeanie Deans's refusal to save a sister's life by a lie. We might, in the abstract, approve or disapprove of her solution of the problem. Truth is of ancient nobility, and the devil has been called the Father of Lies. On the other hand, the question "What is truth?", voiced at the most passionate moment of Christian history, indicates anything but simplicity in the character of truth; and even Peter's thrice-told lie was a good deal more than an unscrupulosity of the tongue. But our concern again is not with the problem in the abstract, but with the concrete context the author provides for it. Is the question of the lie, as dealt with in this book, handled in such a way as to animate and complicate and enrich our perception of the difficulty and drama of truth?

The context gives us one possible point of view, that of the "conditioning" we have spoken of. The pressure placed on our actions by "conditions" is of the greatest dramatic and moral interest: it provided the most powerful source of ambiguity in ancient Greek tragedy, and it does so again today in the novels of Faulkner. But the "conditioning" of Jeanie Deans is not used as a source of ambiguity; it is, indeed, not *used* by Scott at all in the structure of the book. It is an element existing in the book; we are allowed to know and understand Jeanie's training in verbal scrupulosity; but we are not led thereby to penetrate into the complexity of our destiny as "conditioned" and yet morally independent creatures, as we are led to do by Sophocles and by Faulkner. Jeanie's Cameronian training is a mere bit of local color. But real confusion arises from this "mereness." Unfortunately, attitudes toward truth and falsehood are not "merely" local color; they are profoundly and universally important in our destinies. Scott *assumes* that they are important, and he *assumes* that Jeanie's decision to tell the truth contains a vital human attitude toward truth, but he neglects to explore this assumption in the aesthetic context he provides.

We cannot undertake to rewrite schematically Scott's novel, but we might speculate on a possibility of the following sort: had Jeanie been presented as the cultural product of a small sect pushed to the margins of the world, a sect that had developed a fantasy of prestige based on the singularity of its strictness of conduct, a presentation of this kind might, if taken up and made significant in the structure of the whole work, have brought Jeanie into the realm of moral interest, where men acquire guilt even in aspiring toward truth, are treasonable in ignorance and dishonorable in a passion for spiritual order; for such a presentation could have made acknowledgment of the unpredictable complexity and tragedy of serious moral choices. The context offers us also another, related, suggestion. After all, there is Effie, whose life is at stake and who is innocent of the alleged crime. How much is a life worth in scruples as to the absolute "truth" of the voiced word? Or we may turn the same point of view about: how much is a verbal truth or falsehood worth in the poundage of another person's life? How deep and how fine is the connection between "verbal" truth and other kinds of truth? These are most serious and disturbing questions, and they are the questions automatically raised by Scott's pivotal problem, which, as artist or even as intelligently conscientious craftsman, he pledges himself to explore. But, again, he refuses to explore them in the concrete terms of aesthetic structure—presumably because he does not know that they are there. His neglect of their inherence in his materials is an index of confusion. Our view, as readers, is arbitrarily deflected from what the book initially offers us to look at. Instead, we are given highwaymen and kidnaping and queens and colorful eccentrics. This deflection of vision is what we mean by disorderliness and disorganization of structure. It illustrates that dependence, spoken of early in this essay, between aesthetic coherence in the novel and a coherent view of life.

In *Pride and Prejudice,* in materials that appeared at first to be of the simplest, we witnessed extraordinary complexity cohering in a major rhythm that controlled and united all minor rhythms. In *The Heart of Mid-Lothian,* in a wealth of materials, we witness a disorganization that falsifies the materials and in which they separately fall away into unrelated genres of their own: into little ballad-like dramas, like Jeanie's going to London to see the king's face that gives grace (the motif is from the ballad "Johnnie Armstrong"), or, on a larger scale, like Effie's own early story—her seduction by a highwayman lover, her grievous pregnancy and harsh travail, her disposal of her child (a ballad on this subject would have seized advantage of the tragedy of motive here, and Effie would have done away with her child, but Scott, though a collector of ballads, himself had not really the ballad-stomach; he produces an inconceivable harridan, Meg Murdockson, to do the dirty work), her conviction for murder, and her pitiful road to the gallows, where she would have been in the company of other ballad heroines; or they fall into the picaresque genre, as do Jeanie's adventures on the way to London; or into the comic, like the scenes of the old laird's death and the young laird's wooing. These, and other materials in the book, considered separately, carry on occasion the conviction of imaginative reality, but they do not cohere in a common rhythm for the mind; their juxtaposition does not *mean* anything.

The "crime," for instance, which Effie commits is, as we have said, the same "crime" which Shakespeare treats so ambiguously in *Measure for Measure*—she yields herself to her lover's bed. But never in the book is it even implicitly suggested that this *is* the crime; only the notable punishment which Effie suffers from torment of conscience, and in which even Providence seems to be interested, by afflicting her with a barren womb, insists that we look for a crime, for where there is such punishment there must be a crime; and we can find no other but this one. We have, then, two obscurities, or rather obscurations, in this case: a crime which the book refuses to acknowledge structurally and to place in rhythm with the punishment; and an absurd obscuration of whatever meaning sexual indulgence on the part of a person like Effie might have. The ambiguous meaning of sexual indulgence in *Measure for Measure* is not *obscure* meaning; it is complex meaning, difficult meaning. Despite structural anomalies in the play that have no relevance for us here, the play does provide a significant context for the problems raised by the illicit sexual act; it gives the act an environment stressing sexual ugliness, and it places this specially created ugliness in a meaningful rhythm with the counter-horror of death and with the mana of abstinence. Thus it contrives that the sexual problem, as presented, should probe our own deepest instincts and resistances, uniquely opening them up to our view. In Effie's case, though illicit sexual indulgence contributes, so far as we can see, the only structural motivation for Effie's long punishment, it has no "meaning" except that punishment. In other words, sex must be punished, and that is all there is to it. This is to obscure whatever real problem may exist here by a particularly unpleasant and facile kind of romanticism which attempts to interest us in the punishment as a kind of snuff to take away the odor of the offending deed.

One important aspect of the "conception of life" which the book holds is that of Providential care: Providence rewards sturdy little Jeanie for her leg work and her humility of aspiration; it punishes Effie with barrenness and remorse (although, to our confusion of attitude toward this Providential conception of life, it gives Effie a *succès de furor* in London and abroad, and endows her with taste and passion and susceptibility to beauty, so that Effie's punishment seems preferable to Jeanie's reward); it provides that George Staunton's horse shall throw him and break his leg when George wishes to give himself up to the law in order to ransom Effie—for the wicked must not be flattered by the indulgence of their good impulses; and nicely it arranges that George should be killed by the hand of his own son, and even that the son himself, illegitimate issue, should come to a bad end. Providence is a watering down of Calvinistic deity, an illucid gruel-like intermixture of the person of God with theological predestination, so that God is not quite clearly there (His presence might cause the discomfort of intellectual lucidity and spiritual doubt) nor the cruelty of predestination clearly conceived, but both are cheerfully obscured in the more domestic implications of "providing" and "provision." Nevertheless, a Providential universe is haunted by Calvin as by an embarrassed conscience: where Providence provides all, individual willing is a derogation of Providential function; it is absurd to will or to do. And yet, in the Providential universe of Scott's book, the central determination of our attitudes is Jeanie Deans's immense exertion of stubborn will power in legging it to London to upset whatever work Providence may have had in mind regarding Effie. R. H. Tawney, in *Religion and the Rise of Capitalism,* speaks of "the central paradox of religious ethics" as the fact that "only those are nerved with the courage to turn the world upside down who are convinced that already, in a higher sense, it is disposed for the best by a power of which they are the humble instruments." [1] An artist like Jane Austen uses his materials in the sense that he *uses them up,* exhausts their potentialities for meaning or carries that exhaustion so far that we can respect even his failures. In Scott's book there is this staring paradox of a Providential conception of life in which self-reliance is the paramount virtue, but Scott does not use the paradox. Because he ignores it, the work is sentimental, in the sense that it sets up feelings about a Providential kind of life—feelings of hope, trust, gratitude, and humility, let us say—while concretely it exhibits a

[1] New York: Harcourt, Brace & Company, Inc., 1926, p. 109.

way of life in which Providence has no part, a way of life in which the individual determines destiny, by using his legs if not his head.

Scott's literary influence was enormous. More important than his exploitations of history was his opening up, for the novelistic craft, the possibilities lying in physical description or "local color." Scott's own "local color" provides the real entertainment of his books, but it exists in them *ab extra*. Balzac, who admired Scott, turned physical description to the uses of genius; while Scott touristed in landscape and architecture, Balzac made the physical conditions of human lives their spiritual symbol, their passion and their jail. Stendhal, who loathed Scott, used Scott's bounty with both hands; the town of Verrières, in *The Red and the Black*, the cathedral, the seminary, Julien's cave in the mountains, are the transformed gift of Scott—transformed again by the uses of genius, whereas Scott had been able to make of his gift only the small uses of talent. In other fields than literature his influence was epochal. Cardinal Newman, in his *Apologia*, gives careful attention to that releasing of the emotions to new objects and new perspectives for which Scott, among others, was responsible in a time of spiritual poverty and emotional starvation. Bernard Bosanquet says, in *The Growth of Modern Philosophy*,

> It would seem, perhaps, absurd to fix upon the most unreflective of writers, Sir Walter Scott, as the chief initiator of a philosophical influence; but I believe there is little doubt that historical humanism in England, as on the Continent, received an epoch-making impulse from his writings.[2]

We are, however, in this study, concerned with a book and not an influence. Critics have named variously Scott's defect as a novelist: he failed in conveying the sense of an abiding destiny going on beyond the characters described (V. S. Pritchett, in *The Living Novel*); he seldom or never transcended the conventional, the accepted (Sir Herbert Grierson, in his biography of Scott); to go back to Hazlitt, Scott was interested in half of life only, in the past of man and not in what he might become; or to Coleridge, Scott had diversity of fancy but suffered from the blankest absence of imagination. As so frequently happens, it is Coleridge's observation that is the most useful here. To Coleridge, imagination was the

[2] Quoted by Sir Herbert Grierson in *Sir Walter Scott, Bart.* (New York: Columbia University Press, 1938), p. 312.

faculty likest in kind to the primary faculty of perception which gives spatial and temporal and causal organization to the world; a creative faculty because synthetic in function, a maker of unities. In Scott he found a grave defect of this faculty—and it is the defect which we, too, have been tracing in our review of the aesthetic and conceptual confusions in *The Heart of Mid-Lothian,* for confusion and unity are opposed terms. Coleridge was most concerned with Scott's failure to imagine character; that is, to conceive character not as a set of circumstances and accidents (such as Jeanie's Cameronian upbringing, or her falling in with Meg's gang), but as an inwardly complex agent out of whose human complexity evolve the event and the destiny. Coleridge goes on to make the pregnant and far-reaching statement that it is precisely this defect and this failure which

> has done more for Sir Walter Scott's European, yea, plusquam-European popularity, than ever the abundance of [imagination] effected for any former writer. His age is an age of *anxiety* from the crown to the hovel, from the cradle to the coffin; all is an anxious straining to maintain life, or *appearances*—to *rise,* as the only condition of not falling.

Scott's popularity, Coleridge says, is a phase of the desire to be amused, to forget oneself, in an "age of anxiety," and he continues,

> The great felicity of Sir Walter Scott is that his own intellect supplies the place of all intellect and all character in his heroes and heroines, and *representing* the intellect of his readers, supersedes all motive for its exertion, by never appearing alien, whether as above or below.[3]

This unblinking statement, damning as it is, clarifies the air around Scott. For our own purposes, it sets in a wider field of significance the aesthetic category to which, for the sake of objectivity, we have tried to confine ourselves; for it extends to our own historical condition, our own "age of anxiety," the implications of incoherence in the work of art.

[3] *Miscellaneous Criticism* (Cambridge: Harvard University Press, 1936), p. 335.

ON *Great Expectations*

"The distinguishing quality of Dickens's people," says V. S. Pritchett,

is that they are solitaries. They are people caught living in a world of their own. They soliloquize in it. They do not talk to one another; they talk to themselves. The pressure of society has created fits of twitching in mind and speech, and fantasies in the soul . . . The solitariness of people is paralleled by the solitariness of things. Fog operates as a separate presence, houses quietly rot or boisterously prosper on their own . . . Cloisterham believes itself more important than the world at large, the Law sports like some stale and dilapidated circus across human lives. Philanthropy attacks people like a humor or an observable germ. The people and the things of Dickens are all out of touch and out of hearing of each other, each conducting its own inner monologue, grandiloquent or dismaying. By this dissociation Dickens brings to us something of the fright of childhood . . .[1]

Some of the most wonderful scenes in *Great Expectations* are those in which people, presumably in the act of conversation, raptly soliloquize; and Dickens' technique, in these cases, is usually to give the soliloquizer a fantastic private language as unadapted to mutual understanding as a species of pig Latin. Witness Mr. Jaggers' interview with Joe Gargery, in which the dignified lawyer attempts to compensate Joe financially for his part in Pip's upbringing, and Joe swings on him with unintelligible pugilistic jargon.

"Which I meantersay . . . that if you come into my place bull-baiting and badgering me, come out! Which I meantersay as sech if you're a man, come on! Which I meantersay that what I say, I meantersay and stand or fall by!"

[1] *The Living Novel* (New York: Reynal & Hitchcock, 1947), p. 88.

Or Miss Havisham's interview with Joe over the question of Pip's wages; for each question she asks him, Joe persists in addressing his reply to Pip rather than herself, and his replies have not the remotest relation to the questions. Sometimes, by sheer repetition of a phrase, the words a character uses will assume the frenzied rotary unintelligibility of an idiot's obsession, as does Mrs. Joe's "Be grateful to them which brought you up by hand," or Pumblechook's mincing "May I?—May I?" The minimal uses of language as an instrument of communication and intellectual development are symbolized by Pip's progress in the school kept by Mr. Wopsle's great-aunt, where the summit of his education consists in his copying a large Old-English "D," which he assumes to be the design for a belt buckle; and by Joe's pleasure in the art of reading, which enables him to find three "J's" and three "O's" and three "J-O, Joes" in a piece of script.

> "Give me [he says] a good book, or a good newspaper, and sit me down afore a good fire, and I ask no better. Lord! when you *do* come to a J and a O, and says you, 'Here, at last, is a J-O, Joe,' how interesting reading is!"

There is, perhaps, no purer expression of solipsism in literature. The cultivation of the peculiar Dickensian values of language reaches its apogee when the convict Magwitch, with a benefactor's proud delight, asks Pip to read to him from a book in a foreign language, of which he understands no syllable.

From *Don Quixote* on, the novels that we have read in this series of studies have frequently drawn our attention to the ambiguities of language and the varieties of its expressive relationship to life—from the incongruities between Quixote's and Sancho's understanding of the meaning of words, to the hopeless lapse of verbal understanding between Walter and Toby Shandy, and to the subtly threatening divergencies of meaning in the constricted language of Jane Austen's characters. Language as a means of communication is a provision for social and spiritual order. You cannot make "order" with an integer, one thing alone, for order is definitively a relationship among things. Absolute noncommunication is an unthinkable madness for it negates all relationship and therefore all order, and even an ordinary madman has to create a kind of order for himself by illusions of communication. Dickens' soliloquizing characters, for all their funniness (aloneness is inexorably funny, like the aloneness of the man who slips on a banana peel, seen from the point of view of togetherness), suggest a world of isolated integers, terrifyingly alone and unrelated.

The book opens with a child's first conscious experience of his aloneness. Immediately an abrupt encounter occurs—Magwitch suddenly comes from behind a gravestone, seizes Pip by the heels, and suspends him upside down.

> "Hold your noise!" cried a terrible voice, as a man started up from among the graves at the side of the church porch. "Keep still, you little devil, or I'll cut your throat!"

Perhaps, if one could fix on two of the most personal aspects of Dickens' technique, one would speak of the strange languages he concocts for the solitariness of the soul, and the abruptness of his tempo. His human fragments suddenly shock against one another in collisions like those of Democritus' atoms or of the charged particles of modern physics. Soldiers, holding out handcuffs, burst into the blacksmith's house during Christmas dinner at the moment when Pip is clinging to a table leg in an agony of apprehension over his theft of the pork pie. A weird old woman clothed in decayed satin, jewels and spider webs, and with one shoe off, shoots out her finger at the bewildered child, with the command: "Play!" A pale young gentleman appears out of a wilderness of cucumber frames, and daintily kicking up his legs and slapping his hands together, dips his head and butts Pip in the stomach. These sudden confrontations between persons whose ways of life have no habitual or logical continuity with each other suggest the utmost incohesion in the stuff of experience.

Technique is vision. Dickens' technique is an index of a vision of life that sees human separatedness as the ordinary condition, where speech is speech *to* nobody and where human encounter is mere collision. But the vision goes much further. Our minds are so constituted that they insist on seeking in the use of language an exchange function, a delivery and a passing on of perceptions from soul to soul and generation to generation, binding them in some kind of order; and they insist on finding cause and effect, or *motivation,* in the displacements and encounters of persons or things. Without these primary patterns of perception we would not have what we call minds. And when these patterns are confused or abrogated by our experience, we are forced, in order to preserve some kind of psychic equilibrium, to seek them in extraordinary explana-

127

tions—explanations again in terms of mutual exchange and cause and effect. Dickens saw his world patently all in pieces, and as a child's vision would offer some reasonable explanation of why such a world was that way—and, by the act of explanation, would make that world yield up a principle of order, however obscure or fantastic—so, with a child's literalism of imagination, he discovered organization among his fragments.

Dickens lived in a time and an environment in which a full-scale demolition of traditional values was going on, correlatively with the uprooting and dehumanization of men, women, and children by the millions—a process brought about by industrialization, colonial imperialism, and the exploitation of the human being as a "thing" or an engine or a part of an engine capable of being used for profit. This was the "century of progress" which ornamented its steam engines with iron arabesques of foliage as elaborate as the antimacassars and aspidistras and crystal or cut-glass chandeliers and bead-and-feather portieres of its drawing rooms, while the human engines of its welfare groveled and bred in the foxholes described by Marx in his *Capital*. (Hauntingly we see this discordance in the scene in *Great Expectations* where Miss Havisham, sitting in her satin and floral decay in the house called Satis, points her finger at the child and outrageously tells him to "play." For though the scene is a potent symbol of childish experience of adult obtuseness and sadism, it has also another dimension as a social symbol of those economically determined situations in which the human soul is used as a means for satisfactions not its own, under the gross and transparent lie that its activity is its happiness, its welfare and fun and "play"—a publicity instrument that is the favorite of manufacturers and insurance agencies, as well as of totalitarian strategists, with their common formula, "We're just a happy family.") The heir of the "century of progress" is the twentieth-century concentration camp, which makes no bones about people being "things."

Dickens' intuition alarmingly saw this process in motion, a process which abrogated the primary demands of human feeling and rationality, and he sought an extraordinary explanation for it. People were becoming things, and things (the things that money can buy or that are the means for making money or for exalting prestige in the abstract) were becoming more important than people. People were being de-animated, robbed of their souls, and things were usurping the prerogatives of animate creatures—governing the lives of their owners in the most literal sense. This picture, in which the qualities of things and people were reversed, was a picture of a daemonically motivated world, a world in which "dark" or occult forces or energies operate not only in people (as modern psycho-analytic psychology observes) but also in things: for if people turn themselves or are turned into things, metaphysical order can be established only if we think of things as turning themselves into people, acting under a "dark" drive similar to that which motivates the human aberration.

There is an old belief that it takes a demon to recognize a demon, and the saying illustrates the malicious sensibility with which things, in Dickens, have felt out and imitated, in their relationship with each other and with people, the secret of the human arrangement. A four-poster bed in an inn, where Pip goes to spend the night, is a despotic monster that straddles over the whole room,

> putting one of his arbitrary legs into the fireplace, and another into the doorway, and squeezing the wretched little washing-stand in quite a Divinely Righteous manner.

Houses, looking down through the skylight of Jaggers' office in London, twist themselves in order to spy on Pip like police agents who presuppose guilt. Even a meek little muffin has to be "confined with the utmost precaution under a strong iron cover," and a hat, set on a mantelpiece, demands constant attention and the greatest quickness of eye and hand to catch it neatly as it tumbles off, but its ingenuity is such that it finally manages to fall into the slop basin. The animation of inanimate objects suggests both the quaint gaiety of a forbidden life and an aggressiveness that has got out of control—an aggressiveness that they have borrowed from the human economy and an irresponsibility native to but glossed and disguised by that economy.

Dickens' fairly constant use of the pathetic fallacy (the projection of human impulses and feelings upon the nonhuman, as upon beds and houses and muffins and hats) might be considered as incidental stylistic embellishment if his description of people did not show a reciprocal metaphor: people are described by nonhuman attributes, or by such an exaggeration of or emphasis on one part of their appearance that they seem to be reduced wholly to that part, with an effect of having become "thinged" into one of their own bodily members or into an article of their clothing or into some inanimate object of which they have made a fetish. Dickens' devices for producing this transposition of attributes are

129

various.) To his friend and biographer, Forster, he said that he was always losing sight of a man in his diversion by the mechanical play of some part of the man's face, which "would acquire a sudden ludicrous life of its own." Many of what we shall call the "signatures" of Dickens' people—that special exaggerated feature or gesture or mannerism which comes to stand for the whole person—are such dissociated parts of the body, like Jaggers' huge forefinger which he bites and then plunges menacingly at the accused, or Wemmick's post-office mouth, or the clockwork apparatus in Magwitch's throat that clicks as if it were going to strike. The device is not used arbitrarily or capriciously. In this book, whose subject is the etiology of guilt and of atonement, Jaggers is the representative not only of civil law but of universal Law, which is profoundly mysterious in a world of dissociated and apparently lawless fragments; and his huge forefinger, into which he is virtually transformed and which seems to act like an "it" in its own right rather than like a member of a man, is the Law's mystery in all its fearful impersonality. Wemmick's mouth is not a post-office when he is at home in his castle but only when he is at work in Jaggers' London office, where a mechanical appearance of smiling is required of him. And as Wemmick's job has mechanized him into a grinning slot, so oppression and fear have given the convict Magwitch a clockwork apparatus for vocal chords.

(Or this general principle of reciprocal changes, by which things have become as it were daemonically animated and people have been reduced to thing-like characteristics—as if, by a law of conservation of energy, the humanity of which people have become incapable had leaked out into the external environment—may work symbolically in the association of some object with a person so that the object assumes his essence and his "meaning.") Mrs. Joe wears a large apron, "having a square impregnable bib in front, that was stuck full of pins and needles"—she has no reason to wear it, and she never takes it off a day in her life. Jaggers flourishes a large white handkerchief—a napkin that is the mysterious complement of his blood-smeared engagements. Estella—who is the star and jewel of Pip's great expectations—wears jewels in her hair and on her breast; "I and the jewels," she says, as if they were interchangeable. (This device of association is a familiar one in fiction; what distinguishes Dickens' use of it is that the associated object acts not merely to *illustrate* a person's qualities symbolically—as novelists usually use it—but that it has a necessary metaphysical function in Dickens' universe; in this universe objects ac-

tually usurp human essences; beginning as fetishes, they tend to—and
sometimes quite literally do—devour and take over the powers of the
fetish-worshiper.)

The process of conversion of spirit into matter that operates in the
Dickens world is shown working out with savage simplicity in the case of
Miss Havisham. Miss Havisham has been guilty of aggression against life
in using the two children, Pip and Estella, as inanimate instruments of
revenge for her broken heart—using them, that is, as if they were not
human but things—and she is being changed retributively into a fungus.
The decayed cake on the banquet table acts, as it were, by homeopathic
magic—like a burning effigy or a doll stuck with pins; its decay parallels
the necrosis in the human agent. "When the ruin is complete," Miss
Havisham says, pointing to the cake but referring to herself, she will be
laid out on the same table and her relatives will be invited to "feast on"
her corpse. But this is not the only conversion. The "little quickened
hearts" of the mice behind the panels have been quickened by what was
Miss Havisham, carried off crumb by crumb.

(The principle of reciprocal changes, between the human and the
nonhuman, bears on the characteristic lack of complex "inner life" on
the part of Dickens' people—their lack of a personally complex psychology.)
It is inconceivable that the fungoid Miss Havisham should have a complex
inner life, in the moral sense. But in the *art* of Dickens (distinguishing
that moral dialectic that arises not solely from the "characters" in a novel
but from all the elements in the aesthetic structure) there is a great deal
of "inner life," transposed to other forms than that of human character:
partially transposed in this scene, for instance, to the symbolic activity of
the speckle-legged spiders with blotchy bodies and to the gropings and
pausings of the black beetles on Miss Havisham's hearth. Without benefit
of Freud or Jung, Dickens saw the human soul reduced literally to the
images occupying its "inner life.")

Through the changes that have come about in the human, as humanity has leaked out of it, the atoms of the physical universe have become
subtly impregnated with daemonic aptitude.)Pip, standing waiting for
Estella in the neighborhood of Newgate, and beginning dimly to be aware
of his implication in the guilt for which that establishment stands—for
his "great expectations" have already begun to make him a collaborator
in the generic crime of using people as means to personal ends—has the
sensation of a deadly dust clinging to him, rubbed off on him from the

environs, and he tries to beat it out of his clothes. Smithfield, that "shameful place," "all asmear with filth and fat and blood and foam," seems to "stick to him" when he enters it on his way to the prison. The nettles and brambles of the graveyard where Magwitch first appears "stretch up cautiously" out of the graves in an effort to get a twist on the branded man's ankles and pull him in. The river has a malignant potentiality that impregnates everything upon it—discolored copper, rotten wood, honeycombed stone, green dank deposit. The river is perhaps the most constant and effective symbol in Dickens, because it establishes itself so readily to the imagination as a daemonic element, drowning people as if by intent, disgorging unforeseen evidence, chemically or physically changing all it touches, and because not only does it act as an occult "force" in itself but it is the common passage and actual flowing element that unites individuals and classes, public persons and private persons, deeds and the results of deeds, however fragmentized and separated. Upon the river, one cannot escape its action; it may throw the murderer and his victim in an embrace. At the end of *Great Expectations,* it swallows Compeyson, while, with its own obscure daemonic motivation, though it fatally injures Magwitch, it leaves him to fulfill the more subtle spiritual destiny upon which he has begun to enter. The river scene in this section, closely and apprehensively observed, is one of the most memorable in Dickens.

It is necessary to view Dickens' "coincidences" under the aspect of this wholesale change in the aptitudes of external nature. Coincidence is the violent connection of the unconnected. Life is full of violent connections of this sort, but one of the most rigorous conventions of fictional and dramatic art is that events should make a logically sequential pattern; for art is the discovery of order. Critics have frequently deplored Dickens' use of coincidences in his plots. But in a universe that is nervous throughout, a universe in which nervous ganglia stretch through both people and their external environment, so that a change in the human can infect the currents of the air and the sea, events and confrontations that seem to abrogate the laws of physical mechanics can logically be brought about. In this sense, the apparent coincidences in Dickens actually obey a causal order—not of physical mechanics but of moral dynamics.

What connection can there be [Dickens asks in another novel] between many people in the innumerable histories of this world, who, from opposite sides of great gulfs, have, nevertheless, been very curiously brought together!

What brings the convict Magwitch to the child Pip, in the graveyard, is more than the convict's hunger; Pip (or let us say simply "the child," for Pip is an Everyman) carries the convict inside him, as the negative potential of his "great expectations"—Magwitch is the concretion of his potential guilt. What brings Magwitch across the "great gulfs" of the Atlantic to Pip again, at the moment of revelation in the story, is their profoundly implicit compact of guilt, as binding as the convict's leg iron which is its recurrent symbol. The multiplying likenesses in the street as Magwitch draws nearer, coming over the sea, the mysterious warnings of his approach on the night of his reappearance, are moral projections as "real" as the storm outside the windows and as the crouched form of the vicious Orlick on the dark stairs. The conception of what brings people together "coincidentally" in their seemingly uncaused encounters and collisions —the total change in the texture of experience that follows upon any act, public or private, external or in thought, the concreteness of the effect of the act not only upon the conceiving heart but upon the atoms of physical matter, so that blind nature collaborates daemonically in the drama of reprisal—is deep and valid in this book.

In a finely lucid atmosphere of fairy tale, Dickens uses a kind of montage in *Great Expectations,* a superimposing of one image upon another with an immediate effect of hallucination, that is but one more way of representing his vision of a purely nervous and moral organization of reality. An instance is the scene in which Estella walks the casks in the old brewery. Estella's walking the casks is an enchanting ritual dance of childhood (like walking fence rails or railroad ties), but inexplicably present in the tableau is the suicidal figure of Miss Havisham hanging by her neck from a brewery beam. Accompanying each appearance of Estella—the star and the jewel of Pip's expectations—is a similarly disturbing ghost, an image of an unformed dread. When Pip thinks of her, though he is sitting in a warm room with a friend, he shudders as if in a wind from over the marshes. Her slender knitting fingers are suddenly horribly displaced by the marred wrists of a murderess. The technique of montage is that of dreams, which know with awful precision the affinities between the guilt of our desires and the commonplaces of our immediate perceptions.

This device, of doubling one image over another, is paralleled in the handling of character. In the sense that one implies the other, the glittering frosty girl Estella, and the decayed and false old woman, Miss Havisham, are not two characters but a single one, or a single essence with dual aspects, as if composed by montage—a spiritual continuum, so to speak. For inevitably wrought into the fascinating jewel-likeness of Pip's great expectations, as represented by Estella, is the falsehood and degeneracy represented by Miss Havisham, the soilure on the unpurchased good. The boy Pip and the criminal Magwitch form another such continuum. Magwitch, from a metaphysical point of view, is not outside Pip but inside him, and his apparition is that of Pip's own unwrought deeds: Pip, having adopted "great expectations," will live by making people into Magwitches, into means for his ends. The relationship between Joe Gargery, saintly simpleton of the folk, and Orlick, dark beast of the Teutonic marshes (who comes "from the ooze"), has a somewhat different dynamics, though they too form a spiritual continuum. Joe and Orlick are related not as two aspects of a single moral identity, but as the opposed extremes of spiritual possibility—the one unqualified love, the other unqualified hate—and they form a frame within which the actions of the others have their ultimate meaning. A commonplace of criticism is that, as Edmund Wilson puts it, Dickens was usually unable to "get the good and bad together in one character." [2] The criticism might be valid if Dickens' were a naturalistic world, but it is not very relevant to Dickens' daemonically organized world. In a naturalistic world, obeying mechanical laws, each character is organically discrete from every other, and presumably each contains a representative mixture of "the good and bad." But in Dickens' thoroughly nervous world, that does not know the laws of mechanics but knows only spiritual law, one simple or "flat" character can be superimposed upon another so that together they form the representative human complexity of good-in-evil and evil-in-good.

Two kinds of crime form Dickens' two chief themes, the crime of parent against child, and the calculated social crime. They are formally analogous, their form being the treatment of persons as things; but they are also inherent in each other, whether the private will of the parent is to be considered as depraved by the operation of a public institution, or the social institution is to be considered as a bold concert of the depravities of individual "fathers." In *Great Expectations* the private crime against

2 *The Wound and the Bow* (Boston: Houghton Mifflin Company, 1941), p. 65.

134

the child is Mrs. Joe's and Pumblechook's and Wopsle's, all "foster parents" either by necessity or self-conceit; while the social crime is the public treatment of Magwitch. That the two kinds of crime are inherent in each other we are made aware of as we are led to identify Magwitch's childhood with Pip's; the brutality exercised toward both children was the same brutality, though the "parents" in the one case were private persons, and in the other, society itself. Complicating the meaning of "the crime" still further, Magwitch also has taken upon himself the role of foster parent to Pip, and whether, as parent, he acts in charity or impiousness, or both, is a major ambiguity which the drama sets out to resolve.

"The crime," in Dickens, is evidently a permutation of multiple motivations and acts, both public and private, but always with the same tendency to convert people into things, and always implying either symbolically or directly a child-parent situation. The child-parent situation has been disnatured, corrupted, with the rest of nature; or rather, since the child-parent situation is the dynamic core of the Dickens world, the radical disnaturing here is what has corrupted the rest. His plots seldom serve to canalize, with the resolution of the particular set of plotted circumstances, the hysteria submerged in his vision of a nature gone thoroughly wrong; the permutations of the crimes are too many, and their ultimate cause or root is evasive, unless one would resort to some dramatically unmanageable rationale such as original sin. The Dickens world requires an act of redemption. A symbolic act of this kind is again and again indicated in his novels, in the charity of the uncherished and sinned-against child for the inadequate or criminal father—what might be called the theme of the prodigal father, Dickens' usual modification of the prodigal son theme. But the redemptive act should be such that it should redeem not only the individual "fathers," but society at large. One might almost say—thinking of Dickens' caricatures of the living dead, with their necrotic members and organs, their identifications of themselves with inanimate objects—that it should be such as to redeem the dead. *Great Expectations* is an exception among his novels in that here the redemptive act is adequate to and structural for both bodies of thematic material—the sins of individuals and the sins of society.

Pip first becomes aware of the "identity of things" as he is held suspended heels over head by the convict; that is, in a world literally turned upside down. Thenceforth Pip's interior landscape is inverted by his guilty knowledge of this man "who had been soaked in water, and smothered in mud, and lamed by stones, and cut by flints, and stung by nettles, and torn by briars." The apparition is that of all suffering that the earth can inflict, and that the apparition presents itself to a child is as much as to say that every child, whatever his innocence, inherits guilt (as the potential of his acts) for the condition of man. The inversion of natural order begins here with first self-consciousness: the child is heir to the sins of the "fathers." Thus the crime that is always pervasive in the Dickens universe is identified in a new way—not primarily as that of the "father," nor as that of some public institution, but as that of the child—the original individual who must necessarily take upon himself responsibility for not only what is to be done in the present and the future, but what has been done in the past, inasmuch as the past is part and parcel of the present and the future. The child is the criminal, and it is for this reason that he is able to redeem his world; for the world's guilt is his guilt, and he can expiate it in his own acts.

The guilt of the child is realized on several levels. Pip experiences the psychological *form* (or feeling) of guilt before he is capable of voluntary evil; he is treated by adults—Mrs. Joe and Pumblechook and Wopsle —as if he were a felon, a young George Barnwell (a character in the play which Wopsle reads on the night when Mrs. Joe is attacked) wanting only to murder his nearest relative, as George Barnwell murdered his uncle. This is the usual nightmare of the child in Dickens, a vision of imminent incarceration, fetters like sausages, lurid accusatory texts. He is treated, that is, as if he were a thing, manipulable by adults for the extraction of certain sensations: by making him feel guilty and diminished, they are able to feel virtuous and great. But the psychological *form* of guilt acquires spiritual *content* when Pip himself conceives the tainted wish—the wish to be like the most powerful adult and to treat others as things. At the literal level, Pip's guilt is that of snobbery toward Joe Gargery, and snobbery is a denial of the human value of others. Symbolically, however, Pip's guilt is that of murder; for he steals the file with which the convict rids himself of his leg iron, and it is this leg iron, picked up on the marshes, with which Orlick attacks Mrs. Joe; so that the child does inevitably overtake his destiny, which was, like George Barnwell, to murder his nearest relative. But the "relative" whom Pip, adopting the venerable criminality of society, is, in the widest symbolic scope of intention, destined to murder is not Mrs. Joe but his "father," Magwitch—to murder in the socially chronic fashion of the Dickens world, which consists in the dehumanization of the weak, or in moral acquiescence to such murder. Pip is, after all, the ordinary mixed human being, one more Everyman in the long succession of them that literature has represented, but we see this Everyman as he develops from a child; and his destiny is directed by the ideals of his world—toward "great expectations" which involve the making of Magwitches—which involve, that is, murder. These are the possibilities that are projected in the opening scene of the book, when the young child, left with a burden on his soul, watches the convict limping off under an angry red sky, toward the black marshes, the gibbet, and the savage lair of the sea, in a still rotating landscape.

In Dickens' modification of the folk pattern of the fairy wishing, Magwitch is Pip's "fairy godfather" who changes the pumpkin into a coach. Like all the "fathers," he uses the child as a thing in order to obtain through him vicarious sensations of grandeur. In relation to society, however, Magwitch is the child, and society the prodigal father; from the time he was first taken for stealing turnips, the convict's career has duplicated brutally and in public the pathos of the ordinary child. Again, in relation to Pip, Magwitch is still the child; for, spiritually committed by his "great expectations" to that irresponsibility which has accounted for the Magwitches, Pip is projectively, at least, answerable for Magwitch's existence and for his brutalization. Pip carries his criminal father within him; he is, so to speak, the father of his father. The ambiguities of each term of the relationship are such that each is both child and father, making a fourfold relationship; and the act of love between them at the end is thus reinforced fourfold, and the redemption by love is a fourfold redemption: that is to say, it is symbolically infinite, for it serves for all the meanings Dickens finds it possible to attach to the central child-father situation, the most profound and embracing relationship that, in Dickens' work, obtains among men.

As the child's original alienation from "natural" order is essentially mysterious, a guilty inheritance from the fathers which invades first awareness, so the redemptive act is also a mysterious one. The mysterious nature of the act is first indicated, in the manner of a motif, when Mrs. Joe, in imbecile pantomime, tries to propitiate her attacker, the bestial Orlick. In Orlick is concretized all the undefined evil of the Dickens world, that has nourished itself underground and crept along walls, like the ancient stains on the house of Atreus. He is the lawlessness implied in the unnatural conversions of the human into the nonhuman, the retributive death that invades those who have grown lean in life and who have exercised the powers of death over others. He is the instinct of aggression and destruction, the daemonism of sheer external Matter as such; he is pure "thingness" emerging without warning from the ooze where he has been unconsciously cultivated. As Orlick is one form of spiritual excess —unmotivated hate—Joe Gargery is the opposed form—love without reservation. Given these terms of the spiritual framework, the redemptive act itself could scarcely be anything but grotesque—and it is by a grotesque gesture, one of the most profoundly intuitive symbols in Dickens, that Mrs. Joe is redeemed. What is implied by her humble propitiation of the beast Orlick is a recognition of personal guilt in the guilt of others, and of its dialectical relationship with love. The motif reappears in the moment of major illumination in the book. Pip "bows down," not to Joe Gargery, toward whom he has been privately and literally guilty, but to the wounded, hunted, shackled man, Magwitch, who has been guilty toward himself. It is in this way that the manifold organic relationships among men are revealed, and that the Dickens world—founded in fragmentariness and disintegration—is made whole.

ON *Vanity Fair*

Almost exactly a century separates *Tom Jones* from *Vanity Fair;* but with *Vanity Fair,* so far as technical developments in the novel are concerned, it is as if there had been none. We are in the story telling convention of the "omniscient author" sanctioned by Fielding's great example, but with a damaging difference that is due, not so much to an inherent inadequacy of that convention itself, as the spiritual incoherency of another age. It is true that the technique of omniscient authorship can allow a relaxed garrulity—what James called "the terrible fluidity of self-revelation"—for if the author can enter the story in his own voice, there is nothing to keep him from talking. After discussing Becky's adolescent designs on Jos Sedley, and her visions of shawls and necklaces and aristocratic company which she imagines will be the rewards of marriage with Jos, Thackeray comments,

> Charming Alnaschar visions! it is the happy privilege of youth to construct you, and many a fanciful young creature besides Rebecca Sharp has indulged in these delightful day-dreams ere now!

The comment is both inane and distracting—distracting our attention from the tense mental operations of Becky and turning it upon the momentarily flaccid mentality of her author. The effect is one of rather surprised irritation, as it is again when, having described Jos's wardrobe, his pains in dressing, his vanity and shyness, Thackeray remarks,

> If Miss Rebecca can get the better of *him,* and at her first entrance into life, she is a young person of no ordinary cleverness.

What we feel is that two orders of reality are clumsily getting in each other's way: the order of imaginative reality, where Becky lives, and the

139

order of historical reality, where William Makepeace Thackeray lives. The fault becomes more striking in the following unforgivable parenthesis. Jos has just presented Amelia with flowers.

> "Thank you, dear Joseph," said Amelia, quite ready to kiss her brother, if he were so minded. (And I think for a kiss from such a dear creature as Amelia, I would purchase all Mr. Lee's conservatories out of hand.)

The picture of Thackeray himself kissing Amelia pulls Amelia quite out of the created world of *Vanity Fair* and drops her into some shapeless limbo of Thackerayan sentiment where she loses all aesthetic orientation.

Nevertheless, the conventions employed in a work of art cannot fairly be judged by themselves; they can be judged only as instrumental to a vision. The time in which Thackeray wrote was, compared with Fielding's time, itself looser in what we might call cultural composition; its values were less integrated in a common philosophical "style" or tenor of mind. In *Tom Jones,* the convention of the author's appearance in his book as "gregarious eye," stage manager, and moralist, is a strategy that is used with a highly formal regularity of rhythm, and it animates every turn of Fielding's language, as the ironic life of the language. Most important, the convention had benefited by an age's practice of and belief in form, form in manners and rhetoric and politics and philosophy—that is, by an age's coherently structured world view. The set of feelings and ideas of which Fielding acts as vehicle, when he makes his personal appearances in his book, is a set of feelings and ideas with the stamp of spiritual consistency upon them. They do not afflict us with a sense of confused perspectives between the author's person and his work, his opinions and his creation, as do Thackeray's. Whereas Thackeray seems merely to be victimized or tricked by his adopted convention into a clumsy mishandling of perspectives, Fielding manipulates the same convention deliberately to produce displacements of perspective as an organic element of composition. This is not to say that Fielding's creative perceptions are, on the whole, more penetrating and profound than Thackeray's; indeed, Thackeray's seem to reach a good deal deeper into the difficulties, compromises, and darkness of the human estate; but Fielding's have the organizing power to make an ancient oral convention of storytelling an appropriate instrument of his vision, whereas the same convention—actually one that is most sympathetic to Thackeray's gift of easy, perspicacious, ranging talk—

becomes a personal convenience for relaxation of aesthetic control, *even a means to counterfeit* his creative vision.

Becky ruminates, "I think I could be a good woman if I had five thousand a year," and adds with a sigh,

> "Heigho! I wish I could exchange my position in society, and all my relations, for a snug sum in the Three per Cent. Consols."

Here she is as true to herself psychologically as is Moll Flanders; but she is more complex than Moll, and we know perfectly that, at this promising stage in her career, the sigh is only a casual fantasy—arising chiefly out of boredom with the tedious business of cultivating the good graces of people much less intelligent than herself—and that if the "snug sum" were offered, she would not really exchange her prospects for it, for her temperament is not at present to be satisfied with snugness. There are to be pearl necklaces, presentation at court, a *succès fou* at Gaunt House. But Thackeray interprets for us.

> It may, perhaps, have struck her that to have been honest and humble, to have done her duty, and to have marched straightforward on her way, would have brought her as near happiness as that path by which she was striving to attain it.

This is a doctrine with which, in principle, we have no cause either to agree or disagree; a novel is not made of doctrines and principles, but of concretely imagined life, and whatever moral principle may be honestly adduced from that life must be intrinsic to it, concretely qualitative within it. *Vanity Fair* is strong with life, but in those concretions where it is alive there is nothing to suggest that to be "honest and humble" can possibly bring happiness. Becky is the happiest person in the book; she is alive from beginning to end, alive in intelligence and activity and *joie de vivre*, whether she is throwing Dr. Johnson's dictionary out of a coach window, in superb scorn of the humiliations of the poor, or exercising her adulterous charm on General Tufto, whether she is prancing to court to be made an "honest woman" (in stolen lace), or hiding a cognac bottle in a sordid bed. From Becky's delighted exercise in being alive, we can learn nothing about the happiness to be derived from humble dutifulness. On the other hand, from Amelia's humble dutifulness we can learn nothing that convinces us doctrinally that happiness lies in such a way of life. For it is not only that the brisk gait and vivid allure of Becky's egoistic and aggressive way of life make Amelia look tepid, tear sodden, and compromised: this effect would not occur if the book were soundly structured, if its compositional center (what James called the "commanding centre" of the composition) were entirely firm and clear.

The actually functioning compositional center of *Vanity Fair* is that node or intersection of extensive social and spiritual relationships constituted by Becky's activities: her relationships with a multitude of individuals—Jos and Amelia and George, old Sir Pitt and Rawdon and Miss Crawley and the Bute Crawleys and the Pitt Crawleys, Lady Bareacres, Lord Steyne, and so on—and, through these individuals, her relationships with large and significant blocks of a civilization: with the middle-class Sedley block, that block which is in the process of physical destruction because of its lack of shrewdness in an acquisitive culture; with the other middle-class Osborne block, that block which has displaced the Sedley block through its own acquisitive shrewdness and through the necessarily accompanying denial of the compassionate and sympathetic human impulses; with the aristocratic Crawley block, in all its complexity of impotence and mad self-destruction, and (in young Sir Pitt, with the "gooseberry eyes") canny self-renovation through connivance with the economy and morality of the dominant middle class; with the ambiguous Steyne block, that is above the economic strife and therefore free of conventional moral concerns, but in its social freedom, "stained" deeply in nerves and blood. (In the names he gives people, Thackeray plays—like many novelists —on punning suggestion, as he does in the name of the crawling Crawleys, "raw-done" Rawdon, Sharp, Steyne, O'Dowd, etc.) This social relationship, concretized through Becky's relationship with individuals, is the hub of the book's meanings, its "compositional center." But beside this violently whirling and excited center is another, a weak and unavailing epicenter, where Amelia weeps and suffers and wins—wins Dobbin and solvency and neighborhood prestige and a good middle-class house with varnished staircases. Organized around the two centers are two plots, which have as little essentially to do with each other as Thackeray's creative imagination had to do with his sentimental, morally fearful reflections. He cannot bear to allow the wonderfully animated vision of Becky's world to speak for itself, for its meaning is too frightening; he must add to it a complementary world—Amelia's—to act as its judge and corrector. One thinks, in comparison, of Balzac, who was writing almost contemporaneously. Balzac was both as skeptical and as sentimental as Thackeray, but he was a passionate rationalist as well, and a much bolder dramatic formalist. In Balzac, the weak and the suffering and the pure in heart do not win. They have no pretensions to effective moral dynamism in the evil Balzacian world, which uses them as illustrative examples of the impotence of an "honest and humble" way of life.

As the convention of the omniscient author allows Thackeray to keep up a maladroit "sound track" of personal interpolations, so it also collaborates with his confusion as to where the compositional center of his book lies; for though the Becky-world and the Amelia-world, having no common motivation, confront each other with closed entrances, so to speak, yet the author is able, by abuse of his rights of omniscience, to move facilely through these closed doors. We assume that, in Thackeray's plan, the compositional center of the book was to be the moral valence between the two worlds. But there is no valence between them, nothing in either to produce a positive effect of significance on the other. The only effect is negative: the Amelia-plot pales into a morally immature fantasy beside the vivid life of the Becky-plot. For Becky is the great morally meaningful figure, the moral symbol, in the book, and beside her there is room and meaning for Amelia only as victim—certainly not as "success figure." The word "moral," which we have used rather frequently in these studies, needs perhaps a somewhat closer attention here. Becky is not virtuous, and in speaking of her as a morally significant figure, we cannot possibly confuse her moral meaning with the meaning of "virtue." She is a morally meaningful figure because she symbolizes the morality of her world at its greatest intensity and magnitude. The greediness that has only a reduced, personal meaning in Mrs. Bute Crawley, as she nags and blunders at old Miss Crawley's deathbed, acquires, through Becky's far more intelligent and courageous greed—as she encounters international techniques for the satisfaction of greed with her own subtle and knowing and superior techniques—an extensive social meaning. The corruption that, in old Sir Pitt, has meaning at most for the senility of a caste, becomes, in Becky's prostitution and treason and murderousness, the moral meaning of a culture. For Becky's activities are designed with intelligent discrimination and lively intuition, and they are carried through not only with unflagging will power but with joy as well. By representing her world at its highest energetic potential, by alchemizing all its evil but stupid and confused or formless impulses into brilliantly controlled intention, she endows her world with meaning. The meaning is such as to inspire horror; but the very fact that we conceive this horror intellectually and objectively is an acknowledgment of Becky's morally symbolic stature.

There is a French criticism of the English novel, that, in the English novel's characteristic concern with the social scene, it fails to explore "the deeper layers of personality." One understands the motivation of this criticism, if one compares representative French and English novels of approximately the same periods, although the criticism itself does not seem to be well thought out. *The Pilgrim's Progress* is populated with social "types," sparsely limned sketches that isolate certain traits, whereas, almost contemporaneously, Madame de Lafayette's *La Princesse de Clèves* is concentrated upon a depth illumination of the tortured psyche of a delicate woman who, in a loveless marriage, is moved by an illicit passion. Even *Clarissa Harlowe,* which is commonly thought of as an exhaustive representation of a young woman's emotions, is, because of its mythical qualities, rather more of a vision into the social soul than into that of a credible individual; and the difference is brought out by comparison with the almost contemporaneous *Manon Lescaut,* by the Abbé Prevost, in which the subject has certain affinities with that of *Clarissa* (except that it is the girl, here, who is the libertine, and the young man who is the afflicted one), but which is again—like so many French novels —a concentrated depth drawing of personal psychology rather than a social vision. One could pursue a number of other examples in the same way. But the difference is a relative difference only. For the "deeper layers of personality" are meaningless unless they can be related, at least by inference, to aspects of life that have some social generality; while social life is meaningless unless it finds embodiment in individuals. A more significant difference between classical French novels and classical English novels is one of method. The English novel has tended traditionally to symbolize certain phases of personality through the concrete image (Christian as the "man in rags" with a burden on his back; the Philosopher Square standing among Molly's "other female utensils" when the curtain falls in the bedroom; Clarissa, with streaming eyes and disheveled bosom, prostrating herself before Lovelace; Jaggers washing his hands or Miss Havisham beside the rotten bridecake); while the French novel has tended traditionally to a discursive analysis of feeling and motive, as has the French drama. Image and analysis are merely two different ways of mirroring what goes on in the soul. The methods are never exclusive; and we find such significant exceptions to the general tendency as Flaubert's *Madame Bovary,* where the image dominates, and Conrad's *Lord Jim,* where analysis dominates.

Let us illustrate, from *Vanity Fair,* the method of the image and what it is able to imply as to the "deeper layers of personality." Characteristically, in this book, the social concern is paramount. We have spoken of the various "blocks" of this civilization, some slipping into rubble by the crush of the others or by internal decay, some thrusting themselves up by the neighboring defaultment. But governing all the movements is one ethos of aggressive egoism, articulated through the acquisition of cash and through the prestige fantasies born of cash. Becky herself is a member of no particular class and confined to no particular "block." (Significantly, she is the daughter of a Bohemian artist and a French music-hall singer.) She is more mobile than any of the other characters, because of her freedom from caste, and thus is able to enter into a great variety of class relationships: this is the peculiar novelistic virtue of the picara and picaro, and the enduring source of virility of the picaresque form—the protagonist's freedom of movement. Still acting under the same ethos as that governing the whole civilization, Becky is able to represent its tendencies without class pretenses. Thus Becky, like Moll Flanders, though a strongly individualized character, is the type of a whole civilization, a small-scale model of a world, a microcosm in which the social macrocosm is subtilized and intensified and made significant. With this predominantly social bearing of the novel, the characters—even Becky—tend to be depicted in a relatively "external" way: that is, there is relatively little discussion of the nuances of their feelings and their motivations; they are not self-analytical characters, as characters in French novels tend to be, nor do they spend much time in deliberate analysis of each other; they appear to us physically, in action; and—with some generalized interpretive help from the author himself (whose interpretations, as we have noted, we cannot always trust)—we enter into their motives and states of feeling by our own intuition. Examples are manifold. There is Becky's meeting of George's eyes in the mirror as she and Amelia, Jos and George, are leaving for Vauxhall: a flashing, accidental illumination of his vanity and vulnerability—and though here might be an excellent opportunity for Becky to engage in psychological speculations and deliberations, little of the kind occurs. There is the physical flash, the illumination by image only, and Becky has George's number. And yet later, when George and Amelia, Becky and Rawdon, meet on their honeymoon trips at Brighton, and Becky with almost unconscious slyness encourages George to make love to her, the early image of the meeting of eyes in a mirror plays on the reader's understanding of motivation, as it does again when we see Becky in overt sexual aggressiveness at the Brussels ball. There has been no need of discursive analysis of motive; the image does the work.

Or—another instance of the work of the image—there is Jos, in his obesity and his neckcloths and his gorgeous waistcoats. We should not expect Jos to analyze himself, nor anyone else to have an interest in analyzing what he feels, for he is below the level of what is rationally interesting; and yet, from the physical picture alone, we are made intuitively aware of deeply disturbed "layers of personality" in Jos. He is one of the most complicated psychological portraits in the book (more complicated, for instance, than that of another voluptuary, the Marquis of Steyne, who has more refined opportunities than Jos and a better head), extremely unpleasant, with suggestions of impalpable submerged perversities, pathetic, with a pathos that is at the same time an outrage to our feeling for what is humanly cognizable in pathos—for Jos is a glandularly suffering animal, with the "human" so hidden in his tortured fat that we feel it to be obscene, while we must still recognize it as human. Jos offering his neck to Isidore's razor (in the passage we have quoted in the general introduction to the present volume) is a complex image of a kind of fear so muddied, an image of a psychological state so profoundly irrational, that we react to it with an impulse of horrified laughter—the intuitive horror having no other outlet than in a sense of the absurd. At the same time that these physical images of Jos flash to the mind's eye an impression of something deep and possible in individual personality, they are made by Thackeray to represent to the social reason an extremely significant phase of a culture. We see in Jos's obesity the sickness of a culture, the sickness due to spiritual gourmandism, or, in simpler but still metaphorical words, to "overeating"; in his shyness of women, the repressions and abnormalities of a sick culture; in his stupidity and febrile conceit, the intellectual numbing and tubercular euphoria of a culture. Thus the physical image, here, mirrors most fearful depths of the personal and, at the same time, most threatening perspectives of the social life.

We shall cite a few more illustrations of this method of the "image," as Thackeray uses it, keeping in mind its double significance, its significance for personal psychology (the "deeper layers of personality") and its social significance. But in preparation for these particular citations, we. should speak of one singularly important theme of *Vanity Fair,* and that is a theme which we shall call the theme of the "fathers." In the eighteenth-century novels that we have read, the "father" has appeared in a light that is rather different from the light that is thrown on the "father" in nineteenth-century novels. There is Squire Allworthy, for instance, who, as "father," though he may have his failures of insight, is still an affirmative moral reference in the *Tom Jones* system of values; he is idealized, but this itself is significant of the fact that the "father" still represents a moral ideal. In the eighteenth century, the idea of the "father" was not, on the whole, ambiguous, or suggestive of doubts or deficiencies or culpability—that is, as this idea is reflected in literature. Mr. Harlowe, in *Clarissa,* is the most exceptional example; but even here, the daughter's return to her "Father's house," on the elevated stage of the divine, is an affirmation and sanction of the usual parental-filial relationship of authority and obedience which is esteemed to be universally valid; Mr. Harlowe made a mistake, but so did Clarissa make a mistake; informed by Clarissa's passion, it is to be hoped that no other daughters or fathers will ever make such mistakes. In *Tristram Shandy,* the "father," Walter Shandy, is a freak, yet he is presented only under the aspect of general human freakishness, pleasant and interesting eccentricity, and we are led in no way to think of him in terms of parental culpability; indeed, as "father," he takes his responsibility most enormously—to be the right kind of father and to bring up the right kind of son are his devouring concern; the inquiries and devotions of fatherhood—as to conditions of conception, size of the son's nose, the son's name, his education—form the whole shape of Walter Shandy's mental activities, his very eccentricity. Similarly in Smollett's *Humphry Clinker,* where the "father" (an uncle, in this case) is a querulous hypochondriac, leading his life in a tone of objection to everything, we are "on his side," we object when he objects, with a grain of salt for his elderly fury; and the book has its moral equipoise in the rightness of this "father's" perceptions.

We see, in the notion of the father in eighteenth-century literature, a reflection of social trust: of trust in and reliance upon and devotion to a general social system of values—that coherent "world view" of the eighteenth century that we have spoken of earlier in this essay. For, under our anciently inherited patriarchal organization of the family, an organization that inevitably extended itself into political organization and philosophic organization, the "father-imago" has acquired vast symbolic extension beyond domestic life and into general social life: our "fathers" are not only our individual fathers but all those who have come before us—society as it has determined our conditions of existence and the problems we have to confront. *Vanity Fair,* with its panorama of western European international society as backdrop to the heroine's activities, is full of "fathers," sick fathers, guilty fathers.

Curiously enough, we have seen the inception of the theme of the "fathers" in Jane Austen, despite her eighteenth-century social sensibility; and it is—along with her inception of modern technique in the handling of the "point of view"—a striking mark of her modernity. In *Pride and Prejudice,* the father, Mr. Bennet, is anything but the morally idealized figure of Squire Allworthy; and even as an "eccentric" or "humorous" character (in the older sense), he casts moral shadows that, for instance, Walter Shandy—another "eccentric"—does not cast. Mr. Bennet, as father, is guilty. In Dickens' *Great Expectations,* we have seen that the theme of the "father" dominates the meanings of the book, and we have seen how many inflections Dickens is able to get out of this theme. Crossing language boundaries, we find in Stendhal's *The Red and the Black* (1830) various implementations of the same theme: Julien's revolt against the peasant grossness of his own father, and his finding of a "spiritual father" in a Jansenist monk, who himself is under suspicion from the religious institution to which he belongs (here the father who is worthy of respect is himself virtually a social outcast). In Balzac's *Père Goriot*—whose title is indicative of the "father" theme—the actual father, Goriot, is a degenerative victim of corrupt social ideas, while the "spiritual father" of the hero is an out-and-out criminal. Turgenev's *Fathers and Sons* announces the same theme by its title; and again here the "fathers" are inadequate. In Dostoevski's *The Brothers Karamazov,* the sons' murder of the father is the focus of plot, and we have the famous question, on the part of Ivan Karamazov, "Who doesn't desire his father's death?" The title of D. H. Lawrence's *Sons and Lovers* indicates again the modern preoccupation with the parental-filial relationship. Joyce's *Portrait of the Artist* and his *Ulysses* carry out the same preoccupation: in the former, the hero's actual father goes to pieces and the family disintegrates with him; in the latter, the hero's "spiritual father" is a Jew, emotionally an alien in the Dublin

148

of the book, without integration with the social body, and as lost and wandering as the son.

It is significant of the vital intuitiveness of Thackeray's *Vanity Fair* that the theme of the "fathers" should have such importance: in this book, an immensely impressive female, herself quite fatherless, manages to articulate in her career the most meaningful social aspects of the "father" theme. We need, in this view of the book, to free ourselves from the narrower Freudian aspects of the theme and to think in terms of Thackeray's broad social perspective, where the "fathers" are such variants as Mr. Sedley, Mr. Osborne, old Sir Pitt, even the Marquis of Steyne: in other words, such variants as to include all the older, authoritative, and determinative aspects of society.

And now, with this general notion of the significance of the theme of parental authority, we can consider what Thackeray manages to get out of the "image" of old Mr. Osborne and his daughters coming down the stairs, in their evening ritual, to dinner.

> The obedient bell in the lower regions began ringing the announcement of the meal. The tolling over, the head of the family thrust his hands into the great tail-pockets of his great blue coat and brass buttons, and without waiting for a further announcement, strode downstairs alone, scowling over his shoulder at the four females.
>
> "What's the matter now, my dear?" asked one of the other, as they rose and tripped gingerly behind the sire.
>
> "I suppose the funds are falling," whispered Miss Wirt; and so, trembling and in silence, this hushed female company followed their dark leader.

In the lines just before this there is one other, inconspicuous, touch: in the drawing room where they are waiting for dinner is a chronometer "surmounted by a cheerful brass group of the sacrifice of Iphigenia." The depths which are suggested by this picture, but quite as if accidentally, are the depths of Greek tragedy and, still further back, of Freud's dim, sub-human, imagined "primitive horde": the "dark leader" with his "hushed female company," and the ridiculous but furious Victorian clock "cheerfully" symbolizing the whole. Antiquity's dark brooding over the monstrous nature of man is made to take on, in this incidental image of a family's going to dinner, the unwholesomeness and perversity that have been added to man's classical monstrosity by "falling funds," a drop in the stock market.

There is the recurrent incident in the hall outside the bedroom where old Miss Crawley is sick, Becky tending her, everyone—including Becky —waiting for and speculating on the "reversionary spoils."

> Captain Rawdon got an extension of leave on his aunt's illness, and remained dutifully at home. He was always in her ante-chamber. (She lay sick in the state bedroom into which you entered by the little blue saloon.) His father was always meeting him there; or if he came down the corridor ever so quietly, his father's door was sure to open, and the hyaena face of the old gentleman to glare out. What was it set one to watch the other so? A generous rivalry, no doubt, as to which should be most attentive to the dear sufferer in the state bedroom. Rebecca used to come out and comfort both of them—or one or the other of them rather.

Short and unemphasized as the passage is (outside of one ironic line, it consists only of an image, the image of Rawdon opening a door and looking into the corridor, of the old man's "hyaena face" instantly looking out from an opposite door, of Becky coming down the hall to "comfort" them), it contains a pregnant and disturbing meaning, both for personal psychology and for social psychology. Later, when Becky will attempt to inform Sir Pitt about her clandestine marriage, but without telling him the name of her husband, he will be uproariously amused; but as soon as she tells him the name—his son, Rawdon—he goes mad with inexplicable fury. We look back mentally to the incidents in the hall outside Miss Crawley's sickroom, where son and father glare at each other, and where Becky comes to comfort them *separately,* holding each in suspense as to her amorous favor. And we look forward also to that horrible line in Becky's letter to Rawdon (after the disclosure to Sir Pitt), where she says, "I might have been somebody's mamma, instead of— Oh, I tremble, I tremble . . ." What is contained here is probably the most excruciatingly primitive father-son battle in literature, with one of the most sensitively feminine but perversely sentimental reflections upon it. How are we to say, in such a case, whether what we are observing is the "deeper layers of personality" or the social scene?

And then there is the description of the turmoil surrounding old Sir

Pitt's death. It consists of a succession of images: Miss Horrocks flitting in ribbons through "the halls of their fathers"; again Miss Horrocks

> of the guilty ribbons, with a wild air, trying at the presses and escritoires with a bunch of keys.—

while upstairs they are "trying to bleed" Sir Pitt (the "trying to" suggests unknown but repulsive derangements); the servant girl screaming and making faces at him in private while he whimpers. The cumulation of these images, scattered and casual as they are, makes the face of a gorgon of destiny. The personal and social idea of the "father" (an idea which is inextricably both personal and social) is made the nasty companion of the ribbon-flitting Miss Horrocks; when Sir Pitt gives the family pearls to Lady Jane ("Pretty pearls—never gave 'em to the ironmonger's daughter"), marital relationships, with all they mean for the security created for us by our elders, are referred back retrospectively to Sir Pitt's chronic tipsiness and Lady Crawley's worsted knitting—an "enormous interminable piece of knitting"—

> She worked that worsted day and night . . . She had not character enough to take to drinking . . . ;

drawers are tried while the "father" is bled; and finally—so great is the prestige of this "father" and baronet—the servant girl has full amplitude to scream obscenities and make faces at him, for he has turned into "a whimpering old idiot put in and out of bed and cleaned and fed like a baby."

The burden of Thackeray's intuition into personal psychology and its social meaning falls on images like these, and they are innumerable in *Vanity Fair*. But the greatness of *Vanity Fair* is not in scattered images, sensitive as these are. They are all gathered up in Becky Sharp. Becky does for Jos, murderously, at the end; and what she does to Jos is only cancerously implicit in himself and the civilization that has made him; she is the darkness—shining obsidianly in an intelligent personality—in old Mr. Osborn's dense sadism against his daughters and his corruption of the meaning of paternal responsibility toward his son; she manipulates the insane father-son conflict between Sir Pitt and Rawdon; and she is the "guilty ribbons" of Miss Horrocks (instead of a servant's ribbons she has a courtesan's pearls) and at the same time the whimpering idiocy of the dying Sir Pitt (paralleling his repulsive attack of mortality, she inflicts a similarly repulsive mortality on Jos)—for she is at once all the imperatively aggressive, insanely euphoric impulses of a morally sick civilization, and an individual condensation of that civilization. We question whether we would understand her at all, or be charmed by her buoyancy or appalled by her destructiveness, if her impulses were not memorabilia of our own and her civilization our heritage.

ON *Wuthering Heights*

Emily Brontë's single novel is, of all English novels, the most treacherous for the analytical understanding to approach. It is treacherous not because of failure in its own formal controls on its meaning—for the book is highly wrought in form—but because it works at a level of experience that is unsympathetic to, or rather, simply irrelevant to the social and moral reason. One critic has spoken of the quality of feeling in this book as "a quality of suffering":

> It has anonymity. It is not complete. Perhaps some ballads represent it in English, but it seldom appears in the main stream, and few writers are in touch with it. It is a quality of experience the expression of which is at once an act of despair and an act of recognition or of worship. It is the recognition of an absolute hierarchy. This is also the feeling in Aeschylus. It is found amongst genuine peasants and is a great strength. Developing in places which yield only the permanent essentials of existence, it is undistracted and universal.[1]

We feel the lack of "completeness," which this critic refers to, in the nature of the dramatic figures that Emily Brontë uses: they are figures that arise on and enact their drama on some ground of the psychic life where ethical ideas are not at home, at least such ethical ideas as those that inform our ordinary experience of the manners of men. They have the "anonymity" of figures in dreams or in religious ritual. The attitude toward life that they suggest is rather one of awed contemplation of an unregenerate universe than a feeling for values or disvalues in types of human intercourse. It is an attitude that is expressed in some of the great Chinese paintings of the Middle Ages, where the fall of a torrent from an enormous

[1] G. D. Klingopulos, "The Novel as Dramatic Poem (II): 'Wuthering Heights,'" in *Scrutiny* XIV:4 (1946–1947).

height, or a single huge wave breaking under the moon, or a barely indicated chain of distant mountains lost among mists, seems to be animated by some mysterious, universal, half-divine life which can only be "recognized," not understood.

The strangeness that sets *Wuthering Heights* apart from other English novels does not lie alone in the attitude that it expresses and the level of experience that it defines, for something of the same quality of feeling exists, for instance, in Conrad's work. Its strangeness is the perfect simplicity with which it presents its elemental figures almost naked of the web of civilized habits, ways of thinking, forms of intercourse, that provides the familiar background of other fiction. Even Conrad's adventurers, no matter how far they may go into the "heart of darkness," carry with them enough threads of this web to orient them socially and morally. We can illustrate what we mean by this simplicity, this almost nakedness, if we compare Emily Brontë's handling of her materials with Richardson's handling of materials that, in some respects, are similar in kind. For example, the daemonic character of Heathcliff, associated as it is with the wildness of heath and moors, has a recognizable kinship with that of Lovelace, daemonic also, though associated with town life and sophisticated manners. Both are, essentially, an anthropomorphized primitive energy, concentrated in activity, terrible in effect. But Emily Brontë insists on Heathcliff's gypsy lack of origins, his lack of orientation and determination in the social world, his equivocal status on the edge of the human. When Mr. Earnshaw first brings the child home, the child is an "it," not a "he," and "dark almost as if it came from the devil"; and one of Nelly Dean's last reflections is, "Is he a ghoul or a vampire?" But Richardson's Lovelace has all sorts of social relationships and determinations, an ample family, economic orientation, college acquaintances, a position in a clique of young rakes; and Richardson is careful, through Lovelace's own pen, to offer various rationalizations of his behavior, each in some degree cogent. So with the whole multifold *Clarissa*-myth: on all sides it is supported for the understanding by historically familiar morality and manners. But *Wuthering Heights* is almost bare of such supports in social rationalization. Heathcliff might *really* be a demon. The passion of Catherine and Heathcliff is too simple and undeviating in its intensity, too uncomplex, for us to find in it any echo of practical social reality. To say that the motivation of this passion is "simple" is not to say that it is easy to define: much easier to define are the motivations that are somewhat complex and devious, for this is the familiar nature of human motivations. We might associate perfectly "simple" motivations with animal nature or extrahuman nature, but by the same token the quality of feeling involved would resist analysis.

But this nakedness from the web of familiar morality and manners is not quite complete. There is the framework formed by the convention of narration (the "point of view"): we see the drama through the eyes of Lockwood and Nelly Dean, who belong firmly to the world of practical reality. Sifted through the idiom of their commonplace vision, the drama taking place among the major characters finds contact with the temporal and the secular. Because Lockwood and Nelly Dean have witnessed the incredible violence of the life at the Heights, or rather, because Nelly Dean has witnessed the full span and capacity of that violence and because Lockwood credits her witness, the drama is oriented in the context of the psychologically familiar. There is also another technical bulwark that supports this uneasy tale in the social and moral imagination, and that is its extension over the lives of two generations and into a time of ameliorated and respectable manners. At the end, we see young Cathy teaching Hareton his letters and correcting his boorishess (which, after all, is only the natural boorishness consequent on neglect, and has none of the cannibal unregeneracy of Heathcliff in it); the prospect is one of decent, socially responsible domesticity. For this part of the tale, Lockwood alone is sufficient witness; and the fact that now Nelly Dean's experienced old eyes and memory can be dispensed with assures us of the present reasonableness and objectivity of events, and even infects retrospection on what has happened earlier—making it possible for the dream-rejecting reason to settle complacently for the "naturalness" of the entire story. If ghosts have been mentioned, if the country people swear that Heathcliff "walks," we can, with Lockwood at the end, affirm our skepticism as to "how anyone could ever imagine unquiet slumbers for the sleepers in that quiet earth."

Let us try to diagram these technical aspects of the work, for the compositional soundness of *Wuthering Heights* is owing to them. We may divide the action of the book into two parts, following each other chronologically, the one associated with the earlier generation (Hindley and Catherine and Heathcliff, Edgar and Isabella Linton), the other with the later generation (young Cathy and Linton and Hareton). The first of these actions is centered in what we shall call a "mythological romance"

—for the astonishingly ravenous and possessive, perfectly amoral love of Catherine and Heathcliff belongs to that realm of the imagination where myths are created. The second action, centered in the protracted effects of Heathcliff's revenge, involves two sets of young lives and two small "romances": the childish romance of Cathy and Linton, which Heathcliff manages to pervert utterly; and the successful assertion of a healthy, culturally viable kind of love between Cathy and Hareton, asserted as Heathcliff's cruel energies flag and decay. Binding the two "actions" is the perduring figure of Heathcliff himself, demon-lover in the first, paternal ogre in the second. Binding them also is the framing narrational convention or "point of view": the voices of Nelly Dean and Lockwood are always in our ears; one or the other of them is always present at a scene, or is the confidant of someone who was present; through Lockwood we encounter Heathcliff at the beginning of the book, and through his eyes we look on Heathcliff's grave at the end. Still another pattern that binds the two actions is the repetition of what we shall call the "two children" figure—two children raised virtually as brother and sister, in a vibrant relationship of charity and passion and real or possible metamorphosis The figure is repeated, with variation, three times, in the relationships of the main characters. Of this we shall speak again later. The technical continuities or patterning of the book could, then, be simplified in this way:

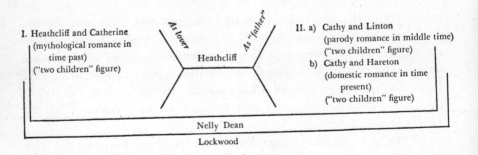

What, concretely, is the effect of this strict patterning and binding? What does it "mean"? The design of the book is drawn in the spirit of intense compositional rigor, of *limitation*; the characters act in the spirit of passionate immoderacy, of *excess*. Let us consider this contrast a little

156

more closely. Essentially, *Wuthering Heights* exists for the mind as a tension between two kinds of reality: the raw, inhuman reality of anonymous natural energies, and the restrictive reality of civilized habits, manners, and codes. The first kind of reality is given to the imagination in the violent figures of Catherine and Heathcliff, portions of the flux of nature, children of rock and heath and tempest, striving to identify themselves as human, but disrupting all around them with their monstrous appetite for an inhuman kind of intercourse, and finally disintegrated from within by the very energies out of which they are made. It is this vision of a reality radically alien from the human that the ancient Chinese landscape paintings offer also. But in those ancient paintings there is often a tiny human figure, a figure that is obviously that of a philosopher, for instance, or that of a peasant—in other words, a human figure decisively belonging to and representing a culture—who is placed in diminutive perspective beside the enormously cascading torrent, or who is seen driving his water buffalo through the overwhelming mists or faceless snows; and this figure is outlined sharply, so that, though it is extremely tiny, it is very definite in the giant surrounding indefiniteness. The effect is one of contrast between finite and infinite, between the limitation of the known and human, and the unlimitedness of the unknown and the nonhuman. So also in *Wuthering Heights:* set over against the wilderness of inhuman reality is the quietly secular, voluntarily limited, safely human reality that we find in the gossipy concourse of Nelly Dean and Lockwood, the one an old family servant with a strong grip on the necessary emotional economies that make life endurable, the other a city visitor in the country, a man whose very disinterestedness and facility of feeling and attention indicate the manifold emotional economies by which city people particularly protect themselves from any disturbing note of the ironic discord between civilized life and the insentient wild flux of nature in which it is islanded. This second kind of reality is given also in the romance of Cathy and Hareton, where book learning and gentled manners and domestic charities form a little island of complacence. The tension between these two kinds of reality, their inveterate opposition and at the same time their *continuity* one with another, provides at once the content and the form of *Wuthering Heights*. We see the tension graphically in the diagram given above. The inhuman excess of Heathcliff's and Catherine's passion, an excess that is carried over into the second half of the book by Heathcliff's revenge, an excess everywhere present in language [2]—in verbs and modifiers and metaphors that seethe with a brute fury—this excess is held within a most rigorous pattern of repeated motifs and of what someone has called the "Chinese box" of Nelly Dean's and Lockwood's interlocution. The form of the book, then—a form that may be expressed as a tension between the impulse to excess and the impulse to limitation or economy—*is* the content. The form, in short, is the book itself. Only in the fully wrought, fully realized, work of art does form so exhaust the possibilities of the material that it identifies itself with these possibilities.

If there has been any cogency in what we have said above, we should ask now how it is that the book is able to represent dramatically, in terms of human "character," its vision of the inhuman. After all, Catherine and Heathcliff *are* "characters," and not merely molecular vibrations in the primordial surge of things; indeed, they are so credibly characterized that Hollywood has been able to costume and cosmeticize them. As "characters," what are they? As lovers, what kind of love is theirs? They gnash and foam at each other. One could borrow for them a line from a poem by John Crowe Ransom describing lovers in hell: "Stuprate, they rend each other when they kiss." This is not "romantic love," as that term has popular meaning; and it is not even sexual love, naturalistically considered —the impulse to destruction is too pure in it, too simple and direct. Catherine says she *is* Heathcliff, and the implication is not of the possibility of a "mating," for one does not "mate" with oneself. Similarly, after her death, when Heathcliff howls that he cannot live without his *life*, he cannot live without his *soul* (and Nellie says that he "howled, not like a man, but like a savage beast"), the relationship and the destiny suggested are not those of adult human lovers, because the complex attendant motivations of adult life are lacking. But the emotional implications of Catherine's and Heathcliff's passion are never "adult," in the sense of there being in that passion any recognition of the domestic and social responsibilities, and the spiritual complexities, of adult life. Whatever could happen to these two, if they could be happily together, would be something altogether asocial, amoral, savagely irresponsible, wildly impulsive: it would be the enthusiastic, experimental, quite random activity of child-

[2] Mark Schorer examines this aspect of *Wuthering Heights* in his essay "Fiction and the 'Analogical Matrix,'" in *Critiques and Essays on Modern Fiction* (New York: The Ronald Press Company, 1952).

hood, occult to the socialized adult. But since no conceivable *human* male and female, not brutish, not anthropologically rudimentary, could be together in this way as adults, all that we can really imagine for the grown-up Catherine and Heathcliff, as "characters" on the human plane, is what the book gives of them—their mutual destruction by tooth and nail in an effort, through death, to get back to the lost state of gypsy freedom in childhood.

Caught in the economical forms of adult life—concepts of social and intellectual "betterment" (such as lead Catherine to marry Edgar Linton), the frames of wealth and property ownership (which Heathcliff at first exploits in order to "raise" himself to Catherine's standard, and then as an engine of revenge against both the Earnshaws and the Lintons), marital relationships, and parenthood—they are, for the imagination, "humanized," endowed with "character," at least to the extent that we see their explosive confusions, resistances, and misery convulsing the forms usual to human adulthood. Their obsession, their prime passion, is also "human" although it is utterly destructive of the values signified by that word: the passion to lose the self in some "otherness," whether in complete identification with another person (an identification for which "mating" is a surrogate only of a temporary and lapsing kind), or by absorption into "nature"—but it is a passion that is tabooed for the socialized adult, disguised, held in check by the complex cultural economics, safely stabled in the unconscious, at best put to work in that darkness to turn the mill of other objectives. This regressive passion is seen in uncompromised purity in Catherine and Heathcliff, and it opens the prospect of disintegration—disintegration into the unconsciousness of childhood and the molecular fluidity of death—in a word, into anonymous natural energy.

If the story of Catherine and Heathcliff had not been a story told by an old woman as something that had had its inception many years ago, if the old woman who tells the story had not been limited in imagination and provincial in her sympathies, if the story had been dramatized immediately in the here-and-now and not at a temporal remove and through a dispassioned intermediator, it is doubtful that it would resonate emotionally for us or carry any conviction—even any "meaning." Because of the very fact that the impulses it represents are taboo, they can conveniently be observed only at a remove, as someone else's, as of the past, and from the judicial point of view of conventional manners. The "someone else's" and the "long ago" are the mind's saving convention for making a distance with itself such as will allow it perspective. Thus the technical *displacement* of Heathcliff's and Catherine's story into past time and into the memory of an old woman functions in the same way as dream displacements: it both censors and indulges, protects and liberates.

Significantly, our first real contact with the Catherine-Heathcliff drama is established through a dream—Lockwood's dream of the ghost-child at the window. Lockwood is motivated to dream the dream by the most easily convincing circumstances; he has fallen asleep while reading Catherine's diary, and during his sleep a tempest-blown branch is scratching on the windowpane. But why should Lockwood, the well-mannered urbanite, dream *this?*

> I pulled its wrist on to the broken pane, and rubbed it to and fro till the blood ran down and soaked the bedclothes . . .

The image is probably the most cruel one in the book. Hareton's hanging puppies, Heathcliff's hanging the springer spaniel, Hindley's forcing a knife between Nelly's teeth or throwing his baby over the staircase, Catherine's leaving the blue print of her nails on Isabella's arm, Heathcliff stamping on Hindley's face—these images and others like them imply savagery or revengefulness or drunkenness or hysteria, but always a motivating set of emotional circumstances. But this is the punctilious Lockwood—whose antecedents and psychology are so insipid that we care little about them—who scrapes the dream-waif's wrist back and forth on broken glass till the blood runs down and soaks the bedclothes. The cruelty of the dream is the gratuitousness of the violence wrought on a child by an emotionally unmotivated vacationer from the city, dreaming in a strange bed. The bed is an old-fashioned closet bed ("a large oak case . . . it formed a little closet" with a window set in it): its paneled sides Lockwood has "pulled together" before going to sleep. The bed is like a coffin (at the end of the book, Heathcliff dies in it, behind its closed panels); it had been Catherine's bed, and the movable panels themselves suggest the coffin in which she is laid, whose "panels" Heathcliff bribes the sexton to remove at one side. Psychologically, Lockwood's dream has only the most perfunctory determinations, and nothing at all of result for the dreamer himself, except to put him uncomfortably out of bed.

But poetically the dream has its reasons, compacted into the image of the daemonic child scratching at the pane, trying to get from the "outside" "in," and of the dreamer in a bed like a coffin, released by that deathly privacy to indiscriminate violence. The coffin-like bed shuts off any interference with the wild deterioration of the psyche. Had the dream used any other agent than the effete, almost epicene Lockwood, it would have lost this symbolic force; for Lockwood, more successfully than anyone else in the book, has shut out the powers of darkness (the pun in his name is obvious in this context); and his lack of any dramatically thorough motivation for dreaming the cruel dream suggests those powers as existing autonomously, not only in the "outsideness" of external nature, beyond the physical windowpane, but also within, even in the soul least prone to passionate excursion.

The windowpane is the medium, treacherously transparent, separating the "inside" from the "outside," the "human" from the alien and terrible "other." Immediately after the incident of the dream, the time of the narrative is displaced into the childhood of Heathcliff and Catherine, and we see the two children looking through the window of the Lintons' drawing room.

> "Both of us were able to look in by standing on the basement, and clinging to the ledge, and we saw—ah! it was beautiful—a splendid place carpeted with crimson, and crimson-covered chairs and tables, and a pure white ceiling bordered by gold, a shower of glass-drops hanging in silver chains from the centre, and shimmering with little soft tapers. Old Mr. and Mrs. Linton were not there; Edgar and his sister had it entirely to themselves. Shouldn't they have been happy? We should have thought ourselves in heaven!"

Here the two unregenerate waifs look *in* from the night on the heavenly vision of the refinements and securities of the most privileged human estate. But Heathcliff rejects the vision: seeing the Linton children blubbering and bored there (*they* cannot get *out!*), he senses the menace of its limitations; while Catherine is fatally tempted. She is taken in by the Lintons, and now it is Heathcliff alone outside looking through the window.

> "The curtains were still looped up at one corner, and I resumed my station as a spy; because, if Catherine had wished to return, I intended

shattering their great glass panes to a million of fragments, unless they let her out. She sat on the sofa quietly . . . the woman-servant brought a basin of warm water, and washed her feet; and Mr. Linton mixed a tumbler of negus, and Isabella emptied a plateful of cakes into her lap . . . Afterwards, they dried and combed her beautiful hair . . ."

Thus the first snare is laid by which Catherine will be held for a human destiny—her feet washed, cakes and wine for her delectation, her beautiful hair combed (the motifs here are limpid as those of fairy tale, where the changeling in the "otherworld" is held there mysteriously by bathing and by the strange new food he has been given to eat). By her marriage to Edgar Linton, Catherine yields to that destiny; later she resists it tormentedly and finds her way out of it by death. Literally she "catches her death" by throwing open the window.

> "Open the window again wide: fasten it open! Quick, why don't you move?" [she says to Nelly].
> "Because I won't give you your death of cold," I answered.
> "You won't give me a chance of life, you mean," she said . . .

In her delirium, she opens the window, leans out into the winter wind, and calls across the moors to Heathcliff,

> "Heathcliff, if I dare you now, will you venture? . . . Find a way, then! . . . You are slow! . . . you always followed me!"

On the night after her burial, unable to follow her (though he digs up her grave in order to lie beside her in the coffin from which the side panels have been removed), he returns to the Heights *through the window* —for Hindley has barred the door—to wreak on the living the fury of his frustration. It is years later that Lockwood arrives at the Heights and spends his uncomfortable night there. Lockwood's outcry in his dream brings Heathcliff *to the window,* Heathcliff who has been caught ineluctably in the human to grapple with its interdictions long after Catherine has broken through them. The treachery of the window is that Catherine, lost now in the "other," can look through the transparent membrane that separates her from humanity, can scratch on the pane, but cannot get "in," while Heathcliff, though he forces the window open and howls into the night, cannot get "out." When he dies, Nelly Dean discovers the window swinging open, the window of that old-fashioned coffin-like bed where Lockwood had had the dream. Rain has been pouring in during the night, drenching the dead man. Nelly says,

> I hasped the window; I combed his black long hair from his forehead; I tried to close his eyes: to extinguish, if possible, that frightful, life-like gaze of exultation before any one else beheld it. They would not shut: they seemed to sneer at my attempts . . .

Earlier, Heathcliff's eyes have been spoken of as "the clouded windows of hell" from which a "fiend" looks out. All the other uses of the "window" that we have spoken of here are not figurative but perfectly naturalistic uses, though their symbolic value is inescapable. But the fact that Heathcliff's eyes refuse to close in death suggests the symbol in a metaphorical form (the "fiend" has now got "out," leaving the window open), elucidating with simplicity the meaning of the "window" as a separation between the daemonic depths of the soul and the limited and limiting lucidities of consciousness, a separation between the soul's "otherness" and its humanness.

There is still the difficulty of defining, with any precision, the quality of the daemonic that is realized most vividly in the conception of Heathcliff, a difficulty that is mainly due to our tendency always to give the "daemonic" some ethical status—that is, to relate it to an ethical hierarchy. Heathcliff's is an archetypal figure, untraceably ancient in mythological thought—an imaged recognition of that part of nature which is "other" than the human soul (the world of the elements and the animals) and of that part of the soul itself which is "other" than the conscious part. But since Martin Luther's revival of this archetype for modern mythology, it has tended to forget its relationship with the elemental "otherness" of the outer world and to identify itself solely with the dark functions of the soul. As an image of soul work, it is ethically relevant, since everything that the soul does—even unconsciously, even "ignorantly" (as in the case of Oedipus)—offers itself for ethical judgment, whereas the elements and the animals do not. Puritanism perpetuated the figure for the imagination; Milton gave it its greatest aesthetic splendor, in the fallen angel through whom the divine beauty still shone; Richardson introduced it, in the person of Lovelace, to an infatuated middle class; and always the figure was ethically relevant through the conception of "sin" and "guilt." (Let us note here, however, the ambivalence of the figure, an ambivalence that the medieval devil does not have. The medieval devil is a really ugly customer, so ugly that he can even become a comedy figure —as in the medieval moralities. The daemonic archetype of which we are speaking here is deeply serious in quality because of his ambivalence: he is a fertilizing energy and profoundly attractive, and at the same time horribly destructive to civilized institutionalism. It is because of his ambivalence that, though he is the "enemy," ethically speaking, he so easily takes on the stature and beauty of a hero, as he does in the Satan of *Paradise Lost*.) In Byron's *Manfred,* the archetype underwent a rather confusing sea-change, for Manfred's crime is, presumably, so frightful that it cannot be mentioned, and the indefinable nature of the crime blurs the edges of the figure and cuts down its resonance in the imagination (when we guess that the crime might be incest, we are disposed to find this a rather paltry equation for the Byronic incantation of guilt); nevertheless, the ethical relevancy of the figure remains. Let us follow it a little further, before returning to Emily Brontë's Heathcliff. In the later nineteenth century, in the novels of Dostoevski, it reappears with an enormous development of psychological subtlety, and also with a great strengthening and clarification of its ethical significance. In the work of André Gide, it undergoes another sea-change: the archetypal daemonic figure now becomes the principle of progress, the spirit of free investigation and creative experience; with this reorientation, it becomes positively ethical rather than negatively so. In Thomas Mann's *Doctor Faustus,* it reverts to its earlier and more constant significance, as the type of the instinctive part of the soul, a great and fertilizing power, but ethically unregenerate and therefore a great danger to ethical man.

Our interest in sketching some phases of the history of this archetype has been to show that it has had, in modern mythology, constantly a status in relation to ethical thought. The exception is Heathcliff. Heathcliff is no more ethically relevant than is flood or earthquake or whirlwind. It is as impossible to speak of him in terms of "sin" and "guilt" as it is to speak in this way of the natural elements or the creatures of the animal world. In him, the type reverts to a more ancient mythology and to an earlier symbolism. *Wuthering Heights* so baffles and confounds the ethical sense because it is not informed with that sense at all: it is profoundly informed with the attitudes of "animism," by which the natural world—that world which is "other" than and "outside of" the consciously individualized human—*appears* to act with an energy similar to the energies of the soul; to be permeated with soul energy but of a mysterious and alien kind that the conscious human soul, bent on securing itself through civilization, cannot identify itself with as to purpose; an energy that can be propitiated, that can at times be canalized into humanly purposeful channels, that *must* be given religious recognition both for its enormous fertility and its enormous potential destructiveness. But Heathcliff does have human shape and human relationships; he is, so to speak, "caught in" the human; two kinds of reality intersect in him—as they do, with a somewhat different balance, in Catherine; as they do, indeed, in the other characters. Each entertains, in some degree, the powers of darkness—from Hindley, with his passion for self-destruction (he, too, wants to get "out"), to Nelly Dean, who in a sense "propitiates" those powers with the casuistry of her actions, and even to Lockwood, with his sadistic dream. Even in the weakest of these souls there is an intimation of the dark Otherness, by which the soul is related psychologically to the inhuman world of pure energy, for it carries within itself an "otherness" of its own, that inhabits below consciousness.

The imagery of the windowpane is metamorphic, suggesting a total change of mode of being by the breaking-through of a separating medium that exists between consciousness and the "other." The strangest and boldest and most radiant figuration that Emily Brontë has given to her subject is the "two children" figure, also a metamorphic figure of break-through and transformation. The *type* or classic form of this figure is a girl with golden hair and a boy with dark hair and shadowed brow, bound in kinship and in a relationship of charity and passion, and with a metamorphosis of some kind potential in the relationship. The beautiful dark boy will be brightened, made angelic and happy, by the beautiful golden girl: this, apparently, is what *should* happen. But the dynamics of the change are not perfectly trustworthy. In one of Emily Brontë's poems, describing a child who might be the child Heathcliff, the ambivalent dark boy will evidently sink further into his darkness.

> *I love thee, boy; for all divine,*
> *All full of God thy features shine.*
> *Darling enthusiast, holy child,*
> *Too good for this world's warring wild,*
> *Too heavenly now but doomed to be*
> *Hell-like in heart and misery.*[3]

[3] *The Complete Poems of Emily Jane Brontë*, edited by C. W. Hatfield (New York: Columbia University Press, 1941), p. 121.

In the 1850 printing of the Brontë poems (the printing supervised by the Brontë sisters) two companion pieces appear under the title "The Two Children," in the first of which the dark boy is still unchanged.

> *Frowning on the infant,*
> *Shadowing childhood's joy,*
> *Guardian angel knows not*
> *That melancholy boy . . .*[4]

In the second of these companion pieces, the golden child is evoked, and now the change in the dark one is promised.

> *Child of Delight! with sunbright hair,*
> *And seablue, seadeep eyes;*
> *Spirit of Bliss, what brings thee here,*
> *Beneath these sullen skies?*
>
> *Thou shouldest live in eternal spring,*
> *Where endless day is never dim;*
> *Why, Seraph, has thy erring wing*
> *Borne thee down to weep with him?*

She answers that she is "not from heaven descended," but that she has seen and pitied "that mournful boy."

> *And I swore to take his gloomy sadness,*
> *And give to him my beamy joy . . .*[5]

Here, with the change of the dark child, the golden child will be changed also, for she will take his "gloomy sadness." In another set of verses, the light-dark contrast is turned around bewilderingly.

> *And only* he *had locks of light,*
> *And* she *had raven hair;*
> *While now, his curls are dark as night,*
> *And hers as morning fair.*[6]

What really seems to be implied by all these shifts is not a mere exchange of characteristics but a radical identification of the two children, so that each can appear in the mode of the other, the bright one in the mode of darkness and the dark one in the mode of light.

[4] *Ibid.,* p. 229.
[5] *Ibid.,* p. 230.
[6] *Ibid.,* p. 174.

In still another of those poems that dramatize affairs in the kingdom of Gondal that occupied Emily Brontë's youthful fantasy, a brooding
phantom figure haunts the moonlit grounds of a castle. Its face is "divinely
fair," but on its "angel brow"

> *Rests such a shade of deep despair*
> *As nought divine could ever know.*

Apparently the cause of his death was adoration of another man's wife
("Lord Alfred's idol queen"), and it is for this reason that his spirit is
"shut from heaven—an outcast for eternity." The woman for whom he
died is represented as an "infant fair," looking from a golden frame in a
portrait gallery.

> *And just like his its ringlets bright,*
> *Its large dark eye of shadowy light,*
> *Its cheeks' pure hue, its forehead white,*
> *And like its noble name.*

A deliberate confusion of the planes of reality—a shifting into the life
inside the picture frame (like the shifts "through the window" in *Wuthering Heights*), and with it a shifting from despairing adulthood into childhood—is suggested with the following questions:

> *And did he never smile to see*
> *Himself restored to infancy?*
>
> *Never part back that golden flow*
> *Of curls, and kiss that pearly brow,*
> *And feel no other earthly bliss*
> *Was equal to that parent's kiss?* [7]

The suggestions are those of metamorphic changes, but all under the aspect of frustration: the despairing lover cannot get through the picture
frame where the child is. Other motifs here are reminiscent of those of
Wuthering Heights. The spectral lover is an ambivalent figure, of divine
beauty, but an outcast from heaven. Kinship is suggested between him
and the child in the picture ("And just like his its ringlets bright . . .
And like its noble name"), and one is left to imagine that "Lord Alfred's
idol queen" was his sister, wherefore the frustration of their love. The
last stanza quoted above remarks ambiguously on the parental feeling

[7] *Ibid.,* pp. 177–178.

involved in the relationship: is it not the infant who is the "parent" here? Parental charity is the feeling of the golden "guardian angel" for her dark charge in "The Two Children" poems, as it is, in a degree, of Catherine for Heathcliff during their childhood, and of young Cathy first for Linton and then for Hareton. The fact that, in the poem, both the infant and the spectral lover have golden hair seems, in this elusive fantasy, to be a mark of perversion of the metamorphic sequence, at least of its having gone awry (as in the case, too, of young Cathy and Linton, who is not dark but fair).

In the relationship of Catherine and Heathcliff, the fantasy has its typical form. She is golden, he is dark. His daemonic origin is always kept open, by reiterations of the likelihood that he is really a ghoul, a fiend, an offspring of hell, and not merely so in behavior. And Catherine also, like the guardian child in "The Two Children" poems, is "not from heaven descended": she has furious tantrums, she lies, she bites, her chosen toy is a whip. They are raised as brother and sister; there are three references to their sleeping in the same bed as infants. She scolds and orders and mothers and cherishes him ("much too fond of him" as a child, Nelly says). The notions of somatic change and discovery of noble birth, as in fairy tale, are deliberately played with; as, when Catherine returns from her first sojourn at the Lintons' and Heathcliff asks Nelly to "make him decent," he says, comparing himself with Edgar,

> "I wish I had light hair and a fair skin, and was dressed and behaved as well, and had a chance of being as rich as he will be!"

and Nelly answers,

> "You're fit for a prince in disguise . . . Were I in your place, I would frame high notions of my birth . . ."

(If Heathcliff is really of daemonic origin, he is, in a sense, indeed of "high birth," a "prince in disguise," and might be expected, like the princes of fairy tale, to drop his "disguise" at the crisis of the tale and be revealed in original splendor: the dynamics of the "two children" figure also points to that potential transformation.) Some alluring and astonishing destiny seems possible for the two. *What* that phenomenon might be or mean, we cannot know, for it is frustrated by Catherine's marriage to Edgar, which dooms Heathcliff to be "hell-like in heart and misery."

168

Catherine's decision dooms her also, for she is of the same daemonic substance as Heathcliff, and a civilized marriage and domesticity are not sympathetic to the daemonic quality.

With the second generation, the "two children" figure is distorted and parodied in the relationship of Catherine's daughter and Heathcliff's son. Young Cathy, another "child of delight, with sunbright hair," has still some of the original daemonic energy, but her "erring wing" has brought her down to "weep with" a *pale-haired* and pallid little boy whose only talents are for sucking sugar candy and torturing cats. She does her best, as infant mother, to metamorphose him, but he is an ungrateful and impossible subject. Her passionate charity finally finds her "married" to his corpse in a locked bedroom. With Cathy and Hareton Earnshaw, her cousin on her mother's side, the "two children" are again in their right relationship of golden and dark, and now the pathos of the dark child cures the daemon out of the golden one, and the maternal care of the golden child raises the dark one to civilized humanity and makes of him a proper husband.

In these several pairs, the relation of kinship has various resonances. Between Catherine and Heathcliff, identity of "kind" is greatest, although they are foster brother and sister only. The foster kinship provides an imaginative implicit reason for the unnaturalness and impossibility of their mating. Impassioned by their brother-and-sisterlike identity of kind, they can only destroy each other, for it is impossible for two persons to *be* each other (as Catherine says she "is" Heathcliff) without destruction of the physical limitations that individualize and separate. In Emily Brontë's use of the symbolism of the incest motive, the incestual impulse appears as an attempt to make what is "outside" oneself identical with what is "inside" oneself—a performance that can be construed in physical and human terms only by violent destruction of personality bounds, by rending of flesh and at last by death.

With Catherine's daughter and young Linton, who are cousins, the implicit incestuousness of the "two children" figure is suggested morbidly by Linton's disease and by his finally becoming a husband only as a corpse. With Cathy and Hareton Earnshaw, also cousins, Victorian "ameliorism" finds a way to sanction the relationship by symbolic emasculation; Cathy literally teaches the devil out of Hareton, and "esteem" between the two takes the place of the old passion for identification. With this successful metamorphosis and mating, the daemonic quality has been completely suppressed, and, though humanity and civilization have been secured for the "two children," one feels that some magnificent bounty is now irrecoverable. The great magic, the wild power, of the original two has been lost.

We are led to speculate on what the bounty might have been,[8] had the windowpane not stood between the original pair, had the golden child and the dark child not been secularized by a spelling book. Perhaps, had the ideal and impossible eventuality taken place, had the "inside" and the "outside," the bright child and the dark one, become identified in such a way that they could freely assume each other's modes, then perhaps the world of the animals and the elements—the world of wild moor and barren rock, of fierce wind and attacking beast, that is the strongest palpability in *Wuthering Heights*—would have offered itself completely to human understanding and creative intercourse. Perhaps the dark powers that exist within the soul, as well as in the outer elemental world, would have assumed the language of consciousness, or consciousness would have bravely entered into companionship with those dark powers and transliterated their language into its own. Emily Brontë's book has been said to be nonphilosophical—as it is certainly nonethical; but all philosophy is not ethics, and the book seizes, at the point where the soul feels itself cleft within and in cleavage from the universe, the first germs of philosophic thought, the thought of the duality of human and nonhuman existence, and the thought of the cognate duality of the psyche.

[8] A stimulating and enlightening interpretation of the book is to be found in Richard Chase's "The Brontës, or Myth Domesticated," in *Forms of Modern Fiction,* edited by William Van O'Connor (Minneapolis: University of Minnesota Press, 1948).

ON *Adam Bede*

In Chapter 17 of *Adam Bede,* "the story pauses a little" and George Eliot sets forth her aim as a novelist, an aim which she describes as "the faithful representing of commonplace things," of things *as they are,* not "as they never have been and never will be"; and we are reminded of a similar aim as expressed by Defoe's Moll Flanders, who said, "I am giving an account of what was, not of what ought or ought not to be." It is the vocation of the "realistic" novelist to represent life in this way; it is at the furthest possible remove from the work of marvel making that we have just witnessed in *Wuthering Heights;* but, as Defoe brought us to a consideration of the shaping changes which the "real" undergoes as it is submitted to art, even to the most "realistic" art, so George Eliot brings us back to the same consideration of the transforming effect of composition upon things-as-they-are. Her strongest effort, she says, is to avoid an "arbitrary picture," and

> to give a faithful account of men and things as they have mirrored themselves in my mind. The mirror is doubtless defective; the outlines will sometimes be disturbed, the reflection faint or confused; but I feel as much bound to tell you as precisely as I can what that reflection is, as if I were in the witness-box, narrating my experience on oath.

We cannot avoid observing that the "mirror" is at times defective, but since it is for the most part clear and well lighted we are not primarily concerned with the defects; more interesting is the analogy of the mirror itself—the novelist's mind as a mirror from whose "reflections" of "men and things" he draws his account. Men and things, then, do not leap to his page directly out of the "real" but, before they get there, take a journey through the "mirror." But the mirror which the mind offers is

171

not at all like other mirrors; even—leaving out of consideration defective glasses—very clear minds are not like very clear mirrors. Dangerous as analogies are, a spoon would be a better one, where, in the concave, as we tip it toward us, we see our head compressed and a half-moon scooped out of it on top as if it were a dime-store flowerpot for our viney hair, our body tapered to vanishing at the hips, and the whole upside down; or, in the convex, our eyelids are as large as foreheads, our forehead is as small as an eyelid, our cheeks hang down from our face like shoulders, and our shoulders hide under them like little ears. The "mirror" of the mind shapes what it sees. It does not passively "reflect" things-as-they-are, but creates things-as-they-are. Though we can clearly discriminate the quality of intention shown by a realistic art—and it usually reduces finally to a choice of materials from the field of the quotidian, the commonplace, the mediocre—yet its aim of veraciousness is necessarily one of veraciousness to what the artist sees in the shape-giving, significance-endowing medium of his own mind, and in this sense the mythopoeic art of *Wuthering Heights* is as veracious as the realistic art of *Adam Bede*.

The singularity of the world of *Wuthering Heights* is its innocence of "good" and "evil" in any civilized ethical meaning of these terms; it is a world shaped by kinetic rather than by ethical forces, and its innocence is that of the laws of dynamics (Catherine's fatal choice, for instance, is essentially a choice of stasis and a denial of motion; it is as if an electron or a star should "choose" to stand still). *Adam Bede* offers the radical contrast of a world shaped through and through by moral judgment and moral evaluation. We are prone, perhaps, to think of a perfectly amoral vision, such as Emily Brontë's, as a vision not of things-as-they-are but as a subjective creation of things-as-they-never-were-but-might-be, and, on the other hand, to think of an ethical vision, such as George Eliot's, as closer to things-as-they-are, more "objective," because of our own familiar addiction to moral judgments (however inapropos or cliché) and our difficulty in turning ethics out of doors. But, on a thought, it should be clear that a through and through ethically shaped world is as "created" a world as the other. The question is not one of *whether* things are really this way or that way, for either vision touches responsive similitudes within us, and God knows what things really are. The question is one of different organizations and different illuminations of the infinite possible qualities of things-as-they-are.

Technique is that which selects among the multitude of possible qualities, organizes them in the finite world of the novel, and holds them in a shape that can catch the light of our own awareness, which, without shapes to fall upon, is ignorant. Technique is like the concave or convex surface of the spoon, and the different turnings and inclinations to which it is liable; technique elongates or foreshortens, and while the rudimentary relationships of common experience remain still recognizable, it reveals astonishing bulges of significance, magnifies certain parts of the anatomy of life, of whose potentialities we had perhaps not been aware, humbles others. The massively slow movement of *Adam Bede* is one such shape-making technique. It is true that we are generally persuaded of the *actual* slow movement of rural life, and it is rural life —the life of villagers, tenant farmers, and peasantry—that George Eliot describes; but Dickens, in the first part of *Great Expectations,* is also dealing with people in a rural community, and yet the tempo or "pace" which he sets for these lives is one of shockingly abrupt accelerations.

> "Hold your noise!" cried a terrible voice, as a man started up from among the graves at the side of the church porch. "Keep still, you little devil, or I'll cut your throat!"

Emily Brontë deals with even more rurally isolated lives, but here the movement is one of furious assault: beasts attack, the tempest whirls and suffocates, emotions express themselves in howls, biting, kicking, trampling, bloodletting, homicidal and suicidal violence. In the context of this comparison let us set almost any random paragraph from *Adam Bede.* The movement is one of a massive leisureliness that gathers up as it goes a dense body of physical and moral detail, adding particle to particle and building layer upon layer with sea-depth patience.

> In the large wicker-bottomed arm-chair in the left-hand chimney-nook sat old Martin Poyser, a hale but shrunken and bleached image of his portly black-haired son—his head hanging forward a little, and his elbows pushed backwards so as to allow the whole of his fore-arm to rest on the arm of the chair. His blue handkerchief was spread over his knees, as was usual indoors, when it was not hanging over his head; and he sat watching what went forward with the quiet *outward* glance of healthy old age, which, disengaged from any interest in an inward drama, spies out pins upon the floor, follows one's minutest motions with an unexpectant purposeless tenacity, watches the flickering of the flame or the sun-gleams on the wall, counts the quarries on the

floor, watches even the hand of the clock, and pleases itself with detecting a rhythm in the tick.

And here are the Poysers going to church.

> There were acquaintances at other gates who had to move aside and let them pass: at the gate of the Home Close there was half the dairy of cows standing one behind the other, extremely slow to understand that their large bodies might be in the way; at the far gate there was the mare holding her head over the bars, and beside her the liver-coloured foal with its head towards its mother's flank, apparently still much embarrassed by its own straddling existence. The way lay entirely through Mr. Poyser's own fields till they reached the main road leading to the village, and he turned a keen eye on the stock and the crops as they went along, while Mrs. Poyser was ready to supply a running commentary on them all . . .
>
> The damp hay that must be scattered and turned afresh tomorrow was not a cheering sight to Mr. Poyser, who during hay and corn harvest had often some mental struggles as to the benefits of a day of rest; but no temptation would have induced him to carry on any field-work, however early in the morning, on a Sunday; for had not Michael Holdsworth had a pair of oxen "sweltered" while he was ploughing on Good Friday? That was a demonstration that work on sacred days was a wicked thing; and with wickedness of any sort Martin Poyser was quite clear that he would have nothing to do, since money got by such means would never prosper.
>
> "It a'most makes your fingers itch to be at the hay now the sun shines so," he observed, as they passed through the "Big Meadow." "But it's poor foolishness to think o' saving by going against your conscience. There's that Jim Wakefield, as they used to call 'Gentleman Wakefield,' used to do the same of a Sunday as o' week-days, and took no heed to right or wrong, as if there was nayther God nor devil. An' what's he come to? Why, I saw him myself last market-day a-carrying a basket wi' oranges in't."
>
> "Ah, to be sure," said Mrs. Poyser, emphatically, "you make but a poor trap to catch luck if you go and bait it wi' wickedness. The money as is got so's like to burn holes i' your pocket. I'd niver wish us to leave our lads a sixpence but what was got i' the rightful way. And as for the weather, there's One above makes it, and we must put up wi't: it's nothing of a plague to what the wenches are."
>
> Notwithstanding the interruption in their walk, the excellent habit which Mrs. Poyser's clock had of taking time by the forelock,

had secured their arrival at the village while it was still a quarter to two, though almost every one who meant to go to church was already within the churchyard gates.

It would be difficult to quote at less length for these illustrations, for a leisurely pace can be illustrated only by its own leisureliness.

But what does "pace" *mean?* Of what is it the expressive signature? We have examined slightly, in the study of *Great Expectations,* what the tempo of that book means—how its abrupt shocks of timing, its ballet-like leaps, express the mysterious movements of a non-naturalistic world in which guilt has an objective being as palpable as that "fearful man, all in coarse grey, with a great iron on his leg" who starts up from among the graves; a world in which the secret inner life of the spirit does not wait on the slow processes of analysis and of naturalistic cause and effect, but suddenly appears before one on the staircase with hands stretched out, saying, "My boy! my dear boy!"; in short, an absurd world, quite contradicting commonsense, and one, therefore, in which things and people do not walk by the clock but dance pantomimic dances in the outrageous tempo of the absurd. In *Wuthering Heights,* the pace of assault is so deeply at the core of the book's feeling that comment seems superfluous: we cannot imagine this novel as moving otherwise than by violent attack—than by verbs of "snatching," "grinding," "crashing," "smashing," "thundering," "choking," "burning," "torturing," "murdering": for such excess is of the nature of that nonhuman Otherworld which, in Emily Brontë's vision, erupts grotesquely into the limited, the civilized, the moral, the static. And now, before attempting to define the expressive value of a very different kind of pace, let us consider somewhat more closely the types of material that, in *Adam Bede,* present themselves with the patient rhythms of day and night, of the seasons, of planting and harvest, of the generations of men, and of the thoughts of simple people who are bound by deep tradition to soil and to community.

We enter the description of Hall Farm in Chapter 6 at "the drowsiest time of the year, just before hay-harvest," and at "the drowsiest time of the day, too, for it is close upon three by the sun, and it is half-past three by Mrs. Poyser's handsome eight-day clock." If the reader will turn back to the passage quoted above, describing old Martin Poyser, he will find the clock again: old Martin watches its hands, not through engagement with time but through disengagement from it; he pleases himself with "detecting a rhythm in the tick" as he does with watching the sun-gleams on the wall and counting the quarries on the floor. And again, in the passage describing the Poysers on their way to church, we are told of "the excellent habit which Mrs. Poyser's clock had of taking time by the forelock," so that, despite interruptions in their walk, they arrive at the village "while it was still a quarter to two." The mechanism of the eight-day clock works in sympathy with the week, with the rhythm of workdays and Sabbath, and we are reminded in the same passage of that other scheduling of man's time which holds him to Sabbath observance no matter if the hay wants turning, for, as Mrs. Poyser says, "as for the weather, there's One above makes it, and we must put up wi't." We shall return to the clock, but we wish to note now the *kind* of life that this great mass of slow time carries with it. It is a kind of life that is signified by that wonderful kitchen at Hall Farm, with its polished surfaces of oak table and, of course, the oak clockcase—not "any of your varnished rubbish," but polished with "genuine 'elbow polish' "—the great round pewter dishes ranged on the shelves above the long deal dinner table, the jasper-shining hobs of the grate, mellow oak and bright brass; and it is signified by the Hall Farm dairy,

> such coolness, such purity, such fresh fragrance of new-pressed cheese, of firm butter, of wooden vessels perpetually bathed in pure water; such soft coloring of red earthenware and creamy surfaces, brown wood and polished tin, grey limestone and rich orange-red rust on the iron weights and hooks and hinges.

It is a kind of life that is signified, too, by the funeral of Thias Bede, that deeply reverend magical rite at which

> none of the old people held books—why should they? not one of them could read. But they knew a few "good words" by heart, and their withered lips now and then moved silently, following the service without any very clear comprehension indeed, but with a simple faith in its efficacy to ward off harm and bring blessing . . .

while old Lisbeth is comforted in her grief by "a vague belief that the psalm was doing her husband good," for

> it was part of that decent burial which she would have thought it a greater wrong to withhold from him than to have caused him many

unhappy days while he was living. The more there was said about her husband, the more there was done for him, surely the safer he would be.

It is a kind of life that is signified by the chapter describing the school-master, Bartle Massy, and his pupils—the stone sawyer, the brickmaker, the dyer—

> three big men, with the marks of their hard labour about them, anxiously bending over the worn books, and painfully making out, "The grass is green," "The sticks are dry," "The corn is ripe" . . . It was almost as if three rough animals were making humble efforts to learn how they might become human.

Bartle Massy himself has no critical place in the plot, but, like the school-master in Goldsmith's "The Deserted Village," he is one more significant member of a community; and his kindness, his depth of feeling, his long habits of sacrifice and self-discipline, even his eccentricity, are of the richest texture of the community life. For it is the community that is the protagonist of this novel, the community as the repository of certain shared and knowledgeable values that have been developed out of ages of work and care and common kindness. The kitchen at Hall Farm shines in the sun, the dairy is clean and fragrant, Lisbeth's grief is alleviated by the funeral, and Bartle Massy's pupils make their toilsome efforts "to learn how they might become human," because of a moral development that has been made possible only by slow and difficult centuries of accreted recognitions, limitations, modulations, techniques.

Therefore the eight-day clock, with its minute rhythms for an old man's ear, with its rhythm for the daily work that starts at half past four, when the mowers' bottles have to be filled and the baking started, and with its weekly rhythm for the Sabbath. The clock is a monument not to time merely as time, but to the assured and saving values stored up through ages of experience. In one of her books George Eliot says, "There is no private life which has not been determined by a wider public life." In *Adam Bede,* this is the mute recognition by which the community lives: as imaginatively realized here, it is a recognition that personal good has communal determinations, that it is contingent upon the preservation of common values. But the statement bears also its converse, which might be phrased thus: "There is no public life which has not been determined by the narrower private life"; for the story of *Adam Bede* is a story of the irreparable damage wrought on the community by a private moment's frivolity.

Mrs. Poyser's clock at Hall Farm, the clock which has sublimated all time into good, is set for daylight saving (it has the "excellent habit" of "taking time by the forelock"). Not so the clocks of the gentlefolk at the Chase. Throughout that Thursday when Arthur twice meets Hetty in the wood, the clock is watched irritably. It is "about ten o'clock" when Arthur, time irritable and bored on his hands, goes to the stables; the "twelve o'clock sun" sees him galloping toward Norburne to see a friend; but Hetty is on his mind, and "the hand of the dial in the courtyard had scarcely cleared the last stroke of three" when he is again home; so that "it was scarcely four o'clock" when he is waiting at the gate of the wood. Hetty comes daily to learn lace mending of Mrs. Pomfret, the maid at the Chase, at four o'clock, and she tells Arthur that she always sets out for the farm "by eight o'clock." They exchange a look: "What a space of time those three moments were, while their eyes met and his arms touched her!" Arthur meditates irresolutely "more than an hour" on the false impression he feels he has created in the girl; but "the time must be filled up," and he dresses for dinner, "for his grandfather's dinner-hour was six"; meanwhile Hetty too is watching the clock, and at last "the minute-hand of the old-fashioned brazen-faced timepiece was on the last quarter of eight." In the shadows of the wood he kisses her. Then he pulls out his watch: "I wonder how late it is . . . twenty minutes past eight—but my watch is too fast." Back at the farm, Mrs. Poyser exclaims,

> "What a time o'night this is to come home, Hetty . . . Look at the clock, do; why, it's going on for half-past nine, and I've sent the gells to bed this half-hour, and late enough too . . ."
>
> "I did set out before eight, aunt," said Hetty, in a pettish tone, with a slight toss of her head. "But this clock's so much before the clock at the Chase, there's no telling what time it'll be when I get here."
>
> "What! you'd be wanting the clock set by gentle-folks's time, would you? an' sit up burnin' candle, an' lie a-bed wi' the sun a-bakin' you like a cowcumber i' the frame? The clock hasn't been put forrard for the first time to-day, I reckon."

The pace of *Adam Bede* is set to Mrs. Poyser's clock, to all that slow toil and patient discipline that have made daylight—and living—valuable. Slower, organically, invisibly slow, are the months of Hetty's pregnancy; the Poysers' clock, the clock at the Chase, do not keep this time, with their eights and nines and half past nines. This other, deep, hidden, animal time drags the whole pace down to that of poor Hetty's "journey in despair," a blind automatism of animal night where the ticking of the human clock cannot be heard.

Hetty's very fragility is her claim to the saving disciplines of a traditional way of life. It is by her mediocrity that their value is tested, for without them she is abandoned to chaos. There is probably no other work that explores human suffering at the organic level with such deep authority as the chapter describing Hetty's journey from Oxford to Stonyshire. It is a suffering that has no issue in "illumination," no spiritual value for the sufferer, for Hetty is not the kind of character that sustains "illumination" through suffering. If she were, we should not have had the particular insight that *Adam Bede* affords into the moral meaning of time and tradition in the lives of simple people. Hetty is lost because she is more fragile than the others and therefore more dependent on the community disciplines (far more fragile, because of her class, than "Chad's Bess" of the village, for instance, who, with her looseness and silliness and—like Hetty—with false garnets in her ears, has a secure and accustomed place in the village life); lost from the only values that can support her mediocrity, she sinks into the chaos of animal fear, which, in the human being, is insanity. Other novelists have explored other kinds of suffering; one might draw up a chart or a dissertation, of no mean interest, that would show the hierarchies of human suffering as represented in literature and their psychological, ethical, and spiritual significance; surely Hetty's would be at the bottom of the scale (even lower, one would think, than that of some of the least human characters in Faulkner's novels, for Faulkner is interested in the "illumination" of which even idiots are capable). But its lowness and blindness in the scale of human suffering is its moving power. For Hetty is very human, very real, and if knowledge of suffering did not include hers, it would not include the broadest and commonest layer of human existence.

It is improbable that any but an English novelist would have interested himself in Hetty as a figure of tragic pathos. Flaubert would have despised her: the luxury fantasies of Emma Bovary (a French Hetty) have a richness and complexity of cultural experience, and a play of sensibility, that make Hetty's dreams of standing beside Arthur Donnithorne as a bride look thin indeed; and the fatality of Hetty's pregnancy would not have occurred to the author of *Madame Bovary,* nor all the mess of child murder, for these are quite English habits of interest (as we have been able to witness those habits in *The Heart of Mid-Lothian*—to whose plot *Adam Bede* is confessedly indebted—and shall again in Hardy's *Tess*); though Emma Bovary's adulterous experiences give her a far wider range of opportunity than Hetty's few moments with Arthur Donnithorne allow, Emma's child is a child by marriage and its existence has ironic rather than tragic significance; and the interest of Emma's adulteries is an interest in the adulterous psychology rather than an interest in spermatic and ovarian operations. Dostoevski could not have used Hetty, for she has less of God in her, a more meager spiritual capacity, than his imbeciles and whores; she is not capable even of that kind of "recognition" which leads the abused child in *The Possessed* and the carpenter in *Crime and Punishment* to hang themselves.

But the massy line of the book is deflected toward the end. ("The mirror," George Eliot says, "is doubtless defective; the outlines will sometimes be disturbed, the reflection faint or confused.") By Mrs. Poyser's clock, Hetty's last-minute reprieve cannot really be timed with a time integral to the rest of the novel, nor can Adam's marriage with Dinah. Henry James says of these events that he doubts very much "whether the author herself had a clear vision" of them, and suggests that the reason may be that George Eliot's perception

> was a perception of nature much more than of art, and that these particular incidents do not belong to nature (to my sense at least); by which I do not mean that they belong to a very happy art . . . they are a very good example of the view in which a story must have marriages and rescues in the nick of time, as a matter of course.[1]

We should add Arthur Donnithorne's return in his interesting and picturesque ill-health. Hetty's reprieve, the marriage of Dinah and Adam, Arthur's reconstruction through such suffering as Arthur is able to suffer —these are no compensation for and no real "illumination" of the tragedy

[1] *Partial Portraits* (London, 1911), p. 53.

of Hetty. They are the artificial illumination which so many Victorian novels indulged in, in the effort to justify to man God's ways or society's ways or nature's ways. But still there is left the ticking of the oak-cased clock, rubbed by human "elbow-polish," that paces the book through its greater part: the realization of value, clean as the clock-tick, radiant as the kitchen of Hall Farm, fragrant as the dairy; and the tragic realization of the loss of however simple human values, in Hetty's abandoned footsteps as she seeks the dark pool and caresses her own arms in the desire for life.

With Meredith's *The Egoist* we enter into a critical problem that we have not before faced in these studies. That is the problem offered by a writer of recognizably impressive stature, whose work is informed by a muscular intelligence, whose language has splendor, whose "view of life" wins our respect, and yet for whom we are at best able to feel only a passive appreciation which amounts, practically, to indifference. We should be unjust to Meredith and to criticism if we should, giving in to the inertia of indifference, simply avoid dealing with him and thus avoid the problem along with him. He does not "speak to us," we might say; his meaning is not a "meaning for us"; he "leaves us cold." But do not the challenge and the excitement of the critical problem as such lie in that ambivalence of attitude which allows us to recognize the intelligence and even the splendor of Meredith's work, while, at the same time, we experience a lack of sympathy, a failure of any enthusiasm of response?

The difficulty is not that the Meredithian prose places too much demand upon the reader's attentiveness. There is no "too much" of this kind that a work of art can require of us. *Tristram Shandy* requires as much or more. Even *Pride and Prejudice*, for all its simplicity of surface, asks that we read with as alert an attentiveness to the word. Henry James offers more sinuous verbal paths than Meredith, paths that demand more of concentration inasmuch as they may be marked only by commas or question marks or dots that signify a suspension or attenuation of the track of communication, where Meredith would set up crusty substantives for the mind's grasp to help it around corners. "The enjoyment of a work of art," James said,

> the acceptance of an irresistible illusion, constituting, to my sense, our highest experience of "luxury," the luxury is not greatest, by my conse-

quent measure, when the work asks for as little attention as possible. It is greatest, it is delightfully, divinely great, when we feel the surface, like the thick ice of the skater's pond, bear without cracking the strongest pressure we throw on it.[1]

And, indeed, it seems to be precisely where Meredith offers the toughest stylistic going that we enjoy him the most. This is true at least of *The Egoist,* if not of later work. Curiously, our very sense of a *virtue* of excrescence in the style is symptomatic of that failure of thoroughly significant communication which we feel in Meredith. It is symptomatic, but let us insist that it is not the failure itself; for to be felt as excrescence, even fine excrescence, style must be related to *something else* in the work to which it seems to be perilously appended—just as building ornament is sensed as excrescent only as we see it in relation to the building.

Nor is the difficulty a lack of sensitive craft and pattern. *The Egoist* is a beautifully planned novel. Its pace is assured and powerful; from the opening incident, when Willoughby, on the terrace with Constantia Durham, snubs the marine lieutenant and tosses off, "I'll send him a check," to the last, when he deliciously misfires his revenge in all directions at once, events march their complicated route with a large inevitability. The spatial, or plastic, conception of the book is as fine as its movement in time: Willoughby's fantastic rigidity is set around, like a Maypole, with a gay and urgent dance on ribbons; the flat-footed, muscle-bound, blown-jowled monolith of his self-importance is host to a lawn festival of delicate searchings, bright scurryings, mobile strategies of the intelligences whose living occasions he has tried to halter at his center.

Nor should we confuse Meredith's failure with his deliberate limitation of the comic drama to the scope of a lawn festival, or, as he says, in his "Prelude" on the Comic Spirit, to

> human nature in the drawing-room of civilized men and women, where we have no dust of the struggling outer world, no mire, no violent crashes . . .

In this "Prelude," he merely puts into manifesto a limitation which Jane Austen made; and in our reading of *Pride and Prejudice* we have sufficiently examined that limitation so that we should not need, now, to bring

[1] In *The Art of the Novel,* James's Critical Prefaces edited by R. P. Blackmur (New York: Charles Scribner's Sons, 1934), p. 304.

any question against a novelist on the grounds that he confines his interest to "human nature in the drawing-room." Human nature is as human there as anywhere else, its opportunities as full and as menacing as in a slum or a coal mine or a dust bowl or a snake pit. It is perhaps strategic to remind ourselves of this fact again here, before we go on to Henry James, for our understanding of James would indeed be stultified if we retained still any facile notion that "life" is deeper and thicker in certain material conditions than in others, among the masses than among the classes, on a street corner than in a drawing room, in a chamber pot than in a porcelain cup.

Mr. Wilson Follett, in his introduction to the Modern Library edition of *The Egoist*, approaches Meredith's dwindled reputation in another way, from the point of view of certain vast generational changes in philosophical and psychological assumptions as to the nature of personality. He says,

> The central fact, the change behind all changes, is the modern annihilation of the Will, both as a valid concept and as a working tool. Up to our own generation man had embraced the belief . . . that he was at least partly the master of his own fate; and, acting on that belief, he had often made his conviction actually work. It had the important pragmatic sanction that it made him feel at home in his world, a world of moral choice. It is among the ruins of that world that we now grope. We see ourselves as lost and rootless in a universe without meaning—victims of malevolently blind forces, in and outside ourselves, that predetermine our actions and reduce our will and our vaunted reason to mere delusive reflexes, behavioristic phenomena. Meredith represents a world of Will, a society of lives modifiable by Will; and that fact alone is enough to give our time the sensation of being divided from him by a span computable in nothing less than light-years.[2]

How, then, are we to understand the fact that George Eliot's universe, where moral choice traces its significant reign, is not similarly divided from us? Or, to use a modern example, how are we to justify our response of excited intelligence and conviction to a book like Albert Camus's *La Peste*, where the vocation of man, even man in despair, is seen as altruistic *willing*? It might, indeed, be argued that, in a world denuded of values

[2] New York: 1947, pp. xii–xiii. Reprinted with permission.

and meanings, dramas in which the will is an operative factor would have a greater poignancy of significance—at least potentially—than they could have in a world which took for granted the measurable effects of willing. It might be argued that, as the conception of the will has become more complicated, complicated by our knowledge that we act under "blind forces" which are our will while yet we will against them, dramas of human relationships under the aspect of personally willed modification would have a more intense interest for us because we would find in them a more complex significance, a greater ambiguity, than would be possible if the personal will were thought of as morally univocal and psychologically undivided. The fiction that has attracted us most in an "absurd" world whose expressive signature is the concentration camp is fiction in which the will, though viewed variously, is still the moral center of the composition: this is true—to take extreme cases—of those fictions in which the personal will is defeated, "absurdly" defeated, as in Kafka and Hardy; it is true of Hemingway's fictions, where the very meagerness of the area within the Nothing where the will can operate is the sign of its tragic nobility; it is true of those fictions that explore the possibilities of self-knowledge (knowledge of what it is that we "will," or of the will's capacity for modification, or of its need for reteaching by experience of the emotions and instincts it has neglected or denied), as in Conrad and James and much of Thomas Mann; it is true of those that explore the epic corruption of the will, as in Melville and Dostoevski. Generational changes in assumptions as to what the will is, how it works, whether it is practically operative or not, do not explain our distance from Meredith, for—so far as moral significance in fiction is concerned—our interest is still intensely in the concept of the will. It is probable that indifference to a work of art (after we have considered the work well) is never explained by the *kind* of "world view" or "life view" that it holds, no matter how alien from our own, but only by the lack of self-substantial coherency of that view of things as represented in the aesthetic form.

In connection with Meredith's view of the human world as a place where choices made by the personal will perceptibly affect reality, *The Egoist* offers, in its major elements, special reasons for a rapport with the modern reader which is nevertheless lacking. There are, in the book, two chief modes in which the effective will appears, represented by Willoughby's immalleable self-will, aspiring to a simplification of the universe on his own measure, and by Clara Middleton's delicate, mobile, searching will, aspiring to air, opportunity, multiplicity. As for Willoughby's effectiveness,

> *Through very love of self himself he slew,*

as his epitaph has it—certainly a pronounced victory of volition. The "comic drama of the suicide" illustrated by Willoughby's career is a drama that, in clinical rather than in English country-house materials, is fairly obsessive to modern interest. It is a drama that Dr. Karl Menninger has traced, uncomically, in *Man against Himself*. We find the note of it in W. H. Auden's poem "September 1, 1939."

> *The windiest militant trash*
> *Important Persons shout*
> *Is not so crude as our wish:*
> *What mad Nijinsky wrote*
> *About Diaghilev*
> *Is true of the normal heart;*
> *The error bred in the bone*
> *Of each woman and each man*
> *Craves what it cannot have,*
> *Not universal love,*
> *But to be loved alone.*[3]

Of the craving "to be loved alone" Meredith's Willoughby makes the necessary conversion into self-love, since we cannot be loved alone by anybody but ourselves. With Clara,

> He dragged her through the labyrinths of his penetralia, in his hungry coveting to be loved more and still more, more still, until imagination gave up the ghost, and he talked to her plain hearing like a monster.

Willoughby is the fetus in full panoply, clothing himself "at others' expense," enjoying, or seeking to enjoy, "without incurring the immense debtorship for a thing done," possessing "without obligation to the object possessed." These phrases are Meredith's description of the sentimentalist, Willoughby being the prime example; they are also descriptive of an embryo. Willoughby is the monster of the womb, imposing on drawing room and lawn his unearned adulthood, his fetal vaporousness supported by name, wealth, and "a leg," and his demands for osmotic nourish-

[3] *The Collected Poetry of W. H. Auden* (New York: Random House, Inc., 1945), p. 58.

ment as if society were but one huge placenta designed for his shelter and growth. With Willoughby we *should* have the utmost rapport, for we have learned fiercely to understand him, through our so broadly ramified education in the fetal and infantile proclivities of the adult.

Willoughby must be delivered, but unfortunately not as in a normal birth, from the womb to the world, for he has been wearing the world as a custom-made womb. His delivery is the delivery of other people from him, from the extravagance of their courtesy in allowing him to occupy them. Willoughby is the difficult occasion for other people to dis-entrail themselves, by the exercise of intelligence, from a strangling, homomorphic Cause; he is the occasion in revolt against which individuality and variety of will are realized. By courtesy, faith, habit, and social exigency Clara Middleton and Vernon Whitford and Laetitia Dale find themselves in the kissing arms of this octopus, fanned on by the aunts, by Dr. Middleton's taste in port, and by a society of submarine fantasies and chattering twilight expectations. They extricate themselves, with difficulty, by learning to recognize meaning in experience and by acting on the recognition. "The drama of Meredith's characters," Ramon Fernandez says,

> is always and essentially the drama of an exacting sensibility. They begin by going straight ahead, in the direction of life, along the road of action. Their first acts, however rich and generous they may be, are simple, normal, not to say conventional . . . Since they can live only by acting, they act at first in perfect harmony with the circle in which tradition has caused them to be born. But then sensibility, at the first collision, is awakened. They feel confusedly that they can no longer live in the conditions which at first they accepted. And there they are, thrown back upon themselves, attentive, on the alert, seeking anxiously among the echoes of experience the key to the enigma which shall deliver them. To live for them is to seek to think, but to think in order to be able afresh to breathe, act, and bloom.[4]

The nobility, the interest, the viability of this conception of character we cannot but acknowledge, and we make the acknowledgment the more readily as Meredith's view of life touches off with electric irony, and almost as if allegorically, certain grim features, both psychological and political, of our own condition.

[4] *Messages* (New York: Harcourt, Brace & Company, Inc., 1927), p. 175.

Why, then, do we find ourselves indifferent? "Not a difficulty met," James said of Meredith, speaking as a novelist about a novelist,

> not a figure presented, not a scene constituted—not a dim shadow condensing once into audible or visible reality—making you hear for an instant the tap of its feet on the earth.[5]

This is perhaps to go too far, particularly between novelists who are so much akin—in respect at least of stylistic elaboration, the social setting, the delicate development of a consciousness of values—as James is to Meredith in *The Egoist*. But it is indicative. Willoughby is a victim in wax model, Virginia Woolf said, not flesh and blood: he "is turned slowly round before a steady fire of scrutiny and criticism which allows no twitch on the victim's part to escape it" [6]—a process that, on description, looks as unfair as other destructive magical rites, as unfair as torture for confession. The fact is that Willoughby is treated as a perfectly lonely aberration, a freak; nobody (neither we as readers nor anyone in the book) knows how he came about, how he happened, what he is for, what connection there might be between his psychological peculiarities and the human soul at large. We do not really supply the connections when we say, "There is a Willoughby in each of us," for though the statement seems valid enough, its validity lies outside the book and not structurally within it: *within* the book there are no Willoughbys except Willoughby. Meredith makes similarly extraneous statements about Willoughby's human representativeness, but they remain dogmatic, without internal aesthetic corroboration. From the earliest note we have of his youth,

> "When he was a child he one day mounted a chair, and there he stood in danger, would not let us touch him, because he was taller than we, and we were to gaze. Do you remember him, Eleanor? 'I am the sun of the house!' It was inimitable!"

he is uncaused, a prodigy; and his career in maturity has only an external relatedness—a relatedness of exploitation—to other people; he is an obstacle to them, an ingratiating and portentous obstacle, but quite definitively outside of them, not inside. That we are not, *aesthetically*, given

[5] Quoted by Siegfried Sassoon, in *Meredith* (New York: The Viking Press, Inc., 1948), p. 232.

[6] *The Second Common Reader* (New York: Harcourt, Brace & Company, Inc., 1932), pp. 252–253.

any insight as to what subtle internal bonds there might be between Willoughby and society—what, in the social soul, was itself Willoughby in order to fertilize this monster—or as to what taint of identity there might be between the soul of Willoughby and the soul of anybody else, makes us restless with his image, powerfully as that image is drawn, for he has evidently much too important a symbolic potential to be left so without spiritual relations, so unproliferative of the possible meanings he might have either for the constitution of the body politic or for that of the private psyche.

Like the giant of *Jack and the Beanstalk,* he is an external menace only, not a suffered portion of self or of the cultural conditions of self. That giant's feet did not touch the earth, because, after the scramble of escape, the stalk was cut down at a single blow. At the end of *The Egoist,* a dozen people—all the world—take whacks with free conscience at the beanstalk. Jane Austen's Mr. Collins, in *Pride and Prejudice,* is a monster quite in the fetal style of Willoughby, but Mr. Collins has the spiritual support of a society of other monsters with common economic causes, and the menace that he offers is one that, graded from grotesque obviousness to inconspicuous subtlety, is distributed through the social organism, pervasive in the private soul, providing the common stuff of the very language—thus truly dangerous because unconsciously environing. Mr. Collins—that is, the representative qualities of Mr. Collins, the complacencies of egoism backed by desperations of economic footing and caste, in a culture contracted to their measure—cannot really be escaped, even by happy marriages and removals, but must be dealt with alertly at every moment as the condition of existence.

Henry James's Osmond, in *The Portrait of a Lady,* also affords parallels with Willoughby, and again the difference in treatment is significant of Meredith's failure to give his egoist a spiritual context. *The Egoist* is of the year 1877; *The Portrait of a Lady,* 1881. We should not wish to force an unwarranted meaning upon these dates, but they do provide a curious comment on the parallels between the two books, particularly in view of James's opinion of Meredith. Health, wealth, and beauty are the qualifications Willoughby demands in his bride; she must also

> come to him out of cloistral purity . . . out of an egg-shell, somewhat more astonished at things than a chick . . . and seeing him with her sex's eyes first of all men.

It is a note sounded also by Osmond, in James's *Portrait,* and we hear in it almost the same comic exaggeration. He asks, concerning Isabel, who has been suggested to him as a possible bride,

> "Is she beautiful, clever, rich, splendid, universally intelligent and unprecedentedly virtuous? It's only on those conditions that I care to make her acquaintance."

Contempt for "the world" is the breath of life to both Willoughby and Osmond; their need to scorn it and set themselves and their possessions apart from it is the inspiration of their existence, on the principle that "the world" must admire where it is scorned and pay to the scorner the tribute of its own helpless vulgarity. For Willoughby,

> The breath of the world, the world's view of him, was partly his vital breath, his view of himself . . . [He was] born to look down upon a tributary world, and to exult in being looked to. Do we wonder at his consternation in the prospect of that world's blowing foul upon him? Princes have their obligations to teach them they are mortal, and the brilliant heir of a tributary world is equally enchained by the homage it brings him . . .

And for Osmond,

> To surround his interior with a sort of invidious sanctity, to tantalise society with a sense of exclusion, to make people believe his house was different from every other, to impart to the face that he presented to the world a cold originality—this was the ingenious effort of the personage to whom Isabel had attributed a superior morality . . . under the guise of caring only for intrinsic values Osmond lived exclusively for the world . . .

These parallelisms—and others—almost suggest that James deliberately used the pattern conceived by Meredith. But how much more he discovered in it! The difference lies in a sense of spiritual context. Willoughby appears without "internal relations" with the society he dominates or with the individuals whose self-development he attempts to suffocate; he is, moreover, personally valueless, a formal abstraction of conceit without any other palpable qualification than a "leg." Osmond is incomparably a subtler evil, for he does represent values, and when he says—in the magnificent scene in which he forbids Isabel to go to England—

> "I think we should accept the consequences of our actions, and what I value most in life is the honour of a thing!"

the gravity of his sincerity, speaking, as Isabel realizes, in the name of "something sacred and precious," is in perfect measure with his blasphemy against *precisely the same values* as his wife interprets them. The menace that he offers is a menace within Isabel herself, in her recognition of the spiritual density and integrity of a man so corrupt. Osmond speaks her own language, for it is in "the honour of a thing" and in accepting "the consequences of her actions" that she finds her own moral identity; the menace, the confusion that cripples decision, lies in the formal similarity of their moral aspirations and the appalling dissimilarity of the interpretations these yield to each. Osmond has roots and ramifications: he is supported not only by human accomplices in his peculiarly subtle guilt, but by ages of value growth thoroughly intelligential, by Rome itself, by Europe, by Isabel's own passion for a finer experience. It is Osmond's spiritual context, his "internal relations" with society and with individuals, that make him so meaningful a figure. It is Willoughby's lack of such context that makes him a *bibelot* of literature.

The prose style of *The Egoist,* intensely nervous and packed, constantly inventive, has somewhat the same status of an abnormal and eccentric growth as does Willoughby, and in this sense Siegfried Sassoon's remark that the phraseology of the book "is an artifice which seems appropriate" [7] has an unintended rightness. The style is beautifully wrought, as is the figure of Willoughby himself; we cannot deny it its qualities of virtu. Again and again the vivid and witty image concretizes a state of mind. There is Willoughby's agony over the threatened defection of Clara.

> The fact that she was a healthy young woman returned to the surface of his thoughts like the murdered body pitched into the river, which will not drown, and calls upon the elements of dissolution to float it.

Or the quality of his pathos with Laetitia:

[7] *Op. cit.,* p. 208.

> As his desire was merely to move her without an exposure of himself, he had to compass being pathetic as it were under the impediments of a mailed and gauntleted knight, who can not easily heave the bosom, or show it heaving.

Or his torments of decision:

> Laocoon of his own serpents, he struggled to a certain magnificence of attitude in the muscular net of constrictions he flung round himself.

It is of this kind of stylistic virtuosity that Ramon Fernandez speaks when he says that Meredith's "artifice" consists

> in representing the most concrete possible equivalent for a mental movement . . . Meredith fills in the intervals of the action with little symbolical actions because he is anxious above all not to let his thought and that of the reader lose their dramatic rhythm.[8]

His images, Fernandez says, thus constitute "a defense system against abstraction." Since the definitive and suicidal characteristic of the egoist is his abstraction from the living world, a style so full of concrete images and tough little verbal dramas has its peculiar logic here, for it keeps the egoist within our ken; he might otherwise lose his liveliness and dissolve into his own sentimental vapor. Yet, attractive as is this rationalization of style, one asks if there is not a fallacy in throwing so much of the burden of concreteness upon style and if the concreteness most necessary to fiction does not lie in that spiritual *contextualism* of lives which we have noticed as lacking in *The Egoist*. Where such context strongly exists and style subserves it, is not the concreteness there too—the concreteness that makes the created world of a novel excitedly meaningful "for us"? Where it does not exist, and style is called upon to substitute for it by energy and picture, is not style forced into an unnatural position where it figures as a kind of "egoist" itself—a separated, self-willed, self-regarding element? In what is surely one of the most abstract vocabularies in fiction, and one of the least "image-making" of styles, Jane Austen evoked a concrete world that is meaningful "for us" because, like a world, it exists in the autonomy of its own internal relations.

On Meredith's style is imposed a somewhat desperate function of

8 *Op. cit.*, p. 171.

keeping author, characters, and reader in a state of awareness, not so much of what is going on, but of each other, a function of keeping us awake to the fact that we are reading a brilliant book by an exceptionally intelligent author about highly burnished characters—all of which the style makes us ever so ready to admit. One thinks of Milton here, for Meredith's style has its brilliance as Milton's has its "grandness," and in reading Milton one has to hang on by the words and the astonishing verbal manipulation if sometimes by nothing else. What Desmond McCarthy said of Meredith might be said of Milton: "It must be remembered in reading Meredith that half his touches are not intended to help you to realize the object so much as to put power into the form." [9] The statement applied to Meredith makes only a fumbling kind of sense, inasmuch as it divides the "form" from the "object," and what we see as failure in Meredith is just this division of form and object, the division of the elegant pattern and splendid style of the book from potential meaning, from potential relationships between characters and thus potential relationships with ourselves. Applied to Milton, it has a good deal more sense, and the difference lies here. One feels that, in a highly special and deeply meaningful way, the Miltonic style *is* "the object"; one feels that the verbal manipulation is the mind's desperate exhibition of its independence and strength, working on the plastic stuff of the word in a frightful vacuum of other stuff adequately tough to reward the worker's gift and exertion—the mind is with its "back to the wall," so to speak, in the position of Lucifer; one feels that this is the moral kinetics which, in Milton, is profoundly "the object," and that the "power" of Milton's language is the same as that satanic power which moved a causeway through empty space from hell to earth. We cannot say so much of Meredith. Style is here a brilliant manner, and, with some embarrassment—for we would not be without the pleasures Meredith provides—we would quote Dr. Middleton on style in the author's own admirably intelligent style:

> "You see how easy it is to deceive one who is an artist in phrases. Avoid them, Miss Dale; they dazzle the penetration of the composer. That is why people of ability like Mrs. Mountstuart see so little; they are bent on describing brilliantly."

[9] Quoted by Siegfried Sassoon, *op. cit.,* p. 210.

ON *Tess of the D'Urbervilles*

It was Hardy who said of Meredith that "he would not, or could not —at any rate did not—when aiming to represent the 'Comic Spirit,' let himself discover the tragedy that always underlies comedy if you only scratch deeply enough." Hardy's statement does not really suggest that comedy is somehow tragedy *manqué*, that writers of comedy would write tragedies if they only "scratched deeply enough." What he says is what Socrates said to Aristophanes and Agathon at the end of the *Symposium* —that the genius of tragedy is the same as that of comedy. It is what Cervantes knew, whose great comic hero, Quixote, walks in the same shades with Orestes and Oedipus, Hamlet and Lear. It is what Molière knew. Even Jane Austen knew it. The precariousness of moral consciousness in its brute instinctual and physical circumstances, its fragility as an instrument for the regeneration of the will: this generic disproportion in the human condition comedy develops by grotesque enlargement of one or another aberrated faculty; tragedy, by grotesque enlargement of the imbalance between human motive and the effect of action. The special point to our purpose is, however, another: neither tragic figure nor comic figure is merely phenomenal and spectacular if it truly serves the function common to both genres—the catharsis; acting as scapegoats for the absurdity of the human dilemma, they are humanity's thoughtful or intuitive comment on itself. We return, thus, deviously by way of the kinship of tragedy and comedy, to the matter of "internal relations." The human condition, whether in the "drawing-room of civilized men and women" or on a wild heath in ancient Britain, shows, if scratched deeply enough, the binding ironies that bind the spectacular destiny of the hero with the unspectacular common destiny; and it is in the internal relations of the art form, the aesthetic structure, that these bonds have symbolic representation. The aesthetic failure of *The Egoist* is thus a diagnostic mark of a crucial failure of vision, a weakness and withdrawal of vision before the common dilemma and the common destiny.

To turn to one of Hardy's great tragic novels is to put "internal relations" in the novel to peculiar test, for there is perhaps no other novelist, of a stature equal to Hardy's, who so stubbornly and flagrantly foisted upon the novel elements resistant to aesthetic cohesion. We shall want to speak of these elements first, simply to clear away and free ourselves from the temptation to appraise Hardy by his "philosophy"—that is, the temptation to mistake bits of philosophic adhesive tape, rather dampened and rumpled by time, for the deeply animated vision of experience which our novel, *Tess*, holds. We can quickly summon examples, for they crop out obviously enough. Before one has got beyond twenty pages one finds this paragraph on the ignominy and helplessness of the human estate:

> All these young souls were passengers in the Durbeyfield ship—entirely dependent on the judgment of the two Durbeyfield adults for their pleasures, their necessities, their health, even their existence. If the heads of the Durbeyfield household chose to sail into difficulty, disaster, starvation, disease, degradation, death, thither were these half-dozen little captives under hatches compelled to sail with them—six helpless creatures, who had never been asked if they wished for life on any terms, much less if they wished for it on such hard conditions as were involved in being of the shiftless house of Durbeyfield. Some people would like to know whence the poet whose philosophy is in these days deemed as profound and trustworthy as his song is sweet and pure, gets his authority for speaking of "Nature's holy plan."

Whenever, in this book, Hardy finds either a butt or a sanction in a poet, one can expect the inevitable intrusion of a form of discourse that infers proofs and opinions and competition in "truth" that belongs to an intellectual battlefield alien from the novel's imaginative concretions. On the eve of the Durbeyfield family's forced deracination and migration, we are told that

> to Tess, as to some few millions of others, there was ghastly satire in the poet's lines:

> *Not in utter nakedness*
> *But trailing clouds of glory do we come.*

To her and her like, birth itself was an ordeal of degrading personal compulsion, whose gratuitousness nothing in the result seemed to justify, and at best could only palliate.

Aside from the fact that no circumstances have been suggested in which Tess could have had time or opportunity or the requisite development of critical aptitudes to brood so formidably on Wordsworth's lines, who are those "few millions" who are the "like" of Tess? as, who are the "some people" in the previous quotation? and in what way do these statistical generalizations add to the already sufficient meaning of Tess's situation? At the end of the book, with the "Aeschylean phrase" on the sport of the gods, we feel again that intrusion of a commentary which belongs to another order of discourse. The gibbet is enough. The vision is deep and clear and can only be marred by any exploitation of it as a datum in support of abstraction. We could even do without the note of "ameliorism" in the joined hands of Clare and Tess's younger sister at the end: the philosophy of an evolutionary hope has nothing essential to do with Tess's fate and her common meaning; she is too humanly adequate for evolutionary ethics to comment upon, and furthermore we do not believe that young girls make ameliorated lives out of witness of a sister's hanging.

What philosophical vision honestly inheres in a novel inheres as the signifying form of a certain concrete body of experience; it is what the experience "means" because it is what, structurally, the experience *is*. When it can be loosened away from the novel to compete in the general field of abstract truth—as frequently in Hardy—it has the weakness of any abstraction that statistics and history and science may be allowed to criticize; whether true or false for one generation or another, or for one reader or another, or even for one personal mood or another, its status as truth is relative to conditions of evidence and belief existing outside the novel and existing there quite irrelevant to whatever body of particularized life the novel itself might contain. But as a structural principle active within the particulars of the novel, local and inherent there through a maximum of organic dependencies, the philosophical vision has the unassailable truth of living form.

We wish to press this difference a bit further by considering—deliberately in a few minor instances, for in the minor notation is the furthest reach of form—the internality and essentiality of Hardy's vision, just as we have previously considered instances of its externalization and devitalization. Significantly, his "ideas" remain the same in either case. They are abruptly articulated in incident, early in the book, with the death of Prince, appearing here with almost ideographical simplicity.

> The morning mail-cart, with its two noiseless wheels, speeding along these lanes like an arrow, as it always did, had driven into [Tess's] slow and unlighted equipage. The pointed shaft of the cart had entered the breast of the unhappy Prince like a sword, and from the wound his life's blood was spouting in a stream, and falling with a hiss into the road.
> In her despair Tess sprang forward and put her hand upon the hole, with the only result that she became splashed from face to skirt with the crimson drops . . .

The mail cart leaves, and she remains alone on the road with the ruin.

> The atmosphere turned pale; the birds shook themselves in the hedges, arose, and twittered; the lane showed all its white features, and Tess showed hers, still whiter. The huge pool of blood in front of her was already assuming the iridescence of coagulation; and when the sun rose, a million prismatic hues were reflected in it. Prince lay alongside still and stark, his eyes half open, the hole in his chest looking scarcely large enough to have let out all that had animated him.

With this accident are concatenated in fatal union Tess's going to "claim kin" of the D'Urbervilles and all the other links in her tragedy down to the murder of Alec. The symbolism of the detail is naïve and forthright to the point of temerity: the accident occurs in darkness and Tess has fallen asleep—just as the whole system of mischances and cross-purposes in the novel is a function of psychic and cosmic blindness; she "put her hand upon the hole"—and the gesture is as absurdly ineffectual as all her effort will be; the only result is that she becomes splashed with blood—as she will be at the end; the shaft pierces Prince's breast "like a sword"—Alec is stabbed in the heart with a knife; with the arousal and twittering of the birds we are aware of the oblivious manifold of nature stretching infinite and detached beyond the isolated human figure; the iridescence of the coagulating blood is, in its incongruity with the dark human trouble, a note of the same indifferent cosmic chemistry that has

198

brought about the accident; and the smallness of the hole in Prince's chest, that looked "scarcely large enough to have let out all that had animated him," is the minor remark of that irony by which Tess's great cruel trial appears as a vanishing incidental in the blind waste of time and space and biological repetition. Nevertheless, there is nothing in this event that has not the natural "grain" of concrete fact; and what it signifies—of the complicity of doom with the most random occurrence, of the cross-purposing of purpose in a multiple world, of cosmic indifference and of moral desolation—is a local truth of a particular experience and irrefutable as the experience itself.

In the second chapter of *Tess* the gathering for the May-day "club-walking" is described, a debased "local Cerealia" that has lost its ancient motive as fertility rite and that subsists as a social habit among the village young people. Here Clare sees Tess for the first time, in white dress, with peeled willow wand and bunch of white flowers. But it is too late for him to stop, the clock has struck, he must be on his way to join his companions. Later, when he wants to marry Tess, he will tell his parents of the "pure and virtuous" bride he has chosen, when her robe is no longer the white robe of the May-walking but the chameleon robe of Queen Guinevere,

> *That never would become that wife*
> *That had once done amiss.*

In the scene of the May-walking, the lovers are "star-crossed" not by obscure celestial intent but by ordinary multiplicity of purposes and suitabilities; but in the submerged and debased fertility ritual—ironically doubled here with the symbolism of the white dress (a symbolism which Clare himself will later debase by his prudish perversity)—is shadowed a more savage doom brought about by a more violent potency, that of sexual instinct, by which Tess will be victimized. Owing its form entirely to the vision that shapes the whole of Tess's tragedy, the minor incident of the May-walking has the assurance of particularized reality and the truth of the naturally given.

Nothing could be more brutally factual than the description of the swede field at Flintcomb-Ash, nor convey more economically and transparently Hardy's vision of human abandonment in the dissevering earth.

> The upper half of each turnip had been eaten off by the live-stock, and it was the business of the two women to grub out the lower or earthy half of the root with a hooked fork called a hacker, that this might

be eaten also. Every leaf of the vegetable having previously been consumed, the whole field was in color a desolate drab; it was a complexion without features, as if a face, from chin to brow, should be only an expanse of skin. The sky wore, in another color, the same likeness; a white vacuity of expression with the lineaments gone.

The visitation of the winter birds has the same grain of local reality, and yet all the signifying and representative disaster of Tess's situation—its loneliness, its bleak triviality, its irrelevance in the dumb digestion of earth—is focused in the mirroring eyes of the birds.

> . . . strange birds from behind the North Pole began to arrive silently . . . gaunt spectral creatures with tragical eyes—eyes which had witnessed scenes of cataclysmal horror in inaccessible polar regions, of a magnitude such as no human being had ever conceived, in curdling temperatures that no man could endure; which had beheld the crash of icebergs and the slide of snow-hills by the shooting light of the Aurora; been half blinded by the whirl of colossal storms and terraqueous distortions; and retained the expression of feature that such scenes had engendered. These nameless birds came quite near to Tess and Marian, but of all they had seen which humanity would never see they brought no account. The traveller's ambition to tell was not theirs, and, with dumb impassivity, they dismissed experiences which they did not value for the immediate incidents of this upland—the trivial movements of the two girls in disturbing the clods with their fragile hackers so as to uncover something or other that these visitants relished as food.

There is the same sensitive honesty to the detail and expression of fact, the same inherence of vision in the particulars of experience, in the description of the weeds where Tess hears Clare thrumming his harp.

> The outskirt of the garden in which Tess found herself had been left uncultivated for some years, and was now damp and rank with juicy grass which sent up mists of pollen; and tall blooming weeds, emitting offensive smells—weeds whose red and yellow and purple hues formed a polychrome as dazzling as that of cultivated flowers. She went stealthily as a cat through this profusion of growth, gathering cuckoo-spittle on her skirts, brushing off snails that were climbing the apple-tree stems, staining her hands with thistle-milk and slug-slime, and rubbing off upon her naked arms sticky blights that, though snow-

white on the tree-trunks, made blood-red stains on her skin; thus she drew quite near to Clare, though still unobserved of him.

The weeds, circumstantial as they are, have an astonishingly cunning and bold metaphorical function. They grow at Talbothays, in that healing procreative idyl of milk and mist and passive biology, and they too are bountiful with life, but they stain and slime and blight; and it is in this part of Paradise (an "outskirt of the garden"—there are even apple trees here) that the minister's son is hidden, who, in his conceited impotence, will violate Tess more nastily than her sensual seducer: who but Hardy would have dared to give him the name Angel, and a harp too? It is Hardy's incorruptible feeling for the actual that allows his symbolism its amazingly blunt privileges and that at the same time subdues it to and absorbs it into the concrete circumstance of experience, real as touch.

The dilemma of Tess is the dilemma of morally individualizing consciousness in its earthy mixture. The subject is mythological, for it places the human protagonist in dramatic relationship with the nonhuman and orients his destiny among preternatural powers. The most primitive antagonist of consciousness is, on the simplest premise, the earth itself. It acts so in *Tess,* clogging action and defying conscious motive; or, in the long dream of Talbothays, conspiring with its ancient sensuality to provoke instinct; or, on the farm at Flintcomb-Ash, demoralizing consciousness by its mere geological flintiness. But the earth is "natural," while, dramatically visualized as antagonist, it transcends the natural. The integrity of the myth thus depends, paradoxically, upon naturalism; and it is because of that intimate dependence between the natural and the mythological, a dependence that is organic to the subject, that Hardy's vision is able to impregnate so deeply and shape so unobtrusively the naturalistic particulars of the story.

In *Tess,* of all his novels, the earth is most actual as a dramatic factor —that is, as a factor of causation; and by this we refer simply to the long stretches of earth that have to be trudged in order that a person may get from one place to another, the slowness of the business, the irreducible reality of it (for one has only one's feet), its grimness of soul-wearying fatigue and shelterlessness and doubtful issue at the other end of the journey where nobody may be at home. One thinks, in immediate comparison, of Egdon Heath in *The Return of the Native*. Except for one instance—when Mrs. Yeobright has a far walk to Clym's cottage, and Clym, unforewarned, fails to meet her, and she turns away—the heath in *The Return* exists peripherally and gratuitously in relation to the action, on the one hand as the place where the action happens to happen (an action has to happen somewhere), and on the other, as a metaphor—a metaphorical reflection of the loneliness of human motive, of the inertia of unconscious life, of the mystery of the enfolding darkness; but it is not a dramatically causative agent and its particular quality is not *dramatically* necessary. In *The Mayor of Casterbridge,* the Roman ruins round about the town of Casterbridge are a rather more complicated metaphor, for they are works of man that have fallen into earth; they speak mutely of the anonymity of human effort in historical as well as in geological time; their presence suggests also the classic pattern of the Mayor's tragedy, the ancient repetitiveness of self-destruction; and they provide thus a kind of guarantee or confirming signature of the heroism of the doomed human enterprise. But the Mayor could have had his tragedy in a town with no Roman ruins about it at all; they are, even more than Egdon Heath, gratuitous, and their gratuitousness leads Hardy into some pedantry of documentation to support their metaphorical standing in the story. In *Tess* the earth is *primarily not a metaphor but a real thing* that one has to move on in order to get anywhere or do anything, and it constantly acts in its own motivating, causational substantiality by being there in the way of human purposes to encounter, to harass them, detour them, seduce them, defeat them.

In the accident of Prince's death, the road itself is, in a manner of speaking, responsible, merely by being the same road that the mail cart travels. The seduction of Tess is as closely related, causally, to the distance between Trantridge and Chaseborough as it is to Tess's naïveté and to Alec's egoism; the physical distance itself causes Tess's fatigue and provides Alec's opportunity. The insidiously demoralizing effect of Tess's desolate journeys on foot as she seeks dairy work and field work here and there after the collapse of her marriage, brutal months that are foreshortened to the plodding trip over the chalk uplands to Flintcomb-Ash, is, again, as directly as anything, an effect of the irreducible *thereness* of the territory she has to cover. There are other fatal elements in her ineffectual trip from the farm to Emminster to see Clare's parents, but fatal above all is the distance she must walk to see people who can have no foreknowledge of her coming and who are not at home when she gets there. Finally, with the uprooting and migration of the Durbeyfield family on Old Lady Day, the simple fatality of the earth as earth, in its measure-lessness and anonymousness, with people having to move over it with no place to go, is decisive in the final event of Tess's tragedy—her return to Alec, for Alec provides at least a place to go.

The dramatic motivation provided by natural earth is central to every aspect of the book. It controls the style: page by page *Tess* has a wrought density of texture that is fairly unique in Hardy; symbolic depth is communicated by the physical surface of things with unhampered transparency while the homeliest conviction of fact is preserved ("The upper half of each turnip had been eaten off by the live-stock"); and one is aware of style not as a specifically verbal quality but as a quality of observation and intuition that are here—very often—wonderfully identical with each other, a quality of lucidity. Again, it is because of the *actual* motivational impact of the earth that Hardy is able to use setting and atmosphere for a symbolism that, considered in itself, is so astonishingly blunt and rudimentary. The green vale of Blackmoor, fertile, small, enclosed by hills, lying under a blue haze—the vale of birth, the cradle of innocence. The wide misty setting of Talbothays dairy, "oozing fatness and warm ferments," where the "rush of juices could almost be heard below the hiss of fertilization"—the sensual dream, the lost Paradise. The starved uplands of Flintcomb-Ash, with their ironic mimicry of the organs of generation, "myriads of loose white flints in bulbous, cusped, and phallic shapes," and the dun consuming ruin of the swede field—the mockery of impotence, the exile. Finally, that immensely courageous use of setting, Stonehenge and the stone of sacrifice. Obvious as these symbolisms are, their deep stress is maintained by Hardy's naturalistic premise. The earth exists here as Final Cause, and its omnipresence affords constantly to Hardy the textures that excited his eye and care, but affords them wholly charged with dramatic, causational necessity; and the symbolic values of setting are constituted, in large part, by the responses required of the characters themselves in their relationship with the earth.

Generally, the narrative system of the book—that is, the system of episodes—is a series of accidents and coincidences (although it is important to note that the really great crises are psychologically motivated: Alec's seduction of Tess, Clare's rejection of her, and the murder). It is accident that Clare does not meet Tess at the May-walking, when she was "pure" and when he might have begun to court her; coincidence that the mail cart rams Tess's wagon and kills Prince; coincidence that Tess and Clare meet at Talbothays, *after* her "trouble" rather than before; accident that the letter slips under the rug; coincidence that Clare's parents are not at home when she comes to the vicarage; and so on. Superficially it would seem that this type of event, the accidental and coincidental, is the very least credible of fictional devices, particularly when there is an accumulation of them; and we have all read or heard criticism of Hardy for his excessive reliance upon coincidence in the management of his narratives; if his invention of probabilities and inevitabilities of action does not seem simply poverty-stricken, he appears to be too much the puppeteer working wires or strings to make events conform to his "pessimistic" and "fatalistic" ideas. It is not enough to say that there is a certain justification for his large use of the accidental in the fact that "life is like that"—chance, mishap, accident, events that affect our lives while they remain far beyond our control, are a very large part of experience; but art differs from life precisely by making order out of this disorder, by finding causation in it. In the accidentalism of Hardy's universe we can recognize the profound truth of the darkness in which life is cast, darkness both within the soul and without, only insofar as his accidentalism *is not itself accidental* nor yet an ideology-obsessed puppeteer's manipulation of character and event; which is to say, only insofar as the universe he creates has aesthetic integrity, the flesh and bones and organic development of a concrete world. This is not true always of even the best of Hardy's novels; but it is so generally true of the construction of *Tess*—a novel in which the accidental is perhaps more preponderant than in any other Hardy—that we do not care to finick about incidental lapses. The naturalistic premise of the book—the condition of earth in which life is placed—is the most obvious, fundamental, and inexorable of facts; but because it is the physically "given," into which and beyond which there can be no penetration, it exists as mystery; it is thus, even as the basis of all natural manifestation, itself of the quality of the supernatural. On the earth, so conceived, coincidence and accident constitute order, the prime terrestrial order, for they too are "the given," impenetrable by human *ratio*, accountable only as mystery. By constructing the *Tess*-universe on the solid ground (one might say even literally on the "ground") of the earth as Final Cause, mysterious cause of causes, Hardy does not allow us to forget that what is most concrete in experience is also what is most inscrutable, that an overturned clod in a field or the posture of herons standing in a water mead or the shadows of cows thrown against a wall by evening sunlight are as essentially fathomless as the procreative yearning, and this in turn as fathomless as the sheerest accident in event. The accidentalism and coincidentalism in the narrative pattern of the book stand, thus, in perfectly orderly correlation with the grounding mystery of the physically concrete and the natural.

But Hardy has, with very great cunning, reinforced the *necessity* of this particular kind of narrative pattern by giving to it the background of the folk instinctivism, folk fatalism, and folk magic. If the narrative is conducted largely by coincidence, the broad folk background rationalizes coincidence by constant recognition of the mysteriously "given" as what "was to be"—the folk's humble presumption of order in a rule of mishap. The folk are the earth's pseudopodia, another fauna; and because they are so deeply rooted in the elemental life of the earth—like a sensitive animal extension of the earth itself—they share the authority of the natural. (Whether Hardy's "folk," in all the attributes he gives them, ever existed historically or not is scarcely pertinent; they exist here.) Their philosophy and their skills in living, even their gestures of tragic violence, are instinctive adaptations to "the given"; and because they are indestructible, their attitudes toward events authoritatively urge a similar fatalism upon the reader, impelling him to an imaginative acceptance of the doom-wrought series of accidents in the foreground of the action.

We have said that the dilemma of Tess is the dilemma of moral consciousness in its intractable earthy mixture; schematically simplified, the signifying form of the *Tess*-universe is the tragic heroism and tragic ineffectuality of such consciousness in an antagonistic earth where events shape themselves by accident rather than by moral design; and the *mythological* dimension of this form lies precisely in the earth's antagonism—for what is persistently antagonistic appears to have its own intentions, in this case mysterious, supernatural, for it is only thus that the earth can seem to have "intentions." The folk are the bridge between mere earth and moral individuality; of the earth as they are, separable conscious ego does not arise among them to weaken animal instinct and confuse response— it is the sports, the deracinated ones, like Tess and Clare and Alec, who are morally individualized and who are therefore able to suffer isolation, alienation, and abandonment, or to make others so suffer; the folk, while they remain folk, cannot be individually isolated, alienated, or lost, for they are amoral and their existence is colonial rather than personal. (There is no finer note of this matter—fine in factual and symbolic precision, and in its very inconspicuousness—than the paragraph describing the loaded wagons of the migrating families:

> The day being the sixth of April, the Durbeyfield wagon met many other wagons with families on the summit of the load, which was built on a well-nigh unvarying principle, as peculiar, probably, to the rural laborer as the hexagon to the bee. The groundwork of the arrangement was the position of the family dresser, which, with its shining handles, and finger marks, and domestic evidences thick upon it, stood importantly in front, over the tails of the shaft-horses, in its erect and natural position, like some Ark of the Covenant which must not be carried slightingly.

Even in the event of mass uprooting, the folk character that is preserved is that of the tenacious, the colonial, the instinctive, for which Hardy finds the simile of the hexagon of the bee, converting it then, with Miltonic boldness, to its humanly tribal significance with the simile of the Ark of the Covenant.) Their fatalism is communal and ritual, an instinctive adaptation as accommodating to bad as to good weather, to misfortune as to luck, to birth as to death, a subjective economy by which emotion is subdued to the falling out of event and the destructiveness of resistance is avoided. In their fatalism lies their survival wisdom, as against the death direction of all moral deliberation. There is this wisdom in the cheerful compassion of the fieldwomen for Tess in her time of trouble: the trouble "was to be." It is in Joan Durbeyfield's Elizabethan ditties of lullaby:

> *I saw her lie do-own in yon-der green gro—ve;*
> *Come, love, and I'll tell you where.*

—the kind of ditty by which women of the folk induce maturity in the child by lulling him to sleep with visions of seduction, adultery, and despair. It is in the folk code of secrecy—as in Dairyman Crick's story of the widow who married Jack Dollop, or in Joan's letter of advice to her daughter, summoning the witness of ladies the highest in the land who had had their "trouble" too but who had not told. Tess's tragedy turns on a secret revealed, that is, on the substitution in Tess of an individualizing morality for the folk instinct of concealment and anonymity.

While their fatalism is a passive adaptation to the earthy doom, the folk magic is an active luxury: the human being, having a mind, however incongruous with his animal condition, has to do something with it—and if the butter will not come and someone is in love in the house, the coexistence of the two facts offers a mental exercise in causation (though this is not really the "rights o't," about the butter, as Dairyman Crick himself observes; magical lore is not so dainty); yet the magic is no less a survival wisdom than the fatalism, inasmuch as it does offer mental exercise in causation, for man cannot live without a sense of cause. The magic is a knowledgeable mode of dealing with the unknowledgeable, and it is adaptive to the dooms of existence where moral reason is not adaptive, for moral reason seeks congruence between human intention and effect and is therefore always inapropos (in Hardy's universe, tragically inapropos), whereas magic seeks only likenesses, correspondences, analogies, and these are everywhere. Moral reason is in complete incommunication with the "given," for it cannot accept the "given" as such, cannot accept accident, cannot accept the obscure activities of instinct, cannot accept doom; but magic can not only accept but rationalize all these, for the correspondences that determine its strategies are themselves "given"—like is like, and that is the end of the matter. As the folk fatalism imbues the foreground accidents with the suggestion of necessity, the folk magic imbues them with the suggestion of the supernaturally motivated; and motivation of whatever kind makes an event seem "necessary," suitable, fitting. The intricate interknitting of all these motifs gives to Hardy's actually magical view of the universe and of human destiny a backing of concrete life, as his evocation of the earth as Cause gives to his vision the grounding of the naturalistic.

The folk magic is, after all, in its strategy of analogy, only a specialization and formalization of the novelist's use of the symbolism of natural detail, a symbolism of which we are constantly aware from beginning to end. Magical interpretation and prediction of events consist in seeing one event or thing as a "mimicry" of another—a present happening, for instance, as a mimicry of some future happening; that is, magic makes a system out of analogies, the correlative forms of things. Poets and novelists do likewise with their symbols. Burns's lines: "And my fause luver staw my rose, / But ah! he left the thorn wi' me," use this kind of mimicry, common to poetry and magic. When a thorn of Alec's roses pricks Tess's chin, the occurrence is read as an omen—and omens properly belong to the field of magic; but the difference between this symbol which is an omen, and the very similar symbol in Burns's lines, which acts only reminiscently, is a difference merely of timing—the one "mimics" a

seduction which occurs later, the other "mimics" a seduction and its consequences which have already occurred. And there is very little difference,
functionally, between Hardy's use of this popular symbol as an *omen*
and his symbolic use of natural particulars—the chattering of the birds
at dawn after the death of Prince and the iridescence of the coagulated
blood, the swollen udders of the cows at Talbothays and the heavy fertilizing mists of the late summer mornings and evenings, the ravaged
turnip field on Flintcomb-Ash and the visitation of the polar birds. All
of these natural details are either predictive or interpretive or both, and
prediction and interpretation of events through analogies are the profession of magic. When a piece of blood-stained butcher paper flies up in the
road as Tess enters the gate of the vicarage at Emminster, the occurrence is
natural while it is ominous; it is realistically observed, as part of the
"given," while it inculcates the magical point of view. Novelistic symbolism
is magical strategy. In *Tess,* which is through and through symbolic, magic
is not only an adaptive specialization of the "folk," but it also determines
the reader's response to the most naturalistic detail. Thus, though the story
is grounded deeply in a naturalistic premise, Hardy's use of one of the commonest tools of novelists—symbolism—enforces a magical view of life.

Logically accommodated by this view of life is the presentation of
supernatural characters. Alec D'Urberville does not appear in his full
otherworldly character until late in the book, in the episode of the planting fires, where we see him with pitchfork among flames—and even then
the local realism of the planting fires is such as almost to absorb the
ghostliness of the apparition. The usual form of his appearance is as a
stage villain, complete with curled mustache, checked suit, and cane; and
actually it seems a bit easier for the reader to accept him as the Evil
Spirit itself, even with a pitchfork, than in his secular accouterments of
the villain of melodrama. But Hardy's logic faces its conclusions with
superb boldness, as it does in giving Angel Clare his name and his harp
and making him a minister's son; if Alec is the Evil One, there will be
something queer about his ordinary tastes, and the queerness is shown
in his stagy clothes (actually, this melodramatic stereotype is just as valid
for a certain period of manners and dress as our own stereotype of the
gunman leaning against a lamppost and striking a match against his
thumbnail). Alec is the smart aleck of the Book of Job, the one who goes
to and fro in the earth and walks up and down in it, the perfectly deracinated one, with his flash and new money and faked name and ag-

gressive ego. If he becomes a religious convert even temporarily it is because he is not really so very much different from Angel (the smart aleck
of the Book of Job was also an angel), for extreme implies extreme, and
both Angel and Alec are foundered in egoism, the one in idealistic egoism, the other in sensual egoism, and Angel himself is diabolic enough in
his prudery. When Alec plays his last frivolous trick on Tess, lying down
on one of the slabs in the D'Urberville vaults and springing up at her
like an animated corpse, his neuroticism finally wears, not the stagy traditional externals of the Evil Spirit, but the deeply convincing character of
insanity—of that human evil which is identifiable with madness. Both
Angel and Alec are metaphors of extremes of human behavior, when
the human has been cut off from community and has been individualized
by intellectual education or by material wealth and traditionless independence.

Between the stridencies of Angel's egoism and Alec's egoism is Tess
—with her Sixth Standard training and some anachronistic D'Urberville
current in her blood that makes for spiritual exacerbation just as it makes
her cheeks paler, "the teeth more regular, the red lips thinner than is
usual in a country-bred girl": incapacitated for life by her moral idealism,
capacious of life through her sensualism. When, after Alec's evilly absurd
trick, she bends down to whisper at the opening of the vaults, "Why am I
on the wrong side of this door?" her words construct all the hopelessness
of her cultural impasse. But her stabbing of Alec is her heroic return
through the "door" into the folk fold, the fold of nature and instinct, the
anonymous community. If both Alec and Angel are spiritually impotent in
their separate ways, Tess is finally creative by the only measure of creative-
ness that this particular novelistic universe holds, the measure of the instinctive and the natural. Her gesture is the traditional gesture of the revenge of
instinct, by which she joins an innumerable company of folk heroines who
stabbed and were hanged—the spectacular but still anonymous and common gesture of common circumstances and common responses, which we, as
habitual readers of newspaper crime headlines, find, unthinkingly, so
shocking to our delicate notions of what is "natural." That she goes, in
her wandering at the end, to Stonehenge, is an inevitable symbolic going—as all going and doing are symbolic—for it is here that the earthiness
of her state is best recognized, by the monoliths of Stonehenge, and that
the human dignity of her last gesture has the most austere recognition, by
the ritual sacrifices that have been made on these stones.

To go from Hardy's *Tess* to James's *The Portrait of a Lady* is to go from Stonehenge to St. Peter's and from a frozen northern turnip field, eyed hungrily by polar birds, to the Cascine gardens where nightingales sing. Though both books concern the "campaign" of a young woman—a campaign that, expressed most simply, is a campaign *to live* —a greater difference of atmosphere could scarcely be imagined nor of articulation of what it means *to live*. The gaunt arctic birds in *Tess* have witnessed, with their "tragical eyes," cataclysms that no human eye might see, but of which they retain no memory. The birds offer a symbol of Tess's world: a world inimical to consciousness, where one should have no memory (Tess's fatal error is to remember her own past), where the eye of the mind should remain blank, where aesthetic and moral perceptivity is traumatic. The nightingales that sing to Isabel Archer and her lover in the "grey Italian shade" also offer a symbol of a world: they are the very voice of memory, of an imperishable consciousness at once recreating and transcending its ancient, all-human knowledge. It is to the tutelage of the European memory that Isabel Archer passionately surrenders herself in her campaign *to live*, that is, to become conscious; for, in James's world, the highest affirmation of life is the development of the subtlest and most various consciousness. In doing so, she must—like the girl in the barbarous legend of the nightingale, who, likewise in a foreign land, read an obscene crime in the weaving of a tapestry—come into knowledge of an evil which, in its own civilized kind, is as corrupting and implacable as that in the old tale. But consciousness here, as an activity nourished by knowledge, transcends the knowledge which is its content: and this too

211

is in analogy with the ancient symbolic tale, where knowledge of evil is transcended, in the very doom of its reiteration, by the bird's immortal song.

   The Portrait is not, like *Tess*, a tragedy, but it is as deeply informed with the tragic view of life: that tragic view whose essence is contained in the words, "He who loses his life shall find it," and "Except a corn of wheat fall into the ground and die, it abideth alone: but if it die, it bringeth forth much fruit." We associate tragic seriousness of import in a character's destiny with tension between the power of willing (which is "free") and the power of circumstances ("necessity") binding and limiting the will; and if either term of the tension seems lacking, seriousness of import fails. Apparently, no two authors could be at further antipodes than James and Hardy in the respective emphases they place on these terms. In Hardy, the protagonist's volition founders at every move on a universally mechanical, mysteriously hostile necessity; it is only in Tess's last acts, of blood sacrifice and renunciation of life, that her will appallingly asserts its freedom and that she gains her tragic greatness. In James's *Portrait,* and in his other novels as well, the protagonist appears to have an extraordinarily unhampered play of volition. This appearance of extraordinary freedom from the pressure of circumstances is largely due to the "immense deal of money" (the phrase is taken from an early page of *The Portrait*) with which James endows his world—for, in an acquisitive culture, money is the chief symbol of freedom. The vague rich gleams of money are on every cornice and sift through every vista of the world of *The Portrait,* like the muted gold backgrounds of old Persian illuminations; and the human correlative of the money is a type of character fully privileged with easy mobility upon the face of the earth and with magnificent opportunities for the cultivation of aesthetic and intellectual refinements. It is by visualizing with the greatest clarity the lustrously moneyed tones of the James universe that we make ourselves able to see the more clearly what grave, somber shapes of illusion and guilt he organizes in this novel. The tension between circumstances and volition, "necessity" and "freedom," is demonstrated at the uppermost levels of material opportunity where, presumably, there is most freedom and where therefore freedom becomes most threatening—and where necessity wears its most insidious disguise, the disguise of freedom.

   In following the previous studies, the reader will perhaps have been impressed with the fact that the novel as a genre has shown, from *Don*

Quixote on, a constant concern with the institutions created by the circulation of money and with the fantasies arising from the having of it, or, more especially, the not having it; a concern not always so direct as that of *Moll Flanders* and *Vanity Fair*, but almost inevitably implicit at least, expressed in indirect forms of aspiration and encitement to passion. As the definitively middle-class literary genre, the novel purchased its roots in a money-conscious social imagination. The wealth shining on the James world is a kind of apogee of the novel's historical concern with money, showing itself, in *The Portrait*, as a grandly sweeping postulate of possession: as if to say, "Here, now, is all the beautiful money, in the most liberating quantities: what ambition, what temptation, what errors of the will, what evil, what suffering, what salvation still denote the proclivities of the human even in a world so bountifully endowed?"

The "international myth" [1] that operates broadly in James's work, and that appears, in this novel, in the typical confrontation of American innocence and moral rigor with the tortuosities of an older civilization, gives its own and special dimension to the moneyed prospect. James came to maturity in a post-Civil War America euphoric with material achievement. In terms of the Jamesian "myth," American wealth is now able to buy up the whole museum of Europe, all its visible "point" of art objects and culture prestige, to take back home and set up in the front yard (we need look no further, for historical objectification of this aspect of the "myth," than to William Randolph Hearst's epic importation of various priceless chunks of Europe to California). If the shadows of the physically dispossessed—the sweat and the bone-weariness and the manifold anonymous deprivation in which this culture-buying power had its source—are excluded from James's money-gilded canvas, the shadow of spiritual dispossession is the somber shape under the money outline. We are not allowed to forget the aesthetic and moral impoverishment that spread its gross vacuum at the core of the American acquisitive dream—the greed, the obtuse or rapacious presumption, the disvaluation of values that kept pace to pace with material expansion. James's characteristic thematic contrasts, here as in other novels, are those of surface against depth, inspection against experience, buying power against living power, the American tourist's cultural balcony against the European abyss of

---

[1] Discussion of James's "international myth" will be found in *The Question of Henry James*, edited by F. W. Dupee (New York: Henry Holt & Company, Inc., 1945), and Philip Rahv's *Image and Idea* (New York: New Directions, 1949).

history and memory and involved motive where he perilously or callously teeters. In *The Portrait,* the American heroine's pilgrimage in Europe becomes a fatally serious spiritual investment, an investment of the "free" self in and with the circumstantial and binding past, a discovery of the relations of the self with history, and a moral renovation of history in the freedom of the individual conscience. It is a growing of more delicate and deeper-reaching roots and a nourishment of a more complex, more troubled, more creative personal humanity. It is, in short, what is ideally meant by "civilization," as that word refers to a process that can take place in an individual.

The postulate of wealth and privilege is, in revised terms, that of the second chapter of Genesis (the story of Adam in the garden)—that of the optimum conditions which will leave the innocent soul at liberty to develop its potentialities—and, as in the archetype of the Fall of Man, the postulate is significant not as excluding knowledge of good and evil, but as presenting a rare opportunity for such knowledge. It is the bounty poured on Isabel Archer (significantly, the man who gives her the symbolical investiture of money is a man who is fatally ill; significantly, also, she is under an illusion as to the giver) that makes her "free" to determine her choice of action, and thus morally most responsible for her choice; but it is the very bounty of her fortune, also, that activates at once, as if chemically, the proclivity to evil in the world of privilege that her wealth allows her to enter—it is her money that draws Madame Merle and Osmond to her; so that her "freedom" is actualized as imprisonment, in a peculiarly ashen and claustral, because peculiarly refined, suburb of hell. Isabel's quest had, at the earliest, been a quest for happiness—the naïvely egoistic American quest; it converts into a problem of spiritual salvation, that is, into a quest of "life"; and again the Biblical archetype shadows forth the problem. After eating of the fruit of the tree of knowledge of good and evil, how is one to regain access to the tree of life?

The great fairy tales and saints' legends have identified life with knowledge. For the fairy-tale hero, the fruit of the tree of life that is the guerdon of kingdom is the golden fleece or the golden apples that his wicked stepmother or usurping uncle have sent him in quest of; and to achieve the guerdon he must go through all tormenting knowledge— of serpents, floods, fire, ogres, enchantment, and even of his own lusts and murderous capacities. The ordeal of the heroes of saints' legends is also an ordeal of knowledge of evil, and the guerdon is life. As do these ancient tales, *The Portrait* identifies life with the most probing, dangerous, responsible awareness—identifies, as it were, the two "trees," the tree of the Fall and the tree of the Resurrection. The heroine's voluntary search for fuller consciousness leads her, in an illusion of perfect freedom to choose only "the best" in experience, to choose an evil; but it is this that, by providing insight through suffering and guilt, provides also access to life—to the fructification of consciousness that is a knowledge of human bondedness. At the very end of the book, Caspar Goodwood gives passionate voice to the illusion of special privileges of choice and of a good to be had by exclusion and separateness: he says to Isabel,

> "It would be an insult to you to assume that you care for . . . the bottomless idiocy of the world. We've nothing to do with all that; we're quite out of it . . . We can do absolutely as we please; to whom under the sun do we owe anything? What is it that holds us, what is it that has the smallest right to interfere . . . ? The world's all before us— and the world's very big."

Isabel answers at random, "The world's very small." What attitude of mind takes her back to Rome, back to old evil and old servitude, is not described; we know only that she does go back. But it is evident that she does so because the "small" necessitous world has received an extension, not in the horizontal direction of imperial mobility that Caspar Goodwood suggests, but an invisible extension in depth, within her own mind—an extension into the freedom of personal renunciation and inexhaustible responsibility. The knowledge she has acquired has been tragic knowledge, but her story does not stop here, as it would if it were a tragedy—it goes on out of the pages of the book, to Rome, where we cannot follow it; for the knowledge has been the means to "life," and having learned to live, she must "live long," as she says. It is only the process of the learning that the portrait frame itself holds.

The title, *The Portrait*, asks the eye to see. And the handling of the book is in terms of seeing. The informing and strengthening of the eye of the mind is the theme—the ultimate knowledge, the thing finally "seen," having only the contingent importance of stimulating a more subtle and various activity of perception. The dramatization is deliberately "scenic," moving in a series of recognition scenes that are slight and low-keyed at first, or blurred and erroneous, in proportion both to the innocence of the heroine and others' skill in refined disguises and obliquities; then, toward the end, proceeding in swift and livid flashes. For in adopting as his compositional center the growth of a consciousness, James was able to use the bafflements and illusions of ignorance for his "complications," as he was able to use, more consistently than any other novelist, "recognitions" for his crises. Further, this action, moving through errors and illuminations of the inward eye, is set in a symbolic construct of things to be seen by the physical eye—paintings and sculptures, old coins and porcelain and lace and tapestries, most of all buildings: the aesthetic riches of Europe, pregnant with memory, with "histories within histories" of skills and motivations, temptations and suffering. The context of particulars offered to physical sight (and these may be settings, like English country houses or Roman ruins, or objects in the setting, like a porcelain cup or a piece of old lace draped on a mantel, or a person's face or a group of people—and the emphasis on the visual is most constant and notable not in these particulars, extensive as they are, but in the figurative language of the book, in metaphors using visual images as their vehicle) intensifies the meaning of "recognition" in those scenes where *sight* is *insight,* and provides a concrete embodiment of the ambiguities of "seeing."

In James's handling of the richly qualitative setting, it is characteristically significant that he suggests visual or scenic traits almost always in such a way that the emphasis is on *modulations of perception in the observer.* The "look" of things is a response of consciousness and varies with the observer; the "look" of things has thus the double duty of representing external stimuli, by indirection in their passage through consciousness, and of representing the observer himself. For instance, when Ralph takes Isabel through the picture gallery in the Touchett home, the "imperfect" but "genial" light of the bracketed lamps shows the pictures as "vague squares of rich colour," and the look of the pictures is Isabel's state at the moment—her eager and innately gifted sensibility and her almost complete ignorance, her conscious orientation toward an unknown "rich" mode of being that is beautiful but indeterminate. Let us take another example from late in the book. Directly after that conversation with Madame Merle when Isabel learns, with the full force of evil revelation, Madame Merle's part in her marriage, she goes out for a drive alone.

She had long before this taken old Rome into her confidence, for in a world of ruins the ruin of her happiness seemed a less unnatural catastrophe. She rested her weariness upon things that had crumbled for centuries and yet still were upright; she dropped her secret sadness into the silence of lonely places, where its very modern quality detached itself and grew objective, so that as she sat in a sun-warmed angle on a winter's day, or stood in a mouldy church to which no one came, she could almost smile at it and think of its smallness. Small it was, in the large Roman record, and her haunting sense of the continuity of the human lot easily carried her from the less to the greater. She had become deeply, tenderly acquainted with Rome: it interfused and moderated her passion. But she had grown to think of it chiefly as the place where people had suffered. This was what came to her in the starved churches, where the marble columns, transferred from pagan ruins, seemed to offer her a companionship in endurance and the musty incense to be a compound of long-unanswered prayers.

Here the definition of visible setting—churches and marble columns and ruins, and comprehending all these, Rome—though it is full, is vague and diffuse, in the external sense of the "seen"; but in the sense that it is a setting evoked by Isabel's own deepened consciousness, it is exactly and clearly focused. It is Rome *felt*, felt as an immensity of human time, as a great human continuum of sadness and loneliness and passion and aspiration and patience; and it has this definition by virtue of Isabel's personal ordeal and her perception of its meaning. The "vague squares of rich colour" have become determinate.

The theme of "seeing" (the theme of the developing consciousness) is fertile with ironies and ambiguities that arise from the natural symbolism of the act of seeing, upon which so vastly many of human responses and decisions are dependent. The eye, as it registers surfaces, is an organ of aesthetic experience, in the etymological sense of the word "aesthetic," which is a word deriving from a Greek verb meaning "to perceive"—to perceive through the senses. James provides his world with innumerable fine surfaces for this kind of perception; it is a world endowed with the finest selective opportunities for the act of "seeing," for aesthetic cultivation. But our biological dependence upon the eye has made it a symbol of intellectual and moral and spiritual perception, forms of perception which are—by the makers of dictionaries—discriminated radically from aesthetic perception. Much of James's work is an exploration of the profound identity of the aesthetic and the moral. (In this he is at variance with the makers of dictionaries, but he has the companionship of Socrates' teacher Diotima, as her teaching is represented by Plato in the

Symposium. Diotima taught that the way to spiritual good lay through the hierarchies of the "beautiful," that is, through graduations from one form of aesthetic experience to another.) Aesthetic experience proper, since it is acquired through the senses, is an experience of *feeling*. But so also moral experience, when it is not sheerly nominal and ritualistic, is an experience of *feeling*. Neither one has reality—has psychological depth —unless it is "felt" (hence James's so frequent use of phrases such as "felt life" and "the very *taste* of life," phrases that insist on the feeling-base of complete and integrated living). Furthermore, both aesthetic and moral experience are nonutilitarian. The first distinction that aestheticians usually make, in defining the aesthetic, is its distinction from the useful; when the aesthetic is converted to utility, it becomes something else, its value designation is different—as when a beautiful bowl becomes valuable not for its beauty but for its capacity to hold soup. So also the moral, when it is converted to utility, becomes something else than the moral —becomes even immoral, a parody of or a blasphemy against the moral life (in our richest cultural heritage, both Hellenic and Christian, the moral life is symbolically associated with utter loss of utility goods and even with loss of physical life—as in the Gospel passage, "Leave all that thou hast and follow me," or as in the career of Socrates, or as in Sophocles' *Antigone*). Moral and aesthetic experience have then in common their foundation in feeling and their distinction from the useful. The identity that James explores is their identity in the most capacious and most integrated—the most "civilized"—consciousness, whose sense relationships (aesthetic relationships) with the external world of scenes and objects have the same quality and the same spiritual determination as its relationships with people (moral relationships). But his exploration of that ideal identity involves cognizance of failed integration, cognizance of the many varieties of one-sidedness or one-eyedness or blindness that go by the name of the moral or the aesthetic, and of the destructive potentialities of the human consciousness when it is one-sided either way. His ironies revolve on the ideal concept of a spacious integrity of feeling: feeling, ideally, is *one*—and there is ironic situation when feeling is split into the "moral" and the "aesthetic," each denying the other and each posing as *all*.

There is comic irony in Henrietta Stackpole's moral busybodyness as she flutters and sputters through Europe obtaining feature materials for her home-town newspaper, "featuring" largely the morally culpable un-Americanism of Europeans to serve her readers as a flattering warning against indulgence in the aesthetic. Henrietta is a stock James comedy character, and she is essential. Without Henrietta's relative incapacity to "see" more than literal surfaces, the significant contrast between surface and depth, between outward and inward "seeing," between undeveloped and developed consciousness, would lose a needed demonstration. (But let us say for Henrietta that, like Horatio in *Hamlet,* she is employed by the dramatist for as many sorts of purposes as his scenes happen to demand; when a foil of obtuseness is wanted, Henrietta is there, and when a foil of good interpretive intelligence or plain charitable generosity is wanted, Henrietta is also there. She is the type of what James technically called the *ficelle,* a wholly subordinate character immensely useful to take in confidences from the principals and to serve other functions of "relief"—"relief" in that sense in which the lower level of a relievo provides perspective for the carved projections.) In Mrs. Touchett, what appears at first as the comic irony of absolute aesthetic insensitivity accompanied by a rugged moral dogmatism ("she had a little moral account-book—with columns unerringly ruled and a sharp steel clasp—which she kept with exemplary neatness") becomes at the end of the book, with her son's death, the tragic irony of that kind of ambiguous misery which is an inability to acknowledge or realize one's own suffering, when suffering is real but the channels of feeling have become nearly atrophied by lack of use. At the midday meal, when Isabel and Mrs. Touchett come together after the night of Ralph's death,

Isabel saw her aunt not to be so dry as she appeared, and her old pity for the poor woman's inexpressiveness, her want of regret, of disappointment, came back to her. Unmistakably she would have found it a blessing to-day to be able to feel a defeat, a mistake, even a shame or two. [Isabel] wondered if [her aunt] were not even missing those enrichments of consciousness and privately trying—reaching out for some aftertaste of life, dregs of the banquet; the testimony of pain or the old recreation of remorse. On the other hand perhaps she was afraid; if she should begin to know remorse at all it might take her too far. Isabel could perceive, however, how it had come over her dimly that she had failed of something, that she saw herself in the future as an old woman without memories. Her little sharp face looked tragical.

Mrs. Touchett's habitual moralistic denial of feeling as an aesthetic indulgence has left her deserted even by herself, even by her love of her son, even by memory, even by suffering. She is stranded in a morality that is tragically without meaning.

In Madame Merle and Osmond the ironies intrinsic to James's theme receive another turn. Madame Merle first appeals to Isabel's admiration by her capacity for "feeling"—for that kind of feeling to which the term "aesthetic" has been specially adapted in common modern use: feeling for the arts, the sensuous perceptivity underlying the arts, and, by extension, feeling for the finer conventions of manners as "arts of living." (Madame Merle "knew how to feel . . . This was indeed Madame Merle's great talent, her most perfect gift.") At Gardencourt, when she is not engaged in writing letters, she paints (she "made no more of brushing in a sketch than of pulling off her gloves") or she plays the piano (she "was a brave musician") or she is "employed upon wonderful tasks of rich embroidery." (The presentation is just a bit insidious, not only because of Madame Merle's so very great plasticity in going from one art to another, but also in the style of the phrases: the suggestion of conventional fluidity in the comparison of her ease in painting with the ease of "pulling off her gloves," the word "brave"—an honorific word in certain places, but carrying here the faintest note of bravado—and the word "employed," suggesting, as it reverberates, Madame Merle's not disinterested professional aestheticism.) Her senses are active and acute: walking in the English rain, she says,

> "It never wets you and it always smells good." She declared that in England the pleasures of smell were great . . . and she used to lift the sleeve of her British overcoat and bury her nose in it, inhaling the clear, fine scent of the wool.

Just how acute her perceptions are is shown never more clearly than in that scene in which she learns of the distribution of property after Mr. Touchett's death, occurring in Chapter 20 of Volume I. Mrs. Touchett has just told her that Ralph, because of the state of his health, had hurried away from England before the reading of the will, in which Isabel had been left half of the fortune accruing to him. With this news, Madame Merle "remained thoughtful a moment, her eyes bent on the floor," and when Isabel enters the room, Madame Merle kisses her—this being "the only allusion the visitor, in her great good taste, made . . . to her young friend's inheritance." There are no other signs than these (and the episode is typical of James's minor "recognition scenes") of just how quickly and acutely Madame Merle's senses—her perception, her intuition—have functioned in apprising her of the possibilities of exploitation now opened, and in apprising her also of the fact that Ralph is the real donor of Isabel's fortune, a fact of which Isabel herself remains ignorant until Madame Merle viciously informs her. Madame Merle's feeling for situation is so subtly educated that she needs but the slightest of tokens in order to respond. And yet, with a sensitivity educated so exquisitely and working at such high tension she is morally insensible —or almost so; not quite—for, unlike Osmond, whose damnation is in ice where the moral faculty is quite frozen, she still has the spiritual capacity of those whose damnation is in fire, the capacity to know that she is damned.

Madame Merle and Osmond use their cultivated aestheticism for utility purposes—Madame Merle, to further her ambition for place and power; Osmond, to make himself separate and envied. Their debasement of the meaning of the aesthetic becomes symbolically vicious when it shows itself in their relationships with people—with Isabel, for instance, who is for them an object of virtu that differs from other objects of virtu in that it bestows money rather than costs it. This is the evil referred to by Kant in his second Categorical Imperative: the use of persons as means —an evil to which perhaps all evil in human relationships reduces. In the case of Madame Merle and Osmond, it has a peculiar and blasphemous ugliness, inasmuch as the atmosphere of beauty in which they live —beauty of surroundings and of manners—represents the finest, freest product of civilization and is such, ideally, as to induce the most reverential feeling for people as well as for things. Isabel first appeals to Osmond as being "as smooth to his general need of her as handled ivory to the palm": it is an "aesthetic" image suggesting his fastidiousness but, ironically, suggesting at the same time his coarseness—for while ivory, like pearls, may be the more beautiful for handling, "handled ivory" might also be the head of a walking stick, and it is in some sort as a walking stick that he uses Isabel. An extension of the same figure, without the aesthetic and with only the utilitarian connotation, indicates Osmond's real degeneracy: Isabel finally realizes that she has been for him "an applied handled hung-up tool, as senseless and convenient as mere wood and iron." But the evil is not one that can be isolated or confined; it is automatically proliferative. Morally dead himself, incapable of reverence for the human quality in others, Osmond necessarily tries to duplicate his death in them, for it is by killing their volition that he can make them useful; dead, they are alone "beautiful." He urges upon Isabel the obscene suggestion that she, in turn, "use" Lord Warburton by exploiting Warburton's old love for herself in order to get him to marry Pansy; and Osmond can find no excuse for her refusal except that she has her private designs for "using" the Englishman. But it is in Osmond's use of Pansy, his daughter, that he is most subtly and horribly effective. He has made her into a work of art, the modeling materials being the least artful of childish qualities—her innocence and gentleness; and he has almost succeeded in reducing her will to an echo of his own. The quaint figure of Pansy, always only on the edge of scenes, is of great structural importance in the latter half of the book; for she shows the full measure of the abuse that Isabel resists, and it is to nourish in her whatever small germ of creative volition may remain—to salvage, really, a life—that Isabel returns to Rome and to Osmond's paralyzing ambiance.

The moral question that is raised by every character in the book is a question of the "amount of felt life" that each is able to experience, a question of how many and how various are the relationships each can, with integrity, enter into. Or, to put the matter in its basic metaphor, it is a question of how much each person is able to "see," and not only to see but to compose into creative order. The moral question, since it involves vision, feeling, and composition, is an aesthetic one as well. Madame Merle and Osmond are blind to certain relations: "I don't pretend to know what people are meant for," Madame Merle says, ". . . I only know what I can do with them." Mrs. Touchett is blind to certain others. Let us stop for a moment with Henrietta Stackpole's comic crudity of vision, for the "eye" is all-important, and the ranges of vision really begin with an eye like that of Henrietta. It is "a peculiarly open, surprised-looking eye." "The most striking point in her appearance was the remarkable fixedness of this organ."

> She fixed her eyes on [Ralph], and there was something in their character that reminded him of large polished buttons—buttons that might have fixed the elastic loops of some tense receptacle: he seemed to see the reflection of surrounding objects on the pupil. The expres-

sion of a button is not usually deemed human, but there was something in Miss Stackpole's gaze that made him, a very modest man, feel vaguely embarrassed—less inviolate, more dishonoured, than he liked.

Henrietta, with her gregariously refractive button-sight, has also "clear-cut views on most subjects . . . she knew perfectly in advance what her opinions would be." Henrietta's is the made-up consciousness, the pseudo consciousness, that is not a process but a content hopelessly once and for all given, able to refract light but not to take it in. (We can understand Henrietta's importance, caricatural as she is, by the fact that she is the primitive form of the pseudo consciousness which Madame Merle and Osmond, in their so much more sophisticated ways, exhibit: theirs too is the made-up consciousness, a rigidified content, impervious and uncreative.) The Misses Molyneux, Lord Warburton's sisters, have "eyes like the balanced basins, the circles of 'ornamental water,' set, in parterres, among the geraniums." Let us note that the figure is drawn from an "aesthetic" arrangement, that of formal gardens—and in this sense has directly opposite associations to those of Henrietta's buttons (presumably very American, very *useful* buttons). The Misses Molyneux's eyes, like Henrietta's, also merely reflect surrounding objects, and reflect more limitedly, far less mobiley; but the image is significant of certain kinds of feeling, of "seeing," that Henrietta is incapable of, and that have derived from ancient disciplines in human relationships—contemplative feeling, reverence, feeling for privacy and for grace. Extremely minor figures such as these, of the buttons and the basins, are pregnant with the extraordinarily rich, extraordinarily subtle potentialities of the theme of "seeing" as an infinitely graduated cognizance of relations between self and world.

In this book, the great range of structural significance through figurative language is due to the fact that whatever image vehicle a figure may have—even when the image is not itself a visual one—the general context is so deeply and consistently characterized by acts of "seeing" that every metaphor has this other implied extension of meaning. For example, a very intricate and extensive symbolic construct is built on a metaphor of opening doors. Henrietta, Ralph says, "walks in without knocking at the door." "She's too personal," he adds. As her eyes indiscriminately take in everything that is literally to be seen, so she walks

223

in without knocking at the door of personality: "she thinks one's door should stand ajar." The correspondence of eyes and doors lies in the publicity Henrietta assumes (she is a journalist): her eye is public like a button, and responds as if everything else were public, as if there were no doors, as if there were nothing to be seen but what the public (the American newspaper public) might see without effort and without discomfort. In James's thematic system of surfaces and depths, "sight" is something achieved and not given, achieved in the loneliness of the individual soul and in the lucidity of darkness suffered; privacy is its necessary stamp, and it cannot be loaned or broadcast any more than can the loneliness or the suffering. "I keep a band of music in my ante-room," Ralph tells Isabel.

> "It has orders to play without stopping; it renders me two excellent services. It keeps the sounds of the world from reaching the private apartments, and it makes the world think that dancing's going on within."

The notation has its pathos through Ralph's illness. Isabel "would have liked to pass through the ante-room . . . and enter the private apartments." It is only at the end, through her own revelations of remorse and loss, that those doors open to her.

The ironic force of the metaphor of doors, as it combines with the metaphor of "seeing," has a different direction in the crucial scene in Chapter 51 of the second volume—one of the major "recognition scenes" in the book, where Isabel sees Osmond's full malignancy, a malignancy the more blighting as it takes, and sincerely takes, the form of honor, and where Osmond sees unequivocally the vivid, mysterious resistance of a life that he has not been able to convert into a tool. Isabel comes to tell him that Ralph is dying and that she must go to England. She opens the door of her husband's study without knocking.

> "Excuse me for disturbing you," she said.
> "When I come to your room I always knock," he answered, going on with his work.
> "I forgot; I had something else to think of. My cousin's dying."
> "Ah, I don't believe that," said Osmond, looking at his drawing through a magnifying glass. "He was dying when we married; he'll outlive us all."

Osmond is here engaged in an activity representative of a man of taste and a "collector"—he is making traced copies of ancient coins (the fact that it is an act of tracing, of copying, has its own significance, as has the object of his attention: coins). What he "sees" in the situation that Isabel describes to him is quite exactly what he sees in the fact that she has opened the door without knocking: a transgression of convention; and what he does not see is the right of another human being to feel, to love, to will individually. Further, what he appallingly does not see is his dependence, for the fortune Isabel has brought him, on the selfless imagination of the dying man, Ralph; or, even more appallingly (for one can scarcely suppose that Madame Merle had left him ignorant of the source of Isabel's wealth), what he does not see is any reason for the moral responsibility implied by "gratitude," a defect of vision that gives a special and hideous bleakness to his use of the word "grateful," when he tells Isabel that she has not been "grateful" for his tolerance of her esteem for Ralph. The metaphor of the "doors" thus goes through its changes, each associated with a depth or shallowness, a straightness or obliquity of vision, from Henrietta's aggressive myopia, to Ralph's reticence and insight, to Osmond's refined conventionalism and moral astigmatism.

Let us consider in certain other examples this reciprocity between theme and metaphor, insight and sight, image and eye. Isabel's native choice is creativity, a "free exploration of life," but exploration is conducted constantly—vision is amplified constantly—at the cost of renunciations. It is in the "grey depths" of the eyes of the elder Miss Molyneux, those eyes like the balanced basins of water set in parterres, that Isabel recognizes what she has had to reject in rejecting Lord Warburton: "the peace, the kindness, the honour, the possessions, a deep security and a great exclusion." Caspar Goodwood has eyes that "seemed to shine through the vizard of a helmet." He appears always as an armor-man: "she saw the different fitted parts of him as she had seen, in museums and portraits, the different fitted parts of armoured warriors—in plates of steel handsomely inlaid with gold." "He might have ridden, on a plunging steed, the whirlwind of a great war." The image is one of virility, but of passion without relation, aggressive energy without responsibility. The exclusions implied by Casper's steel-plated embrace are as great as those implied by the honor and the peace that Lord Warburton offers; and yet Isabel's final refusal of Caspar and of sexual possession is tragic, for it is to a sterile marriage that she returns.

Architectural images, and metaphors whose vehicle (like doors and windows) is associated with architecture, subtend the most various and complex of the book's meanings; and the reason for their particular richness of significance seems to be that, of all forms that are offered to sight and interpretation, buildings are the most natural symbols of civilized life, the most diverse also as to what their fronts and interiors can imply of man's relations with himself and with the outer world. Osmond's house in Florence has an "imposing front" of a "somewhat incommunicative character."

> It was the mask, not the face of the house. It had heavy lids, but no eyes; the house in reality looked another way—looked off behind . . . The windows of the ground-floor, as you saw them from the piazza, were, in their noble proportions, extremely architectural; but their function seemed less to offer communication with the world than to defy the world to look in . . .

(One notes again here the characteristic insistence on *eyes* and *looking*.) The description, perfectly fitting an old and noble Florentine villa, exactly equates with Osmond himself, and not only Isabel's first illusional impression of him—when it is his renunciatory reserve that attracts her, an appearance suggesting those "deeper rhythms of life" that she seeks—but also her later painful knowledge of the face behind the mask, which, like the house, is affected with an obliquity of vision, "looked another way—looked off behind." The interior is full of artful images; the group of people gathered there "might have been described by a painter as composing well"; even the footboy "might, tarnished as to livery and quaint as to type, have issued from some stray sketch of old-time manners, been 'put in' by the brush of a Longhi or a Goya"; the face of little Pansy is "painted" with a "fixed and intensely sweet smile." Osmond's world, contained within his eyeless house, is "sorted, sifted, arranged" for the eye; even his daughter is one of his arrangements. It is a world bred of ancient disciplines modulating through time, selection and composition, to the purest aesthetic form.

> [Isabel] carried away an image from her visit to his hill-top . . . which put on for her a particular harmony with other supposed and divined things, histories within histories . . . It spoke of the kind of personal issue that touched her most nearly; of the choice between objects,

subjects, contacts—what might she call them?—of a thin and those of a rich association . . . of a care for beauty and perfection so natural and so cultivated together that the career appeared to stretch beneath it in the disposed vistas and with the ranges of steps and terraces and fountains of a formal Italian garden . . .

The illusion is one of a depth and spaciousness and delicacy of relationships, an illusion of the civilized consciousness.

But while Osmond's world suggests depth, it is, ironically, a world of surfaces only, for Osmond has merely borrowed it. The architectural metaphor shifts significantly in the passage (Chapter 42 of Volume II) in which Isabel takes the full measure of her dwelling. "It was the house of darkness, the house of dumbness, the house of suffocation."

> She had taken all the first steps in the purest confidence, and then she had suddenly found the infinite vista of a multiplied life to be a dark, narrow alley with a dead wall at the end. Instead of leading to the high places of happiness . . . it led rather downward and earthward, into realms of restriction and depression where the sound of other lives, easier and freer, was heard as from above . . .

"When she saw this rigid system close about her, draped though it was in pictured tapestries . . . she seemed shut up with an odour of mould and decay." Again the architectural image changes its shape in that passage (quoted earlier in this essay) where Isabel takes her knowledge and her sorrow into Rome, a Rome of architectural ruins. Here also are depth of human time, "histories within histories," aesthetic form, but not "arranged," not borrowable, not to be "collected"—only to be *lived* in the creative recognitions brought to them by a soul itself alive. The image that accompanies Ralph through the book—"his serenity was but the array of wild flowers niched in his ruin"—gains meaning from the architectural images so frequent in the Roman scenes (as, for instance, from this:

> [Isabel] had often ascended to those desolate ledges from which the Roman crowd used to bellow applause and where now the wild flowers . . . bloom in the deep crevices . . .)

Whereas Osmond's forced "arrangements" of history and art and people are without racination, blighting and lifeless, Ralph's "array of wild flowers" is rooted, even if precariously rooted in a ruin; it is a life *grown,* grown in history, fertilized in the crevices of a difficult experience. The metaphor is another version of St. John's "Except a corn of wheat fall into the ground and die, it abideth alone; but if it die, it bringeth forth much fruit." Isabel, still seeking that freedom which is growth, goes back to Osmond's claustral house, for it is there, in the ruin where Pansy has been left, that she has placed roots, found a crevice in which to grow straightly and freshly, found a fertilizing, civilizing relationship between consciousness and circumstances.

ON *Lord Jim*

Marlow's last view of Jim, on the coast of Patusan, is of a white figure "at the heart of a vast enigma." Jim himself is not enigmatic. The wonder and doubt that he stirs, both in Marlow and in us, are not wonder and doubt as to what *he* is: he is as recognizable as we are to ourselves; he is "one of us." Furthermore, he is not a very complex character, and he is examined by his creator with the most exhaustive conscientiousness; he is placed in every possible perspective that might help to define him. The enigma, then, is not what Jim is but what we are, and not only what we are, but "how to be" what we are.

Jim's shocking encounter with himself at the moment of his jump from the *Patna* is a model of those moments when the destiny each person carries within him, the destiny fully molded in the unconscious will, lifts its blind head from the dark, drinks blood, and speaks. There is no unclarity in the shape that Jim saw at that moment: he had jumped —it is as simple as that. But because the event is a paradigm of the encounters of the conscious personality with the stranger within, the stranger who is the very self of the self, the significance of Jim's story is *our own* significance, contained in the enigmatic relationship between the conscious will and the fatality of our acts. Jim's discovery of himself was a frightful one, and his solution of the problem of "how to be" was to exorcise the stranger in a fierce, long, concentrated effort to be his opposite. The oracle spoke early to Oedipus, too, in his youth in Corinth, telling him who he was—the man destined to transgress most horribly the saving code of kinship relations—and Oedipus's solution of the problem of "how to be" was the same as Jim's: he fled in the opposite direction from his destiny and ran straight into it.

Jim is one of the most living characters in fiction, although his presentation is by indirection, through Marlow's narrative; that indirection is itself uniquely humanizing, for we see him only as people can see each other, ambivalently and speculatively. He is nevertheless an extraordinarily simplified *type,* obsessed with a single idea, divested of all psychological attributes but the very few that concretize his relationship with his idea. The simplification is classical; it is a simplification like that of Aeschylus' Orestes, possessed by the divine command, and like that of Sophocles' Oedipus, possessed by his responsibility for finding out the truth. Conrad is able thus to imply a clear-cut formal distinction between the man and his destiny (his acts), even though he conceives destiny as immanent in the man's nature and in this sense identical with him. Here is Jim, "clean-limbed, clean-faced, firm on his feet, as promising a boy as the sun ever shone on," and there are his acts—the destruction of his best friend, the destruction of himself, the abandonment of the Patusan village to leaderlessness and depredation. Similarly Orestes and Oedipus, human agents simplified to a commanding ethical idea, are analytically separable from their destinies, the *anankē* or compelling principle fatally inherent in their acts. This subtle but tangible distinction between the human agent and his destiny allows the classical dramatists to orient clearly what we may call the metaphysical significance of the hero's career, the universal problem and the law of life which that career illustrates. We see the hero as an ideal human type (literally "idealized" through his devotion to an idea of ethical action); but his fate is pitiful and terrible—a fate that, if a man's deserts were to be suited to his conscious intentions, should fall only on malicious, unjust, and treasonable men; and the problem, the "enigma," thus raised is the religious problem of the awful incongruity between human intention and its consequences in action, between ethical effort and the guilt acquired through such effort; and the law—if a law appears—will be the law that justifies, to man's reason and and feeling, that appearance of awful incongruity. Conrad's treatment of Jim's story is classical in this sense, in that he sees in it the same problem and orients the problem in the same manner.

"In the destructive element immerse," Stein says, voicing his own solution of the problem of "how to be." There is no way "to be," according to Stein, but through the ideal, the truth as it appears, what he calls "the dream," although it is itself "the destructive element." "Very funny this terrible thing is," Stein says,

> "A man that is born falls into a dream like a man who falls into the sea. If he tries to climb out into the air as inexperienced people

endeavour to do, he drowns—*nicht wahr?* . . . No! I tell you! The way is to the destructive element submit yourself, and with the exertions of your hands and feet in the water make the deep, deep sea keep you up. So if you ask me—how to be? . . . I will tell you! . . . In the destructive element immerse."

Stein's words are but one outlook on the universal problem that is Jim's, but it is the outlook dramatized in Jim's own actions. It is that dramatized by Sophocles also. Oedipus "submitted" himself to his ideal of the responsible king and citizen, self-sworn to the discovery of the truth. It was the "destructive element," bringing about the terrible revelation of his guilt. So also Jim submits himself to his dream of heroic responsibility and truth to men, fleeing from port to port, and finally to Patusan, to realize it. And, again, the ideal is the "destructive element," bringing about the compact with Brown (a compact made in the profoundest spirit of the dream) and inevitably, along with the compact, destruction. The irony is that Jim, in his destructiveness, was "true." This is the classical tragic irony: the incongruity and yet the effective identity between the constructive will and the destructive act.

Whether Conrad goes beyond that particular tragic incongruity to the other ancient tragic perception, of ennoblement through suffering, is doubtful. The "enigma" that Marlow finds in Jim's career has this other dark and doubtful aspect. When, at the end, after receiving Doramin's bullet, "the white man sent right and left at all those faces a proud and unflinching glance," is he really fulfilled in nobility in our sight? Has his suffering, entailed in his long and strenuous exile and his guilt and his final great loss, given him the knowledge, and with the knowledge the nobility, which is the mysterious and sublime gift of suffering? The answer is doubtful. We need to bring to bear on it the fairly inescapable impression that the only character in the book in whom we can read the stamp of the author's own practical "approval" is the French lieutenant who remained on board the *Patna* while it was being towed into port. The French lieutenant would not have acted as Jim did in the last events on Patusan—indeed is inconceivable in the Patusan circumstances. If, in Conrad's implicit evaluation of his material, the French lieutenant represents the ethically "approved" manner of action and the only one, Jim can scarcely support the complete role of the tragic hero of the classical type, the hero who achieves unique greatness through suf-

fering. (The French lieutenant suffers only for lack of wine.) For our notion of what constitutes a "hero" is thus surely divided: if the French
lieutenant's heroism is the true heroism, Jim's is not, and conversely. No
doubt the division—and it seems to be real in our response to the book—
is associated with a division of allegiance on Conrad's part,[1] between emotional allegiance to Jim's suffering and struggling humanity, in all its
hybristic aspiration, and intellectual allegiance to the code represented
by the lieutenant, in all its severe limitation and calm obscurity. With
this division in mind, it is impossible to identify the "view of life" in
the book as a whole with Stein's view of life, impressive as Stein is in his
broad and enlightened sensitivity: for the French lieutenant knows nothing of a "destructive element," and if he did—which he could not—
would doubtless think that to talk of "submitting" oneself to it was sheer
twaddle.

What intervenes between Conrad's ambivalent attitude toward Jim's
story and the attitudes of Aeschylus and Sophocles toward their subjects
is modern man's spiritual isolation from his fellows. Jim's isolation is profound, most profound and complete at that last moment when he "sent
right and left at all those faces a proud and unflinching glance": here his
aloneness in his dream—his illusion—of faith to men is unqualified, for
the material fact is that he has allowed a brigand to slaughter Dain Waris
and his party, and that he has left the village open to ravage. Moral isolation provides a new inflection of tragedy. Orestes freed Argos from a tyranny, and Oedipus freed Thebes from a plague. Their guilt and suffering
had a constructive social meaning; they had acted for the positive welfare of
the citizens; and that social version of their heroism, internal to the dramas
in which they appear, is the immediate, literal basis of our (because it is
the citizen-chorus's) appraisal of their heroism. But Jim—to use parallel
terms—destroys his city. Thus there is nothing structurally internal to
Jim's story that matches the positive moral relationship, in the ancient
dramas, between the social destiny and the hero's destiny, the relationship
that is presented concretely in the fact that the hero's agony is a saving
social measure. There is nothing to mediate, practically and concretely,
between Jim's "truth" and real social life, as a benefit to and confirma-
tion of the social context. Jim is alone.

And yet one asks, is his last act, when he "takes upon his head" the

---

[1] Albert Guerard discusses this division of allegiance in his *Joseph Conrad* (New
York: New Directions, 1947).

blood-guilt, an atonement? If it were so, it would be atonement not in quite the same sense that the madness and exile of Orestes and the blinding and banishment of Oedipus were atonements, for these involved the restoration of community health, whereas Jim's final act brings about (projectively) the destruction of the community—but in the necessary modern sense, necessitated by the fact of the disintegration of moral bonds between men: an atonement for that social sterility, a sacrifice offered in the name of moral community. If it were so, Jim would still be, metaphorically speaking, the savior of the city. No doubt Sophocles, civic-minded gentleman, did not "approve" of Oedipus: when parricide and incest occur in the leading families, what are the rest of us to do? how is the world's business to be kept up decently? what model shall we look to? But the Greek cities were said to have carried on quarrels over the burial place of Oedipus, for his presence brought fertility to the land. So also the story of Lord Jim is a spiritually fertilizing experience, enlightening the soul as to its own meaning in a time of disorganization and drought; and Conrad's imagination of Jim's story has the seminal virtue of the ancient classic.

In James's *The Portrait of a Lady* we watched the creation of a self. In Conrad's austerely pessimistic work, the self stands already created, the possibilities are closed. Again and again, and finally on Patusan, a "clean slate" is what Jim thinks he has found, a chance to "climb out," to begin over, to perform the deed which will be congruent with his ideal of himself. "A clean slate, did he say?" Marlow comments; "as if the initial word of each our destiny were not graven in imperishable characters upon the face of a rock." The tension, the spiritual drama in Conrad, lie in a person's relation with his destiny. The captain in "The Secret Sharer" acknowledges his profound kinship with a man who has violently transgressed the captain's professional code (the man has murdered another seaman during a voyage, and murder at sea is, in Conrad, something worse than murder; whatever its excuses, it is an inexcusable breach of faith with a community bound together by common hazard); but by the acknowledgment he masters his own identity, integrates, as it were, his unconscious impulses within consciousness, and thereby realizes self-command and command of his ship. In contrast with the captain of "The Secret Sharer," Jim repudiates the other-self that has been revealed to him; at no time does he consciously acknowledge that it *was* himself who jumped from the *Patna*—it was only his body that had jumped; and his career thenceforth is an attempt to prove before men that the gross fact of the jump belied his identity.

James works through recognitions; the self-creating character in James develops by taking into consciousness more and more subtle relations—"seeing" more in a world of virtually infinite possibilities for recognition, and thus molding consciousness, molding himself. Conrad works through epiphanies, that is, through dramatic manifestations of elements hidden or implicit in the already constructed character. The difference of method is suggestive of the difference of world view: in James, the world ("reality" as a whole) being, as it were, an open and fluid system, essentially creative; in Conrad, a closed and static system, incapable of origination though intensely dramatic in its revelations. (Paradoxically, the environments in James's open world are the closed environments of city and house, while those in Conrad's closed world are those of the open, the mobile sea.) The word "epiphany" implies manifestation of divinity, and this meaning of the term can serve us also in analyzing Conrad's method and his vision, if we think of the "dark powers" of the psyche as having the mysterious absoluteness that we associate with the daemonic, and if we think mythologically of a man's destiny both as being carried within him, and, *in effect*—since his acts externalize his destiny—as confronting him from without.

The sunken wreck that strikes the *Patna* is one such epiphany in *Lord Jim,* and this manifestation of "dark power" is coincident with and symbolically identifiable with the impulse that makes Jim jump, an impulse submerged like the wreck, riding in wait, striking from under. Outer nature seems, here, to act in collusion with the hidden portion of the soul. But Conrad's supreme mastery is his ability to make the circumstance of "plot" the inevitable point of discharge of the potentiality of "character." [2] The accident that happens to the *Patna* is not merely a parallel and a metaphor of what happens to Jim at that time, but it is the objective circumstance that discovers Jim to himself. The apparent "collusion" between external nature and the soul, that gives to Conrad's work its quality of the marvelous and its religious temper, is thus, really, only the inevitable working out of character through circumstance.

Another major epiphany is the appearance of Brown on Patusan. The appearance of Brown is, in effect, an externalization of the complex

[2] Morton Dauwen Zabel points this out in his Introduction to *The Portable Conrad* (New York: The Viking Press, Inc., 1947).

of Jim's guilt and his excuses for his guilt, for he judges Brown as he judged himself, as a *victim of circumstances* (the distinction is radical) rather than as a character exposed by circumstances, at least to be given that benefit of doubt which would discriminate intention from deed, ethos from the objective ethical traits to be seen in a man's actions. Therefore he gives Brown a "clean slate," a chance to "climb out"—from himself! But Jim's compact with Brown is more than a compact with his own unacknowledged guilt; it is at the same time, and paradoxically, a lonely act of faith with the white men "out there," the men of Jim's race and traditions, the men upon the sea whose code he had once betrayed, the "home" from which a single impulse of nerves had forever exiled him. Brown is the only white man who has appeared on Patusan to put to test Jim's ethical community with his race and his profession, and in "taking upon his head" responsibility for Brown's honor, he is superbly "true" to that community. But his truth is, effectively, betrayal; it is "the destructive element." Since only a chance in thousands brings Brown to Patusan, again outer nature seems to have acted in collusion with the "dark power" within Jim's own psyche, in order to face him once more with his unacknowledged identity when he is in the full hybris of his truth and his courage. But again the apparent collusion is only the working out of character through circumstance.

The impossibility of escape from the dark companion within leaves a man more perfectly alone in this world because he has that companion —who is always and only himself. The physical settings of Jim's career concretize his isolation. In constant flight from the self that he reads on men's lips but that he refuses to acknowledge except as a freakish injustice of circumstances, and, as he flees, pursuing the heroic ideal which would reconstitute him in the ranks of men where his salvation lies (for, as Conrad says, "in our own hearts we trust for our salvation in the men that surround us"), he comes finally to Patusan, ascends the river to the heart of the island, unarmed (why carry a loaded revolver when it is only oneself that one must face?)—ascends, that is, the dark paths of his own being back to its source: [3] "thirty miles of forest shut it off."

The first description that Marlow gives of the interior of the island is of a conical hill that is "split in two, and with the two halves leaning slightly apart," and in his reminiscences he returns frequently to the image of the hill (it is, indeed, the hill up which Jim hauled the cannon,

[3] The observation is made by Mr. Guerard in *Joseph Conrad*, cited above.

in his first great exploit when he won the faith of the natives and became their protector), particularly to a scene of moonlight when the moon is rising behind the fissured mass.

> On the third day after the full, the moon, as seen from the open space in front of Jim's house . . . rose exactly behind these hills, its diffused light at first throwing the two masses into intensely black relief, and then the nearly perfect disc, glowing ruddily, appeared, gliding upwards between the sides of the chasm, till it floated away above the summits, as if escaping from a yawning grave in gentle triumph. "Wonderful effect," said Jim by my side. "Worth seeing. Is it not?"
>
> And this question was put with a note of personal pride that made me smile, as though he had had a hand in regulating that unique spectacle. He had regulated so many things in Patusan! Things that would have appeared as much beyond his control as the motions of the moon and the stars.

On Marlow's last night on the island he sees the same spectacle again, but the mood is different, oppressive.

> I saw part of the moon glittering through the bushes at the bottom of the chasm. For a moment it looked as though the smooth disc, falling from its place in the sky upon the earth, had rolled to the bottom of that precipice: its ascending movement was like a leisurely rebound; it disengaged itself from the tangle of twigs; the bare contorted limb of some tree, growing on the slope, made a black crack right across its face. It threw its level rays afar as if from a cavern, and in this mournful eclipse-like light the stumps of felled trees uprose very dark, the heavy shadows fell at my feet on all sides . . .

Together Jim and Marlow watch "the moon float away above the chasm between the hills like an ascending spirit out of a grave; its sheen descended, cold and pale, like the ghost of dead sunlight." Carried to the mind by the image of the fissured hill, with the suspiciously ghostlike moon floating out of the chasm, is the relentless solitude of Jim's fate. He is not only an outcast from his kind but he is also an outcast from himself, cloven spiritually, unable to recognize his own identity, separated from himself as the two halves of the hill are separated. And the rebounding moon, in which he has so much pride, "as though he had had a hand in regulating that unique spectacle," remains in the mind as a figure of the ego-ideal, even that ideal of truth by which, Marlow says, Jim approached "greatness as genuine as any man ever achieved": its illusionariness, and the solitude implied by illusion. At the end, after all —when the silver ring that is the token of moral community falls to the floor, and through Jim's "truth" his best friend has been killed and the village under his protection betrayed—Jim is only what he has been; he is of the measure of his acts. To be only what one has been is the sentence of solitary confinement that is passed on everyman. It is in this sense, finally, that Jim is "one of us."

Since Jim is "one of us," the truth about Jim will be—within the scope of the expressiveness of Jim's story—a truth about life; and in view of this responsibility, Conrad's task of evaluation demands that *all* the accessible evidence be presented and that it be submitted to mutually corrective hypotheses of its meaning. There are Jim's actions, which are concrete enough and simple as the concrete is simple. But the significance of action is significance in the judgments of men, which are various; and as soon as judgment is brought to the act, the act becomes not simple but protean. *What, then, is the act?* The question defines Conrad's method in this book, his use of reflector within reflector, point of view within point of view, cross-chronological juxtapositions of events and impressions. Conrad's technical "devices," in this case, represent much more than the word "device" suggests: they represent extreme ethical scrupulosity, even anxiety; for the truth about a man is at once too immense and too delicate to sustain any failure of carefulness in the examiner.

The omniscient early chapters give briefly the conditions of Jim's up-bringing, his heroic dreams, two incidents in his sea training, the *Patna* voyage up to the moment when the submerged wreck strikes, and the courtroom scene with Jim in the dock: that is, the first chapters take us up to the point where the accused is placed before us and the processes of judgment have to begin. From here, Marlow takes over. Marlow is unofficial attorney both for the defense and the prosecution. He selects, objectifies, and humanizes the evidence on both sides, but he lets it— intensified and set in perspective through his intelligent, freely roaming curiosity—speak for itself. Marlow is the most familiar narrative mecha-nism in Conrad's work; and in this particular book *Marlow has to exist.* For Jim's "case" is not an absolute but a relative; it has a being only in relation to what men's minds can make of it. And Marlow provides the necessary medium of an intelligent consciousness, at once a symbol of that relativity, a concretization of the processes by which just judgment may be evoked, and—through his doubt and reverence—an acknowledgment of the irony of judgment of the relative.

The few particulars that are given of Jim's home environment are all we need to give the word "home" potency for this chronicle: there is the parsonage, its decency, its naïveté, its faith, its sterling morality, its representativeness of "the sheltering conception of light and order which is our refuge." In the thirty-fifth chapter, where Marlow takes final farewell of Jim, and Jim says,

> "I must stick to their belief in me to feel safe and to—to" . . . He cast about for a word, seemed to look for it on the sea . . . "to keep in touch with" . . . His voice sank suddenly to a murmur . . . "with those whom, perhaps, I shall never see any more. With—with—you, for instance."

the parsonage home, as well as the community of men upon the sea, contains the "those" with whom Jim must keep in touch through faithfulness in word and act. "Home" is the ethical code which enables men to live together through trust of each other, and which, in so binding them, gives them self-respect. The exclusiveness and naïveté of the parsonage background interpret the symbol of "home" in all its own relativity, its merely provisional status in the jungle of the universe. When we close the book, the symbol of "home" is as ghostlike as the moon over Patusan. But it is the only provision for salvation, in the sense in which Conrad uses the word salvation when he says, "In our own hearts we trust for our salvation in the men that surround us."

The two incidents in Jim's early sea training, the storm in Chapter 1, when he was "too late," and, in Chapter 2, his disablement at the beginning of a hurricane week, when he "felt secretly glad he had not to go on deck," counterpoint his belief in himself with actualities of frustration. A certain distinct polarity is already established, between his dreams and the "facts"; and when, in Chapter 2, Jim suddenly decides to ship as mate on the *Patna*, it is as if we saw a bar magnet curved into a horseshoe and bent until its poles closed, sealing personal will and the fatality of circumstances in a mysterious identity that is the man himself; for his unexplained choice of the *Patna* is in more than one sense a choice of exile. He could have gone back to the home service, after his convalescence;

but he throws in his lot with the men he has seen in that Eastern port (and disdained) who "appeared to live in a crazy maze of plans, hopes, dangers, enterprises . . . in the dark places of the sea," and with those others who had been seduced by "the eternal peace of Eastern sky and sea," who talked "everlastingly of turns of luck . . . and in all they said —in their actions, in their looks, in their persons—could be detected the soft spot, the place of decay . . ." Moreover, on the *Patna* he is in a special sense a man alone, alone with a dream that is unsharable because he is among inferiors: the third chapter presents "the *Patna* gang" from Jim's point of view—"those men did not belong to the world of heroic adventure . . . he rubbed shoulders with them, but they could not touch him; he shared the air they breathed, but he was different . . ." Is his choice of the *Patna* a measure taken to protect his dream from reality? Is it thus significant of his "soft spot"? There is no choice but reality, and actually none but the single, circumscribed, only possible choice that is one's own reality—witnessed by Jim's jump from the *Patna,* as by his shipping on the *Patna* in the first place.

When Sophocles, in his old age, wrote of Oedipus again, he had Oedipus assert his innocence and curse those who had banished him; for Oedipus had acted in ignorance of the circumstances, and therefore could not be held guilty for them. Jim puts up a fight as Oedipus did, and the causes involved are the same: is the self deducible from circumstances? is one guilty for circumstances? is one guilty for oneself when one has no choice but to be oneself? is one guilty for oneself when one is in ignorance of what oneself is? if, with lifelong strife, one refuses to acquiesce in the self, is one guilty for the self? who has a right to pronounce this judgment?

Obviously from this point another device of presentation must be used, other than either objective presentation by the author or subjective presentation through Jim, for Jim is too youthful, idealistic, and ingenuous to throw light on himself, and "objectivity"—the objectivity of the camera and the sound recorder—is hopelessly inadequate to the solution of these questions. Marlow has to take up the case, and Marlow—intelligent professional man of the sea, and insatiably curious psychological observer— brings to bear on it not only Jim's own evidence (and his friendship with Jim draws from Jim much more than he could ever say for himself— brings out gestures and tones, situations and impulses, that only sympathy could bring out), and not only the reactions of the judges (and the judges are more in number than those in the courtroom), but also a marvelously sensitive registration of the concrete detail of life, bits of color and form and movement, a chin, a hand, a shuffle, a vase of dry flowers, a striped pajama suit, that could not be admitted as "evidence" in a formal inquiry, but that are nevertheless essential psychological evidence to the sensitive investigator.

The *Patna* gang has to be presented over again, not now from Jim's point of view but from Marlow's. So far as the *Patna* gang is concerned, the question is, is Jim one of them or "one of us"? Marlowe has only to see the group on a street corner to know that Jim is not one of them; but he pushes further—he is around when the fat captain, in his night-suit, squeezes into the ramshackle gharry and disappears, "departed, disappeared, vanished, absconded; and absurdly enough it looked as though he had taken that gharry with him." It is Marlow's impression of the obscenely ridiculous captain that conveys to us the captain's sur-reality: he is, through Marlow's view, not simply stupid and inferior as he appeared to Jim, but a frightful manifestation of underground evil, as mysterious and unaccountable in its apparition as the captain's vanishing with the gharry is complete; that the captain wears a sleeping suit (like the murderer in "The Secret Sharer") emphasizes the psychological, that is to say spiritual, symbolism of his evil; he is another epiphany, a "showing" from the daemonic underground of the psyche—but he is only that, and the psyche, Jim's psyche, is more than the obscene man in the sleeping suit.

Then Marlow interviews the chief engineer in the hospital, the man with the noble head and the pink toads under his bed. The effort is an effort again to test his perception that Jim is not one of them, but "one of us"; for the initial perception alone is scarcely to be trusted, since Jim, whatever his excuses, had identified himself with the *Patna* gang by jumping from the ship. The pink toads under the chief engineer's bed are a fearful inversion of Jim's own dream: they too are a dream—and the dreamer has a noble head. The pink toads are a horrible degeneration of the dream. They serve as a commentary on the dream that cannot be evaded (no more than can the captain in the sleeping suit). But Jim had stayed for the trial, while the captain had disappeared, the chief engineer had cultivated the d.t.'s, and the second engineer wasn't around (the little man will reappear later, for the act is immortal). It is Jim's dream that makes him stay for the trial, and therefore Jim's dream cannot be identified with the chief engineer's, however identifiable they are in illusionary quality and spiritual potency. Marlow's visit with the chief engineer fixes this judgment of a difference, as well as of a similarity.

These two observations of Marlow's project the question of identity (the question "Who am I?" that is Oedipus' as well as Jim's), that can only be decided by comparison of like things and different things, discrimination of congruences and incongruences. Two identifications of Jim with other persons have been rejected—although even the impulse to distinguish suggests subtle similarities between the objects compared, and we can never forget that Jim was in the lifeboat with the *Patna* gang, though at the other end. The rest of the narrative moves through a devious course of identifications and distinctions. Brierly, the unimpeachable professional seaman, in some astounding way identifies himself with the accused man, Jim, and commits suicide. Is this another version of Jim's "jump"? If so, in avoiding by suicide the possibility of being Jim, Brierly succeeds merely in being what he was trying to avoid; this is Jim's "case" all over again. The loathsome Chester also identifies himself with Jim; Chester instantly spots him as the man for his job—fantastic exile on a guano island; "He is no earthly good for anything," Chester says,—"he would just have done for me"; the man has a "soft spot," and for men with a soft spot, as Jim himself had observed, "death was the only event of their fantastic existence that seemed to have a reasonable certitude of achievement"; for Chester, Jim is "one of us" in a sense that disgusts Marlow, and Marlow's disgust with Chester and therefore with Chester's appraisal of the man helps us to measure Jim: but the fact that Marlow, during those grueling hours in the hotel room when he is writing factitious letters in order to give Jim a chance for privacy with his ordeal, can hesitate between recommending Jim for a decent job and turning him over to Chester still suggests a doubt as to what "one of us" means, whether it has Chester's meaning or Marlow's.

The French lieutenant whom Marlow encounters, though he is a sympathetic man, does *not* identify himself with Jim; and curiously, while the French lieutenant represents the approved ethos of the profession (and not only of the profession of the sea, but of the profession of being human, as the author evaluates his material; for, in that evaluation, being human, as humans ought to be, *is* a profession, with an austere Spartan-like discipline.[4]), he is the only person in the book who does not, in some way, identify himself with Jim except for Cornelius and Brown, who hate him

[4] In his *Joseph Conrad*, Mr. Guerard thoroughly clarifies this issue.

as an opposite and as an indictment of their evil (perhaps the captain of the *Patna* and the chief engineer could be included here, but their presentation is more objective and their attitudes less determinable; although the same point would hold): that is to say that the only cases in which subjective identification with Jim does not take place are those of a man —the French lieutenant—who is above Jim's failings by virtue of his mediocrity, and of men who are below Jim's problem by virtue of their psychotic maliciousness. The portrait of the French lieutenant is extremely careful, as all the portraits in the book are done with extreme care, for on the nature of the man who judges depends the validity of the judgment.

> He clasped his hands on his stomach again. "I remained on board that—that—my memory is going (*s'en va*). Ah! *Patt-nà*. *C'est bien ça. Patt-nà. Merci*. It is droll how one forgets. I stayed on that ship thirty hours . . ."

And just a moment before, we have learned that "all the time of towing we had two quartermasters stationed with axes by the hawsers, to cut us clear of our tow in case she . . ." The French lieutenant's failure to remember even the name of the ship, on which he had stayed for thirty hours *after* Jim had jumped, and the laconic tone of the information about the quartermasters' assignment, are a judgment of Jim in terms of Jim's own dream. The French lieutenant's unconscious heroism is the heroism that Jim had made a conscious ideal; and his witness measures Jim's failure by the painful difference of fact. And yet this damning commentary appears as inconclusive as that of the pink toads under the chief engineer's bed; it is as far from and as near to "the case."

The distinguished naturalist Stein offers another approach. Stein has been a hero of action like the French lieutenant, but he is also a hero of the intellect, and, in his way, a psychologist, a philosopher, and an artist. Stein is able to identify himself with Jim through his own profound idealism (as Marlow does through doubt). But Stein's idealism, so far as we know, has never differentiated itself from his actions; he has the gift of nature which is itself ideal; he had known, Marlow says, how "to follow his destiny with unfaltering footsteps." Stein "diagnoses the case" of Jim, making it quite simple "and altogether hopeless" by framing it in the question: "how to be." "I tell you, my friend," he says, "it is not good for you to find you cannot make your dream come true, for the reason that you not strong enough are, or not clever enough. *Ja!* . . . And all the time you are such a fine fellow, too! *Wie?* . . . How can that be? . . ."

The shadow prowling amongst the graves of butterflies laughed boisterously.

Stein gives Jim his great chance to make his dream come true, by sending him to Patusan. This journey is ambiguous: "once before Patusan had been used as a grave," Marlow reflects; while Stein prowls "amongst the graves of butterflies," Brierly's remark about Jim recurs to Marlow's mind: "Let him creep twenty feet underground and stay there"; and there is the fissured hill at the heart of Patusan, whose chasm is like a "yawning grave," from which the moon (the dream) rises "like an ascending spirit out of a grave . . . like the ghost of dead sunlight." The ancient mythical heroes, Odysseus and Aeneas, made the "journey underground" to Hades in search of wisdom, and brought it back to daylight —the wisdom which was knowledge of their own destinies. And shadowily behind them is the barbarous ritual that made a king by burying him and disinterring him, a surrogate perhaps, or a "story" (mythos), to stand for the killing of an old king and his "resurrection" in a new one. In the grave of Patusan—"the secular gloom and the old mankind"—Jim's dream does come true. But the doubt remains as to whether, like the ancient heroes, he brought back to daylight the wisdom of his destiny—or, in other terms, whether in that grave an old self was really buried and from it a new one congruent with his dream was resurrected.

The test of daylight, of the bright sea beyond the dark island, offers itself only through Brown. Jim identifies himself with Brown in two ways, through his guilt, and through his honor: Brown is at once the "dark power" in Jim's psyche and his only effective bond with the brightness outside himself, the community of tradition to which "we trust for our salvation." Brown's ambivalence for Jim is Jim's own ambivalence, and it is, in its most extensive sense, the ambivalence that exists in all historical and personal stages of experience where law (the "code") and the self question each other—as well in the Athens of Thucydides and Euripides as in our own time, and as well, we must surmise, in Conrad as in Jim. The tale Conrad prepared to narrate was a tale in the manner of the older classical dramatists, wherein law—whether divine, as with

Aeschylus, or natural, as with Sophocles—is justified to the self, whatever its agonies of discovery. But he managed to do a tale that put both the law and the self to question, and left them there. At the end (dated July 1900), Stein does not help:

> Stein has aged greatly of late. He feels it himself, and says often that he is "preparing to leave all this; preparing to leave . . ." while he waves his hand sadly at his butterflies.

ON *Sons and Lovers*

Novels, like other dramatic art, deal with conflicts of one kind or another—conflicts that are, in the work of the major novelists, drawn from life in the sense that they are representative of real problems in life; and the usual urgency in the novelist is to find the technical means which will afford an ideal resolution of the conflict and solution of the living problem—still "ideal" even if tragic. Technique is his art itself, in its procedural aspect; and the validity of his solution of a problem is dependent upon the adequacy of his technique. The more complex and intransigent the problem, the more subtle his technical strategies will evidently need to be, if they are to be effective. The decade of World War I brought into full and terrible view the collapse of values that had prophetically haunted the minds of novelists as far back as Dostoevski and Flaubert and Dickens, or even farther back, to Balzac and Stendhal. With that decade, and increasingly since, the problems of modern life have appeared intransigent indeed; and, in general, the growth of that intransigence has been reflected in an increasing concern with technique on the part of the artist. D. H. Lawrence's sensitivity to twentieth-century chaos was peculiarly intense, and his passion for order was similarly intense; but this sensitivity and this passion did not lead him to concentrate on refinements and subtleties of novelistic technique in the direction laid out, for instance, by James and Conrad. Hence, as readers first approaching his work, almost inevitably we feel disappointment and even perhaps shock, that writing so often "loose" and repetitious and such unrestrained emotionalism over glandular matters should appear in the work of a novelist who is assumed to have an important place in the literary canon. "There is no use," Francis Fergusson says, "trying to appreciate [Lawrence] solely as an artist; he was himself too often impatient of the demands of art, which seemed to him trivial

245

compared with the quest he followed." [1] And Stephen Spender phrases the problem of Lawrence in this way: what interested him "was the tension between art and life, not the complete resolution of the problems of life within the illusion of art . . . For him literature is a kind of pointer to what is outside literature . . . This outsideness of reality is for Lawrence the waters of baptism in which man can be reborn." [2] We need to approach Lawrence with a good deal of humility about "art" and a good deal of patience for the disappointments he frequently offers as an artist, for it is only thus that we shall be able to appreciate the innovations he actually made in the novel as well as the importance and profundity of his vision of modern life.

Sons and Lovers appears to have the most conventional chronological organization—the extreme reverse of Conrad's intricate cross-chronology; it is the kind of organization that a naïve autobiographical novelist would tend to use, with only the thinnest pretense at disguising the personally retrospective nature of the material. We start with the marriage of the parents and the birth of the children. We learn of the daily life of the family while the children are growing up, the work, the small joys, the parental strife. Certain well-defined emotional pressures become apparent: the children are alienated from their father, whose personality degenerates gradually as he feels his exclusion; the mother more and more completely dominates her sons' affections, aspirations, mental habits. Urged by her toward middle-class refinements, they enter white-collar jobs, thus making one more dissociation between themselves and their proletarian father. As they attempt to orient themselves toward biological adulthood, the old split in the family is manifested in a new form, as an internal schism in the characters of the sons; they cannot reconcile sexual choice with the idealism their mother has inculcated. This inner strain leads to the older son's death. The same motif is repeated in the case of Paul, the younger one. Paul's first girl, Miriam, is a cerebral type, and the mother senses in her an obvious rivalry for domination of Paul's sensibility. The mother is the stronger influence, and Paul withdraws from Miriam; but with her own victory Mrs. Morel begins to realize the discord she has produced in his character, and tries to release her hold on him by unconsciously seeking her own death. Paul finds another girl, Clara, but the damage is already

---

[1] "D. H. Lawrence's Sensibility," in *Critiques and Essays in Modern Fiction*, edited by John W. Aldridge (New York: The Ronald Press Company, 1952), p. 328.
[2] "The Life of Literature," in *Partisan Review*, December, 1948.

too deeply designed, and at the time of his mother's death, he voluntarily gives up Clara, knowing that there is but one direction he can take, and that is to go with his mother. At the end he is left emotionally derelict, with only the "drift toward death."

From this slight sketch, it is clear that the book is organized not merely on a chronological plan showing the habits and vicissitudes of a Nottinghamshire miner's family, but that it has a structure rigorously controlled by an idea: an idea of an organic disturbance in the relationships of men and women—a disturbance of sexual polarities that is first seen in the disaffection of mother and father, then in the mother's attempt to substitute her sons for her husband, finally in the sons' unsuccessful struggle to establish natural manhood. Lawrence's development of the idea has certain major implications: it implies that his characters have transgressed against the natural life-directed condition of the human animal—against the elementary biological rhythms he shares with the rest of biological nature; and it implies that this offense against life has been brought about by a failure to respect the complete and terminal individuality of persons —by a twisted desire to "possess" other persons, as the mother tries to "possess" her husband, then her sons, and as Miriam tries to "possess" Paul. Lawrence saw this offense as a disease of modern life in all its manifestations, from sexual relationships to those broad social and political relationships that have changed people from individuals to anonymous economic properties or to military units or to ideological automatons.

The controlling idea is expressed in the various episodes—the narrative logic of the book. It is also expressed in imagery—the book's poetic logic. In previous studies we have discussed, from a number of points of view, the function of imagery in novels, but nowhere else do we find the image so largely replacing episode and discursive analysis and taking over the expressive functions of these, as it does in Lawrence. The chief reason for the extraordinary predominance of the image, as an absolute expressive medium, in Lawrence, lies in the character of the idea which is his subject. He must make us aware—sensitively aware, not merely conceptually aware—of the profound life force whose rhythms the natural creature obeys; and he must make us aware of the terminal individuality—the absolute "otherness" or "outsideness"—that is the natural form of things and of the uncorrupted person. We must be made aware of these through the *feelings* of his people, for only in feeling have the biological life force and the sense of identity, either the identity of self or of others, any immediacy

247

of reality. He seeks the objective equivalent of feeling in the image. As Francis Fergusson says, Lawrence's imagination was so concrete that he seems not "to distinguish between the reality and the metaphor or symbol which makes it plain to us." [3] But the most valid symbols are the most concrete realities. Lawrence's great gift for the symbolic image was a function of his sensitivity to and passion for the meaning of real things—for the individual expression that real forms have. In other words, his gift for the image arose directly from his vision of life as infinitely creative of individual identities, each whole and separate and to be reverenced as such.

Let us examine the passage with which the first chapter of *Sons and Lovers* ends—where Mrs. Morel, pregnant with Paul, wanders deliriously in the garden, shut out of the house by Morel in his drunkenness. Mrs. Morel is literally a vessel of the life force that seems to thrust itself at her in nature from all sides, but she is also in rebellion against it and the perfume of the pollen-filled lilies makes her gasp with fear.

> The moon was high and magnificent in the August night. Mrs. Morel, seared with passion, shivered to find herself out there in a great white light, that fell cold on her, and gave a shock to her inflamed soul. She stood for a few moments helplessly staring at the glistening great rhubarb leaves near the door. Then she got the air into her breast. She walked down the garden path, trembling in every limb, while the child boiled within her . . .
>
> She hurried out of the side garden to the front, where she could stand as if in an immense gulf of white light, the moon streaming high in face of her, the moonlight standing up from the hills in front, and filling the valley where the Bottoms crouched, almost blindingly. There, panting and half weeping in reaction from the stress, she murmured to herself over and over again: "The nuisance! the nuisance!"
>
> She became aware of something about her. With an effort she roused herself to see what it was that penetrated her consciousness. The tall white lilies were reeling in the moonlight, and the air was charged with their perfume, as with a presence. Mrs. Morel gasped slightly in fear. She touched the big, pallid flowers on their petals, then shivered. They seemed to be stretching in the moonlight. She put her hand into one white bin: the gold scarcely showed on her fingers by moonlight. She bent down to look at the binful of yellow

---

[3] Fergusson, *op. cit.*, p. 335.

pollen; but it only appeared dusky. Then she drank a deep draught of the scent. It almost made her dizzy.

Mrs. Morel leaned on the garden gate, looking out, and she lost herself awhile. She did not know what she thought. Except for a slight feeling of sickness, and her consciousness in the child, herself melted out like a scent into the shiny, pale air.

She finally arouses Morel from his drunken sleep and he lets her in. Unfastening her brooch at the bedroom mirror, she sees that her face is smeared with the yellow dust of the lilies.

The imagery of the streaming moonlight is that of a vast torrential force, "magnificent" and inhuman, and it equates not only with that phallic power of which Mrs. Morel is the rebellious vessel but with the greater and universal demiurge that was anciently called Eros—the power springing in plants and hurling the planets, giving the "glistening great rhubarb leaves" their fierce identity, fecundating and stretching the lilies. The smear of yellow pollen on Mrs. Morel's face is a grossly humorous irony. This passage is a typifying instance of the spontaneous identification Lawrence constantly found between image and meaning, between real things and what they symbolize.

Our particular culture has evolved deep prohibitions against the expression, or even the subjective acknowledgment of the kind of phallic reality with which Lawrence was concerned—and with which ancient religions were also concerned. Certainly one factor in the uneasiness that Lawrence frequently causes us is the factor of those cultural prohibitions. But these prohibitions themselves Lawrence saw as disease symptoms, though the disease was far more extensive and radical than a taboo on the phallus. It was a spiritual disease that broke down the sense of identity, of "separate selfhood," while at the same time it broke down the sense of rhythm with universal nature. Paul Morel, working his fairly unconscious, adolescent, sexual way toward Miriam, finds that rhythm and that selfhood in the spatial proportions of a wren's nest in a hedge.

He crouched down and carefully put his finger through the thorns into the round door of the nest.

"It's almost as if you were feeling inside the live body of the bird," he said, "it's so warm. They say a bird makes its nest round like a cup with pressing its breast on it. Then how did it make the ceiling round, I wonder?"

When Paul takes his first country walk with Clara and Miriam, the appearance of a red stallion in the woods vividly realizes in unforced symbolic dimension the power which will drive Paul from Miriam to Clara, while the image also realizes the great horse itself in its unique and mysterious identity.

> As they were going beside the brook, on the Willey Water side, looking through the brake at the edge of the wood, where pink campions glowed under a few sunbeams, they saw, beyond the tree-trunks and the thin hazel bushes, a man leading a great bay horse through the gullies. The big red beast seemed to dance romantically through that dimness of green hazel drift, away there where the air was shadowy, as if it were in the past, among the fading bluebells that might have bloomed for Deirdre . . .
>
> The great horse breathed heavily, shifting round its red flanks, and looking suspiciously with its wonderful big eyes upwards from under its lowered head and falling mane . . .

A simple descriptive passage like the following, showing a hen pecking at a girl's hand, conveys the animal dynamics that is the urgent phase of the phallic power working in the boy and the girl, but its spontaneous symbolism of a larger reality is due to its faithfulness to the way a hen does peck and the feeling of the pecking—due, that is, to the actuality or "identity" of the small, homely circumstance itself.

> As he went round the back, he saw Miriam kneeling in front of the hen-coop, some maize in her hand, biting her lip, and crouching in an intense attitude. The hen was eyeing her wickedly. Very gingerly she put forward her hand. The hen bobbed for her. She drew back quickly with a cry, half of fear, half of chagrin.
>
> "It won't hurt you," said Paul.
>
> She flushed crimson and started up.
>
> "I only wanted to try," she said in a low voice.
>
> "See, it doesn't hurt," he said, and, putting only two corns in his palm, he let the hen peck, peck, peck at his bare hand. "It only makes you laugh," he said.
>
> She put her hand forward, and dragged it away, tried again, and started back with a cry. He frowned.
>
> "Why, I'd let her take corn from my face," said Paul, "only she bumps a bit. She's ever so neat. If she wasn't, look how much ground she'd peck up every day."

He waited grimly, and watched. At last Miriam let the bird peck from her hand. She gave a little cry—fear, and pain because of fear—rather pathetic. But she had done it, and she did it again.

"There, you see," said the boy. "It doesn't hurt, does it?"

There is more terse and obvious symbolism, of the typical kind in Lawrence, in that sequence where Clara's red carnations splatter their petals over her clothes and on the ground where she and Paul first make love, but we acquire the best and the controlling sense of Lawrence's gift for the image, as dramatic and thematic expression, in those passages where his urgency is to see *things* and to see them clearly and completely in their most individualizing traits, for the character of his vision is such that, in truly seeing them as they are, he sees through them to what they mean.

We have fairly frequently noticed in these studies the differentiating significance of a writer's treatment of nature—that is, of that part of "nature" which is constituted by earth and air and water and the nonhuman creatures; and we have found that attitudes toward nature were deeply associated with attitudes toward human "good," human destiny, human happiness, human salvation, the characteristic problems of being human. One might cite, for instance, in *Tom Jones*, Fielding's highly stylized treatment of outdoor nature (as in the passage in which Tom dreams of Sophia beside the brook, and Mollie Seagrim approaches): here nature has only generalized attributes for whose description and understanding certain epithets in common educated currency are completely adequate—brooks murmur, breezes whisper, birds trill; nature is really a linguistic construction, and this rationalization of nature is appropriate in Fielding's universe since everything there exists ideally as an object of *ratio*, of reasoning intelligence. We have noticed in Jane Austen's *Pride and Prejudice* (in the description of Darcy's estate, for example) that outdoor nature again has importance only as it serves to express rational and social character—wherefore again the generalized epithet that represents nature as either the servant of intelligence or the space where intelligence operates. In George Eliot's *Adam Bede*, where there is relatively a great deal of "outdoors," nature is man's plowfield, the acre in which he finds social and ethical expression through work; this is only a different variety of the conception of nature as significant by virtue of what man's intelligential and social character makes of it for his ends.

With Emily Brontë, we come nearer to Lawrence, though not very near. In *Wuthering Heights,* nature's importance is due not to its yielding itself up to domestication in man's reason, or offering itself as an instrument by which he expresses his conscience before God or society, but to its fiercely unregenerate difference from all that civilized man is—a difference that it constantly forces on perception by animal-like attacks on and disruptions of human order. In Hardy, nature is also a daemonic entity in its own right, and not only unrationalizable but specifically hostile to the human reason. It is worth noting that, among all English novelists, Hardy and Lawrence have the most faithful touch for the things of nature and the greatest evocative genius in bringing them before the imagination. But there are certain definitive differences of attitude. Both Emily Brontë's and Hardy's worlds are dual, and there is no way of bringing the oppositions of the dualism together: on the one side of the cleavage are those attributes of man that we call "human," his reason, his ethical sensibility; and on the other side is "nature"—the elements and the creatures and man's own instinctive life that he shares with the nonhuman creatures. The opposition is resolved only by destruction of the "human": a destruction that is in Emily Brontë profoundly attractive, in Hardy tragic. But Lawrence's world is multiple rather than dual. Everything in it is a separate and individual "other," every person, every creature, every object (like the madonna lilies, the rhubarb plants, the wren's nest, the stallion); and there is a creative relationship between people and between people and things so long as this "otherness" is acknowledged. When it is denied—and it is denied when man tries to rationalize nature and society, or when he presumptuously assumes the things of nature to be merely instruments for the expression of himself, or when he attempts to exercise personal possessorship over people—then he destroys his own selfhood and exerts a destructive influence all about him.

In *Sons and Lovers,* only in Morel himself, brutalized and spiritually maimed as he is, does the germ of selfhood remain intact; and—this is the correlative proposition in Lawrence—in him only does the biological life force have simple, unequivocal assertion. Morel wants to live, by hook or crook, while his sons want to die. To live is to obey a rhythm involving more than conscious attitudes and involving more than human beings—involving all nature; a rhythm indifferent to the greediness of reason, indifferent to idiosyncrasies of culture and idealism. The image associated with Morel is that of the coalpits, where he descends daily and from which he ascends at night blackened and tired. It is a symbol of rhythmic descent and ascent, like a sexual rhythm, or like the rhythm of sleep and awaking or of death and life. True, the work in the coalpits reverses the natural use of the hours of light and dark and is an economic distortion of that rhythm in nature—and Morel and the other colliers bear the spiritual traumata of that distortion; for Lawrence is dealing with the real environment of modern men, in its complexity and injuriousness. Nevertheless, the work at the pits is still symbolic of the greater rhythm governing life and obedience to which is salvation. Throughout the book, the coalpits are always at the horizon.

> On the fallow land the young wheat shone silkily. Minton pit waved its plumes of white steam, coughed, and rattled hoarsely.
> "Now look at that!" said Mrs. Morel. Mother and son stood on the road to watch. Along the ridge of the great pit-hill crawled a little group in silhouette against the sky, a horse, a small truck, and a man. They climbed the incline against the heavens. At the end the man tipped the waggon. There was an undue rattle as the waste fell down the sheer slope of the enormous bank . . .
> "Look how it heaps together," [Paul says of the pit] "like something alive almost—a big creature that you don't know . . . And all the trucks standing waiting, like a string of beasts to be fed . . . I like the feel of *men* on things, while they're alive. There's a feel of men about trucks, because they've been handled with men's hands, all of them."

Paul associates the pits not only with virility but with being alive. The trucks themselves become alive because they have been handled by men. The symbolism of the pits is identical with that of Morel, the father, the irrational life principle that is unequally embattled against the death principle in the mother, the rational and idealizing principle working rhythmlessly, greedily, presumptuously, and possessively.

The sons' attitude toward the father is ambivalent, weighted toward hate because the superior cultural equipment of the mother shows his crudeness in relief; but again and again bits of homely characterization of Morel show that the children—and even the mother herself—sense, however uncomfortably, the attractiveness of his simple masculine integrity. He has, uninjurable, what the mother's possessiveness has injured in the sons.

"Shut that doo-er!" bawled Morel furiously.

Annie banged it behind her, and was gone.

"If tha oppens it again while I'm weshin' me, I'll ma'e thy jaw rattle," he threatened from the midst of his soapsuds. Paul and the mother frowned to hear him.

Presently he came running out of the scullery, with the soapy water dripping from him, dithering with cold.

"Oh, my sirs!" he said. "Wheer's my towel?"

It was hung on a chair to warm before the fire, otherwise he would have bullied and blustered. He squatted on his heels before the hot baking-fire to dry himself.

"F-ff-f!" he went, pretending to shudder with cold.

"Goodness, man, don't be such a kid!" said Mrs. Morel. "It's *not* cold."

"Thee strip thysen stark nak'd to wesh thy flesh i' that scullery," said the miner, as he rubbed his hair; "nowt b'r a ice-'ouse!"

"And I shouldn't make that fuss," replied his wife.

"No, tha'd drop down stiff, as dead as a door-knob, wi' thy nesh sides."

"Why is a door-knob deader than anything else?" asked Paul, curious.

"Eh, I dunno; that's what they say," replied his father. "But there's that much draught i' yon scullery, as it blows through your ribs like through a five-barred gate."

"It would have some difficulty in blowing through yours," said Mrs. Morel.

Morel looked down ruefully at his sides.

"Me!" he exclaimed. "I'm nowt b'r a skinned rabbit. My bones fair juts out on me."

"I should like to know where," retorted his wife.

"Iv'ry-wheer! I'm nobbut a sack o' faggots."

Mrs. Morel laughed. He had still a wonderfully young body, muscular, without any fat. His skin was smooth and clear. It might have been the body of a man of twenty-eight, except that there were, perhaps, too many blue scars, like tattoo-marks, where the coal-dust remained under the skin, and that his chest was too hairy. But he put his hands on his sides ruefully. It was his fixed belief that, because he did not get fat, he was as thin as a starved rat.

Paul looked at his father's thick, brownish hands all scarred, with broken nails, rubbing the fine smoothness of his sides, and the incongruity struck him. It seemed strange they were the same flesh.

Morel talks the dialect that is the speech of physical tenderness in Law-rence's books.[4] It is to the dialect of his father that Paul reverts when he is tussling with Beatrice in adolescent erotic play (letting the mother's bread burn, that he should have been watching), and that Arthur, the only one of the sons whom the mother has not corrupted, uses in his love-making, and that Paul uses again when he makes love to Clara, the uncomplex woman who is able for a while to give him his sexual manhood and his "separate selfhood." The sons never use the dialect with their mother, and Paul never uses it with Miriam. It is the speech used by Mellors in *Lady Chatterley's Lover;* and, significantly perhaps, Mellors' name is an anagram on the name Morel.

Some of the best moments in the children's life are associated with the father, when Morel has his "good" periods and enters again into the in-timate activity of the family—and some of the best, most simply objective writing in the book communicates these moments, as for instance the pas-sage in Chapter 4 where Morel is engaged in making fuses.

> Morel fetched a sheaf of long sound wheat-straws from the attic. These he cleaned with his hand, till each one gleamed like a stalk of gold, after which he cut the straws into lengths of about six inches, leaving, if he could, a notch at the bottom of each piece. He always had a beautifully sharp knife that could cut a straw clean without hurting it. Then he set in the middle of the table a heap of gun-powder, a little pile of black grains upon the white-scrubbed board. He made and trimmed the straws while Paul and Annie filled and plugged them. Paul loved to see the black grains trickle down a crack in his palm into the mouth of the straw, peppering jollily downwards till the straw was full. Then he bunged up the mouth with a bit of soap—which he got on his thumb-nail from a pat in a saucer—and the straw was finished.

There is a purity of realization in this very simple kind of exposition that, on the face of it, resists associating itself with any *symbolic* function—if we tend to think of a "symbol" as splitting itself apart into a thing and a meaning, with a mental arrow connecting the two. The best in Lawrence carries the authenticity of a faithfully observed, concrete actuality that re-fuses to be so split; its symbolism is a radiation that leaves it intact in itself.

[4] This observation is made by Diana Trilling in her Introduction to *The Portable D. H. Lawrence* (New York: The Viking Press, Inc., 1947).

So, in the passage above, the scene is intact as homely realism, but it radiates Lawrence's controlling sense of the characterful integrity of objects —the clean wheat straws, the whitely scrubbed table, the black grains peppering down a crack in the child's palm, the bung of soap on a thumbnail —and that integrity is here associated with the man Morel and his own integrity of warm and absolute maleness. Thus it is another representation of the creative life force witnessed in the independent objectivity of things that are wholly concrete and wholly themselves.

The human attempt to distort and corrupt that selfhood is reflected in Miriam's attitude toward flowers.

> Round the wild, tussocky lawn at the back of the house was a thorn hedge, under which daffodils were craning forward from among their sheaves of grey-green blades. The cheeks of the flowers were greenish with cold. But still some had burst, and their gold ruffled and glowed. Miriam went on her knees before one cluster, took a wild-looking daffodil between her hands, turned up its face of gold to her, and bowed down, caressing it with her mouth and cheeks and brow. He stood aside, with his hands in his pockets, watching her. One after another she turned up to him the faces of the yellow, bursten flowers appealingly, fondling them lavishly all the while. . . .
> "Why must you always be fondling things!" he said irritably. . . . "Can you never like things without clutching them as if you wanted to pull the heart out of them? . . . You're always begging things to love you. . . . Even the flowers, you have to fawn on them—"
> Rhythmically, Miriam was swaying and stroking the flower with her mouth. . . .
> "You don't want to love—your eternal and abnormal craving is to be loved. You aren't positive, you're negative. You absorb, absorb, as if you must fill yourself up with love, because you've got a shortage somewhere."

The relationship of the girl to the flowers is that of a blasphemous possessorship which denies the separateness of living entities—the craving to break down boundaries between thing and thing, that is seen also in Miriam's relationship with Paul, whom she cannot love without trying to absorb him. In contrast, there is the flower imagery in the eleventh chapter, where Paul goes out into the night and the garden in a moment of emotional struggle.

256

It grew late. Through the open door, stealthily, came the scent of madonna lilies, almost as if it were prowling abroad. Suddenly he got up and went out of doors.

The beauty of the night made him want to shout. A half-moon, dusky gold, was sinking behind the black sycamore at the end of the garden, making the sky dull purple with its glow. Nearer, a dim white fence of lilies went across the garden, and the air all round seemed to stir with scent, as if it were alive. He went across the bed of pinks, whose keen perfume came sharply across the rocking, heavy scent of the lilies, and stood alongside the white barrier of flowers. They flagged all loose, as if they were panting. The scent made him drunk. He went down to the field to watch the moon sink under.

A corncrake in the hay-close called insistently. The moon slid quite quickly downwards, growing more flushed. Behind him the great flowers leaned as if they were calling. And then, like a shock, he caught another perfume, something raw and coarse. Hunting round, he found the purple iris, touched their fleshy throats and their dark, grasping hands. At any rate, he had found something. They stood stiff in the darkness. Their scent was brutal. The moon was melting down upon the crest of the hill. It was gone; all was dark. The corn-crake called still.

The flowers here have a fierce "thereness" or "otherness" establishing them as existences in their own right, as separate, strange selves, and the demiurgic Eros is rudely insistent in their scent. Paul's perception of that independent life puts him into relation with himself, and the moment of catalytic action is marked by the brief sentence: "At any rate, he had found something." The "something" that he finds is simply the iris, dark, fleshy, mysterious, alien. He goes back into the house and tells his mother that he has decided to break off with Miriam.

Darkness—as the darkness of this night in the garden—has in Lawrence a special symbolic potency. It is a natural and universal symbol, but it offers itself with special richness to Lawrence because of the character of his governing vision. Darkness is half of the rhythm of the day, the darkness of unconsciousness is half of the rhythm of the mind, and the darkness of death is half of the rhythm of life. Denial of this phase of the universal tide is the great sin, the sin committed by modern economy and modern rationalism. In acceptance of the dark, man is renewed to himself—and to light, to consciousness, to reason, to brotherhood. But by refusal to accept that half of the rhythm, he becomes impotent, his reason becomes destructive, and he loses the sense of the independence of others which is essential to brotherhood. In the thirteenth chapter of *Sons and Lovers* there is a passage that realizes something of what we have been saying. It occurs just after Paul has made love to Clara in a field.

> All the while the peewits were screaming in the field. When he came to, he wondered what was near his eyes, curving and strong with life in the dark, and what voice it was speaking. Then he realized it was the grass, and the peewit was calling. The warmth was Clara's breathing heaving. He lifted his head, and looked into her eyes. They were dark and shining and strange, life wild at the source staring into his life, stranger to him, yet meeting him; and he put his face down on her throat, afraid. What was she? A strong, strange, wild life, that breathed with his in the darkness through this hour. It was all so much bigger than themselves that he was hushed. They had met, and included in their meeting the thrust of the manifold grass-stems, the cry of the peewit, the wheel of the stars . . .
>
> . . . after such an evening they both were very still. . . . They felt small, half afraid, childish, and wondering, like Adam and Eve when they lost their innocence and realized the magnificence of the power which drove them out of Paradise and across the great night and the great day of humanity. It was for each of them an initiation. . . . To know their own nothingness, to know the tremendous living flood which carried them always, gave them rest within themselves. If so great a magnificent power could overwhelm them, identify them altogether with itself, so that they knew they were only grains in the tremendous heave that lifted every grass-blade its little height, and every tree, and living thing, then why fret about themselves? They could let themselves be carried by life, and they felt a sort of peace each in the other. There was a verification which they had had together. Nothing could nullify it, nothing could take it away; it was almost their belief in life.

But then we are told that "Clara was not satisfied . . . She thought it was he whom she wanted . . . She had not got him; she was not satisfied." This is the impulse toward personal possessorship that constantly confuses and distorts human relationships in Lawrence's books; it is a denial of the otherness of people, and a denial, really, of the great inhuman life force, the primal Otherness through which people have their independent definition as well as their creative community. Paul had felt that "his experience had been impersonal, and not Clara"; and he had wanted the same impersonality in Clara, an impersonality consonant with that of the manifold grass stems and the peewits' calling and the wheel of the stars. André Malraux, in his preface to the French translation of *Lady Chatterley's Lover,* says that this "couple-advocate," Lawrence, is concerned not with his own individuality or that of his mate, but with "being": "Lawrence has no wish to be either happy or great," Malraux says; "he is only concerned with being." [5] The concern with being, with simple being-a-self (as distinguished from imposing the ego or abdicating selfhood in the mass), can be understood only in the context of twentieth-century man's resignation to herd ideologies, herd recreations, herd rationalizations. Lawrence's missionary and prophetic impulse, like Dostoevski's, was to combat the excesses of rationalism and individualism, excesses that have led—paradoxically enough—to the release of monstrously destructive irrationals and to the impotence of the individual. He wanted to bring man's self-definition and creativity back into existence through recognition of and vital relationship with the rhythms that men share with the nonhuman world; for he thought that thus men could find not only the selves that they had denied, but also the brotherhood they had lost.

The darkness of the phallic consciousness is the correlative of a passionate life assertion, strong as the thrust of the grass stems in the field where Paul and Clara make love, and as the dynamics of the wheeling stars. "In the lowest trough of the night" there is always "a flare of the pit." A pillar of cloud by day, the pit is a pillar of fire by night: and the Lord is at the pit top. As a descent of darkness and an ascent of flame is associated with the secret, essential, scatheless maleness of the father, so also the passionate self-forgetful play of the children is associated with a fiery light in the night—an isolated lamppost, a blood-red moon, and behind, "the great scoop of darkness, as if all the night were there." It is this understanding of the symbolism of darkness in Lawrence that gives tragic dignity to such a scene as that of the bringing home of William's coffin through the darkness of the night.

> Morel and Paul went, with a candle, into the parlour. There was no gas there. The father unscrewed the top of the big mahogany oval table, and cleared the middle of the room; then he arranged six chairs opposite each other, so that the coffin could stand on their beds.

[5] In *Criterion,* XII:xlvii (1932–1933), 217.

"You niver seed such a length as he is!" said the miner, and watching anxiously as he worked.

Paul went to the bay window and looked out. The ash-tree stood monstrous and black in front of the wide darkness. It was a faintly luminous night. Paul went back to his mother.

At ten o'clock Morel called:

"He's here!"

Everyone started. There was a noise of unbarring and unlocking the front door, which opened straight from the night into the room.

"Bring another candle," called Morel. . . .

There was the noise of wheels. Outside in the darkness of the street below Paul could see horses and a black vehicle, one lamp, and a few pale faces; then some men, miners, all in their shirt-sleeves, seemed to struggle in the obscurity. Presently two men appeared, bowed beneath a great weight. It was Morel and his neighbour.

"Steady!" called Morel, out of breath.

He and his fellow mounted the steep garden step, heaved into the candle-light with their gleaming coffin-end. Limbs of other men were seen struggling behind. Morel and Burns, in front, staggered; the great dark weight swayed.

"Steady, steady!" cried Morel, as if in pain. . . .

The coffin swayed, the men began to mount the three steps with their load. Annie's candle flickered, and she whimpered as the first men appeared, and the limbs and bowed heads of six men struggled to climb into the room, bearing the coffin that rode like sorrow on their living flesh.

Here the darkness appears in another indivisible aspect of its mystery—as the darkness of death. Perhaps no other modern writer besides Rilke and Mann has tried so sincerely to bring death into relationship with life as Lawrence did, and each under the assumption that life, to know itself creatively, must know its relationship with death; a relationship which the ethos of some hundred and fifty years of rationalism and industrialism and "progress" have striven to exorcise, and by that perversion brought men to an abject worship of death and to holocausts such as that of Hiroshima. *Sons and Lovers* ends with Paul a derelict in the "drift toward death," which Lawrence thought of as the disease-syndrome of his time and of Europe. But the death drift, the death worship, is for Lawrence a hideous distortion of the relationship of death to life. In the scene in which William's coffin is brought home, the front door "opened straight from the night into the room." So, in their rhythmic proportions, life and death open straight into each other, as do the light of consciousness and the darkness of the unconscious, and the usurpation of either one is a perversion of the other. Stephen Spender calls Lawrence "the most hopeful modern writer." His "dark gods," Spender says,

> are symbols of an inescapable mystery: the point of comprehension where the senses are aware of an otherness in objects which extends beyond the senses, and the possibility of a relationship between the human individual and the forces outside himself, which is capable of creating in him a new state of mind. Lawrence is the most hopeful modern writer, because he looks beyond the human to the non-human, which can be discovered within the human.[6]

[6] "The Life of Literature," *op. cit.*

ON *A Portrait of the Artist as a Young Man*

It is not accidental that the two novels with which this series of studies ends, Lawrence's *Sons and Lovers* and Joyce's *Portrait*, are both autobiographical "portraits of the artist as a young man." In a stable culture, the artist inherits certain broad assumptions as to the nature of reality which, in some degree, correspond with empirical experience of the kind of relationships people maintain with themselves, with each other, and with their natural environment. The subjective, introspective impulse is then quiescent; there is no spiritual need, on the part of the individual, to go questing backward over his personal life in an attempt to find in it a meaningful form or unity or direction; for his social environment objectively manifests to him a form, a unity, a direction, that correspond with his feelings. But in a time of cultural crisis, when traditional values no longer seem to match at any point with the actualities of experience, and when all reality is therefore thrown into question, the mind turns inward on itself to seek the shape of reality there—for the thinking and feeling man cannot live without some coherent schematization of reality. Here at least—in one's own memory, emotion, and thought—is empirical ground for such an investigation. The great autobiographical artists, St. Augustine, Montaigne, Pascal, Rousseau, made their self-inventories under historical compulsions of this kind. The dates 1913 for *Sons and Lovers* and 1914 for *Joyce's Portrait* carry their own obvious implication: they mark a time of shocking disclosure of the failure of the social environment as a trustworthy carrier of values.

The autobiographic impulse appeared contemporaneously in the French novel, as in Proust's great work, *A la recherche du temps perdu*, and as in Gide's *L'Immoraliste,* his *Si le grain ne meurt,* direct rather than fictionized autobiography, and later in his *Les Faux-Monnayeurs,* a novel which used a number of autobiographical materials and whose protagonist is a novelist who is deeply engaged in a reformulation of novelistic aesthetics. In this book Gide has his novelist say,

> My novel hasn't got a subject . . . Let's say, if you prefer it, it hasn't got *one subject* . . . Please understand; I should like to put everything into my novel. I don't want any cut of the scissors to limit its substance at one point rather than at another. For more than a year now that I have been working at it, nothing happens to me that I don't put into it—everything I see, everything I know, everything that other people's lives and my own teach me . . .

The passage (though it has to be taken in the merely provisional sense that it has in the context of Gide's book) suggests rather forcibly the kind of motivation of which we have been speaking as the motivation of the "autobiographical" artist: the attempt of the artist, living in an environment that has failed to provide sanctions not only for art but even for life, to test out in the materials of his own experience the possibility of a new conceptual and aesthetic form which will give him imaginative grasp of his world. Proust, in *A la recherche,* and Gide, in *Les Faux-Monnayeurs,* and Joyce, in the *Portrait,* have as a central part of their concern the sanctions of art, a concern that can be formulated in the questions: what is art? what is the relationship between art and life? can one discover the nature of reality through art? The coupling of autobiography with this concern is natural enough; for the novelist is desperately committed to find a valid schematization of the "real," one which will place his own function as artist in organic relationship with the rest of life.

One of the oldest themes in the novel is that language is a creator of reality. There is this theme in *Don Quixote,* as there is there, in one form or another, most of the themes that we have traced in the other novels we have read. Quixote is supremely a man animated by "the word"; and as the words he has read in books send him into action—creating reality for him by determining what he sees and what he feels and what he does—so Quixote in turn has a similar effect upon other people, subtly changing their outlook, creating in them new forms of thought and activity. *Don Quixote* may be looked on as an extensive investigation of the creative effects of language upon life. Joyce's *Portrait* is also an investigation of this kind; appropriately so, for the "artist" whose youthful portrait the book is, is at the end to find his vocation in language; and the shape of reality that gradually defines itself for Stephen is a shape determined primarily by the associations of words. We follow in the circumstances of the boy's life the stages of breakdown and increasing confusion in his external environment, as his home goes to pieces, and the correlative stages of breakdown in his inherited values, as his church and his nation lose their authority over his emotions. Very early the child's mind begins to respond to that confusion by seeking in itself, in its own mental images, some unifying form or forms that will signify what the world *really* is, that will show him the *real* logic of things—a logic hopelessly obscure in external relations. His mental images are largely associations suggested by the words he hears, and in intense loneliness he struggles to make the associations fit into a coherent pattern.

To the very young child, adults seem to possess the secret of the whole, seem to know what everything means and how one thing is related to another. Apparently in command of that secret, they toss words together into esoteric compounds, some words whose referents the child knows and many whose referents are mysterious; and the context of the familiar words guides him in his speculation about the unfamiliar ones, the unfamiliar ones thus taking on their meaning for him in a wondrously accidental and chaotic fashion. These accidents of context, however bizarre, build up his notion of reality and determine his later responses and the bias of his soul. There is the story that Stephen's father tells him about a cow coming down along a road. There is the song about the wild rose blossoming on the green place. He, Stephen, is evidently the "nicens little boy" toward whom the cow designs its path, and he, Stephen, can make the wild rose into a green one by a transposition of adjectives. The world's form, then, is apparently shaped toward him and out from him as its center. But how to put the story and the song intelligibly together, in a superior meaningful pattern of reality, with his father's hairy face looking at him through a glass? or with the queer smell of the oil sheet? or with Dante's two brushes? or with Eileen, the neighbor girl, who has a different father and mother? or with some shadowily guilty thing he has done for which he must "apologize," else eagles will pull out his eyes? In this extremely short sequence at the beginning of the book, the child's sense of insecurity, in a world whose form he cannot grasp, is established—and with insecurity, guilt (he must apologize) and fear (the horrible eagles). With these unpromising emotional elements established in him, the maturing child will try again and again to grasp his world imaginatively as a shape within which he has a part that is essential to its completeness and harmoniousness and meaningfulness.

Immediately there is a transition to the children's playground at Clongowes Wood, the child's earliest experience of a community other than that of the home. Again the auditory impression is predominant—sounds heard, words spoken—and the life-directed attempt of the young mind is to understand their meaning in relation to each other and in relation to a governing design. There are the "strong cries" of the boys and the "thud" of their feet and bodies; then comes a quick succession of references to special oddnesses in the names of things. To the child's laboring apprehension, which assumes all names to have intimate and honest connections with reality, the name "dog-in-the-blanket" for the Friday pudding must represent something about the pudding which is real and which other people know but which is obscured from him; it may have more than one meaning, like the word "belt," which means a strap on a jacket and also "to give a fellow a belt"; or it may have complex, mysterious, and terribly serious associations with destiny, understood by others but dark and anxious to himself, like his own name, Stephen Dedalus, which Nasty Roche says is "queer" with a queerness that puts the social status of Stephen's father in doubt. Through words the world comes to Stephen; through the words he hears he gropes his way into other people's images of reality. Doubts and anxieties arise because the words and phrases are disassociated, their context frequently arbitrary, like that of the sentences in the spelling book:

> Wolsey died in Leicester Abbey
> Where the abbots buried him.
> Canker is a disease of plants,
> Cancer one of animals.

The sentences in the spelling book at least make a rhythm, and a rhythm is a kind of pattern, a "whole" of sorts; they are therefore "nice sentences" to think about. But the threatening, overwhelming problem is the integration of all the vast heap of disassociated impressions that the child's mind is subjected to and out of which his hopeful urgency toward intelligibility forces him, entirely lonely and without help, to try to make superior rhythms and superior unities.

The technique of the "stream of consciousness," or "interior monologue," as Joyce uses it, is a formal aspect of the book which sensitively reflects the boy's extreme spiritual isolation. There is a logical suitability in the fact that this type of technique should arise at a time of cultural debacle, when society has failed to give objective validation to inherited structures of belief, and when therefore all meanings, values, and sanctions have to be built up from scratch in the loneliness of the individual mind. When an author assumes the right to enter his novel in his own voice and comment on his characters—as Fielding does or George Eliot does—we are able to infer a cultural situation in which there are objective points of reference for the making of a judgment; the author and reader enter into overt agreement, as it were, in criticizing and judging the character's actions; and where there is this assumption of agreement, we are in a relatively secure social world. The "gregarious point of view" used by the older novelists reflects a world, comparatively speaking, of shared standards. As the technical point of view adopted by the novelist more and more tends to exclude the novelist's own expression of opinion from his book, the world which he represents tends more and more to be one whose values are in question; and we have, for instance, in the later work of Henry James, a work such as *The Ambassadors*, where the subjective point of view of the main character is dominant, a concentration on a process of mind in which values are reshifted and rejudged from top to bottom, all in the loneliness of an individual's personal experience. The technique of the "interior monologue" is a modification of the subjective point of view. It is not a departure from traditional convention, for even Fielding used this point of view when he wanted to show "from the inside" how a character's mind worked; but it is an employment of the subjective point of view throughout the entire novel—instead of sporadically, as in the older English novel—and it follows more devious and various paths of consciousness than traditional novelists were concerned with. Joyce's concern, in the *Portrait*, is with the associative patterns arising in Stephen's mind from infancy into adolescence. What we need to emphasize, however, is that he is concerned with these only as they show the dialectical process by which a world-shape evolves in the mind. The process is conducted in the absolute solitude of the inside of the skull, for Stephen has no trustworthy help from the objective environment. The technique of the "interior monologue" is the sensitive formal representation of that mental solitude.

"By thinking of things you could understand them," Stephen says to himself when he arrives at the conclusion that the epithet "Tower of Ivory," in the litany of the Blessed Virgin, means what Eileen's hand felt like in his pocket—like ivory, only soft—and that "House of Gold" means what her hair had looked like, streaming out behind her like gold in the sun. Shortly before, he has been puzzling over the fact that Dante does not wish him to play with Eileen because Eileen is a Protestant, and the Protestants "make fun of the litany of the Blessed Virgin," saying, "How could a woman be a tower of ivory or a house of gold?" Who was right then, the Protestants or the Catholics? Stephen's analytical quandary is resolved by the perception of the identity between the feel of Eileen's prying hand and the meaning of "Tower of Ivory." In the same way, by the same dialectical process, his flooding impressions reach a stage of cohesion from moment to moment, a temporary synthesis in which he suddenly sees what they "mean." As Stephen matures, there is mounted on the early association between the Virgin and Eileen an identification between his dream-Mercedes (ideal girl in a rose-cottage) and a whore. By extension, this association holds in it much of Stephen's struggle between other-worldliness and this-worldliness, for it has identified in his imagination flesh and spirit, while his intellect, developing under education, rebels against the identification.[1] Thus "the word"—Tower of Ivory, House of Gold—creates by accident and at random the reality of suffering and act.

Those moments in the dialectical process when a synthesis is achieved, when certain phrases or sensations or complex experiences suddenly cohere in a larger whole and a meaning shines forth from the whole, Joyce—who introduced the word into literary currency—called "epiphanies." They are "showings-forth" of the nature of reality as the boy is prepared to grasp it. Minor epiphanies mark all the stages of Stephen's understanding, as when the feel of Eileen's hand shows him what Tower of Ivory means, or as when the word "Foetus," carved on a school desk, suddenly focuses for him in brute clarity his "monstrous way of life." Major epiphanies, occurring at the end of each chapter, mark the chief revelations of the nature of his environment and of his destiny in it. The epiphany is an image, sensuously apprehended and emotionally vibrant, which communicates instantaneously the meaning of experience. It may contain a revelation of a per-

[1] Irene Hendry points this out in her admirable essay "Joyce's Epiphanies," in *James Joyce: Two Decades of Criticism,* edited by Seon Givens (New York: Vanguard Press, Inc., 1948).

son's character, brief and fleeting, occurring by virtue of some physical trait in the person, as the way big Corrigan looked in the bath:

> He had skin the same colour as the turf-coloured bogwater in the shallow end of the bath and when he walked along the side his feet slapped loudly on the wet tiles and at every step his thighs shook a little because he was fat.

In this kind of use, as revelation through one or two physical traits of the whole mass-formation of a personality, the epiphany is almost precisely duplicable in Dickens, as in the spectacle of Miss Havisham leaning on her crutch beside the rotten bridecake, or of Jaggers flourishing his white handkerchief and biting his great forefinger. The minor personalities in the *Portrait* are reduced to something very like a Dickensian "signature" —as Heron with his bird-beaked face and bird-name, Davin with his peasant turns of speech, Lynch whose "long slender flattened skull beneath the long pointed cap brought before Stephen's mind the image of a hooded reptile." Or the epiphany may be a kind of "still life" with which are associated deep and complex layers of experience and emotion. In the following passage, for instance, the sordor of Stephen's home, the apprehensive and guilty image of the bath at Clongowes, and the bestiality he associates with the bogholes of Ireland, are illuminated simultaneously by a jar of drippings on the table.

> He drained his third cup of watery tea to the dregs and set to chewing the crusts of fried bread that were scattered near him, staring into the dark pool of the jar. The yellow dripping had been scooped out like a boghole, and the pool under it brought back to his memory the dark turfcoloured water of the bath at Clongowes.

Here the whole complex of home, school, and nation is epitomized in one object and shot through with the emotion of rejection. The epiphany is usually the result of a gradual development of the emotional content of associations, as they accrete with others. Among Stephen's childish impressions is that of "a woman standing at the halfdoor of a cottage with a child in her arms," and

> it would be lovely to sleep for one night in that cottage before the fire

of smoking turf, in the dark lit by the fire, in the warm dark, breathing the smell of the peasants, air and rain and turf and corduroy . . .

The early impression enters into emotional context, later, with the story Davin tells him about stopping at night at the cottage of a peasant woman, and Stephen's image of the woman is for him an epiphany of the soul of Ireland: "a batlike soul waking to the consciousness of itself in darkness and secrecy and loneliness." The epiphany is dynamic, activated by the form-seeking urgency in experience, and itself feeding later revelations. At the point of exile, Stephen feels, "under the deepened dusk,"

> the thoughts and desires of the race to which he belonged flitting like bats, across the dark country lanes, under trees by the edges of streams and near the pool mottled bogs.

The major epiphanies in the book occur as the symbolic climaxes of the larger dialectical movements constituting each of the five chapters. As Hugh Kenner has pointed out, in his essay *"The Portrait* in Perspective," [2] each of the chapters begins with a multitude of warring impressions, and each develops toward an emotionally apprehended unity; each succeeding chapter liquidates the previous synthesis and subjects its elements to more adult scrutiny in a constantly enlarging field of perception, and develops toward its own synthesis and affirmation. In each chapter, out of the multitude of elements with which it opens, some one chief conflict slowly shapes itself. In the first, among all the bewildering impressions that the child's mind entertains, the deeper conflict is that between his implicit trust in the authority of his elders—his Jesuit teachers, the older boys in the school, his father and Mr. Casey and Dante—and his actual sense of insecurity. His elders, since they apparently know the meaning of things, must therefore incarnate perfect justice and moral and intellectual consistency. But the child's real experience is of mad quarrels at home over Parnell and the priests, and at school the frivolous cruelty of the boys, the moral chaos suggested by the smugging in the square and the talk about stealing the altar wine, and the sadism of Father Dolan with his pandybat. With Stephen's visit to the rector at the end of the chapter, the conflict is resolved. Justice is triumphant—even a small boy with weak eyes can find it; he is greeted like a hero on his emergence from the rector's office; his consolidation with his human environment is gloriously affirmed.

The second chapter moves straight from that achievement of emo-

[2] In *James Joyce: Two Decades of Criticism,* cited above.

tional unity into other baffling complexities, coincident with the family's removal to Dublin. The home life is increasingly squalid, the boy more lonely and restless. In Simon Dedalus' account of his conversation with the rector of Clongowes about the incident of the pandying, what had seemed, earlier, to be a triumph of justice and an affirmation of intelligent moral authority by Stephen's elders is revealed as cruel, stupid indifference. In the episode in which Stephen is beaten for "heresy," the immediate community of his schoolfellows shows itself as false, shot through with stupidity and sadism. More importantly, the image of the father is corroded. On the visit to Cork, Simon appears to the boy's despairing judgment as besotted, self-deluded, irresponsible—and with the corruption of the father-image his whole picture of society suffers the same ugly damage. On the same visit, Stephen's early dim apprehension of sin and guilt is raised into horrible prominence by the word "Foetus" which he sees inscribed on the desk at Queen's College and which symbolizes for him all his adolescent monstrosity (the more monstrous in that Simon looks with obscene sentimentality on the desk carvings, thus condemning the whole world for Stephen in his own sickened sense of guilt). Meanwhile, his idealistic longings for beauty and purity and gentleness and certitude have concentrated in a vaguely erotic fantasy of the dream-girl Mercedes in her rose-cottage. Again, at the end of the chapter, Stephen's inner conflict is resolved in an emotional unity, a new vision of the relationships between the elements of experience. The synthesis is constituted here by a triumphant integration of the dream of Mercedes with the encounter with the whore. It is "sin" that triumphs, but sublimated as an ideal unity, pure and gentle and beautiful and emotionally securing.

As Hugh Kenner has observed, in the essay cited above, the predominant physical activity in *The Portrait* that accompanies Stephen's mental dialectics, as he moves through analysis to new provisional syntheses, is the activity of walking; his ambulatory movements take him into new localities, among new impressions, as his mind moves correspondingly into new spiritual localities that subsume the older ones and readjust them as parts of a larger whole. Living in Dublin, his walks take him toward the river and the sea—toward the fluid thing that, like the "stream" of his thoughts, seems by its searching mobility to imply a more engrossing reality. At first, in Dublin, the boy

contented himself with circling timidly round the neighbouring square or, at most, going half way down one of the side streets; but

when he had made a skeleton map of the city in his mind he followed
boldly one of its central lines until he reached the Custom House . . .
The vastness and strangeness of the life suggested to him by the bales
of merchandise stocked along the walls or swung aloft out of the holds
of steamers wakened again in him the unrest which had sent him
wandering in the evening from garden to garden in search of Mercedes . . . A vague dissatisfaction grew up within him as he looked
on the quays and on the river and on the lowering skies and yet he
continued to wander up and down day after day as if he really sought
someone that eluded him.

On his visit to Cork with his father, in his wanderings in the brothel section of Dublin, on his seaward walk at the end of the fourth chapter when
his chief revelation of personal destiny comes to him, on his later walks
between home and the university, on his walk with Lynch during which
he recapitulates his aesthetics, and with Cranly when he formulates his
decision not "to serve"—on each of these peripatetic excursions, his mind
moves toward more valid organizations of experience, as his feet carry him
among other voices and images and into more complex fields of perception.

In the third chapter of the book, the hortations to which he is exposed
during the retreat pull him down from his exaltation in sin and analyze
his spiritual state into a multitude of subjective horrors that threaten to
engulf him entirely and jeopardize his immortal soul. The conflict is resolved during a long walk which he takes blindly and alone, and that carries him to a strange place where he feels able to make his confession. A
new synthesis is achieved through his participation in the Mass. Chapter 4
shows him absorbed in a dream of a saintly career, but his previous emotional affirmation has been frittered and wasted away in the performance
of pedantically formal acts of piety, and he is afflicted with doubts, inse-
curities, rebellions. Release from conflict comes with a clear refusal of a
vocation in the church, objectified by his decision to enter the university.
And again it is on a walk that he realizes the measure of the new reality
and the new destiny.

He has abandoned his father to a public house and has set off toward
the river and the sea.

The university! So he had passed beyond the challenge of the
sentries who had stood as guardians of his boyhood and had sought
to keep him among them that he might be subject to them and serve

their ends. Pride after satisfaction uplifted him like long slow waves. The end he had been born to serve yet did not see had led him to escape by an unseen path: and now it beckoned to him once more and a new adventure was about to be opened to him. It seemed to him that he heard notes of fitful music leaping upwards a tone and downwards a diminishing fourth, upwards a tone and downwards a major third, like triple-branching flames leaping fitfully, flame after flame, out of a midnight wood. It was an elfin prelude, endless and formless; and, as it grew wilder and faster, the flames leaping out of time, he seemed to hear from under the boughs and grasses wild creatures racing, their feet pattering like rain upon the leaves. Their feet passed in pattering tumult over his mind, the feet of hares and rabbits, the feet of harts and hinds and antelopes, until he heard them no more and remembered only a proud cadence from Newman:—
    —Whose feet are as the feet of harts and underneath the ever-lasting arms.

The imagery is that of mobile, going things, increasingly passionate and swift—first slow waves, then fitful music leaping, then flames, then racing creatures. A phrase of his own making comes to his lips: "A day of dappled seaborne clouds." The dappled color and the sea movement of the clouds are of the same emotional birth as the images of music and flames. All are of variety and mobility of perception, as against stasis and restriction. Physically Stephen is escaping from his father—and the public house where he has left Simon is the sordid core of that Dublin environment whose false claims on his allegiance he is trying to shake off; at the same time he is realizing a "first noiseless sundering" with his mother, a break that is related to his decision against accepting a vocation in the church. Dublin, the tangible and vocal essence of his nationality, and the Roman church, the mold of his adolescent intellect, have failed to provide him with a vision of reality corresponding with his experience, and he thinks in terms of a movement beyond these—toward another and mysterious possible synthesis. "And underneath the everlasting arms": the phrase from Newman implies an ultimate unity wherein all the real is held in wholeness. Toward this problematic divine embrace Stephen moves, but it is only problematic and he can approach it only by his own movement. The epiphany which confronts him in this moment on the beach is a manifestation of his destiny in terms of a winged movement. He hears his name, Dedalus, called out, and the name seems to be prophetic.

. . . at the name of the fabulous artificer, he seemed to hear the noise
of dim waves and to see a winged form flying above the waves and
slowly climbing the air . . . a hawklike man flying sunward above
the sea, a prophecy of the end he had been born to serve and had been
following through the mists of childhood and boyhood, a symbol of
the artist forging anew in his workshop out of the sluggish matter of
the earth a new soaring impalpable imperishable being . . .

The ending of Chapter 4 presents this new consciousness in terms of
an ecstatic state of sensibility. It is marked by the radiant image of the girl
standing in a rivulet of tide, seeming "like one whom magic had changed
into the likeness of a strange and beautiful seabird . . . touched with
the wonder of mortal beauty," while his own life cries wildly to him, "To
live, to err, to fall, to triumph, to recreate life out of life!" The girl is a
"wild angel" that has appeared to him, to "throw open before him in an
instant of ecstasy the ways of error and glory." The batlike woman-soul of
his race, flitting in darkness and secrecy and loneliness, has given place to
this angelic emissary from "the fair courts of life," of strange seabird
beauty, inviting him to exile across waters and into other languages, as the
sun-assailing and perhaps doomed Icarus. And it is in the flights of birds
that Stephen, standing on the steps of the university library, in the last
chapter, reads like an ancient haruspex the sanction of his exile.

With Chapter 5, Stephen's new consciousness of destiny is subjected to
intellectual analysis. Here, during his long walks with Lynch and Cranly,
all the major elements that have exerted emotional claims upon him—his
family, church, nation, language—are scrutinized dryly, their claims torn
down and scattered in the youthfully pedantic and cruel light of the adolescent's proud commitment to art. Here also he formulates his aesthetics,
the synthesis which he has contrived out of a few scraps of medieval learning. In his aesthetic formulation, the names he borrows from Aquinas for
"the three things needed for beauty"—*integritas, consonantia, claritas*—
are names for those aspects of reality—wholeness, harmoniousness, significant character—that he has been seeking all his life, from earliest childhood. His aesthetic formulation is thus a synthesis of the motivations of
his psychological life from the beginning; and the vocation of artist which
he has chosen is the vocation of one who consciously sets himself the task
of apprehending and then representing in his art whatever wholeness, harmony, and meaning the world has.

In an earlier version of *The Portrait,* called *Stephen Hero,* it is said that the task of the artist is to

> disentangle the subtle soul of the image from its mesh of defining circumstances most exactly and "re-embody" it in artistic circumstances chosen as the most exact for it in its new office . . .

The "new office" of the image is to communicate to others the significant character of a complete and harmonious body of experience. The artist is a midwife of epiphanies. Joyce's doctrine of the epiphany assumes that reality does have wholeness and harmony—even as Stephen as a child premises these, and with the same trustfulness—and that it will radiantly show forth its character and its meaning to the prepared consciousness, for it is only in the body of reality that meaning can occur and only there that the artist can find it. This is essentially a religious interpretation of the nature of reality and of the artist's function. It insists on the objectivity of the wholeness, harmony, and meaning, and on the objectivity of the revelation—the divine showing-forth.

At Clongowes Wood, there had been a picture of the earth on the first page of Stephen's geography, "a big ball in the middle of clouds," and on the flyleaf of the book Stephen had written his name and "where he was."

Stephen Dedalus
Class of Elements
Clongowes Wood College
Sallins
County Kildare
Ireland
Europe
The World
The Universe

His ambulatory, dialectical journey is a quest to find the defining unity, the composing harmony, and the significant character of each of these broadening localities containing Stephen Dedalus, and the intelligible relationships making each functional in the next. It is an attempt, by progressive stages, at last to bring the term "Stephen Dedalus" into relationship with the term "The Universe." Through the book he moves from one geographical and spiritual orbit to another, "walking" in lengthening radius until he is ready to take up flight. As a child at Clongowes it had pained him that he did not know what came after the universe.

> What was after the universe? Nothing. But was there anything round the universe to show where it stopped before the nothing place began? It could not be a wall but there could be a thin thin line there all round everything. It was very big to think about everything and everywhere. Only God could do that. He tried to think what a big thought that must be but he could think only of God. God was God's name just as his name was Stephen. *Dieu* was the French for God and that was God's name too; and when anyone prayed to God and said Dieu then God knew at once that was a French person that was praying. But though there were different names for God in all the different languages in the world and God understood what all the people who prayed said in their different languages still God remained always the same God and God's real name was God.

At the end of the book Stephen is prepared at least to set forth on the "dappled, seaborne clouds" that float beyond Ireland and over Europe. His search is still to find out "what came after the universe." The ultimate epiphany is withheld, the epiphany of "everything and everywhere" as one and harmonious and meaningful. But it is prophesied in "God's real name," as Stephen's personal destiny is prophesied in his own name "Dedalus." It is to be found in the labyrinth of language that contains all human revelation vouchsafed by divine economy, and to be found by the artist in naming the names.

Problems for Study and Discussion

The questions suggested here are directed toward providing concrete opportunities for creative criticism on the part of the student, toward making each novel a really personal possession of his mind, and toward designing a classroom situation in which perceptions and opinions can confront each other dialectically.

The questions are merely suggestive. Various rearrangements, omissions, and additions would no doubt be necessary for each different association of students, depending upon interests. Some of the questions perhaps have no single answers or perhaps have contradictory answers, but complexity of this kind is gain, not loss. In general, the questions are designed to lead to evaluations firmly grounded in the texts of the novels.

Don Quixote

1. As the book opens and the Knight prepares for his first sally,[1] by what details do the manner and techniques of parody become evident? We have likened parody, in its very simplest implications, to debate. What antitheses or "opposites" are implicit in the following: the description of the Knight and the references to and quotations from his reading? the naming of Rosinante? the naming of Dulcinea? We have also suggested that parody involves more than mere antithesis. When the author says that Quixote "was sensible that a knight-errant without a mistress, was a tree without either fruit or leaves, and a body without a soul," what added significance is given to Dulcinea?

2. Beginning with the vigil at the horse trough,[2] enumerate a number of adventures which take place at night.[3] Why, with a hero like Don Quixote, is it appropriate that many of his adventures take place in an atmosphere of night?

3. Enumerate some of the adventures in which Quixote is asleep, or Sancho is asleep, or in which the key words "sleep" and "dream" occur prominently.[4] In each of these episodes, analyze carefully the ambiguities in the reference to the sleeping or dreaming state. How is the use of these words related to the theme of sanity or insanity? What is the psychological relationship between the theme of sanity or insanity, the theme of sleep or dream, and the theme of night?

4. In the encounter with the merchants,[5] when Quixote demands that they swear to the superiority of Dulcinea and they object that they have not seen her, he says, "The importance of the thing lies in oblig-

---

[1] In Pt. 1, Bk. 1, Ch. 1.
[2] Pt. 1, Bk. 1, Ch. 3.
[3] See, for instance, 1-1-8, 1-3-2, 1-3-6, 1-4-8, 2-3-8.
[4] See 1-1-8, 1-3-2, 1-4-8, 2-3-20, 2-3-22.
[5] Pt. 1, Bk. 1, Ch. 4.

ing you to believe it, confess it, affirm it, swear it, and maintain it, without seeing her." Other elements are entwined here with the obvious comic and burlesque element. What is the relation of Quixote's statement to St. Paul's definition of faith: "Now faith is the substance of things hoped for, the evidence of things not seen"? Is Cervantes satirizing faith? Is he satirizing idealism? Or is he, like an organist or a pianist, playing upon many notes at once, *com-posing* many diverse feelings and attitudes?

5. The "literary theme" of *Don Quixote* enters with the inventory of the Knight's library and the burning of the books.[6] In this episode, which closes the Knight's first sally, what is emphasized as the effect of books upon men's minds? In what sense would you say that the effect of books (the "word," the "idea," the Logos) upon Quixote's mind is dramatized in the narrative as the effect of Quixote himself upon his environment and upon the people he knows or meets?

6. Why is it Sancho, an illiterate countryman, who accompanies Quixote, rather than the barber or Carrasco or someone else with a possibility of intellect and ideal to match Quixote's own? Sancho and Quixote offer foils to each other (literate and illiterate, fantastic and practical, and so forth) in the manner in which opposing views confront each other in a debate; but if Sancho is actually the "opposite" of Quixote, why does he follow him and submit to his fantasies? After the adventure of the windmills,[7] Sancho warns Quixote that the same fiasco will happen with the Benedictine monks,[8] but he disregards his own counsel and is thrashed. In the adventure of the bands of sheep,[9] he swallows quite a roll call of epic armies before he penetrates to the fact that the sheep are sheep. In the adventure of the fulling mills,[10] his fear holds him to the Knight's side. Enumerate other adventures in which Sancho is not a perfect "realist." If a true conceptual *opposition* does not seem adequate to interpret the relationship of Sancho and Quixote, what would you suggest as a definition of their relationship and the relationship between "Sanchoism" and "Quixotism"?

7. The following quotations illustrate a typical trait of Cervantes' style (a trait not limited to the English translation, but found in the Span-

6 Pt. 1, Bk. 1, Ch. 6.
7 Pt. 1, Bk. 1, Ch. 8.
8 Pt. 1, Bk. 1, Ch. 8.
9 Pt. 1, Bk. 3, Ch. 4.
10 Pt. 1, Bk. 3, Ch. 6.

ish): [11] ". . . accompanied by my *servant* and many *fancies* . . ."; "I abandoned *home* and *patience* . . ."; ". . . to break *lances* and facilitate *difficulties* . . ."; "But *daylight* and the *hope* of succeeding in their object failed them . . ."; *Maidens* and *modesty* wandered at will alone and unattended . . ."; "Don Quixote and Sancho returned to their *beasts* and to their *state of beasthood*." Bring to class other illustrations of the same trait. How would you describe this stylistic usage? Define the relationship of the coupled nouns: is it a relationship of straight "opposition" of meanings, or a relationship of some other kind? In what sense do you find, in both the linked nouns and the linking of Sancho and Quixote, the same combinations and the same dual aspects of "reality"?

8. In the adventure of the windmills,[12] the theme of "enchantment" first enters. Quixote says, ". . . that cursed Necromancer Freston, who carry'd away my study and my books, has transformed these giants into windmills, to deprive me of the honour of the victory." What is the meaning of "enchantment" (*engaño*) here? Enumerate other adventures in which this type of *engaño* occurs.[13] In what sense is Quixote himself an enchanter? In the 1615 volume, we have an enchanted head that speaks, an enchanted horse that flies, and other instances of enchantment: are these cases quite in the same mode of enchantment as the windmills or fulling mills or the barber's basin of the 1605 volume? What general difference would you point out between the enchantments of 1605 and the enchantments of 1615? Can you suggest any reason why the *engaño* of 1605 is associated with night and dream and solitude, and that of 1615 is associated with daylight and conversation and populous places?

9. The literary theme enters again with the break in the adventure of the Biscayan, where Cervantes says that he picked up, in Alcana de Toledo, the history of Don Quixote written by Cid Hamet Benengali.[14] Suggest a reason for the fact that Cervantes did not start his novel with mention of Cid Hamet Benengali's manuscript, though he could readily have done so, instead of interrupting a combat and leaving the

[11] This type of structure is pointed out by Helmut Hatzfeld in the essay "The Style of *Don Quixote*," in *Cervantes across the Centuries*, edited by Angel Flores and M. J. Benardete (New York: The Dryden Press, Inc., 1947).

[12] Pt. 1, Bk. 1, Ch. 8.

[13] See, for instance, 1-3-7, 1-4-17, 1-4-4.

[14] Pt. 1, Bk. 2, Ch. 1.

opponents with drawn swords, immobilized. Later, in the 1615 volume, Cid Hamet's history of Quixote is dwelt on at greater length; [15] Don Quixote is now a famous character in a book who is also a live man. In what way does this hybrid book-man or man-book dramatize and deepen the relationships which we have been watching in the Sancho-Quixote combination—in the descent of these two upon a common everyday world of inns and highways and houses and cities?

10. In the adventure of the galley slaves,[16] when Gines de Passamonte mentions his autobiography, Quixote asks him if the book is finished, and Gines replies, "How can it be finished when my life is not yet finished?" What is Gines' implication as to the connection between life and books, between material reality and "the word"? In what way is the same implication carried out by Quixote's hybrid status as both a real man and a character in a book?

11. What are the respective eating habits of the Knight and his Squire? What is parodied in this comparison? What bearing on it have the words of the New Testament: "Man does not live by bread alone"? One of the easiest (but probably not the most accurate) things to say about Sancho is that he is a "realist"; and in speaking of Sancho in this way, we are probably giving to the word "realist" the meaning of "normal." The Knight's eating habits are clearly extreme, not "normal"; but as Sancho eats his way through the book, do you find his eating habits perfectly "normal"? What exaggeration is there in Sancho's attitude toward food? How does this question bear on your definition of the relationship between Sancho and Quixote?

12. How does the Knight justify to Sancho the fiasco of the adventure of the fulling mills? [17] Is his justification quite without validity or has it some validity? The adventure is made more grotesque by Sancho's relief of his physiological needs. In the context of the Knight's high-minded vigilance, does Sancho's performance appear to you to exhibit the golden mean of "normality" as against the Knight's extremism? In what sense is this feature of the adventure extreme also?

13. What traits are exaggerated in Maritornes? [18] In what way does Maritornes bear somewhat the same relationship to Dulcinea as Sancho

15 Pt. 2, Bk. 3, Ch. 3.
16 Pt. 1, Bk. 3, Ch. 8.
17 Pt. 1, Bk. 3, Ch. 6.
18 Pt. 1, Bk. 3, Ch. 2.

does to Quixote? Among these extremes, what characters in the book would you say represented the "normal"? By "normal," do you mean here that "normal" or "real" people, people with common sense, the people who presumably constitute the majority of the human race, are those who are immune to gross fleshly appetites and needs and to high ideals also, immune to both irrational impulses and abstract conceptions?

14. The literary theme has extended appearances in the five short novels having to do with Marcela, Cardenio, Dorotea, the "Curious Impertinent," and the Captive. What is the central question on which Marcela bases her discourse to her lovers? [19] Does this question have any relationship with Quixote's attitude toward Dulcinea? What is the connection between Marcela's history and Rosinante's capers with the Galician mares in the section that immediately follows? [20]

15. Is Cardenio's a story [21] of outward or inward action?—that is, is it a story in which external circumstances are most important, or in which subjective moral complications are most important? Cardenio's narration is bipartite, its two parts framing the episode of Quixote's penance. What is the significance of Quixote's penance? [22] In this episode, is Quixote put into action by external circumstances or by purely inward subjective circumstances? What is the physical setting for Cardenio's story and for Quixote's penance? What is the appropriateness of this setting? What appropriateness is there in the use of Cardenio's story as a frame for Quixote's penance?

16. Don Quixote says that in the present age no woman can defend herself from man, though she were to withdraw into a labyrinth. How does Dorotea's story illustrate this statement? [23] Why does Dorotea seek to regain Ferdinand? Dorotea's story starts with a brutal seduction (the sexual impulse under no social controls) and ends in a complacent marriage [24] (the sexual impulse "domesticated" and "socialized"). What outlook does this story illustrate with regard to sex and marriage? What contrast does it offer to the treatment of love in Marcela's history, and what contrast with Quixote's attitude toward love?

[19] Pt. 1, Bk. 2, Ch. 6.
[20] Pt. 1, Bk. 3, Ch. 1.
[21] Pt. 1, Bk. 3, Chs. 10 and 13.
[22] Pt. 1, Bk. 3, Ch. 11.
[23] Pt. 1, Bk. 4, Ch. 1.
[24] Pt. 1, Bk. 4, Ch. 9.

17. In the novel of the "Curious Impertinent," [25] was Anselmo's wife really virtuous (in the old sense, that is, chaste) or really not virtuous? Though a faithful wife at first, was she even then a potential adulteress and therefore really not a faithful wife? Was her virtue an illusion or a reality? If her virtue was an illusion (in the sense that, under testing, she lost her virtue), should Anselmo have remained content with the illusion? In view of the various and conflicting answers which you and other members of the class may offer to these questions, would you say that the story either (1) contained some one definite, absolute, non-contingent, abstract, and more or less universally applicable "truth" concerning women's virtue, or (2) was fundamentally unclear and confused in significance, or (3) contained the negative point only, that there is no definite and absolute "truth" of this kind, or (4) held the positive point, that the "truth" in experience is relative to a specific set of conditions or circumstances? After weighing these possibilities, how would you say Anselmo's story is related to the main narrative of *Don Quixote?*

18. The Captive, in relating his story,[26] says: ". . . never did I abandon the hope of being free, and when what I planned, thought, and put into action did not meet with the success that was intended, then, without succumbing to despair, I sought and imagined another hope that would sustain me, though it were only a weak and feeble one." Does this statement enter into any relationship with the principal narrative of *Don Quixote?* The Captive's story has certain resemblances to Cervantes' own history: Cervantes fought in the battle of Lepanto and was captured and held for ransom by the Moors. The materials of the Captive's story are "heroic" materials, but they are situated in contemporary time. How, then, does this story both resemble and contrast with the heroic romances which provide the impulse for Quixote's adventures?

19. What aspect is shared in common by these events of the 1615 volume: Carrasco poses as the Knight of the Mirrors; [27] Sancho tells Quixote that a farm girl is Dulcinea; [28] Maese Pedro claims preternatural powers for his monkey; [29] Altisidora pretends to be in love with Quix-

25 Pt. 1, Bk. 4, Chs. 6 and 7; and concluding in Ch. 8.
26 Pt. 1, Bk. 4, Chs. 12, 13, and 14.
27 Pt. 2, Bk. 3, Ch. 12.
28 Pt. 2, Bk. 3, Ch. 10.
29 Pt. 2, Bk. 3, Ch. 25.

ote; [30] Don Antonio Moreno has a magic head which is supposed to speak; [31] Sancho is made to believe that he is a governor; [32] Sancho tells Quixote that he has flogged himself when he has really flogged a tree; [33] a false history of Quixote has been written? [34] What is the essential difference between the theme expressed in these incidents and the theme of enchantment in the 1605 volume?

20. Under what common description would you place the following: the cart of strolling players; [35] the puppet show; [36] the representations of Merlin and the Countess Trifaldi; [37] the staging of Altisidora's "death"? [38] What thematic connection do these elements have with the events mentioned in Question 19?

21. On the other hand, many explanations now take place. Sancho's machinations are described; [39] the identity of the Knight of the Mirrors is revealed; [40] Maese Pedro's identity is made clear; [41] the workings of the enchanted head are explained; [42] Quixote explains on his deathbed that he has been mad.[43] How is this theme of "explanation" related to the disappearance, from the 1615 volume, of the themes of night and solitude?

22. Enumerate the occasions in the 1615 volume where money plays an important part. What part does money play in the 1605 volume? Enumerate the occasions, in the 1615 volume, in which the action takes place in a house. With what predominant setting, or settings, of the 1605 volume, does the house offer a contrast?

23. In what way do all the themes and motifs mentioned above—the type of *engaño* indicated in Questions 19 and 20, the "explanations," money and houses—have a common point of reference in the concept of Society (man-in-society rather than man-alone)?

[30] Pt. 2, Bk. 4, Ch. 44.
[31] Pt. 2, Bk. 4, Ch. 62.
[32] Pt. 2, Bk. 4, Ch. 45.
[33] Pt. 2, Bk. 4, Ch. 71.
[34] Pt. 2, Bk. 4, Ch. 59.
[35] Pt. 2, Bk. 3, Ch. 11.
[36] Pt. 2, Bk. 3, Ch. 26.
[37] Pt. 2, Bk. 4, Ch. 34.
[38] Pt. 2, Bk. 4, Ch. 69.
[39] Pt. 2, Bk. 3, Ch. 33.
[40] Pt. 2, Bk. 3, Chs. 14–15.
[41] Pt. 2, Bk. 3, Ch. 27.
[42] Pt. 2, Bk. 4, Ch. 52.
[43] Pt. 2, Bk. 4, Ch. 74.

24. The adventure of the cave of Montesinos [44] offers a striking contrast with the predominantly social context of the 1615 volume. In all Quixote's other adventures, even those of the 1605 book, he has still been in contact with at least a minimum material or social reality. How does the adventure of the cave differ in this respect? How does the loosening of the rope which holds Quixote symbolize that difference? In what way is the adventure of the cave a realization of Quixote's aspiration and a consecration of his efforts? What reason would you suggest for Cervantes' placing the adventure at this point in the book, rather than in one of the more solitary situations of the 1605 volume?

25. Montesinos and Durandarte, whom Quixote sees in the cave, were characters in the old heroic ballads of Spain. The experience of poetry and fiction, like all activities of the imagination, and of memory as well, is an experience in atemporal time—not the time which is felt as an actual and practical factor, but time as conceived in the mind. Quixote's descent into the cave and the hours he spent sleeping mark the actual time of this adventure. In his dream he hears Montesinos marveling that ". . . though I know it to be as sure as day that Durandarte ended his life in my arms [that is, in the old ballad], . . . how comes it that he now moans and sighs from time to time, as if he were still alive?" How does Montesinos' remark accent the coexistence, even the fusion, of two kinds of time, the atemporal time of the imagination and actual time? In the dream, Dulcinea sends one of her companions to ask her lover to lend her "half a dozen reals . . . on this *new dimity petticoat* that I have here." Since a new dimity petticoat would be an object of modern manufacture, how does this request emphasize again the coexistence or simultaneity of different time perspectives?

26. When he returns to the upper world, Quixote encounters Sancho's doubt, and he himself falls into doubt. Later he asks the brass head, ". . . was that which happened to me in the cave of Montesinos the truth or a dream?" and the answer is: ". . . there is much to be said; there is something of both in it." [45] How is the head's answer related to what Quixote says of Mambrino's helmet: [46] "What seems to you a

44 Pt. 2, Bk. 3, Chs. 22–23.
45 Pt. 2, Bk. 4, Ch. 62.
46 Pt. 1, Bk. 3, Ch. 11.

barber's basin, is to me Mambrino's helmet, and to another it will appear to be something else"? In what way do both statements reflect the attitude toward life spoken of by Americo Castro as the theme of *Don Quixote?*

27. Recapitulate, now, some of the more striking sets of contrasts in *Don Quixote*. What giant contrast between two different ways of being, or modes of existence, is offered by the 1605 and 1615 volumes? In what way do the five *novelle* of the 1605 volume carry out, on a smaller scale, the same principle of contrast between different modes of being? In what way does this extensive principle concentrate dramatically in the characters of Quixote and Sancho? In what way does the story of the "Curious Impertinent" (refer to Question 17) suggest, in miniature scope, the significance of this immense system of contrasts between the ways people live in different times and different places and under different conditions? How are the answer of the brass head and Quixote's statement about Mambrino's helmet related to the system of contrasting ways of life found in *Don Quixote?* The answer of the brass head is actually as vague, fatuous, and absurd as the answers of most fortunetellers. Why is this absurdity itself appropriate to the whole tremendous structure of *Don Quixote?*

28. Let us carry our generalizations back now, for testing, to a few specific episodes: (1) Quixote's "rescue" of the peasant boy; [47] (2) his "rescue" of the galley slaves; [48] (3) the episode in which the Knight attempts to act as peacemaker and restorer of reason between the armies of the two towns whose pride is the ability to bray like donkeys; [49] and (4) the quarrel, at the duke's house, between Quixote and the clergyman.[50] Behind each of these episodes, as behind all of *Don Quixote,* lie the latent questions: what is "real" in a situation? what is Reality? what is Truth? As you consider each of these episodes singly, and as you compare them one with another, what would you say was the nature of Reality and Truth as Cervantes presents the raw material for such a judgment?

29. Why does Cervantes, instead of finishing off his hero in a blaze of laughter, allow us to follow Quixote in his sadness and disillusion-

[47] Pt. 1, Bk. 1, Ch. 4.
[48] Pt. 1, Bk. 3, Ch. 8.
[49] Pt. 2, Bk. 3, Ch. 27.
[50] Pt. 2, Bk. 3, Chs. 31–32.

ment, trampled first by bulls [51] and then by hogs? [52] In view of the general principle of contrast in the book, by which a multitude of forms of experience have been juxtaposed with one another, do you think the book would have been complete (an adequate "mirror of life") without this particular type of ending? Why did not Cervantes soften the last adventure, instead of giving it this extreme, grotesque, and beastly form? Do you think that the "meaning" of Quixote's defeat and disillusionment is that the Knight was "wrong" after all and that his ideas (as he himself admits, dying) were folly?

30. In the scene of Don Quixote's deathbed, it is said that ". . . one of the signs by which they came to the conclusion that he was dying was this so sudden and complete return to his senses." With a full consciousness of the complexity of the book, how would you interpret this actually ambiguous statement?

The Pilgrim's Progress

(NOTE: *Since the book has no chapter breaks, reference is somewhat difficult. The references below can best be located with the help of the page headings that appear in most editions.*)

1. Both parts of the story are cast as dreams. The first dream occurs in "a Den," and the margin note tells us this is "the Jail." We may assume a reference here to the Bedford jail where Bunyan spent twelve years; but, remembering perhaps Plato's parable of the cave in the *Republic,* what other meaning might the Den or Jail have? Where does the dream take place in Part II? Does the difference in the place where the dream occurs suggest the difference in atmosphere between the two parts? Notice the Chinese box of dreams in Part II: the dreamer dreams of an old man, who tells him of Christiana's dream. By what naïvely direct means does Bunyan rid himself of the old man so that he can place the tale more immediately before us? Christiana's dream

51 Pt. 2, Bk. 4, Ch. 58.
52 Pt. 2, Bk. 4, Ch. 68.

is a kind of "awakening": does this fact suggest the meaning of Bunyan's use of the dream form?

2. Evangelist, the bringer of the Evangel or Gospel, is not able to save Christian (relieve him of his burden), but what is he able to do for him? Why is it only a good while later and after several adventures that Christian arrives at the Cross where his burden falls off? Why not immediately? Why does he lose his burden here? Why does it roll into the "sepulchre"? Why is Christian given a new coat here? In the final episode of the passage of the river, Christian is weighed down so that he almost goes under; in a sense, then, he is still burdened. Why? Is Bunyan's a Pollyanna version of the Christian life?

3. What humorously ironic double meanings do you find in these comments of Mr. Worldly Wiseman?

I would advise thee, then, that thou with all speed get thyself rid of thy burden; for thou wilt never be settled in thy mind till then; nor canst thou enjoy the benefits of the blessing which God hath bestowed upon thee until then.

Christian tells Mr. W. W. that he got his burden by reading a book. What does Mr. W. W. think about people who read books? You may note, incidentally, that Mr. W. W. offers to help Christian in getting rid of his burden by renting him a house "at reasonable rates." Is Mr. W. W. merely a stick figure or empty mask used to represent an abstract conception, or is he a psychologically coherent character? A psychologically coherent character (even Robinson Crusoe) is inconceivable except as a surrounding social atmosphere, or medium, or context is at least implied for him. What specific kind of social atmosphere is implied for Mr. W. W.? Why does Christian's burden become heavier after leaving Mr. W. W.?

4. The hill from which the fire flashes, frightening Christian, is called Mount Sinai—the mountain where Moses received the tablets of the law. Why does Bunyan place this threat (of "the law") in Christian's way? What does Mr. W. W.'s advice have to do with the law, and in what way does "the law" describe the error into which Christian has fallen? (See what Evangelist has to say, immediately, as to "the works of the law.") What special imaginative effect, characteristic of Bunyan, is produced by placing Mount Sinai, with its miracle of fire, directly

on the road trodden by a character—Mr. W. W.—whom we frequently meet in our own home town?

5. The gate through which Christian must pass is, on the literal plane of the story, a gate anyone might have to go through in crossing rural country, but, like everything else in Part I, it is also a sign of a state of mind. What does the gate—which demands a "crossing over" from one place (or state) to another—signify? Why does Good-Will stand at this particular gate? What is the meaning of the fact that Formalist and Hypocrisy "tumbled over the wall" rather than going through the gate? Would you assign any specific meaning to the Hill Difficulty? What is the significance of Christian's sleep in the arbor at the top of the Hill Difficulty?

6. The House Beautiful probably stands for the church: suggest a reason why Bunyan does not have Christian's conversion take place in the church at the beginning, instead of introducing him into it only after a number of temptations and trials. Why is the supper composed of "fat things" and "wine that was well refined," rather than of the lenten fare we might feel was more appropriate to the tastes of a strict seventeenth-century Puritan? The talk at supper is of the Lord of the Hill, who had "built that house," and who is said to be "such a lover of poor pilgrims, that the like is not to be found from the east to the west." What familiar motif from romances of chivalry is Bunyan using here? What is the significance of the fact that Christian issues from the House Beautiful, no longer as a poor pilgrim, but as a knight in armor? In what part of the journey—before or after his coming to the House Beautiful—are Christian's adventures the more dangerous? Why do the sisters show him this collection of menacing trophies: the hammer and nail with which Jael slew Sisera, the jawbone used by Samson, David's sling and stone?

7. Why is it in the Valley of Humiliation that Christian meets Apollyon? Why has Christian no armor for his back? When Apollyon says that he is the "prince and god" of the country from which Christian has come, what spirit does he identify himself with? Besides merely threatening Christian and advising him to abdicate from his lord, what two chief temptations does Apollyon put into his mind? In the line, "Then Apollyon straddled quite over the whole breadth of the way," where do you find Bunyan's typical diction? On what part of speech does he usually rely for pace and vividness? What romance or fairy-tale motif

do you find in the "leaves of the tree of life" with which Christian salves his wounds and is healed? Remembering the ancient science of herbalism, and those associations that are aroused by the thought of trees and leaves, would you say that Christian's healing by the leaves of the tree of life was arbitrarily allegorical or naturally and spontaneously symbolic?

8. How does Bunyan dramatize this verse from the Twenty-third Psalm: "Yea, though I walk through the valley of the shadow of death . . ."? Noting that Christian's death is not symbolized until much later, at the river, what would you say is the meaning of the Valley of the Shadow of Death in this place in the allegory? You may be familiar with Hawthorne's *Scarlet Letter* and with Dostoevski's *The Brothers Karamazov:* in the first book, Arthur Dimmesdale, when he returns from his appointment with Hester in the forest, finds himself whispering obscenities to staid townsfolk and cannot believe that these come from his own lips; in the second book, Ivan Karamazov, during a severe moral crisis, is visited by the devil, who seems to be an incarnation of all his own doubts and confusions. What resemblance to these two episodes do you find in Christian's experience with the whispering demons in the Valley, and what acute psychological perception, common with Hawthorne's and Dostoevski's, does Bunyan show here?

9. Why is it that, though Faithful's conversion was swift and easy, though he escaped the Slough, though the lions were asleep when he passed them, though he "had sunshine" through the two Valleys, though he did not have to fight with Apollyon, yet he was tempted severely by Madame Wanton and by the daughters (named Lust) of the old Adam—temptations that did not touch Christian? Do you find in this characterization of Faithful—a characterization by the dangers he did *not* have to go through, and by those that really threatened him—a measure of true psychological coherence, making him in some degree recognizable as a human type?

10. Mr. Talkative is apparently a fellow Puritan, for he is in full possession of a theology compatible with that of Christian. What is Bunyan's humorously satirical characterization of him? One of the true novelistic gifts is the gift for characterizing a person through his own words. (One might, for instance, compare Bunyan's method in this respect, with the method of Thackeray, who, though a much more sophisti-

cated novelist, insists on telling the reader everything he ought to know and think about a character before he allows the character to speak for himself.) Where, in the phrases used by Talkative, do you find the man characterizing himself out of his own mouth? What specific turns of idiom, and what specific speech rhythms, would you point to as showing his character? Notice that the meeting with Talkative serves also to characterize both Faithful and Christian a little more fully: what is Faithful's reaction to Talkative, and what is Christian's? In what way are these two different reactions psychologically significant of the differences between Faithful and Christian?

11. What is the meaning of the word "vanity" in the name Vanity Fair? In the list of the commodities sold at Vanity Fair, and of the entertainments that are given, would you say that Bunyan is merely lumping together generalized and random immoralities of urban life, or would you say that the specific items compose a genuine social satire founded on some measure of literal truth? Why do the merchandisers at the fair object to the conduct of the two pilgrims? Why do the examiners believe them mad? In what sense would you say that Christian and Faithful are actually disturbers of the peace and subverters of the status quo? Do you find genuine social satire—again founded on some measure of literal truth—in the speeches of Envy, Superstition, and Pickthank at the trial?

12. Mr. Hold-the-World employs proverbs as discourse: "Let us be wise as serpents," he says; "it is best to make hay when the sun shines; you see how the bee lieth still all winter, and bestirs her only when she can have profit with pleasure," and so forth. Mr. Hold-the-World and his companions are evidently substantial citizens belonging to the Established Church, men who look upon the Puritans as fanatics at the mercy of their emotions and lacking in reason and logic. What is Bunyan's satire in making Mr. Hold-the-World string proverbs together as if they were an argument? What is the satirical treatment of Mr. Money-Love's arguments? After this long passage of social satire, what characteristic contrast does Bunyan achieve by bringing his pilgrims to the "river of the water of life"? What is the meaning of the river and why is it found precisely at this point in the allegory? As the river is described, does it seem to you an arbitrary allegorical emblem (needing to have its meaning pointed out conceptually) or a symbol sponta-

neously calling upon natural associations and spontaneously stirring feelings and attitudes?

13. In leaving the road and taking the path through the meadow beside the way, are Christian and Hopeful further characterized, and are their different attitudes in the matter psychologically coherent with what we know of each? Why, allegorically, does their taking the path result in their imprisonment? (Try to answer this question in terms of some genuine psychology of the moral life.) What is the meaning of the "despair" personified in the Giant Despair, and why does he live in Doubting Castle? With these Biblical quotations in mind—"I will give unto him that is athirst of the fountain of the water of life" (Revelation) and "I am the bread of life" (St. John)—what usage, typical of Bunyan, do you find in the dietary conditions of the prisoners? What significance is there in the fact that the giant, instead of killing his prisoners outright, counsels them to commit suicide? What characteristic synthesis of fairy-tale motif and moral symbolism has Bunyan made in this episode?

14. The shepherds wish that the pilgrims may solace themselves "with the good of these Delectable Mountains," and then, instead of showing them more idyllic pastures and fresh springs, show them several terrible perspectives—men dashed to pieces at the foot of the mountain, blind men stumbling among tombs, and the opening to hell; and only afterwards offer them field glasses through which they may see the Celestial City. What psychological subtlety is there in this collocation of frightful and delightful perspectives in the Delectable Mountains? Why are the pilgrims unable to look steadily through the field glasses or see the Celestial City clearly? In this instance, what characteristic use has Bunyan made of a metaphor in Paul's first epistle to the Corinthians, 13:12? (Look up the Biblical verse.)

15. The subject at the end of Part I, from the entrance of the pilgrims into the country of Beulah to their entrance into the Celestial City, offers very great difficulty, if the author would be convincing; for he must create a sense of supernatural glory that will be emotionally fresh, but he can find no help in "realistic" techniques, inasmuch as the subject itself is "irrealistic," and his chief resource must be traditional apocalyptic imagery, with all its dangers of cliché-dullness, vulgarization in the popular mind, or mere obscurity. Would you say that the last pages

of Part I possessed or lacked intensity of vision? The ending of this little prose epic (Part I) ought surely to be heroic: is it convincingly heroic? What details would you cite to justify your judgment?

16. Although in Part II there is more dallying along the way, and we see Matthew growing up and marrying Mercy, yet there is not the same sense of the passage of time and the aging of a human being as there is in Part I. Is one made to feel that Christian himself changes? How and where? Does Christiana undergo any changes? There would seem to be danger of repetitiousness in Bunyan's taking a second group of characters across the same ground; actually, there is no repetitiousness. Illustrate this fact from the handling in Part II of the Slough, the Hill Difficulty, and the Valley of Humiliation. If we may look upon the terrain as changing with the travelers who cross it, what general explanation would you offer for the fact that the country was far rougher and more threatening for Christian than it is for the female pilgrims? Why, for instance, is the Valley of Humiliation (compare what it was for Christian) a pleasant place for the women and children, green and full of flowers?

17. Explain the psychology of Mr. Fearing, who "lay roaring at the Slough of Despond for about a month together," then, "one sunshine morning," suddenly got over it without quite knowing how he had managed it; who stood for so long trembling and hanging back at the gate; but who "made no stick at" the Hill Difficulty, "nor did he much fear the lions," and who had the happiest part of his pilgrimage in the Valley of Humiliation, but, at the Valley of the Shadow of Death, was "ready to die for fear"; and for whom the waters of the river of death ebbed so low that he scarcely had to get his shoes wet. Why do Christiana and Mercy both find themselves in instant, intimate sympathy with the psychology of Mr. Fearing?

18. Glance over the pages describing the supper at Gaius' house. This is intended to be a very allegorical supper, for an allegorical interpretation is given for each dish of food. Do you feel that the allegorical significance of the scene is its chief effect, or do you feel that the preponderant effect is that of a realistic picture of homely domestic manners and atmosphere? When the pilgrims come to the place where the Giant Despair is buried, they hold a celebration, the two women providing music, and Ready-to-halt dancing with the girls.

So he took Despondency's daughter, named Much-afraid, by the hand, and to dancing they went in the road. True, he could not dance without one crutch in his hand; but, I promise you, he footed it well. Also the girl was to be commended, for she answered the music handsomely.

As for Mr. Despondency, the music was not much to him; he was for feeding rather than dancing, for that he was almost starved. So Christiana gave him some of her bottle of spirits, for present relief, and then prepared him something to eat; and, in a little time, the old gentleman came to himself, and began to be finely revived.

Would this scene be damaged if one removed the allegorical names of the characters and gave them ordinary names? Do you feel that the scene is in any way dependent upon its allegorical intention? In what ways is the scene typical of the atmosphere of Part II?

19. It was in this place on the journey—where the Giant Despair now lies buried—that Christian had a nearly fatal experience. Now, without any shadow of despair, the women and the children, and the feeble and the halt and the lame, have their merriest time. Why should the second group of characters make merry over Despair, while Christian nearly died by him? Does the group motif of Part II indicate some part of the significance of this change? Is the particular make-up of the group significant? As, in retrospect over the book, the reader contemplates such differences as this, does the comparatively "realistic" scene of the merrymaking seem to lack psychological symbolism? On the basis of this comparison, formulate some statement as to the *symbolic* potentialities of "realism."

20. What is the chief difference between the final scene at the river of death in Part I, and the parallel scene in Part II? Note the constitution of the group here, which really falls into two groups: the women and children, Mr. Ready-to-halt, Mr. Despondency and his daughter Much-afraid, Mr. Feeble-mind; and the others, of contrasting temperament, Mr. Great-heart, Mr. Valiant, and so forth. What is the significance of the grouping together of these contrasting types? What effect is achieved by the description of the passage of each across the river, and in what way is this person-by-person description of the *group* coherent with the whole content and handling and meaning of Part II?

Moll Flanders

(NOTE: *Because of the lack of chapter breaks, guided reference is difficult. The page headings in most editions will be helpful in locating the references below.*)

1. Moll has much to say, at various places in the book, about the strife between her "inclinations" and necessity. In the first conversation recorded between Moll and the schoolteacher with whom, as a child, she was put to board in Colchester, when the woman suggests that Moll will have to earn her living in domestic service, what does the child's response tell of her "inclinations"? It has been said that Moll's "criminal habits were not a psychological eccentricity . . . but had behind them the impetus of a genuine social passion." [1] Characterize the particular "social passion" that moves Moll throughout her life. How is this social passion illustrated by her expression of "inclination" in the conversation referred to above? What touch of irony do you find in the nurse's words ". . . and how will you come to be a gentlewoman? What! will you do it by your fingers' ends?" What ironic aspect of her own words is the nurse aware of, and what other ironic aspect of the words is the reader aware of by virtue of his knowledge of later developments in Moll's life?

2. Consider the following love passage from Fielding's *Tom Jones,* a novel written some years later than Defoe's:

[The lover speaks:] "Oh! transporting thought! am I not assured that the blessed day will come, when I shall call you mine; when fears shall be no more; when I shall have that dear, that vast, that exquisite, ecstatic delight of making my Sophia happy?"—"Indeed, sir," said she, "that day is in your own power."—"Oh! my dear, my divine angel," cried he, "these words have made me mad with joy.—But I must, I will thank those dear lips which have so sweetly pronounced my bliss." He then caught her in his arms, and kissed her with an ardour he had never ventured before.

[1] Peter Quennell, in *The New Statesman and Nation,* September 7, 1940, p. 236.

Consider now the following love passage, taken from Moll's first, and only, "romance":

As I stepped forward . . . he was just got to the door, and clasping me in his arms, as if it had been by chance, "Oh, Mrs. Betty," says he, "are you here? . . ." and then, having me in his arms, he kissed me three or four times.—I struggled to get away, and yet did it but faintly neither, and he held me fast, and still kissed me, till he was out of breath, and, sitting down, says he, "Dear Betty, I am in love with you."

Both passages express sincere feeling. How would you differentiate the precise quality of feeling expressed in each? Make a careful, formal analysis of the syntax of the sentence from Fielding beginning "Oh! transporting thought!" and of the sentence from Defoe beginning "I struggled to get away . . ." What is the relationship, in each case, between the syntactical form of the sentence and the character of the emotion expressed? Which passage has the more points of contact with the complexities of civilized life? How do you find these implied by the use of language peculiar to each? If you had only this passage from *Moll Flanders* to judge from, would you be able to speculate imaginatively on some characteristic, or characteristics, of the special world in which Moll lives?

3. One of the sisters admonishes her brother thus:

"I wonder at you, brother," says the sister. "Betty wants but one thing, but she had as good want everything, for the market is against our sex just now; and if a young woman has beauty, birth, breeding, wit, sense, manners, modesty, and all to an extreme, yet if she has not money she's nobody, she had as good want them all; nothing but money now recommends a woman; the men play the game all into their own hands."

What is the older brother's rationalization for advising Moll to marry the younger brother, and for his own inability to marry her? In what way are his convictions entirely consonant with the sister's appraisal of the marriage market? The sister and the brother are two of the typical outlying characters who populate Moll's world and make it a social world. Characterize the ethos of this world, as the sister and the brother express that ethos. Is Moll's own ethos, as witnessed by her whole life, similar to or different from the social ethos expressed here?

4. The sister says, in effect, that the world is against women ("the men play the game all into their own hands"). Actually, are Moll's relationships with men (and the men's "game") antagonistic, or are they collaborative? What place and importance in this world does sex have, and the nucleus of passion, natural feeling, and so forth which "sex" implies? Moll often refers to a male companion as a "lovely person": what does she mean when she calls a man a "lovely person"?

5. There is a "moral" in Moll's behavior in her love affair with the older brother, a moral of which she becomes wisely aware after she realizes the unwisdom of her behavior. The moral does not concern illicit love as such: what does it concern? In what way is the moral lesson, which Moll learns here, of the same type as the morality preached throughout the book?

6. In what way does this statement,

> . . . he (the younger brother) would have me, and I was not obliged to tell him that I was his brother's whore . . .

illustrate not only Moll's own ethos, but the ethos of most of the characters in the book as well; for instance, that of the Lancashire husband? Judging by the following statement,

> I never was in bed with my husband, but I wished myself in the arms of his brother . . . in short, I committed adultery and incest with him every day in my desires . . .

would you say that Moll's understanding of herself and her circumstances was clear sighted and honest, or otherwise? In what way do the two quotations, given above, illustrate understatement? Do you find the same type of understatement in the passage quoted from *Moll Flanders* in Question 2? Why, would you say, is understatement generally suitable to the exigencies of Moll's whole way of life and the world in which she lives?

7. Moll is not without "idealism," in the sense that she has aspirations for "finer things" of a certain order. What "idealism" is illustrated by her junket to Oxford with her linen-draper husband? What social values are conceived here as paramount? What do these values arise

from and what are they dependent on? Moll's marriage to the linen draper lasts two and a quarter years. See the passage in which she describes the end of this marriage. How much does it tell us about her marital life and about the husband himself? What is her evaluation of her experience with this man? In what other of her liaisons and marriages do you find the same pattern illustrated?

8. What is the "moral" of the pages captioned "Advice to a Young Lady," "A Successful Stratagem," and "Counsel to the Ladies"? In what way is this moral related to the moral of Moll's affair with the older brother? What "idealism" does it illustrate? We have suggested that Moll is not an underworld type, but, in all her thoughts and aspirations, a respectable middle-class woman. How is her middle-class respectability illustrated by the moral preachments mentioned here? What does this morality have in common with criminal morality? What irony is there in this identity? How does the episode of the Successful Stratagem illustrate the fact that Moll, far from being in antagonism against her social world, collaborates with all her being in the making of it?

9. In the episode of her marriage with her own brother, Moll becomes very uneasy when she learns of the incestuous nature of her situation. She says,

> I was now the most unhappy of all women in the world. Oh! had the story never been told me, all had been well; it had been no crime to have lain with my husband, if I had known nothing of it . . . In the meantime, as I was but too sure of the fact, I lived therefore in open avowed incest and whoredom, and all under the appearance of an honest wife; and though I was not much touched with the crime of it, yet the action had something in it shocking to nature, and made my husband even nauseous to me

How is the statement ". . . it had been no crime to have lain with my husband, if I had known nothing of it . . ." psychologically and morally consistent with the first statement quoted in Question 6 (". . . he would have me, and I was not obliged to tell him that I was his brother's whore . . .")? Refer to the second quotation in Question 6: in what way is it *inconsistent* with Moll's attitude toward her incestuous marriage? One must remember that, to the mind of Moll's time, the situation referred to in Question 6 is as incestuous as that referred to here—a fact of which Moll is evidently fully aware. Does her inconsistency of attitude indicate a failure on Defoe's part to delineate Moll's character with psychological coherence; or is her inconsistency in this case quite coherent with the rest of her psychology? How would you explain it? Compare what she says, in the passage quoted above, about living "in open avowed incest and whoredom, and all under the appearance of an honest wife," with her conduct with the gentleman at Bath. Is she consistent or inconsistent? When she says, ". . . the action had something in it shocking to nature, and made my husband even nauseous to me," does she reveal a genuinely individual emotional response and moral perception, or, instead, a generalized and conventional horror of the breaking of the taboo, and of a situation not socially "respectable"? If the latter is the case, is her attitude psychologically consistent with her attitudes in other circumstances?

10. Moll afterwards goes to Bath to "mend her circumstances." What is the commodity she has to sell? With the gentleman at Bath, the realm of the moral and of the subjectively qualitative is placed explicitly before us. (In the passage below, the words having reference to emotional and moral qualities are italicized.)

And now he made *deep protestations of a sincere inviolable affection* for me, but *with the utmost reserve for my virtue and his own* . . . He carried it that length that he protested to me, that if he was naked in bed with me, he would as *sacredly preserve my virtue* as he would defend it, if I was assaulted by a ravisher.

Moll's relations with the gentleman remain "within the bounds of the strictest virtue" in the inn at Gloucester, where the two bed together in the same room, then in the same bed; and they remain so still after the return to Bath, where the virtuous experiment is frequently repeated and "all the familiarities of man and wife were common to us." But a time arrives when "the bars of virtue and conscience" are removed. The bars of virtue are removed by purely physical mechanics. In what way does this episode illustrate the typical transformation, in *Moll Flanders,* of the emotionally and spiritually qualitative into the material and quantitative? How does it illustrate ironic structure? Moll says that she now "exchanged the place of friend for that unmusical, harsh-sounding title of whore." In view of the "friendly" relationship preceding the exchange, what irony do you find in the distinction she makes? Is Moll herself ironical in this case? How does the whole episode show Moll's innately "respectable" inclinations? What is meant by "respectability" as illustrated here? In the beginning of her friendship with the gentleman, he shows her a drawer full of guineas and asks her to scoop up a handful. The little scene makes a vivid image. What symbolic value has it?

11. Let us consider what Moll has to say about "inclination" and "necessity"—her favorite philosophical speculation. After the unfortunate end of her affair with the Bath gentleman, she says,

> I wanted to be placed in a settled state of living, and had I happened to meet with a sober, good husband, I should have been as true a wife to him as virtue itself could have formed. If I had been otherwise, the vice came in always at the door of necessity, not at the door of inclination . . .

Again, having been married to "a house well furnished, and a husband in very good circumstances," she reflects,

> O . . . had I not fallen into that poverty which is the sure bane of virtue, how happy I had been . . . for while I lived thus [that is, in "a house well furnished," and with "a husband in very good circumstances"], I was really a penitent for all my life past . . . But, prompted by that worst of evils, poverty, I returned to the vile practice, and made the advantage of what they call a handsome face be the relief to my necessities . . .

After she has begun to build up a little capital by stealing, she says,

> Thus the devil, who began, by the help of an irresistible poverty, to push me into this wickedness, brought me to a height beyond the common rate, even when my necessities were not so terrifying . . .

And finally,

> . . . the temptation of necessity, which is the general introduction of all such wickedness, was now removed; [so] that I had near £500 by me in ready money, on which I might have lived very well, if I had thought fit to have retired; but, I say, I had not so much as the least inclination to leave off . . .

In Moll's observations of this kind, there is sociological truth, acute perception of the relationship between poverty and vice, and so forth;

and a certain base level of our reading of the whole novel is that of sociological realism. But Defoe has built upon this level other structures, which make of the book not a tract in sociology, but a complex, created world. For instance, Moll visualizes a constant strife between "necessity" (poverty, which leads her into crime) and her "inclination" (which is toward respectability); but, considering the following questions, is there really any strife between inclination and necessity in her world? How are "a house well furnished" and "a husband in very good circumstances" related to Moll's inclinations? How are they related to her criminal activities? Are not the objectives of her inclinations and the objectives of her criminal practices fundamentally identical? If the objectives of vice and the objectives of virtue are the same, is there a difference between vice and virtue? Do Moll's rewards after her conversion (the rewards of her inclination toward virtue, that is, "respectability") differ radically from the rewards of her crimes? Define the irony in these identifications. What *practical* differentiation would you say was made in Moll's world between vice and virtue? What irony is there in Moll's statement that when she lived in "a house well furnished" and with "a husband in very good circumstances," she was "really a penitent for all her life past"?

12. In what way is the following passage typical of Moll's affectional life?

> Nothing that ever befell me in my life sank so deep into my heart as this farewell [the Lancashire husband's letter of farewell]. I reproached him a thousand times in my thoughts for leaving me, for I would have gone with him through the world, if I had begged my bread. I felt in my pocket, and there I found ten guineas, his gold watch, and two little rings, one a small diamond ring, worth only about £6, and the other a plain gold ring. I sat down and looked upon these things two hours together, and scarce spoke a word.

13. The following is from the affair at the lying-in hospital, when the proprietress explains her bills. What typical irony do you find in it?

> "Then, madam," says she, "if the child should not live, as it sometimes happens, there is the minister's article [for christening] saved . . ." This was the most reasonable thing that I ever heard of; so I smiled, and told her I would come and be a customer.

Three itemized bills are presented for Moll's consideration here. This is one of the most obvious examples of Defoe's documentary realism. We might say that the three bills are presented in full in order to make the episode look like a report of fact. This is correct, so far as it goes; for the episode does look like a report of fact. But techniques of realism in literature are too often spoken of as if their *aesthetic* justification lay in making fiction look like fact. Fact structure is not art structure, and resemblance to fact (in the way in which a photograph resembles the object photographed, or a news item "resembles" the event reported) is not, simply in itself, a sign of aesthetic or literary function. What other reason would you give for the presentation of the three itemized bills? In what way, or ways, do they contribute to the texture of a special, created, fictional world?

14. Keeping in mind Moll's disposal of her first two children,

My two children were, indeed, taken happily off of my hands by my husband's father and mother, and that was all they got by Mrs. Betty.

and her complacency about the saving of the minister's article, consider Moll's meritorious thoughts about maternal affection and child care:

I wish all those women who consent to the disposing their children out of the way, as it is called, for decency sake, would consider that 'tis only a contrived method for murder; that is to say, killing their children with safety . . . I question not but these are partly the reasons why affection was placed by nature in the hearts of mothers to their children; without which they would never be able to give themselves up, as 'tis necessary they should, to the care and waking pains needful to the support of children.—Since this care is needful to the life of children, to neglect them is to murder them; again, to give them up to be managed by those people who have none of that needful affection placed by nature in them, is to neglect them in the highest degree; nay, in some it goes farther, and is in order to their being lost; so that 'tis an intentional murder, whether the child lives or dies.

Would you say that this extempore sermon of Moll's is hypocritical? Is it psychologically consistent with her "inclinations" toward middle-class respectability? Is Defoe subtly faithful here to the character of his creature, Moll, and to the world she symbolizes, or has he clumsily allowed the characterization to fall apart—the one part, the Moll who "happily" gets her children taken off her hands, and the other part, the Moll who sermonizes on maternal affection? Certainly we recognize some kind of fissure here, some kind of discordance. Is it a psychological and aesthetic discordance (in Moll and in the book), or, paradoxically, is the fissure itself a signature of the integrity, unity, and coherence of Moll and of her world?

15. The following two sentences are characteristic of the prose of *Moll Flanders:*

> The child had a little necklace on of gold beads, and I had my eye upon that, and in the dark of the alley I stopped, pretending to mend the child's clog that was loose, and took off her necklace, and the child never felt it, and so led the child on again . . . [Moll then leaves the child.] And I went through Bartholomew Close, and then turned round to another passage that goes into Long Lane, so away into Charterhouse Yard, and out into St. John's Street; then crossing into Smithfield, went down Chick Lane, and into Field Lane, to Holborn Bridge, when, mixing with the crowd of people usually passing there, it was not possible to have been found out.

Where is the technique of circumstantial realism shown here? What aesthetic justification does it seem to have in this instance? Why should Moll have such an accurate memory for street names? Make a formal analysis of the syntactical structure of the first sentence. In what way is this sentence structure sensitive to the quality of Moll's habits of mind and to the pace and tone and texture of her world?

16. In what way does the "moral" which Moll adduces from the stealing of the child's necklace illustrate the same mental process as that referred to in Question 14? The "moral" drawn from the robbing of the drunken cavalier is extensive in length and defended with eloquence; some thousand words are given to Moll's reflections, and some four thousand to the benign effect of the incident on the gentleman and his family. In view of the length and eloquence of these passages, it is clear that the moral is intended to sink home in the reader's mind. In what way does the expressed moral swerve away from the common ethical sense of the whole occasion? Does the episode itself (including Moll's inventory afterwards, and her conversation with her governess) have

moral significance, or is it amoral? Is this an instance of irony? If so, is it irony on Moll's part, or on Defoe's part, or on the part of the book (the book being neither Moll nor Defoe)?

17. Read over the pages describing Moll's sojourn in Newgate. Do you agree or disagree with what has been said as to the relative abstractness of the description? Knowing that Defoe himself spent some time in Newgate, and knowing his reportorial exactitude, would you say that the Newgate episode showed a singular failure on Defoe's part to employ his familiar technique of circumstantial realism? Or would you say that the description of Newgate, as it is given, is consistent with Moll's capacities for realization and is therefore aesthetically valid?

18. A conviction of sin and the act of penitence are, if they are anything, purely subjective experiences, emotionally concrete. If these states of mind are to be described, they must reflect that subjective qualitativeness and concreteness. Read over the section describing Moll's adoption of Christianity. Again, do you agree or disagree with what has been said as to the abstractness of the description, that is, its lack of subjective quality? Does this mean that Moll is a hypocrite? Or is it to be explained by the total context of her habits of mind and by the integrity of a world which excludes subjectivity?

19. Why does Moll receive more courteous treatment on the ship than the other voyagers? Is it because she is a reformed woman now? The latter part of the book—after Moll's conversion—probably contains more yardage, bales, pounds, bottles, barrels, gold watches, and so forth, by the page, than the earlier part. Explain the fact that, after Moll has gone through her crisis and become a Christian and an "honest woman," the elements of her world remain essentially the same—or the same elements are even increased quantitatively. Is this an illustration of the ironic structure of the book?

20. When Moll first sees her son by her brother-husband, she has what we must call a strongly emotional experience, after her capacities. Keeping in mind her disposal of her other children, the saving of the minister's article, her lecture on child care, and above all, the fact that her son is in "flourishing circumstances," interpret the following passage:

It was a wretched thing for a mother thus to see her own son, a handsome, comely young gentleman in flourishing circumstances, and durst not make herself known to him, and durst not take any notice of him. Let any mother of children that reads this consider it, and but think with what anguish of mind I restrained myself; what yearnings of soul I had in me to embrace him, and weep over him; and how I thought all my entrails turned within me, that my very bowels moved, and I knew not what to do, as I now know not how to express these agonies!

Shall we describe Moll as hypocritical here? Or are we to think of her as "perfectly changed," "another body," as she says of herself after her conversion? Or shall we explain the passage in terms of that strongly defined world which we have come to know in all the preceding contexts?

21. As soon as Moll is able to visit her son, the grandmother's will is pulled out, certain plantations, stock of servants, stock of cattle, and so forth are discussed, and the son tells Moll that he will be able to send her £100 a year from the tobacco raised on the estate she has inherited. Moll thereupon says,

This was all strange news to me, and things I had not been used to; and really my heart began to look up more seriously than I think it ever did before, and to look with great thankfulness to the hand of Providence, which had done such wonders for me, who had been myself the greatest wonder of wickedness perhaps that had been suffered to live in the world. And I must again observe, that not on this occasion only, but even on all other occasions of thankfulness, my past wickedness and abominable life never looked so monstrous to me . . . as when I had a sense upon me of Providence doing good to me . . . But I leave the reader to improve these thoughts.

How would you, as reader, "improve these thoughts"? Considering the fact that conviction of sin, penitence, and the grace of God are mysteries of the spirit, what irony do you find in this passage?

22. With these uplifting thoughts in mind, Moll presents her son with a gold watch.

I did not, indeed, tell him that I stole it from a gentlewoman's side, at a meeting-house in London. That's by the way.—He stood a little while hesitating, as if doubtful whether to take it or no. But I pressed it on him, and made him accept it, and it was not much less worth than his leather pouch full of Spanish gold; no, though it were to be reckoned as if at London, whereas it was worth twice as much there. At length he took it, kissed it, told me the watch should be a debt upon him that he would be paying as long as I lived.

Interpret this passage with those critical instrumentalities which you feel apply to *Moll Flanders*. In what way does the passage mirror Moll's world? Noting the first two statements—"I did not, indeed, tell him that I stole it from a gentlewoman's side, at a meeting-house in London. That's by the way."—in the particular context given them by the episode, attempt to make some speculative judgment as to whether Defoe was altogether innocent, or not altogether innocent, of the systematic ironies which the book exhibits.

23. Attempt to make a definitive statement as to the relationship between Defoe's realistic technique, his style (selection and ordering of words), and his vision of a highly unified, highly specialized world. Are the author's technique and style such that he might employ them on the shaping of visions of other worlds than this one, or are they a technique and a style peculiarly adapted to the projection of that special version of "reality" which we find in *Moll Flanders?*

Clarissa Harlowe

1. From time to time the questions here will refer to the fatality operating in Clarissa's story. Fatality may be thought of in the figure of a circle, whose end is in its beginning: that is, given certain inceptive conditions, certain results fatally follow. First of all, fatality is found in the plot itself, and we shall want to examine some of the details of the plot in order to see its fatal movement. What is Lovelace's first relationship with the Harlowe family? [1] What is the first discord in the relationship? By what minor and incidental means is Clarissa first involved with Lovelace so that continued communication with him is necessary? [2] What is her early attitude toward him? [3] Why does the family

[1] Letters of January 13 and 15, Clarissa to Miss Howe.
[2] January 13, same.
[3] February 27, Miss Howe to Clarissa.

encourage Solmes, as Clarissa's suitor, rather than Lovelace? [4] They want a title: why do they not obtain it through alliance with Lovelace? Though furiously set against Lovelace's suit, why do they connive at Clarissa's continued correspondence with him? [5] How does Lovelace play upon the family situation in order to win Clarissa's confidence? [6] In what sense are all these circumstances, which are beyond Clarissa's control, "fatal" for her?

2. What explains Arabella's harshness toward her sister? What reflection of the Cinderella situation do you find in the relationship of the sisters? What explains the brother's hatred of Lovelace? Having explained this at the literal level of the plot (the narrative sequence), do you find any further suggestion, in the sketch of a myth of caste given in the essay on *Clarissa,* for an explanation of James's hatred of the profligate aristocrat? (Note, in this connection, the ambivalence of the Harlowes' attitude toward the aristocrat: attraction to him on the part of the marriageable daughters, repulsion on the part of the Harlowe males.) [7] Does Clarissa's private inheritance have any effect upon James's attitude? Why does he want her to marry Solmes? Can you find any explanation for the fact that the father delegates his police authority over the daughter to the brother? What psychological explanation would you offer for James's extreme brutality to Clarissa when he becomes her jailer? A very young friend of Richardson's, Sally Wescomb, said to him,

Permit me to say, that it seems a little unnatural that so general an Infatuation shou'd run thro Clarissa's whole Family, as does not often happen, to bring about the Ruin of this admirable young Creature.

In what way does Sally's remark (which we might interpret as an objection to a lack of realistic verisimilitude in the story) touch indirectly on the mythical nature of the Harlowe situation?

3. Clarissa's marriage with Solmes is arranged to take place in a *moated house,* a tactic which is also "a little unnatural," since her incarceration could probably be as well guarded in London as by a moat. Notice that the theme of captivity runs through the book. What are its major

---

4 Approximately March 3 or 4, Clarissa to Miss Howe.
5 January 20, Clarissa to Miss Howe.
6 March 5 and March 18, Clarissa to Miss Howe.
7 March 1, Clarissa to Miss Howe.

instances? Captivity implies the use of force, and in *Clarissa* this theme is inflected as the use of force by men on a young girl in order to marry her or to seduce her. What is the psychological and cultural significance of these associations? What do they imply as a conception of love life?

4. Given the female impasse at the lover's seduction threat and the police authority of father and brother, there must be some canalization for feminine emotion. The expression of the emotion will appear abnormal and artificial because of the various blockages that it suffers. In the following passage (Clarissa's interview with her mother after the Solmes controversy), work out in detail and interpret all the elements of style, image, projection of a social situation, psychology, and symbolism that the passage contains.

> She saw my concern. Holding out her kind arms, as she sat, Come kiss me, my dear, said she, with a smile like a sunbeam breaking through the cloud that overshadowed her naturally benign aspect. Why flutters my jewel so? . . .
>
> O my mamma! was all I could say; and I clasped my arms around her neck, and my face sunk into her bosom.
>
> My child! my child! restrain, said she, your powers of moving! I dare not else trust myself with you.—And my tears trickled down her bosom, as hers bedewed my neck . . .
>
> Lift up your sweet face, my best child, my own Clarissa Harlowe!—O my daughter, best beloved of my heart, lift up a face so ever amiable to me!—Why these sobs?—Is an apprehended duty so affecting a thing . . . ?
>
> You know, my dear, what I every day forego, and undergo, for the sake of peace. Your papa is a very good man, and means well! but he will not be controlled; nor yet persuaded. You have sometimes seemed to pity *me,* that I am obliged to give up every point. Poor man! *his* reputation the less for it; *mine* the greater; yet would I not have his credit, if I could help it, at so dear a rate to *him* and to *myself.* You are a dutiful, a prudent, and a *wise* child . . . ; you would not add, I am sure, to my trouble! you would not wilfully break that peace which costs your mother so much to preserve. Obedience is better than sacrifice. O my Clary Harlowe, rejoice my heart by telling me I have apprehended too much . . . ! I am not prepared for your irresistible expostulation . . .
>
> But on this one quarter of an hour depends the peace of my

future life, the satisfaction of all the family, and your own security from a man of violence: and I charge you *besides,* on my blessing that you think of being Mrs. Solmes.

There went the dagger to my heart, and down I sunk: and when I recovered, found myself in the arms of my Hannah, my sister's Betty holding open my reluctantly opened palm, my laces cut, my linen scented with hartshorn; and my mother gone.[8]

What is the representative psychological and moral situation between husband and wife as Mrs. Harlowe describes it? What do the references to "peace" and "obedience" suggest as to the satisfactions of marital and family life? The dramatic image of Clarissa weeping on her mother's bosom has a later parallel in the picture of Clarissa sleeping on Mrs. Lovick's breast.[9] Both suggest infantile associations; what do they imply as to an ideal of the model daughter and the model young woman? How are these associations carried out in the language of the passage? In what way would you say that Mrs. Harlowe's mixed metaphor—"Why flutters my jewel so?"—is consistent with the psychological tenor of the whole situation? Would you say that her polysyllabism in the statement—"I am not prepared for your irresistible expostulation"—was also consonant with the peculiar psychological blockages and freshets here? Later we shall speak of other images of stabbing, but you may notice that Clarissa uses the image of stabbing as a metaphor in the last paragraph of the passage, and that the cutting of laces—always important in the feminine economy in *Clarissa* —enters associatively into the same image construct.

5. Consider the following collection of representative references. Miss Howe says, "See in Lovelace all that is desirable in figure, in birth, and in fortune: but in his heart a devil!" She tells Clarissa that she would refuse to take a man as her "instructor," even though he might impose himself by the "insolence of his will"; and that she would not "be a wife to any man breathing whom I at present know." [10] Clarissa, at the time of her arrest, cries, "With men! must go with men! I am not used to go with strange men!" [11] In what way does each of these

---

[8] March 3, Clarissa to Miss Howe.

[9] Approximately September 4, Belford to Lovelace, starting "Eight in the evening." The letter is split up.

[10] This and the preceding two quotations, August 29, Miss Howe to Clarissa.

[11] July 16, Belford to Lovelace.

expressions reinforce the symbolism of "the man" and of Lovelace's function in the plot? How do you explain, in terms of this symbolism, the fact that Miss Howe looks upon Clarissa's possible marriage with Lovelace as a "splendid alliance"? [12]

6. What is Lovelace's motivation? Is his motivation sufficiently expressed in the following statement? [13]

I have boasted that I was once in love before:—and indeed, I thought I was. It was in my early manhood—with that quality-jilt, whose infidelity I have vowed to revenge upon as many of the sex as shall come into my power.

Or is it expressed more adequately in this?

Then shall I have all the rascals and rascallesses of the family come creeping to me: I prescribing to them; and bringing that sordidly imperious brother to kneel at the footstool of my throne.

Richardson's and the Harlowes' attitude toward Lovelace is clearly ambivalent (involving both attraction and repulsion), but what does the above statement indicate as to the notion a man of the middle class might hold as to the motivations of the aristocracy? How much of an emphasis would you give to Lovelace's expression of motivation in the following?

All my fear arises from the little hold I have in the heart of this charming frost-piece: such a constant glow upon her lovely features: eyes so sparkling: limbs so divinely turned: health so impenetrable: and *I*, the hitherto successful Lovelace, the addresser— How can it be?

Would you phrase Lovelace's motivation simply, or how many complex elements would you find necessary to ascribe to it? When he says that triumph over Clarissa would be a "triumph over the whole sex," a "rape worthy of Jupiter," what further psychological complexity is added to his motivation? Is his impulse to seduce the female literally an impulse turned against all women, among whom Clarissa is only

[12] July 13, Miss Howe to Clarissa.
[13] All the quotations in Question 6, letter of March 13, Lovelace to Belford.

one? Or does she offer a special symbolism to him, that makes her the object of his obsession?

7. Even before the abduction, by what detailed means does he surround her with his intrigue? [14] How do Lovelace's relatives enter unwittingly into the conspiracy? [15] Why cannot Clarissa appeal for protection to Mrs. Howe? [16] In what sense do these plot circumstances contribute toward the "fatality" of Clarissa's drama? Explain the contrivance of the abduction: is Clarissa to blame at any point? [17] Richardson's intent was to give Clarissa a "tragic flaw," [18] a weakness readily to be condoned in the individual character, but tragically operative at a crisis, so that one might—in raising one's daughters and guarding them against frailties—point to Clarissa's story and say, "Remember what happened to Clary Harlowe!" What is Clarissa's "tragic flaw"?

8. Through a good section of the middle part of the book, while Clarissa is at Mrs. Sinclair's, and before the fire, what is her attitude toward Lovelace? What prevents a marriage proposal and settlement? [19] What specific arrangements does Lovelace prepare at Mrs. Sinclair's so that Clarissa is compromised from the start? [20] What prevents her from writing of her predicament to Cousin Morden? [21] In what sense is "fate" operative in these circumstances? It has been suggested by a number of commentators that Clarissa could have, very early in her troubles, made short work of them if she had made a deposition before her neighbor in Bow Street, Henry Fielding, Justice of the Peace: a comment which indicates merely that Clarissa, the captive and the helpless, need not have been captive and helpless if she were a "real" person. In other words, the postulate of captivity and helplessness, on which the novel depends, is ridiculous from a "realistic" point of view. But the novel that is myth deals in "realities" of a different kind, those of wish and fear and desire and dream. What "reality" of this kind is suggested by Clarissa's captivity at Mrs. Sinclair's (cp. Question 3.)? The infatuation of the Harlowes and Lovelace's subtle intrigues have surrounded

[14] Approximately March 17, Lovelace to Belford.
[15] March 18, Clarissa to Miss Howe.
[16] See May 2, Clarissa to Miss Howe.
[17] Tuesday, probably April 11, Clarissa to Miss Howe, and April 8, Lovelace to Joseph Leman.
[18] See May 4, and Tuesday, probably March 28, Clarissa to Miss Howe.
[19] April 13, Clarissa to Miss Howe, and, probably same date, Lovelace to Belford.
[20] Approximately April 27, Lovelace to Belford.
[21] Approximately May 4–6(?), Clarissa to Miss Howe.

her with fatal circumstances from the beginning, a net from which it is difficult to see (accepting only those possibilities with which the novel itself provides us) how she could escape: in what way does this fatality *on the plot level* technically enforce the *mythical* meaning of *Clarissa?* That is, how does the fatality of the plot urge us to subscribe to the wish fulfillments unconsciously represented in Clarissa's captivity at Mrs. Sinclair's and in Lovelace's assault on her?

9. Conceivably, Lovelace could have incarcerated Clarissa in respectable quarters, where, because of the complex circumstances that prevent her from obtaining other protection, she would still have remained in his power (as the Harlowes could have projected the marriage with Solmes quite safely in London, rather than in a "moated house"); but he chooses to take her to a brothel. How does the placing of her in a brothel sharpen and focus the significance of Lovelace's motivations? In what way is the brothel symbolic of the notion of "love life" in *Clarissa?* Clarissa's duenna is described thus:

The old dragon straddled up to her, with her arms kemboed again, her eyebrows erect like the bristles upon a hog's back, and, scowling over her shortened nose, more than half hid her ferret eyes. Her mouth was distorted. She pouted out her blubber-lips, as if to bellow up wind and sputter into her horse-nostrils, and her chin was curdled, and more than usually prominent with passion.

Would you say that this is a realistic portrait or a mythical evocation? The devil is spoken of as a "dragon" in later books of the Bible, and you will remember that Bunyan gives Apollyon dragon characteristics: in what way do these associations place Mrs. Sinclair symbolically?

10. What is the purpose behind Lovelace's deliberate attempt to make himself sick? [22] Is the fire accidental? [23] What new inflection does the episode of the fire give to the relationship between Lovelace and Clarissa? Is the fire imagery symbolic? In what way does the fire imagery support the significance of Lovelace's motivation and intent?

11. The following passage is from the fire scene, and the student is asked to interpret style, image, psychology of situation, and symbolism.

[22] May 26, Lovelace to Belford.
[23] See Wednesday, June 7, Lovelace to Belford.

When I had flown down to her chamber door, there I beheld the most charming creature in the world . . . sighing, trembling, and ready to faint, with nothing on but an under petticoat, her lovely bosom half open, and her feet just slipped into her shoes . . .

She conjured me, in the most solemn and affecting manner . . . to quit her apartment, and permit her to hide herself from the light, and from every human eye.

I besought her pardon, yet could not avoid offending; and repeatedly vowed, that the next morning's sun should witness our espousals . . . but redoubling her struggles to get from me, in broken accents, and exclamations the most vehement she protested that she would not survive what she called a treatment so disgraceful and villainous; and, looking all wildly round her, as if for some instrument of mischief, espied a pair of sharp pointed scissors on a chair by the bed-side, and endeavoured to catch them up, with design to make her words good on the spot . . .

O the sweet discomposure!—her eyes running over, yet seeming to threaten future vengeance: . . . wilt thou wonder if I resumed the incensed the already too much provoked fair one?

I did; and clasped her once more to my bosom: but, considering the delicacy of her frame, her force was amazing; . . . nor could I prevent her sliding through my arms, to fall upon her knees: which she did at my feet: and there, in the anguish of her soul, her streaming eyes lifted up to my face with supplicating softness, hands folded, dishevelled hair; her lovely bosom too heaving with sighs, and broken sobs, as if to aid her quivering lips, in pleading for her—did she implore my compassion and my honor . . .

Wicked wretch!—Insolent villain!—Yes, she called me insolent villain, although so much in my power! And for what!—only for kissing (with passion indeed) her inimitable neck, her lips, her cheeks, her forehead, and her streaming eyes, as this assemblage of beauties offered itself at once to my ravished sight; she continued kneeling at my feet as I sat.

Indeed you are!—the worst of villains! Help, dear blessed people! and screamed out— No help for a poor creature!

Am I then a villain, madame?—Am I then a villain, say you?— And clasped both my arms about her, offering to raise her to my bounding heart.

O no!—And yet you are!—And again I was her *dear* Lovelace!— Her hands again clasped over her charming bosom: Kill me! Kill me!—If I am odious enough in your eyes to deserve this treatment;

and I will thank you!—Too long, much too long has my life been a burden to me!—Or, wildly looking all around her, give me but the means, and I will instantly convince you, that my honour is dearer to me than my life! . . .

I sat suspended for a moment; by my soul, I thought, thou art, upon full proof, an angel and no woman!

At the level of narrative intention, what is offered in this passage is a picture of a severely virtuous woman defending her chastity under the most trying circumstances. Does the imagery in the following phrases contribute associations appropriate to such an intention: "the most charming creature in the world . . . with nothing on but an under petticoat, her lovely bosom half open"; "her lovely bosom . . . heaving"; "her inimitable neck, her lips, her cheeks . . . this assemblage of beauties offered itself at once to my ravished sight"; "her charming bosom . . ."? How would you describe the erotic associations peculiar to the following phrases: "sighing, trembling, and ready to faint"; "nor could I prevent her sliding through my arms, to fall upon her knees: which she did at my feet: and there, in the anguish of her soul, her streaming eyes lifted up to my face with supplicating softness, hands folded, dishevelled hair, . . ."? When Lovelace asks, "Wilt thou wonder if I resumed the incensed the already too much provoked fair one?" would you answer yes or no? Do you find erotic associations, and of what kind, in the following: "Yes, she called me insolent villain, although so much in my power!"; "Am I then a villain, madame? . . . O no!—And yet you are!—And again I was her *dear* Lovelace!"; "Kill me! Kill me!—If I am odious enough in your eyes to deserve this treatment; and I will thank you!" Dreams often adopt those disguises of wish fulfillment known as "displacement"; that is, some quality or activity is "displaced" from the dreamer onto a character in his dream (so that the dreamer will not have to accuse himself of having that quality or wishing to indulge in that activity), or a dream may attribute to the dreamer himself some gesture which he would like to see in another person (and in this case his conscience is saved from acknowledging his desire to see the other person use the gesture). In Question 12 (below) are some references to Clarissa's typical gestures with sharp instruments. Inasmuch as in the total context of *Clarissa*, erotic passion is conceived as desire to violate the body, what erotic association do you find in her gesture in the passage quoted above, when she makes as if to catch up the "sharp pointed scissors"? How does this gesture contribute to the generally perverse erotic context of the passage?

12. The following passages have reference to Clarissa's constant recourse to weapons of assassination or to thoughts of such weapons:

> She wrung her hands. She disordered her headdress. She tore her ruffles. She was in a perfect phrensy . . .
>
> 'Twill be a mercy, said she, the highest act of mercy you can do, to kill me outright upon this spot—this happy spot, as I will in my last moments call it!—Then baring, with a still more frantic violence, part of her enchanting neck— Here, here, said the soul-harrowing beauty, let thy pointed mercy enter! [24]

Here is a similar passage:

> "Stop where thou art, O vilest and most abandoned of men! Stop where thou art! Nor with that determined face, offer to touch me, if thou wouldst not that I should be a corpse at thy feet!"
>
> To my astonishment, she held forth a penknife in her hand, the point to her own bosom, grasping resolutely the whole handle . . .
>
> She withdrew to the door, and set her back against it, holding the pointed knife to her heaving bosom . . .
>
> "Approach me, Lovelace . . . I dare die. It is in defence of my honour." [25]

Clarissa's disordering of her clothes and exposure of her bosom are, at the plot level, an expression of desperation, but, in the context, is her dishevelment without erotic association? What significance does this association provide for the images of stabbing? Again, at the plot level, Clarissa is resisting Lovelace and defending her honor, but (referring back to the remarks on dream "displacement" in Question 11) in what way would you say that she is also symbolically enacting capitulation to Lovelace? How is this inference supported by her language when she calls on Lovelace to kill her, and when she refers to the spot where she will be assassinated as a "happy spot"?

[24] Part of long and split-up letter, Lovelace to Belford, begun June 18, section dated "Monday night."
[25] Probably June 24 or 25 ("Friday night or rather Saturday morning"), Lovelace to Belford.

13. Keys and keyholes frequently appear in the sequences at Mrs. Sinclair's house. For instance, Lovelace writes,

> I looked through the key-hole, and saw her on her knees . . .[26]

and again,

> I looked through the key-hole at my going by her door, and saw her on her knees, at her bed's feet, her head and bosom on the bed, her arms extended . . .[27]

After the seduction, Clarissa writes incoherently on a scrap of paper,

> . . . when all my doors are fast, and nothing but the key-hole open, and the key of late put into that . . . O wretched, wretched Clarissa Harlowe! [28]

In what way does the imagery of key and keyhole enter into configuration with the phallic imagery of sharp instruments referred to in Question 12? How does it enter into emotional configuration with the captivity theme? The rape itself is a fairly public affair, with the door open and the women of the house looking on.[29] What attitude toward sexual violation is to be inferred from this aspect of the rape as a spectacle, together with the constant peeping and peering at Clarissa from the keyhole?

14. Lovelace uses drugs to accomplish the seduction. In what way is this plot contrivance an instance of what in dreams is called "censorship"? The use of drugs is an employment of force upon the victim. How does this device support the conception of love life suggested in Question 3?

15. Why is Clarissa usually described as wearing white clothes?

> . . . her linen beyond imagination white, considering she had not undressed since she'd been there . . . ; . . . in a white satin nightgown, ever elegant! [30]

[26] Thursday morning, probably June 8, Lovelace to Belford.
[27] Same, Thursday at two.
[28] Fragment addressed "To Mr. Lovelace," among the scraps thrown by Clarissa on the floor after the rape.
[29] July 8, Clarissa to Miss Howe.
[30] July 17, Belford to Lovelace.

What is the symbolic effect of placing her, in her white clothes, in a particularly dirty and sordid garret? After the seduction, she gives away all her clothes (except for the suit with the everlasting laundry guarantee); and Lovelace (who is something of a Freudian) says,

Some disappointed fair ones would have hanged, some drowned themselves. My beloved only revenges herself upon her clothes.[31]

In what way is Clarissa's tearing or giving away of her clothes a symbolic action? If we should say that her white clothes are a correlative of her virginity and her "respectability," is there a radical similarity of attitude toward "virtue" between Clarissa and Moll Flanders, despite the difference in their social status and their usual psychology? Bearing in mind this correlation between clothes and virtue, and noting that, early in the book, Clarissa's various suits are described as very elegant, very expensive, and as gifts from her father, who, her mother tells her, has spent a great deal of money on her clothing, and noting also that Solmes proposes to "add some jewels" to her outfit when she marries him, would you be able to defend the proposition that Clarissa's virginity is an expensive material property belonging (not to her but) to her father and her prospective husband, and that it is for this reason that sexual violation raises such a commotion in the book? Does this speculation have any bearing on the father's curse?

16. Lovelace is not directly to blame for Clarissa's arrest for debt.[32] In what sense, however, has he set forces in motion which make the incident fatally inevitable? Refer back to Question 8, where the technical effect of fatality in the plot circumstances is spoken of. In what way does the tight causal weaving of the plot circumstances, as illustrated for instance in Clarissa's arrest, influence indirectly our feeling of inevitability and fatality in the denouement—that is, in regard to Clarissa's "decline" and death?

17. Consider the following imagery of weakness and debility:

She only eat a little bread and drank a glass of water.[33]

Rowland's wife pressed her to drink tea. She said she had rather have a glass of water . . . The woman brought her a glass, and some bread

31 July 21, Lovelace to Belford.
32 July 15, Lovelace to Belford.
33 Approximately June 8–9, Lovelace to Belford.

and butter. She tried to taste the latter: but could not swallow it: but eagerly drank the water; lifting up her eyes in thankfulness for that! [34]

Her diet is prescribed: water gruel, weak broths, a dish of tea with milk.[35] She is compared to a "half-broken-stalked lily." [36] As she weakens toward the end, many pages are given to a description of her symptoms, her trembling fingers, her misty eyes, her gently panting breath. In what way does imagery such as this enter into configuration with the imagery of Clarissa in white clothes? of Clarissa fainting? of Clarissa weeping on her mother's bosom? In what way does it enter into configuration with the erotic imagery discussed in Question 11? Explain why the condition of ill-health in the heroine appears to be an attractive and desirable attribute. Does the configuration as a whole (one image after another of this kind bombarding us from the beginning of the book to the end) suggest any reason for our acceptance of the inevitability and even the desirability and ideality of Clarissa's death?

18. The following is a portrait of the dying Clarissa:

> We beheld the lady, in a charming attitude. Dressed . . . in her virgin white, she was sitting in her elbow-chair, Mrs. Lovick close by her in another chair, with her left arm round her neck, supporting it, as it were; for, it seems, the lady had bid her do so, saying, she had been a mother to her, and she would delight herself in thinking she was in her mamma's arms . . .
>
> One faded cheek rested upon the good woman's bosom, the kindly warmth of which had over-spread it with a faint, but charming flush; the other paler, and hollow, as if already iced over by death. Her hands white as the lily, with her meandering veins more transparently blue than ever . . . one before her, the other grasped by the right hand of the kind widow, whose tears bedewed the sweet face which her motherly bosom supported . . .[37]

Compare this portrait with that quoted at length in Question 4. There we suggested that the ideal charm of the daughter was the charm of infantilism (note in the passage above: "she would delight herself in thinking she was in her mamma's arms"); here the same charm is asso-

[34] July 16, Belford to Lovelace.
[35] July 27, Belford to Lovelace.
[36] Approximately June 12, Lovelace to Belford.
[37] Approximately September 4, Belford to Lovelace.

ciated with the poetic beauties of moribundity. In the sketch that the essay on *Clarissa* offers of a myth of family life, what suggestions do you find that would bear on the correlation, in the passage quoted above, of an imagery of infantilism and an imagery of death? How does the *Clarissa*-world manage to make infantilism and death ideal?

19. Remembering Moll Flanders' happy associations with men, many men, and her relatively few and unrewarding associations with women, what contrast do you find in Clarissa's relationships with women (her mother, Mrs. Lovick, Miss Howe, the "worthy Norton")? How would you explain the contrast? Dying, Clarissa returns Miss Howe's miniature, and looking upon the picture says, *"Sweet and ever amiable friend—companion—sister—lover!"* [38] (The italics are Richardson's.) The passage continues: "[She] kissed it four several times, once at each tender appellation." Intimate feminine friendships, with their rituals, had more literary representation in the eighteenth century than they have in our own; but, although Richardson is representing the manners of his period, he is engaged in something more than a representation of manners; with the raw materials of manners, he is engaged in creating a meaningful world—a world which, like other fully created worlds in fiction, undoubtedly has more and other meanings than those which he himself consciously designed for it. Looking back to Question 4, and the impasse in feminine emotional life referred to there, in what sense would you say that the emotionalism of Clarissa's relationship with Miss Howe is justified by the particular character of the male-female relationships in Clarissa's world? In her will, Clarissa insists that only members of her own sex touch her body. How does this injunction, on the part of the divine Clarissa, symbolically confirm, sanction, and approve the complex system of emotional relationships between men and women, and women and women, in this world?

20. Early in the book, Clarissa had written to Miss Howe that she would prefer, rather than marry Solmes, to be "bricked up in the vaults of her ancestors." [39] Dying, she places a clause in her will asking to be "placed at the feet of her grandfather." These two expressions of desire—one at the beginning of the book, and one at the end—figuratively enclose her career in a circle, a figure of fate, which, as we suggested in Question 1, is a figure that is expressive because it shows the "end" as in-

[38] Same as above.
[39] Tuesday, probably April 4, Clarissa to Miss Howe.

cipient in the "beginning." In the first instance, Clarissa prefers death to marriage; in the second, she symbolically "returns" to her family (rejecting sexual alliance) in death. What weight would you give to this symbolism in judging Clarissa's story as (a) a description of eighteenth-century manners, and of an unfortunate girl's attempted rebellion against family domination, or as (b) a complex and profound representation, through a mythical drama, of an idealism of death as against the threats and delights of vitality? Does one interpretation necessarily exclude the other? When Clarissa says, "I have more pleasure in thinking of death than of a husband," [40] when she orders her coffin to be placed in her sickroom and concerns herself in the refinement of its decoration [41] (as a bride her bridebed), when she lingers rhetorically in her death throes and in the fullness of the mana which her ability to die has given her, to what degree are we to look upon these matters as (a) the sickly romanticism and sentimentalism of a limited historical period, or as (b) fillips given to a plot ending (one way to end a plot is to kill off the main character), or as (c) a robust and inevitable development of a theme that has been paramount in the book from the beginning? When Clarissa dreams that Lovelace carries her into a churchyard and there stabs her to the heart, then tumbles her into a grave among several half-dissolved carcasses, afterwards throwing in the dirt upon her with his hands and trampling it down with his feet, is the dream merely a random expression of anxiety or is it prescient and symbolic? In what way is it correlated with the erotic imagery referred to in Question 12? In what way is it correlated with her early preference for being "bricked up in the vaults of her ancestors" rather than marry Solmes? When Lovelace, after her death, says that he wants to "open" her and take out her heart,[42] what connection has his necrophilism with his earlier eroticism?

21. Why must Clarissa die? Explain the necessity of her death thoughtfully and carefully, in terms not only of plot fatality but also of that "fatality" or inevitability which lies in the unfolding of theme and in the expectations that are aroused by imagery. Cousin Morden arrives, with plenty of "money bills," and the Harlowe family becomes reconciled to Clarissa, only after her death. Could Cousin Morden's earlier

[40] July 23, Clarissa to Miss Howe.
[41] Thursday and Friday, August 31 and Sept. 1, Belford to Lovelace.
[42] September 9, Lovelace to Belford; September 10, Mowbray to Belford.

arrival, or the family's reconciliation with her, have prevented her death in any case? Given the theme and symbolism of the novel, would it have been possible for the family to become "reconciled" with her except through her death? In bare outline, the plot of *Clarissa* is melodramatic, and melodrama is known as an "aesthetic fallacy." What nevertheless makes of the *Clarissa*-plot a spendid technical instrument for the projection of a world rich in meaning?

Tom Jones

1. In the following passages for reference, trace the ambiguous relationships that are worked out between the physical appearances of people and their "real" nature. Miss Bridget says that she was shocked (I, viii) to see two farmer's daughters with bare necks, and it would be better for them if their faces were seamed with smallpox, as beautiful bodies are merely lures for the devil in man. (Actually, Samuel Richardson himself graciously wished the smallpox on two famous beauties of his day, for the same reason.) Miss Bridget, no beauty herself, is so "discreet" in her conduct "that her prudence was as much on guard as if she had all the snares to apprehend which were ever laid for her whole sex." What is the ironic implication here as to the relation between physical appearance and moral ("inner") traits such as "prudence" or "discretion"? In I, xi, we are told that Captain Blifil's "person" was "not much beholden to nature": "you could not discern what the natural colour of his cheeks was, they being totally overgrown by a black beard, which ascended to his eyes." But, for Miss Bridget, "such were the charms of the captain's conversation, that she totally overlooked the defects of his person." What is ironically implied as to the relative significance of a person's looks and his "conversation" (which presumably represents something "deeper" than looks, namely, a quality of mind)? What sly suggestion is there in the description of the Captain's beard? The Captain, also, is "one of those wise men who regard beauty in the other sex as a very worthless and superficial qualification"; he "very wisely preferred the more solid enjoyments he ex-

pected of this lady, to the fleeting charms of person." What are the "solid enjoyments" that are here contrasted with the "superficialities" of beauty?

2. To continue with the same considerations, Sophia's beauty is described in IV, ii, whereupon we are told: "Such was the outside of Sophia; nor was this beautiful frame disgraced by an inhabitant unworthy of it. Her mind was every way equal to her person; nay, the latter borrowed some charms from the former." And in IX, v, Tom is described as "one of the handsomest young fellows in the world. His face, besides being the picture of health, had in it the most apparent marks of sweetness and good-nature." In these remarks about the beautiful "outsides" of Sophia and Tom, does "appearance" seem to be set in opposition to "nature" or is it a manifestation of it? What is the difference in emphasis between these passages and those cited in Question 1?

3. In II, ix, we are told that Bridget, after her husband's death, "continued a whole month with all the decorations of sickness . . ."

At length, the decent time of sickness and immoderate grief being expired, the doctors were discharged, and the lady began to see company; being altered only from what she was before, by that colour of sadness in which she had dressed her person and countenance.

In what words here do you find a buried clothes metaphor? How does this buried metaphor suggest an ironic attitude about the lady's grief? What irony is there in the diction of the phrase, "the *decent* time of sickness and *immoderate* grief being expired"? In what words in the following passage (III, i) do you find the clothes metaphor working, and what do they suggest as to "appearance" and "reality" in the circumstances?

Mrs. Bridget . . . conducted herself through the whole season in which grief is to make its appearance on the outside of the body with the strictest regard to all the rules of custom and decency, suiting the alterations of her countenance to the several alterations of her habit: for as this changed from weeds to black, from black to gray, from gray to white, so did her countenance change from dismal to sorrowful, from sorrowful to sad, and from sad to serious . . .

How does this context help to determine our attitude toward words such as "strictest regard," "rules," "custom and decency"?

4. What "conditioned response" to Fielding's language has been built up, by the usages referred to in Questions 1 and 3, which determines our interpretation of such phrases as the following: "Miss Bridget had always expressed so great a regard for virtue" (I, iv); Deborah is frequently called "the prudent housekeeper"; Dr. Blifil has a "great appearance of religion" (I, x); Bridget's "conversation was so pure, her looks so sage, and her whole deportment so grave and solemn, that she seemed to deserve the name of saint . . ." (I, x)? Define the effect of such words as "expressed," "appearance," "looks," and "seemed," in these contexts. What connotations have been built up for words like "conversation" and "deportment," which, by themselves, are fairly free of connotation? Words with direct or indirect ethical reference, such as "prudent," "pure," "sage," "grave and solemn," might have very different connotative meaning in another book; what are their connotations here?

5. In I, xi, we are told that, as soon as Captain Blifil had "succeeded with her [Bridget] in private, the more reserved was he in public. And as for the lady, she had no sooner secured her lover than she behaved to him before company with the highest degree of indifference." How does this differentiation between public and private behavior parallel the clothes metaphor spoken of in Question 3? How does it parallel the distinction between physical appearance and "inner," moral qualities spoken of in Questions 1 and 2? What sly bearing on the same differentiation between public and private, "outside" and "inside," appearance and "reality," does the following reference (II, 2) to young Blifil's birth have? Mrs. Bridget was "by reason of a fright, delivered of a fine boy. The child was indeed to all appearances perfect; but the midwife discovered it was born a month before its full time."

6. In the discussion of the intellectual differences between Square and Thwackum in III, iii, what assumption is implied as to the existence of some one universal moral "reality," and what prevents Thwackum and Square from discovering this universal by their methods? What is Square's interpretation of "nature"? What is Thwackum's? What connotations do such words as "rule," "authority," and "system" have as they are used in this context? With what specific philosophical school of the eighteenth century would you associate Square? With what religious group would you place Thwackum? In III, v, we are told that young Blifil "got by heart" all the "principles" of his two schoolmas-

ters, although the "principles" contradicted each other; what does this imply as to the *moral* (or amoral) quality of the intellect when it is divorced from "feeling"? In the fact that Jones is said (III, v) to lack the "outward tokens of respect" toward his masters, and to have "little sobriety in his manners and less in his countenance," what is suggested as to the relationship, in Jones, between outward appearance and "nature"?

7. The question of justice is important in *Tom Jones* (note that Squire Allworthy is justice of the peace); many of the revelations of character occur in situations where justice is in question. In I, vi, when Mrs. Deborah, "putting on the gravity of a judge," calls Jenny an "audacious strumpet" ("proceeding rather to pass sentence on the prisoner than to accuse her"), what *motivates* Mrs. Deborah's particular version of "justice"? In II, v, Captain Blifil and Squire Allworthy discuss charity (mercy, generosity) in terms of "law": the Squire says charity is enjoined both by Christian law and the "law of nature." What *motivates* Captain Blifil's attitude toward charity here? What relation has charity (in this sense, as mercy, generosity of feeling, and so forth) to the Squire's kind of "justice," and how is it illustrated in his handling of Jenny's affairs? What miscarriage of justice is there on Allworthy's part in the affair of Partridge, II, vi? Notice that this miscarriage of justice occurs through the adventitious fact that Jenny, who could have testified for Partridge, has just gone off with a recruiting officer; in this instance, what has Fortune to do with men's "justice"? Is it implied in these contexts that "justice" is an abstract principle that can be used as an absolute rule in all occasions where a question of justice arises, or that justice is a varying characteristic of concrete experience? What have motives, feelings, and mere accidents of circumstance to do with "justice"?

8. In III, ii, the affair of the poaching (notice the frequency of legal language in this chapter and the following one), a new question of justice arises. What is Thwackum's notion of justice and how is it carried out? What does Allworthy think of this kind of justice? How is the question of justice inflected by the fact that Allworthy gives Tom a horse "to make him amends," and that with this gesture of the Squire's, "Tom's guilt now flew in his face more than any severity could make it"? In III, vii, we are told that Mrs. Bridget's open dislike of young Blifil and her open preference for Tom caused Allworthy to develop the

opposite feelings about the two boys—sympathy for Blifil and hardness toward Tom: is there another miscarriage of "justice" here, and what in this case has charity to do with the perversion of justice? In III, viii, the affair of the selling of Tom's horse and the various reactions of Allworthy, Thwackum, and Square to this event, what is the relation between justice and charity? In III, x, where Blifil informs against the gamekeeper, where does Blifil stand as to justice and charity? In these cases, is justice presented as an abstraction or as a concrete aspect of special, complicated psychological circumstances? Why should questions of justice assume particular importance in a book so constantly concerned with "appearance" and "reality," public behavior and private feeling, the "outward" and the "inward"?

9. At the time of Allworthy's illness (V, vii), when he thinks he is dying and makes public his will, we have a scene which Samuel Richardson would have called a "proper occasion" for the display of emotion (remember the scene of Clarissa's death); and we are told Mrs. Deborah, reacting appropriately to the occasion, "dropped her pearls as fast as the Arabian trees their medicinal gums; for this was a ceremonial which that gentlewoman never omitted on a proper occasion." Why the inflated diction here? What is the connotative force of the words "ceremonial" and "proper"? In the immediately following chapter (V, viii), what contrast is set up between the public behavior in the sickroom and Mrs. Deborah's private motivations and feelings? What parallel contrast is recorded with reference to Thwackum and Square? In Jones's drunkenness on this occasion, what relationship has "appearance" to the concrete reality of motivation and feeling? Are they interdependent or are they separate and departmentalized?

10. The following question has to do with the operations of Fortune. In II, viii, where Captain Blifil is calculating his fortune (Allworthy's possessions and the probable date of Allworthy's demise) and suddenly dies of a heart attack, what relationship is suggested between Fortune and man's calculations? Now note a directly opposite relationship: in III, ix, we are told that "misfortunes seldom come single," for on top of Tom's trouble over the sale of the horse, he gets into further trouble by the sale of his Bible; but is the latter "misfortune" the work solely of a mysterious Nemesis, or has human calculation a causal operation here? On the whole, would you say that in this book Fortune is repre-

sented as a capricious superhuman influence or as a humanly explicable concatenation of circumstances? In the episode (V, v) that takes place in Molly's bedroom, in what way is Fortune an agent of comic exposure of "real" character? In the great chapter (V, x) on Tom's encounter with Molly by the brookside, in what way does Fortune act as a malevolent agent in upsetting men's calculations (in this case, Tom's ideals of chaste love)?

11. Here and in Question 12, you are asked to make a fairly close analysis of the two scenes mentioned at the end of the preceding question. First, the scene in Molly's bedroom (V, v). Fielding has just spoken of the literary function of contrast, in his head-chapter for Book V. How is this illustrated, in the present scene, in Molly's impassioned disquisition on fidelity and the ensuing event? Note that, after her discourse, the description of the garret is drawn out in a rather long paragraph, and we get to the fatal accident quite slowly. How does this sober slowness of pace add to the comic effect of the revelation? In the fact that it is the fall of a *curtain* that exposes Square, do you find any reflection of the clothes metaphor suggested in Question 3? What symbolic appropriateness has a *curtain* in the contexts of "appearance" and "reality" that dominate the book thematically? Does this scene suggest what Square's motivations have been in his attempts to blacken Tom's relationship with Molly (he has told Allworthy that Tom's kindness to George's family was a ruse to corrupt the daughter)? In the paragraph analyzing Square's inconsistency (beginning, "But, to confess the truth, this inconsistency is rather imaginary than real. Philosophers are composed of flesh and blood as well as other human creatures," and so forth) what single, tangible, concrete, universal "reality" is set up against all the varieties of abstract theory? How does Square manage to make his philosophical theory rationalize and justify his behavior? What does his manipulation of theory suggest as to the reliability of purely logical "truth" and its relation to "reality"?

12. Now analyze closely the first five paragraphs of V, x—the scene of Tom's encounter with Molly by the brook. In the second paragraph, the description of nature and the account of Tom's amorous imaginings are stereotyped in diction. What clichés do you notice? What do you think is the function of an inflated, stereotyped kind of diction in this place? How is the principle of contrast carried out in the episode?

Is the *deflation* sudden or is it protracted by the diction of the following sentences?

At these words he started up, and beheld—not his Sophia—no, nor a Circassian maid richly and elegantly attired for the grand Signior's seraglio. No; without a gown, in a shift that was somewhat of the coarsest, and none of the cleanest, bedewed likewise with some odoriferous effluvia, the produce of the day's labour, with a pitchfork in her hand, Molly Seagrim approached.

Suppose the break between the inflation and the deflation had been more violent, and instead of the word "bedewed" we should have had "smeared," and instead of "odoriferous effluvia" the simple word "dung," what effect would have been lost? What is the rhetorical structure of the second sentence quoted above? In what way is this sentence like a little "plot," with accreted "complications" and suspended "crisis" and revelation? Would Defoe's style have sufficed for what Fielding is trying to do here? In what way does Fielding's particular style demand an *intellectual* response to his subject—that is, call for constant intellectual objectification of the subject, and "put it at a distance" where it can be measured and judged all around? In what way is this constant sophisticated activity of the style consonant with the theme of the ideal *intelligibility* of "nature," when "nature" allows itself to appear without disguise before men?

13. In the passage introducing Sophia (IV, ii), the description is enormously "idealized" (the diction "elevated," or "embellished," in a parody of the manner of classical tragic and epic poetry), but you will notice that Sophia's forehead is said to be too low and her chin somewhat large. What is the effect of placing these "realistic," not entirely flattering details in the midst of the overblown idealism of the apostrophe? Is Fielding, by his parody here, *merely* mocking at traditional literary idealization of female beauty? Is it implied that the traditional literary treatment is false to life? Or is it implied that life, even with its imperfections, does show the ideal? Thwackum and Square also have "idealistic" theories; what is the difference between their "idealism" and the idealism suggested in the treatment of Sophia's beauty? What is the nature of the contrast between this passage and the scene of Squire Western's dinner conversation about bastards (IV, x) which takes place in his daughter's presence? How does this contrast succeed

in bringing the idealized Sophia down to the size of life? How does Sophia's tumble from her horse (XI, ii) accomplish the same thing?

14. The battle in the churchyard (IV, viii) is a famous example of Fielding's parody of classical epic. How, specifically, is the parody carried out? The function of the parody here is somewhat different from its function in the apostrophe to Sophia, since Sophia herself is an "ideal" subject, while here the subject is "low." What is the particular effect of the "literary" inflation of the description of the battle, in contrast with the grossness of the subject? Has its effect anything to do with the fact that classical poets would not have treated such a plebeian subject? Has it anything to do with the suggestion that "common" events may have "epic" proportions? Certainly, as in the apostrophe to Sophia, "literature" is here brought into some suggestive relationship with "life": what relationship?

15. Though the English novel was for long under the influence of Fielding, the most familiar modern novelistic technique derives from Flaubert, Henry James, and Conrad, who attempted to perfect an art of illusion which would, if carried to some of its conclusions, make it seem that a novel writes itself without help of an author—in other words, that a novel is not a novel but *is* life; the characters would appear to speak and think entirely without author control. Define and illustrate Fielding's deliberate exploitation of authorial management and omniscience in his "assistance" to the reader at the end of I, v; in his disquisition on novel time as against historical time, II, i; in his refusal to reveal secrets, II, vi. In connection with the latter instance, note that, in V, viii, the lawyer Dowling reveals to Blifil the secret of Tom's birth, but the reader is not allowed to learn this until the end of the book; a modern author, in the tradition of Henry James, would feel that this was an abuse of novelistic illusion; how is Fielding's withholding of the secret justified by his generally deliberate treatment of "the novel as a novel," an artifact *made* by an author and not in any sense a competitor or rival of life? But now consider, in this connection, the passage describing Partridge's response to the acting of Garrick in the part of Hamlet, when Tom takes him to the play (XVI, v), and particularly the fourth paragraph from the end of this chapter; Tom asks him which actor he liked best, and Partridge says the king, whereupon Mrs. Miller tells him that all the town agrees that "Hamlet is acted by the best player who ever was on the stage."

"He the best player!" cries Partridge, with a contemptuous sneer; "why, I could act as well as he myself. I am sure, if I had seen a ghost, I should have looked in the very same manner, and done just as he did. And then, to be sure, in that scene, as you called it, between him and his mother, where you told me he acted so fine, why, Lord help me, any man, that is, any good man, that had such a mother, would have done exactly the same. I know you are only joking with me; but indeed, madam, though I was never at a play in London, yet I have seen acting before in the country: and the king for my money; he speaks all his words distinctly, half as loud again as the other.—Anybody may see he is an actor."

What implied comment do you have here on art as a technique of illusion, that is, as a technique of "embodiment" which has the effect, not of artifice, but of "real life"?

16. Fielding's head-chapters also accent that character of literary art which is its character as *literary artifice* rather than *illusion of life*. What are some of the more conspicuous subjects treated by the head-chapters? How does the device of the head-chapter point up ironically the illusionism of the novel as art? This irony has a serious aspect in the actually great influence that books in general and novels in particular have on people's lives. What elements in *Don Quixote* had a similar bearing on the relationship of literature and life? We have noted Fielding's interest in this relationship, in his parodies of traditional literary manners; how, precisely, do the head-chapters show it? The theme of Fielding's comedy of appearance and reality is the necessity of committing "nature" openly to the social intelligence; how does the device of the head-chapter carry out this appeal to intelligence? How do the head-chapters increase the sense of the "objectivity" of the comic spectacle? What does Fielding himself say, in V, i, as to the purpose of the head-chapters? How is the "principle of contrast" carried out in the relation of the head-chapters to the dramatic action?

17. Book VI is concerned with love and matrimony. In the description of Mrs. Western, VI, ii, analyze the particular connotations, largely built up by earlier contexts, in the diction of such phrases as the following: she is a "perfect mistress of manners, customs, ceremonies, and fashions"; she is a "critic" of literature; she has "very competent skill in politics" and can "discourse very learnedly on the affairs of Europe"; she is "excellently well skilled in the doctrine of Amour"; she has con-

sidered matters of love "scientifically." Analyze the incident in VI, v (the interview between Mrs. Western and Sophia), in terms of a small "plot" with "complications," "recognition," and "reversal." What happens, in this scene, to Mrs. Western's scientific knowledge of Amour (a passion, she says, of which she "highly approves")?

18. There is a good deal of play on the word "see" through this part of the book; for instance, Mrs. Western says to Sophia (VI, v),

Consider, you are only revealing to me what I know already, and what I plainly saw yesterday through that most artful of all disguises which you had put on, and which must have deceived any one who had not perfectly known the world.

"Recognition scenes" were important in classical drama, and the example of Sophocles' Oedipus has taught us the meaning of "recognition" or "seeing," and the meaning also of "blindness." What is the trouble with Mrs. Western's "sight"? What are the particular "blinders" which she has on her eyes, and how does her spiritual eye-trouble illustrate the thematic dualism of "appearance" and "reality" (or "nature")? What contrast is set up between the two women, Mrs. Western and Sophia?

19. Following out the motif of "seeing," analyze Squire Western's attitude toward the love complication. What does the following suggest as to his "insight" into love? When Mrs. Western informs him that Sophia is in love with Blifil, he says, "I was never more rejoiced in my life; for nothing can lie so handy together as our two estates." By what is Squire Western "blinded," and how does his particular "blindness" differ from his sister's?

20. Squire Allworthy is not unappreciative of the advantages of Sophia's fortune; we are told (VI, iii) that, "though he was too sober to be intoxicated with it, he was too sensible to despise [it]." Reread the last eight paragraphs of VI, iii, describing and generalizing on Allworthy's attitude. Why does Fielding say that "the wisest man is the likeliest to possess all worldly blessings in an eminent degree"? (Notice that we are not concerned here with whether Fielding is "right" or "wrong," but only with the *contextual* validity of the attitude expressed here.) How does the emphasis on Allworthy's "moderation" set up a contrast with Squire Western's reactions to the love affair? If Allworthy is a man

who has committed "nature" to the intelligence, how does Squire Western (himself by no means weak in "human nature") stand in this respect?

21. What are Blifil's motivations in forcing his suit on Sophia (see VI, iv and VII, vi)? "Animal nature" is apparently not lacking in Blifil, no more than in Tom himself; what, then, is the difference between these two, so far as "animal nature" is concerned, and how does this difference illustrate the thematic dualism of "appearance" and "nature"? If "blindness" may be said, generally, to be the flaw in Mrs. Western and Squire Western (and even in Squire Allworthy at times, under the stress of specially complicated circumstances when it becomes very difficult to "see"), would you say that Blifil's trouble was also "blindness," or would you say that Blifil was simply an example of "natural depravity"—human nature gone wrong from the root up?

22. In the treatment of Sophia by her father—he locks her up—and in Blifil's acquiescence in this treatment, the question of freedom and constraint arises. You will recall the constant motif of captivity in *Clarissa Harlowe;* which is strongest in *Tom Jones,* the motif of captivity or the motif of freedom? How is this illustrated by Sophia's action? How is it illustrated by the long central section of the book, of scenes on the highway (recall the fact that all of the scenes in *Clarissa* are scenes of house interiors, with much business with keys, locking of doors, etc.)? In what way is the motif of free physical action in *Tom Jones* related to the motif of *exposure* (the comic exposure of men's "real" characters) and to the theme of open revelation of "nature" to the light of the social intelligence in such a way that "nature" and "appearance" will not be opposed to each other but will be one and the same thing?

23. What miscarriage of justice, on Allworthy's part, occurs in VI, x and xi? In what way is "injustice" here a function of highly complicated circumstances and devious calculations, and not merely a "flaw" in Allworthy's character? Notice that immediately after this important perversion of justice, we have the scene (VI, xiii) of Black George's "court of conscience," when George argues with himself over keeping Tom's money. How is this scene managed as a parody of legalistic behavior? What is George's final motivation in giving up the money? Does this suggest that ordinary men act on "principles" or by force of less intellectual factors? Are we to understand here that George is, like

Blifil, a case of absolute human depravity, or are we to understand from it rather that "human nature" is ordinarily a product of circumstances and external pressures, changing as circumstances change, rather than remaining some fixed and unchangeable "absolute" of "good" or "bad"? How is this attitude toward "human nature" carried out in the case of Tom himself?

24. Note that Mrs. Honour's "case of conscience" is treated almost immediately after George's. What are the circumstances determining Mrs. Honour's "honor" (see VII, viii and following)? What part has Fortune to do with these circumstances, or are the circumstances themselves the concrete aspect of Fortune? Why, just between these two scenes— that concerning George's case of conscience, and that concerning Honour's—do we have the head-chapter (VII, i) in which the author uses the metaphor of Nature as a theater, in which an actor may play a villainous part on one night and a sympathetic part on another night?

25. The first scene on the highways occurs in VII, x, where Tom is wandering around after an ignorant guide and meets two equally ignorant countrymen who give him confused directions. How does this meeting symbolize the new life on the roads, and how does it symbolize the increased play of Fortune? Inns now become the setting for events, as in Part I of *Don Quixote*. Why is the inn a specially suitable setting for cross-purposed events, complications, mistaken identities, "exposures," and contrasts between "appearances" and "reality"?

26. Analyze, in VII, xiii and VIII, ii, the play on "appearance" and "reality" as shown in the landlady's changing attitudes toward Tom, and in those of the surgeon. What is the only "reality" to the landlady and the surgeon, and what is their criterion of gentlemanly "quality"? Fielding has often been called to account, by critics, for "vulgarity." What would you say was Fielding's own criterion of "vulgarity" in people, as illustrated in the scenes referred to here? (See his footnote on "the mob," I, ix. What does he mean by "the mob"?) In the swift comic contrast, VII, xiii, between the landlady's manner of speech and that of the surgeon, the one "low," the other scientifically "high," what is the ironic implication as to the relative "lowness" or "highness" of either?

27. Like Cervantes, Fielding allows himself to "digress" into a short novelette, with the tale told by the Old Man of the Hill (VIII, xi–xiv). Why is the Old Man's history, if it is relevant to the main narrative at all,

particularly relevant here, where Tom is "out on his feet" in the world? What contrast do you find between the Old Man's attitude toward "human nature" and the attitude generally expressed in Fielding's novel as a whole? In this radical contrast of attitude, do you find any justification for the inclusion of the Old Man's tale in the novel?

28. What is Tom's own criticism, in VIII, xv, of the Old Man's attitude? Notice that Tom is himself, at this moment, a victim of one of "the worst and basest" of the human species—namely, Blifil—a type from whom the Old Man has drawn all his doctrine of what constitutes "human nature"; from what specimens of the species does Tom say a representative picture of human characteristics should be drawn? How does the case of Black George illustrate Tom's thesis in the following?

If there was, indeed, much more wickedness in the world than there is, it would not prove such general assertions against human nature, since much of this arrives by mere accident, and many a man who commits evil is not totally bad and corrupt in his heart.

How does the Old Man's tale set Tom's own career in perspective, and how does Tom's total career give perspective to the Old Man's tale? Would you say, finally, that the Old Man's tale was an inexcusable digression and a flaw in the structure of this novel?

29. In IX, iv and vi, the "clothes metaphor" (see Question 3) appears again, but this time with literal realization in Mrs. Waters' state of undress. How, as shown in the landlady's reactions, does the metaphor again serve to illuminate varying aspects of "appearance" and "reality"? In X, iii, we have again a play on "seeing" and "blindness," when Susan, the chambermaid, says she "saw with her own eyes" Mrs. Waters in bed with Tom, and the landlady replies, "I would not have believed my own eyes against such good gentlefolks," and again, "No, no, I will never believe any harm of such sober good sort of people" (after Tom and Mrs. Waters have just consumed two bottles of the best champagne). What irony does the metaphor of "seeing" have in this context? What determines what the landlady "sees" and what she doesn't "see"? In IX, v, we are told that even heroes "are liable to the worst infirmities, and subject to the vilest offices of human nature"—namely, eating—just before a beafsteak is served up to Tom. How does this statement prepare for the amatory episode that follows?

30. In XIII, vii–ix, where Tom accepts a position as Lady Bellaston's gig-
olo, we have the hero in his least heroic situation in the whole novel.
Considering the fact that Tom is broke, and re-examining Chapter vii,
on the masquerade, and Chapter ix, where his attitude toward the
matter is analyzed, what partial (even if feeble) justifications do you
find for Tom's acceptance of his position? In view of Fielding's deliberate system of contrasts, and particularly in view of the major thematic contrast of "appearance" and "reality," do you find dramatic
justification for his bringing his hero to such a nadir, where the "appearances" that are against him are the worst possible? In what way
does the affair of the highwayman, and Tom's disposal of his first "pay-
ment" from Lady Bellaston (XIII, viii), act compensatorily to keep
him in the reader's sympathies and to show us what the "reality" in
Tom's nature is? In what way does Tom's attitude toward Nightingale's flirtation with Nancy (shown in XIV, iv and vii), and his action
in bringing this unfortunate matter to a happy conclusion, serve also
—like the affair of the highwayman—to brighten up Tom's "real"
character (which so very much needs all the furbishing it can get at this
time)?

31. Having got his hero into apparently unresolvable difficulties, in prison
for murder and presumptively guilty of incest with his mother, Fielding insists (XVII, i) that only "natural" means must be used for the
resolution of these complications. Illustrate the "naturalness" (or unnaturalness) of the steps in the resolution, with reference to:
a. Mrs. Miller's influence on Allworthy's attitude (XVII, ii and vii);
b. Mrs. Waters' sudden arrival and her motivation in visiting Jones
(XVII, ix);
c. Philosopher Square's letter to Allworthy (XVIII, iv);
d. The revelation of the truth about Tom's birth (XVIII, vii);
e. The exposure of Blifil's guilt (XVIII, vii);
f. Squire Western's change of heart toward the marriage of Tom and
Sophia (XVIII, ix).
How many of these involve "recognitions"? In what way does the multiple use of "recognitions" carry out the motifs of "seeing" and "blindness" that we have noticed in the earlier portions of the book? How
does the use of "recognition scenes" carry out the thematic play on
"appearance" and "reality"? Does Tom himself come to any "recognition"? The most decisive of these "recognitions," for the plot as a

whole, is that by which Allworthy recognizes the secret of Tom's birth; in what sense does this particular recognition mark the full sweep of a circle whose starting point was the scene in Allworthy's bedroom at the beginning of the book (I, iii)? (Incidentally, one may note here that Tom is one more example of the archetypal hero whose birth is mysterious and whose story is resolved with the revelation of the secret of his birth. What other heroes of story fall into this class?)

Tristram Shandy

1. Sterne encourages the reader to think that his writing is artless and formless, for in the appearance of formlessness and artlessness lies the illusion of the spontaneous workings of the mind. In other words, the appearance of artlessness is an element of Sterne's art, and the appearance of formlessness an element of form in *Tristram Shandy*. The questions here are all investigations of form, or "structure," and the first four bear particularly on deliberate unifying designs that tie up the beginning and the end of the novel. Compare the first and the last chapter of the novel, noting that common to them both is the theme of procreation.[1] Suggest a reason for Sterne's beginning and ending on this theme. What implicit connection do you find between the procreative theme and that aspect of *Tristram* which is its concern with the "timeless time" of consciousness (as against progressive physical time, which marks the abrupt beginning of phenomena and their abrupt "conclusions")? You will note that while the first chapter has to do with the begetting of a child, the last has to do with the begetting of a calf. Do you find here, on a large structural scale, an illustration of Coleridge's definition of humor? In these variations of the procreative theme, what significant attitude is implied as to the relationship of human nature and animal nature?

2. In the first book, parson Yorick dies. In what way do Sterne's special

---

[1] B. H. Lehman points out in detail the binding function of this theme, in his essay "Of Time, Personality and the Author," in *Studies in Comedy* (Berkeley: University of California Press, 1940).

novelistic assumptions give him the right to resuscitate Yorick immediately as a living character in the novel? Read over the gravediggers'
scene in *Hamlet,* Act V, scene i, and suggest a reason for the fact that
Sterne, like Shakespeare, presents the *jester* under the aspect of death.
In other words, why does Sterne kill Yorick off in the first book? Note
that Yorick has the last word in the novel, and that it is a bawdy word
addressed to Mrs. Shandy and springs from a discussion of procreation.
What logic (not logicians' logic, but logic of the imagination) do you
find in this conception of the jester Yorick who encircles the book with
his death and his bawdy joke? [2]

3. Book II is propelled out of or necessitated by Book I because the question as to *where* Uncle Toby received his wound must be settled, a
question which Book I proposes and which Book II sets out to resolve;
but it is not actually resolved—that is, in its fullest dramatic potentiality and significance—until the final book of the novel. Thus the
location of the place where Toby received his wound provides another
design uniting the beginning and the end of the novel. In the word
"where" (where did Toby receive his wound?) what illustration do you
find of Sterne's concern with the ambiguities of language? What does
the Widow Wadman make of the question? In what way does the
Widow Wadman's interpretation of a preposition bring Toby's amour
to an end? What schematic relationship would you suggest that might
link a study of the ambiguities of language with a study of the processes
of consciousness?

4. Toby, gentle-hearted as he is, is a military man, absorbed in a toy war.
Reread the first three paragraphs of the final chapter of the novel,
where Mr. Shandy expresses himself on the baseness of the means of
the procreation of man, as compared with the gloriousness of the means
of killing him. What two themes, dominant in *Tristram Shandy* and
traditionally thought of as dominant in the life of man, are brought
together here? [3] Suggest a structural reason why Sterne characterizes
Toby as shy of women and exquisitely modest. Why does he keep the
question of the virility of this warrior ambiguous and obscure? Given
the themes suggested above, what structural reason do you find for the
fact that the last book of the novel is concerned, not with Tristram, but
with the warrior in love? Note that Toby, the idealizing lover, falls in

[2] The perception of Yorick's function, as suggested here, is again Mr. Lehman's.
[3] Again, Mr. Lehman's essay is the source of the suggestion.

love by looking into a lady's *eye*. In the last book, while Toby is court-
ing, Trim tells the story of Tom's love affair. How did Tom fall in
love (see Chs. V and VII, Bk. IX)? What inflections of the love theme
does Sterne play on in the comparison of these two amours—in the
comparison of the amorous effects of eyes and sausages? How does the
introduction of Obadiah's cow in the last chapter significantly cap the
affair of Toby and the Widow Wadman?

5. The theme of language—its uses, abuses, ambiguities, and inade-
quacies—appears in Book I overtly with Walter's notional speculations on *naming*. Like magicians and like children, Walter thinks that
power lies in the name a thing has, that the existence and nature of a
thing are somehow inherent in its name. Walter is a kind of wishful
eighteenth-century Adam, who would by naming the lion and the crocodile "lion" and "crocodile" creatively define the nature of the lion and
and the crocodile. What is Walter's theory of names (see Ch. XIX, Bk.
I)? Consult the dictionary to find out why Walter respects the name
Trismegistus and abhors the name Tristram. What other sad fellow
had the name Tristram, and how was the procreative instinct associated with his case? Given Sterne's interest in language (language as the
names of things, actions, and relations), suggest a reason for his quoting
the marriage articles in full (see how he finishes off this quotation in
Chapter XV: "In three words . . ."). What is he satirizing here?
Sterne's interest in satirizing conventions and institutions is only incidental; but in view of his attitude toward man and nature (man in and
of nature), as we see it by implication in his highlighting of the theme
of procreation, what reason would you give for his touching off satir-
ically the formal language of the marriage articles? In what way did the
marriage articles destine Tristram to a flat nose? (It may interest you to
consult a portrait of Sterne, and to see that he has a long nose, like his
own Slawkenbergius.) In this matter of the marriage articles and Tristram's flat nose, would you be able to formulate in a statement the
humorous connection between the theme of language and the procreative theme?

6. In Chapter XX of the first book, Sterne scolds the reader (addressed as
"Madam"!) for inattentiveness to his words, inasmuch as the reader is
assumed not to have taken up the indication that Mrs. Shandy was a
papist. In what way had he indicated that Mrs. Shandy was a papist?
What suggestion, as to mass economy in baptism, does Tristram make?

In what way does this suggestion show Tristram to be a son of Walter Shandy? Make a judgment as to whether Sterne is wholly unserious or partly serious in his scolding of the reader ("Madam") for inattention to the language of the book. Among the books you have read in this series, where would you say *Tristram Shandy* stood with regard to the demands it makes upon the reader's attention to words?

7. In Chapter XXIII of the first book, Sterne advances an imaginative theory of the possibilities for character sketching on the planet Mercury. What is the theory? In what way does this hypothesis identify (in terms of mental predilection) Tristram, the narrator, as the son of Walter Shandy? Where do you find in this passage the accents of a prebender of York Cathedral and a writer of sermons, inheritor of the language and metaphysical conceits of the seventeenth-century divines and poets? Do you find also in this passage Sterne's typically *concretizing* imagination—the imagination of a poet? Where? How does the passage bear on his theory of the explication of character? Formulate a judgment as to the difference between Sterne's novelistic theory, as it pertains to the depiction of character, and that of Richardson or Fielding. Where, by implication, does Richardson or Fielding believe "character" to consist, and where does Sterne believe it to consist? How seriously would you take Sterne's statement in Chapter XXII: "my work is digressive, and it is progressive too,—and at the same time"? What structural justification would you give for the fact that, while Sterne promises to develop the subject of Toby's hobbyhorse in Book II, he does not actually do so until Book VI, where the campaigns of the bowling green are described?

8. In the books we have read so far, let us reconsider briefly the dynamics of event, that aspect which may be put in the question: what makes things happen? In *Don Quixote* and *The Pilgrim's Progress*, things happen because the hero's volitional faculty, his will, which is motivated by an ideal of conduct, is brought into play against a recalcitrant, unpredictable context of physical fact and counter-motivations on the part of other people. In *Moll Flanders*, things happen for somewhat the same reason, that is, the heroine makes choices, exercises her will: but what is the difference in the motivation of the will in this case? Determine similarly the dynamics of event in *Clarissa Harlowe;* in *Tom Jones*. In the latter novel, as we have noticed in our study of it, mere chance or "fortune" is a good deal more operative in bringing

about events than it is in the other books; nevertheless, in the long run, it is clear that chance itself is somehow deeply relevant to, connected with, the character of the hero's will—his "goodness." What makes things happen in *Tristram Shandy?*—for instance, how does it happen that Tristram is born with a flat nose? that he is named Tristram? that he is circumcised? that Toby's love affair falls through? Is chance operative here in the same way as in *Tom Jones,* with precisely the same implications as to ethical will and individual destiny? What difference would you suggest?

9. It would be impossible to imagine a full projection of the characters of Uncle Toby and Walter Shandy out of context with each other and their setting; both live only in the total circumstances of the Shandy household, in the medium of Tristram's consciousness, and in the contrast each offers the other. What, chiefly, is that contrast? What characteristics of each brother highlight those of the other? Illustrate the reciprocal commentary of these two personalities upon each other in:
   a. the last half of Chapter XXI, Book I;
   b. Chapters VI, VII, and XI, Book II;
   c. Chapter XVIII, Book III (a chapter that is significant, also, for the psychological basis of Sterne's novel, and for his notions of time and "duration");
   d. the last two paragraphs of Chapter XXIV, Book III;
   e. Chapter XLI, Book III.

10. In Questions 3, 5, and 6 above, we have suggested certain aspects of Sterne's concern with language. In your comparison of the two brothers, do you find a reflection of the same concern? Much of the activity of the book takes place in the conversations of Toby and Walter: how effective is language as a medium of communication between the two? Do you find here an illustration of Coleridge's notion of humor as arising from the identification of "finite incommensurables"? Compare now, with the conversations of Toby and Walter, those of Toby and Trim, for instance in
   a. Chapters XIX–XXII, Book VIII (Trim's story of the King of Bohemia, and of how he fell in love with the young Beguine);
   b. Chapters IV–VII, Book IX (his story of Tom's love affair).
   Do Toby and Trim have any difficulty in understanding each other through language? Why not? Now consider the conversations of Toby and the Widow Wadman, in Chapters XX, XVIII, and XIX (which fol-

low XXV!), and Chapter XXVI, Book IX: how effective is language as a medium of communication between these two? In Chapters XXVIII and XXIX of Book IX, Trim and Bridget converse: do they understand each other? Now comment on the degree of communication between Walter and Mrs. Shandy, as illustrated, for example, in Chapter XVIII, Book VI (the "bed of justice" on the subject of Tristram's breeches). Reconsidering these comparisons, what would you say was Sterne's idea as to the relationship between the verbal noises one makes ("language") and life as *felt* experience? (You may recall that this was one of Cervantes' preoccupations also.)

11. Given Sterne's conception of the relationship between language and living activity, in what way do you find this conception illustrated in his own style? Reread the first seven paragraphs of Chapter XII, Book III (the critic's criticism of Garrick's soliloquy): how does the passage bear on Sterne's conception of the relationship between language and life? From what, according to the conception we have been illustrating here, does language derive its meaning, or its possibilities of heterogeneous meanings? Where does its effectiveness as an instrument of communication lie? What inhibits its effectiveness? Now reread Chapters XLII and XLIII, Book V (Mr. Shandy on auxiliary verbs). What humorous but significant commentary does this passage make on Sterne's notion of the uses of language? In view of all these considerations, how would you justify Sterne's own highly personal style in terms of his conception of the relationship between language and subjective experience—for instance, the pauses marked by frequent semicolons and apparently slap-happy dashes, the spontaneity of the rhythms of the phrases as they fluctuate around the unforeseen contours of the thought? Formulate a comparison between Fielding's style and Sterne's style which will indicate a fundamental *philosophical* difference between these two writers, their views of life.

12. The following question has to do with a typical trait of the book, namely, the emphasis on physical gesture and attitude. The student is asked to reread the passages listed below and to formulate, with specific reference to these passages, a statement as to the function of the close description of gesture and physical position or attitude. What connection do you see, in each case, between this kind of close description and Sterne's conception of the relationship between language and life (life as subjective experience)?

a. Walter and his pipe, first paragraph of Chapter VII, Book II;
b. Trim reading the sermon, Chapter XVII, Book II;
c. Dr. Slop's vacuous look, fifth paragraph, Chapter I, Book III;
d. Walter's taking out his handkerchief, Chapter II, Book III;
e. Walter's prostration, Chapter XXIX, Book III;
f. Walter's gesture of desperation with thread paper and pincushion, Chapter XLI, Book III;
g. Mrs. Shandy listening at the door, Chapter V, Book V;
h. Walter's shifts with his pillow on the bed of justice, Chapter XVIII, Book VI;
i. Trim's and Toby's activities with the Montero-cap and the pipe, Chapters XXVII and XXVIII, Book VI;
j. The business of Widow Wadman's night-shift, Chapter IX, Book VIII;
k. The corporal's gestures with the Montero-cap, before he begins the story of the King of Bohemia, Chapter XIX, Book VIII.

13. Where, judging from your investigations for Question 12, would you say that Sterne understands the real matter of the novel, as a "mirror of life," to lie? How does he differ, in this respect, from the novelist who lays greatest emphasis on "plot," and from the novelist who lays greatest emphasis on a moral or philosophical thesis?

14. In this and the following questions, you are asked to examine certain scenes and to analyze them as fully as possible. Chapter XII, Book II, contains the famous passage concerning Uncle Toby and the fly. This passage is often used to illustrate Sterne's "sentimentality." In the modern sense, "sentimentality" means inadequately motivated emotionalism, a display of feeling out of proportion to the cause. In Sterne's time, sentimentality meant something else: namely, sensitivity, or sensibility, and particularly delicacy of sensibility. Such sensibility was thought of as valuable and admirable. In the passage referred to, what deliberate exaggeration of situation do you find in Toby's use of the Biblical second-person-singular as he talks to the fly? What exaggeration do you find in Toby's saying, "This world surely is wide enough to hold both thee and me"? (It is obvious, is it not, that the world *is* wide enough to hold both Uncle Toby and a fly?) Do you find perfect ingenuousness in Tristram's statement

I was but ten years old when this happened: but whether it was, that the action itself was more in unison to my nerves at that age of pity, which instantly set my whole frame into one vibration of most pleasurable sensation;—or . . .

(Is the age of ten an "age of pity"?) Precisely how would you describe the attitude shown in the passage? [4]

15. The sermon which Trim reads in Chapter XVII, Book II was one of Sterne's own sermons, and his favorite. In what way do the interruptions of Trim's discourse—interruptions from Dr. Slop, Toby, Walter, and Trim himself—illustrate Sterne's conception of the relationship between language (in this case, the language of the sermon) and the communicative effects of language, that is, understanding? What, from this passage, appears to be Sterne's test of the *effective* meaning of language? How is the test of meaning illustrated in Dr. Slop's comment: " 'Tis only a description, there's not a word of truth in it," and in Trim's literal application of the sermon to his brother Tom's situation? How is Dr. Slop's comment influenced by his papism?

16. What is the issue of the learned conference, Chapters XXVI–XXX, Book IV, on the changing of Tristram's name? In the second paragraph on Chapter XXVI,

"Methinks," said Didius, half rising from his chair, in order to remove a bottle and a tall decanter, which stood in a direct line betwixt him and Yorick—

what typical Sternean stylistic trait do you find? (Note the same trait in the story of Maria, Chapter XXIV, Book IX, where Sterne says of the postillion that he was "leaning his body on one side to let me see her, for he was in a line betwixt us.") [5] What connection do you find between this typical trait, which emphasizes the immediate physical circumstance, however trifling, and the weighty theoretical question at issue in the conference? In what way does the episode illustrate Coleridge's notion of humor as arising from the identification of "finite little" and "finite great"?

[4] These suggestions for analysis of the scene are made by Ernest Nevin Dilworth in *The Unsentimental Journey of Lawrence Sterne* (New York: King's Crown Press, 1948).

[5] The observation, here, of this trait in Sterne's work is owing, again, to suggestions made by Mr. Dilworth.

17. The announcement of Brother Bobby's death might have provided a fine opportunity for "sentiment." How does Sterne handle it—"sentimentally" (see Chs. II and III, Bk. V)? The death of a son is, after all, an adequately motivating cause for emotion. Is Sterne's treatment of the episode brutally unfeeling and therefore in bad taste? Is he attempting to show Walter as a hardhearted, insensible father? In what way does his depiction of the character of Walter, so far in the book, and his evocation of the whole Shandy atmosphere, justify this treatment of the death of Brother Bobby? Bacon, in his essay on death, says,

Groans and convulsions, and discoloured faces, and friends weeping, and blacks, and obsequies, and the like, show Death terrible.

Compare this statement with what Walter has to say about death.[6]

There is no terrour, brother Toby, in its looks, but what it borrows from groans and convulsions—and the blowing of noses and the wiping away of tears with the bottoms of curtains, in a dying man's room.

What has Sterne done to Bacon's sentence to give it its typical Sternean twist and flavor? In which sentence—Bacon's or Sterne's—is the intimate, concrete, domestic atmosphere of the event of death more vividly realized?

18. Turn to Chapter VII in this sequence (Book V). What is the effect of the announcement of Bobby's death upon Susannah? In what way do the first three paragraphs in this chapter illustrate Sterne's interest in language as a medium of communication? How do they illustrate his conception of the relationships between words and "meaning"? words and people? The chapter makes much of Trim's eloquence on the subject of mortality. Does the memorableness of Trim's eloquence lie in the words that he says or in the vivid particularization of the setting in which they are said and the traits of gesture?

19. The story of Le Fever's death, in Chapters VI–X, Book VI, is another famous "sentimental" passage. Note how much the story owes not to its own content but to the setting in which it is recounted—the atmos-

6 This comparison is made by Herbert Read in *The Sense of Glory* (New York: Harcourt, Brace & Company, Inc., 1930).

phere of Toby's room, of sack and toast and tobacco. Near the end of Chapter VII, the possibilities for pathos (and "sentimentality" in the eighteenth-century sense) grow rich, where the dying man gives a ring to his son; but what is the effect here of Toby's comment,—"I wish, said my Uncle Toby, with a deep sigh,—I wish, Trim, I was asleep"? The end of Chapter VIII has been considered by some critics a master-piece of "sentimental" writing—most delicately and touchingly done —while others have felt that Sterne tastelessly overdid his effect with the editorial action of the Recording Angel in blotting out Toby's oath with a tear. Leslie Stephen, for instance, says that the angel

> seems to introduce an unpleasant air as of eighteenth century polite-ness; we fancy that he would have welcomed a Lord Chesterfield to the celestial mansions with a faultless bow and a dexterous compli-ment; and somehow he appears, to my imagination at least, ap-parelled in theatrical gauze and spangles rather than in the genuine angelic costume.[7]

Apparently what many critics have wanted Sterne to do (and the desire leads them to object to the handling of the passage) was what Sterne does not seem to have had any intention of doing—that is, to write perfectly pathetically rather than perfectly jestingly. How would you evaluate the passage? Would you think that it would have been im-proved if Sterne had given the angel the "genuine angelic costume"? What typical Sternean trait do you find in the third paragraph from the end of the chapter, where Toby rises from the side of the bed "with one shoe off" and later "marches the foot which had a shoe on"? In what way does this trait enrich the passage? Evaluate the handling of the end of Chapter X, where Le Fever finally dies and where we should properly get out our handkerchiefs for a good cry.

> Nature instantly ebb'd again,—the film returned to its place,—the pulse fluttered—stopp'd—went on—throbb'd—stopp'd again—moved—stopp'd—shall I go on?—No.

Is this an instance (and it is an old objection to Sterne) of an attempt to be funny in the wrong place, and therefore of tastelessness? What

[7] *Hours in a Library* (London: Putnam & Co., Ltd., 1909), III, 154–155.

similarity do you see between the quoted lines and the end of Tristram's conference with Maria (Ch. XXIV, Bk. IX)?

20. The episode involving the ass of Lyons, in Chapter XXXII, Book VII, is almost equally famous with that concerning the fly and that of Le Fever's death. Analyze and evaluate the passage as fully as you can, in the manner in which we have examined the others.

Pride and Prejudice

1. Clearly it is Elizabeth Bennet who provides the "eyes" of our judgment, our norm of intelligent values. In Chapter XXIV, Elizabeth expresses her estimate of people, thus:

> There are few people whom I really love, and still fewer of whom I think well. The more I see of the world, the more am I dissatisfied with it; and every day confirms my belief of the inconsistency of all human characters, and of the little dependence than can be placed on the appearance of either merit or sense.

In what way does such a statement show the close resemblance and sympathy of mind between Elizabeth and her father? As the novel develops, does it appear that Elizabeth's estimate of people is perfectly correct or is in want of rectification? Is Mr. Bennet's attitude toward people a reliable social judgment or is it in want of rectification? As Elizabeth's character is developed in the book, does she come to resemble her father more closely or less closely? What final comparison would you make between them?

2. In Chapter XVIII, with the party at Netherfield, the submerged conflict between Elizabeth and her family becomes intense, and we begin to see that this is the chief personal conflict in the book. Reread the last few pages of the chapter, beginning where the party sits down to supper. Elizabeth is made very uneasy by her mother's conversation with Lady Lucas, which she knows Darcy has overheard. In terms of plot, what is the effect of this conversation upon Darcy's attitude

toward the Bennet family? What, in turn, is the effect of his attitude upon Jane's relationship with Bingley? In terms of Elizabeth's own sense of values, what particularly distresses her in Mrs. Bennet's conversation? Are Mrs. Bennet's fatuousness and lack of social sensitivity merely "funny" and innocuous, in this case, or seriously harmful? How does the incident illustrate the moral and practical interdependence of the members of the social group (here, the family group)?

3. The following passage is taken from the same context. Mrs. Bennet is discussing the advantages of a marriage between Jane and Bingley. What do the italicized words convey of Mrs. Bennet's own set of values?

It was an animating subject, and Mrs. Bennet seemed incapable of fatigue while *enumerating* the *advantages* of the *match*. His being such a *charming* young man, and so *rich,* and *living but three miles from them,* were the first points of self-gratulation . . . It was, moreover, such a promising thing for her younger daughters, as Jane's marrying so *greatly* must *throw them in the way of* other *rich* men . . . She concluded with many good wishes that Lady Lucas might soon be *equally fortunate,* though evidently and triumphantly believing there was no chance of it.

How does the word "enumerating" contribute, however inconspicuously, to our understanding of Mrs. Bennet's mental processes? What is the effect of the word "charming" in this context? Does the phrase "throw them in the way" seem fortuitous to you, or does it aid in characterizing Mrs. Bennet's taste and morality?

4. Now consider Elizabeth's own thoughts, noted just previously to those of her mother. She is thinking of the same subject, namely, Jane's possible marriage to Bingley.

As Elizabeth had no longer any *interest* of her own to pursue, she turned her attention almost entirely on her sister and Mr. Bingley . . . She saw her in idea *settled* in *that very house,* in all the *felicity* which a *marriage* of *true affection* could *bestow* . . .

While Mrs. Bennet's emphasis is on Bingley's being "rich," what is Elizabeth's emphasis? Do you find any difference in connotation between Mrs. Bennet's word "match" and Elizabeth's word "marriage"? between Mrs. Bennet's word "fortunate" and Elizabeth's word "felicity"? Do the words "settled" and "house" ("that very house"—namely, Netherfield, in all its wealth and comfort) convey anything of Elizabeth's set of values? Are they materialistic? What are the associations of words like "interest" and "bestow"? Do they belong to the same or a different basic idiom as "enumerate" and "equally fortunate" in Mrs. Bennet's speech? In what way does the diction of "settled," "that very house," and "bestow," affect the connotations of "felicity" and "marriage of true affection"? Between these two sets of words is there, or is there not, the same ironic incongruity as between "rich" and "charming" in Mrs. Bennet's conversation?

5. We think of Elizabeth as civilized in feeling and mentality, and of Mrs. Bennet as stupid and vulgar; of Elizabeth as representing the best development of personality in the world of this book, and of Mrs. Bennet as representing—to the point of caricature—the lowest, least examined, least sensitive and critical of common group values. But judging from your analysis of language in Questions 3 and 4, and what the language implies as to what is desirable in life, would you say that the basic idiom of these two women implies an absolute dichotomy between the finest and the grossest values in this world, or that it implies a certain central correspondence of values, by which the extremes of the group are held together in the group life? What, precisely, are the shared values, as indicated by this brief analysis of language? Where does the differentiation lie between Elizabeth's aspirations (for her sister) and those of her mother? Does the correspondence in values between two such different characters suggest that individual development will be easy or difficult?

6. Turning now from the family group to the larger social unit of the neighborhood, consider the description of the Bingleys given in the latter half of Chapter IV. We shall set down a list of phrases from this section, with certain words italicized to indicate the dominant type of reference.

their behavior (that of the Bingley sisters) . . . had not been *calculated* to please
not *deficient* in good humour when they were pleased
had a *fortune* of *twenty thousand pounds*
in the habit of *spending* more than they ought
associating with people of *rank*

were therefore . . . *entitled* to think well of themselves
of a *respectable family*
their brother's *fortune* . . . had been *acquired by trade*
inherited property to the *amount* of nearly an *hundred thousand pounds*
intended to *purchase* an *estate*
he was not *provided* with a *good house*
leave the next *generation* to *purchase*
having an *estate* of his own
he was now *established*

The student is asked to categorize the italicized words under three or four headings that he thinks appropriate. Now turn back to the first chapter; go through the whole chapter categorizing similarly (under the same or related headings) the words whose type of reference is repeated frequently. Judging from the language base, would you say that the Bingleys and the Bennets—despite the difference in social status between the two families—had the same interests and aspirations, that is, the same values? What does this fact imply as to the uniformity and homogeneity of the social world of *Pride and Prejudice?* What does it imply as to the possibilities for individual spiritual development?

7. The last paragraph of Chapter IV speaks of the Bingley sisters' judgment of Jane Bennet, and ends thus:

Miss Bennet was therefore *established* as a *sweet* girl, and their brother felt *authorized* by such commendation *to think* of her *as he chose.*

What ironic trait of the Austen style do you find in the juxtaposition of the word "established" with the phrase "as a sweet girl"? of "authorized" with "to think"? What added irony lies in the phrase "as he chose"? Do you find reflected in the sentence any elements of the thematic conflict between utilitarian, materialistic values and the nonutilitarian values we have spoken of as lying in personal tastes, attitudes, "feelings"? Do the Bingley sisters (as this sentence represents them) feel any such conflict?

8. In the relationships of Jane and Miss Bingley, and Elizabeth and Charlotte Lucas, we have a double representation of the kind of friendship that is available in the world of this book—a world so distinctly de-

349

fined by social interdependence, of which friendship would seem to be one of the finer forms. Is Miss Bingley's falsification of Jane's trust a quite harmless piece of behavior? Judging by the first part of Chapter VI, where Charlotte and Elizabeth discuss marriage, what values does Charlotte prize and what values does she neglect? Do these friendships suggest ease or difficulty for the individual in the maintenance of integrity of feeling?

9. In Chapters XIII and XIV, Mr. Collins is portrayed at full length; but first we are given a kind of prologue to his entrance, with Mrs. Bennet holding forth on the matter of the entail. How is the theme of the entail, here and elsewhere, used to characterize Mrs. Bennet? Does this theme gain its comic properties through its actual appositeness to the immediate affairs of the family, or through its inappositeness? What comic irony, involved with the marriage problem, is built up by Mrs. Bennet's attitude toward Mr. Collins before she meets him? When he arrives, he and Mrs. Bennet find themselves in the best rapport. Seriously—that is, outside their common comic grotesquerie—where does their rapport lie? what values do they share?

10. One critic has called the Austen grotesques, such as Mrs. Bennet and Mr. Collins, "society's embarrassing unconscious comment on itself." [1] Do you find in this book other characters who are equally, or almost equally, grotesque? How would you summarize the common characteristic elements among them? We have several times suggested the difficulty that faces the sensitively developed individual who tries to live with any personal integrity in this world crudely dominated by stupidity and subtly dominated throughout its whole range by materialistic attitudes. One character like Mrs. Bennet might, in her manifest absurdity, not seem to offer much of a threat; but we have observed that her activity is not altogether harmless. With the multiplication of similar grotesques, what potential for harm is given to stupidity and egotism? Why, in a world whose central group values—shared to some extent by the most intelligent and sensitive—are materialistic, should stupidity and egotism have an exaggerated capacity for creating spiritual disaster? Where do characters like Miss Bingley and Charlotte Lucas stand, in terms of intelligence and sensitivity, in relation to the

[1] D. W. Harding, "Regulated Hatred: An Aspect of the Work of Jane Austen," in *Scrutiny*, March, 1940. The analysis here of the shadings between the "grotesques" and the "real" people is owing to Mr. Harding's article.

truly grotesque characters? Does the fact that they are less exaggerated and more like "real people" make this world (the world of this book) a morally easier world to live in, or a morally more difficult world?

11. Here are a few of the significant expressions from Mr. Collins' letter (Chapter XIII):

a. distinguished by the patronage
b. bounty and beneficence
c. preferred me to the valuable rectory
d. my late honored father
e. misfortune
f. heal the breach
g. disrespectful
h. good terms
i. I have been so fortunate
j. it shall be my earnest endeavour to demean myself with grateful respect
k. my duty to promote and establish the blessing of peace
l. on these grounds I flatter myself
m. my present overtures of good will
n. the offered olive branch
o. I cannot be otherwise than concerned at being the means of
p. your amiable daughters
q. beg leave to apologize
r. I propose myself the satisfaction
s. shall probably trespass on your hospitality . . . which I can do without any inconvenience, as Lady Catherine is far from objecting

Summarize what can be gathered from these phrases alone as to Mr. Collins' habits of mind. Specifically what is the function of language in d), f), and n)? What somewhat different function do you find in the diction and syntactical construction of j) and o)? Do you find that the references in a), b), c), e), h), and i) reflect anything of that general language base we have spoken of at the end of our discussion of the book and again in Questions 3, 4, and 6? Does Mr. Collins' language, absurd as it is in this document, suggest that his assumptions as to the cultural amenities are radically different from those of Miss Bingley, for instance? What common element would you point out between the absurd language of Mr. Collins' letter and the ordinary mode of expression of the intelligent as well as the stupid members of the Bennet family? Insofar as a repeated type of vocabulary reflects common mental processes and value assumptions, would you say that even a monster of fatuity like Mr. Collins is actually an integrated member of the culture group represented in this novel, or that he is so caricatured as to provide merely "comic relief" with no serious significance for the group life?

12. In Chapter XV we are told that Mr. Collins, in seeking a reconciliation with the Bennets,

> had a wife in view, as he meant to chuse one of the daughters, if he found them as handsome and amiable as they were represented by common report. This was his plan of amends—of atonement—for inheriting their father's estate; and he thought it an excellent one, full of eligibility and suitableness . . .

In this sketch of Mr. Collins' intentions, what elements do you find that substantiate his "good will," or that obliquely show him as a man of purely self-seeking will? What elements in the passage illustrate the conflict between materialistic or utilitarian values and the civilized need for expression in terms of refined sentiments? In what way has the cultivation of "refined sentiments" made Mr. Collins dishonest? Mr. Bennet, we are told, is pleased with Mr. Collins.

> His cousin was as absurd as he had hoped, and he listened to him with the keenest enjoyment.

As you consider Mr. Collins' intentions, the support given him by Mrs. Bennet, the state of the family finances, the prospects of the girls, and the rivalry of the Lucas family, what judgment would you make of Mr. Bennet's attitude toward Mr. Collins? Is it a responsible attitude?

13. In the scene in Chapter XVIII where Collins insists on introducing himself to Darcy, he tells Elizabeth,

> "I have found out . . . that there is now in the room a near relation of my patroness . . . I am most thankful that the discovery is made in time for me to *pay my respects* to him, which I am now going to do, and trust he will excuse my not having done it before. My total ignorance of the *connection* must *plead my apology.*"

Elizabeth, trying to dissuade him, tells him that the first gesture of recognition should belong to Darcy, who is the "superior in consequence." How do the phrases *"pay* my respects" and *"plead* my apology" operate connotatively, in terms of the general language base and in terms of Mr. Collins' psychology? In this part of the book, what evaluation does Darcy himself put upon "connections"—particularly upon Elizabeth's "connections"? Is Mr. Collins' view of the value of "connections" very different from that of Darcy? How does this commonality of opinion, as to the value of "connections," linking two such opposed characters as Darcy and Collins, illustrate the cultural consistency of the world of this book? Is Darcy portrayed in terms of caricature, as is Mr. Collins, or is he portrayed as a "real person" (using Elizabeth as our criterion of rounded human reality)? You will note that Elizabeth herself places distinct emphasis on difference in social rank, by warning Collins that Darcy is "superior in consequence." Interpreting general cultural assumptions by such phrases, would you say that Elizabeth, too, shared some of the values of the loathsome Mr. Collins? What distinction, if any, would you make between Elizabeth's anguished discrimination of the social proprieties here, and Mr. Collins' type of discrimination? In Chapter XXIX, Mr. Collins tells Elizabeth that Lady Catherine de Bourgh will not think the worse of her for being simply dressed, because she (Lady Catherine) "likes to have the distinction of rank preserved." If this is Austen irony on snobbery of social status, how do you account—in terms of a consistent world of values—for Elizabeth's serious warning of Collins as to the proprieties due to people who are "superior in consequence"?

14. In Chapter XIX, we are given the scene of Collins' proposal to Elizabeth. The scene is "comic" in the most obvious sense, through the juxtaposition of incongruities. But aside from the obvious comic aspect, is there a sense in which the scene shows us in heightened dramatic form the subtle and profound conflict reigning in this world? How does Charlotte Lucas' acceptance of Collins accent the seriousness of Elizabeth's situation? At the end of Chapter XXII, Charlotte gives her reasons for accepting him.

"I am not romantic, you know . . . I ask only a *comfortable home;* and considering Mr. Collins's character, *connections, and situation in life,* I am convinced that my *chance* of happiness with him is *as fair as most people can boast of on entering the marriage state."*

Comparing Charlotte's ideas with Elizabeth's thoughts about her sister's marriage as we have considered them in Question 4, for instance, would you say that Charlotte and Elizabeth shared certain ideas of happiness, and if so, how would you differentiate their notions of what is desirable in marriage? Given the certain commonality of aspiration between Charlotte and Elizabeth, would you say that maintenance of integrity of feeling, for a person like Elizabeth, was more difficult or less difficult than if her values were radically and altogether different from those of her friend and the rest of her social world? Notice Charlotte's use of the word "chance": at the end of Chapter XLIX, Elizabeth despairs of "rational happiness" for Lydia in marriage, and in Chapter LV we are told that she believes Jane's and Bingley's expectations of happiness to be "rationally founded": how would you analyze the difference in taste and in integrity of moral outlook suggested by Charlotte's word "chance" ("I am convinced that my chance of happiness with him is as fair as most people can boast of on entering the marriage state") and Elizabeth's phrase "rational happiness"? How do the conjugal relations of Mr. and Mrs. Bennet supply an implicit frame of reference for the attitudes of Charlotte and Elizabeth toward marriage to Mr. Collins? What compromise with her world has Charlotte made?

15. In Chapter XXIII, when Mr. Bennet hears the news of Charlotte's engagement, we are told that

> Mr. Bennet's emotions were much more tranquil on the occasion, and such as he did experience he pronounced to be of a most agreeable sort; for it gratified him, he said, to discover that Charlotte Lucas, whom he had been used to think tolerably sensible, was as foolish as his wife, and more foolish than his daughter!

What serious difference in sensibility and attitude, between Elizabeth and her father, is suggested by their different responses in this case? In what sense is Mr. Bennet's attitude, however cynically intelligent, nevertheless a frivolous and irresponsible one? How does it accent the real dangers in this world? What do the words "rectitude" and "delicacy" mean in the following sentence:

> [Elizabeth's] disappointment in Charlotte made her turn with fonder regard to her sister, of whose rectitude and delicacy she was sure her opinion could never be shaken . . .

16. At the end of Chapter XXIV, Mr. Bennet compliments Elizabeth on her fondness for Wickham in these terms: "He is a pleasant fellow and would jilt you creditably." What typical Austen linguistic irony, and what peculiarity of Mr. Bennet's psychology, do you find in the phrase "jilt you creditably"? Judging from the following passage, from the same context, what would you say were the symptoms of Wickham's lack of "rectitude and delicacy"?

> They saw him often, and to his other recommendations was now added that of general unreserve. The whole of what Elizabeth had already heard, his claims on Mr. Darcy, and all that he had suffered from him, was now openly acknowledged and publicly canvassed; and everybody was pleased to think how much they had always disliked Mr. Darcy before they had known anything of the matter.

In the Austen world, what direct association has "rectitude" with "delicacy"? Does Elizabeth's attraction to Wickham show her own delicacy of judgment? In other words, is she the heroine of this novel because she is impeccable in taste and rationality?

17. At the beginning of Chapter XXVI, Elizabeth's aunt, Mrs. Gardiner, warns her against involving herself in affection for Wickham, "an affection which the want of fortune would make so very imprudent." In view of Mrs. Gardiner's emphasis on the need of "fortune" for happiness in marriage, how would you discriminate her attitude from the vulgarly acquisitive attitude of people like Mrs. Bennet or even of Charlotte Lucas? In reading *Tom Jones,* we spoke of Fielding's association of "fortune" and "good nature," an association which constitutes a kind of "myth" in the sense in which myth represents a dramatic synthesis of values that dominates an author's view of the world. Do you find something of the same sort of "myth" in *Pride and Prejudice?* What differences would you point out between the Austen "myth" and the Fielding "myth"?

18. We have been hearing about Lady Catherine de Bourgh through half the book before she appears in person. At the end of Chapter XXVIII, Eliza Lucas summons Elizabeth in a violent hurry, telling her that "there is such a sight to be seen!" and Elizabeth runs down the stairs "in quest of this wonder," only to see two ladies in a phaeton at the gate. "And is this all?" she cries; "I expected at least that the pigs were

got into the garden, and here is nothing but Lady Catherine and her daughter!" What is the dramatic effectiveness of Elizabeth's remark, in making the final preparation for the portentous appearance of Lady Catherine? How would you interpret Elizabeth's thoughts on seeing Miss de Bourgh?

"I like her appearance . . . She looks sickly and cross.—Yes, she will do for him very well. She will make him a very proper wife."

Would you say that this is merely the amused cynicism that would be characteristic of Elizabeth's father, or—in view of Elizabeth's relationship with Darcy—does it have another, more subtle psychological aspect?

19. In Chapter XXIX, describing an evening spent with Lady Catherine, what is the quantitative proportion between stupidity and intelligence, vulgarity and civilized feeling among the members of the party? What irony lies in Sir William Lucas' cult of "elegant breeding" as exhibited here? What are Lady Catherine's values? Is intelligence among them? Does the boredom and loneliness besetting intelligence, when it is environed by stupidity and vulgarity, seem to you a theme of any weight or significance, as dramatized for instance in this chapter, or does it seem shallow and without vitality?

20. In Chapter XXV, where the Gardiners visit the Bennets, we were told that "Mrs. Bennet had so carefully provided for the entertainment of her brother and sister, that they did not once sit down to a family dinner." What is the typical irony here? Comparing Mrs. Bennet as hostess with Lady Catherine as hostess, would you say that the difference in social rank between these two ladies represented a difference between grossness and fineness of social feeling? In view of the fact that Darcy is first alienated from Elizabeth because of her mother's vulgarity, suggest some structural reason for the characterization that is given to Darcy's aunt.

21. At the beginning of Chapter XLII, we are given Elizabeth's judgment of her father: she had never been blind to "the *impropriety* of her father's behaviour" and to his continual breach of "conjugal obligation and *decorum*." Consider, now, Mr. Bennet's attitude toward Lydia's Brighton trip, as shown in Chapter XLI: he says, for instance, of Lydia: "she cannot grow many degrees worse, without authorizing us to lock

her up for the rest of her life," and this is the philosophical thought which justifies him in allowing Lydia to go to Brighton. Words like "propriety" and "decorum" are key words in Austen, but their precise meanings can be determined only by the contexts they are given. With reference to Lydia's Brighton trip, in what way would you say that Mr. Bennet showed "impropriety" of behavior and lack of "decorum"? These words represent certain important aspects of that system of values which we have spoken of as lying in civilized refinement of feeling. As they apply to Mr. Bennet's behavior toward his family, particularly in the Brighton episode, would you say that they imply shallow effete values, or that they represent—in the world created in this book —values of some profundity, that cannot be disregarded without danger? How does the Brighton episode illustrate that danger? Is it a danger involving only one ignorant and flighty girl, who might be considered "expendable," or does its real seriousness lie in the consequences it has, or might have, for others?

22. Refer to Question 19 and to Lady Catherine's dinner party (Chapter XXIX). In this chapter we are given, perhaps in a more heightened manner than elsewhere in the book, the typical "polite" drawing room scene, with vulgarity and stupidity rampant; yet, at this point, these qualities still appear innocuous, incapable of more serious injury than the affliction of boredom and loneliness. How does the Brighton episode articulate dramatically the potential for injury that lies precisely in "mere" vulgarity and stupidity?

23. The naturalistic novelist, who, presumably, cuts a "slice of life" just as "nature" gives it, might have followed Lydia and Wickham on their sordid adventure, representing it in detail and for its own sake as "life." Jane Austen handles the episode by indirection only, showing it by its effects on the neighborhood, the Bennet family, and particularly on Elizabeth and Darcy. Is the Austen method, in this case, a sign of puritanical revulsion from the illicit, the brutal, and the "crude," and of the author's inability to cut down "deep" into life, or is the method justified by the basic themes of the book?

24. After Lydia has been safely married, we are told that the news was borne in the neighborhood "with decent philosophy."

To be sure it would have been more for the advantage of conversation, had Miss Lydia Bennet come upon the town; or, as the happiest

357

alternative, been secluded from the world, in some distant farm house. But there was much to be talked of, in marrying her; and the good-natured wishes for her well-doing, which had proceeded before from all the spiteful old ladies in Meryton, lost but little of their spirit in this change of circumstances, because with such a husband, her misery was considered certain.

What is the meaning of the phrase "come upon the town"? In this description of the villagers' reaction, do you find Jane Austen's technique inadequate for coping with the "dark" and "crude" elements in life, or do you find it the reverse? If we had been given a chapter on the illicit sex life of Lydia and Wickham in cheap boardinghouses, do you think we would have been put in closer touch with the "dark" realities of life than by this single paragraph describing the effect of the escapade on the emotions of the neighborhood? What is that particular kind of human "darkness" into which Jane Austen has clear insight?

25. In terms of the main love plot, why is the Brighton episode in the book at all? How does it function as a "test" of Darcy and Elizabeth, and as that crucial experience by which both self-knowledge and deeper social understanding are achieved? How does it confirm Darcy's early strictures against Elizabeth's "connections"? What new and more complex meaning does it assign to "connections"? How does it develop in Darcy a much deeper sense of moral realities than was contained in his earlier attitude toward the Bennets—however just that attitude was? If we should say that at the beginning of the book, Elizabeth showed a tendency to fall into her father's faults—into witty cynicism at the expense of insight, and into complacency of intellect at the expense of responsibility—how does the Brighton episode function toward developing in her the deeper understanding necessary for the full rounding of personality? Summarize the relationship of this central episode to the theme of the interdependence between the individual and his social environment.

26. Chapter LI describes Lydia's triumphant home-coming. If the Brighton episode has been a crucial "test" for Elizabeth and Darcy and has developed in them the moral capacities that might otherwise have remained latent or gone into atrophy, what has the episode meant for Lydia? for Mrs. Bennet? Do you think that Jane Austen would have shown a more or a less "realistic" understanding of human behavior if

she had represented Lydia and Mrs. Bennet as morally affected by the Brighton episode?

27. At the end of Chapter LIII, where Mrs. Bennet puts on her usual show before Bingley and Darcy, we are told that

> Elizabeth's misery increased at such unnecessary, such officious attention! Were the same fair prospect to arise at present, as had flattered them a year ago, everything, she was persuaded, would be hastening to the same vexatious conclusion. At that instant she felt, that years of happiness could not make Jane or herself amends, for moments of such painful confusion.

The story is here almost at its conclusion, but has there been any change in the social context that environs the protagonists? If the social context has not changed, what, precisely, has changed?

28. Darcy's second proposal to Elizabeth, and her acceptance of him, provide the resolution of conflict and the final, symbolic, reconciling act. Note the stylistic handling of the episode: we are not given the direct words of the lovers, when they acknowledge their love, but we are told that Darcy "expressed himself on the occasion, as sensibly and as warmly as a man violently in love can be supposed to do." This is certainly a cool treatment of a love scene, although it is a sympathetic treatment. What typical wry bite of the Austen style do you find in the coolness and indirection of the treatment, in conjunction with the use of the words "warmly" and "violently"? In view of basic themes and values, would you say that this treatment of the final love scene (Chapter LVIII) was appropriate here and consistent with the rest of the book, or would you say that the book would have been more appropriately expressive if it had presented the lovers in emotional exaltation and erotic throes?

29. Before the final roundup of destinies, Mrs. Bennet offers, at the end of Chapter LIX, her conclusive commentary. "Oh, my sweetest Lizzy!" she cries,

> "how rich and how great you will be! What pin-money, what jewels, what carriages you will have! . . . I am so pleased—so happy! Such a charming man!—so handsome! so tall!—Oh, my dear Lizzy! pray apologize for my having disliked him so much before . . . A house in town! Every thing that is charming! Three daughters married!

359

Ten thousand a year! Oh, Lord! what will become of me. I shall go distracted."

What is the dramatic appropriateness of this lyrical explosion as the book ends? How does it serve to reiterate the terms of the primary conflict—both the conflict between persons and the conflict in values? We have spoken of the marriage of Darcy and Elizabeth as marking a "resolution" of the central conflict. How is it possible to speak of a "resolution" of conflict when, at the end, Mrs. Bennet is able to reiterate all over again, with exaltation, those attitudes which have constituted the most serious spiritual, as well as practical, dangers for the protagonists? Make a summary statement of the "moral realism" exhibited by this book.

The Heart of Mid-Lothian

1. In the Wilson-Robertson-Porteous episode, which starts the story moving (Chapters 2–4), what sympathies and antipathies for the characters are aroused? Explain the reason for the response in each case. Summarize the kind of "values" (values lying in a certain way of life, or in a certain type of emotional reaction to situation) which the episode raises to view. Do you find the same values operating elsewhere in the book?

2. Suggest a structural reason for the fact that the book starts with an episode of outlawry.[1] (Note that a structural reason, here, would have to show that outlawry—with the special implications given it by the opening episode—is a way of life and an attitude that offer some significance for, and illuminate in some way, other attitudes and types of action in the book.) Let us say that we have in the book two kinds of "law," the law of the courts and the law of conscience, and that we have therefore by implication two kinds of "outlaw" (or the "outlaw" might be a breaker of both kinds of "law"). Is Effie an "outlaw," and if so, of what kind? Why does she refuse liberation from the Tol-

[1] Chapters 2, 3, and 6.

booth? [2] Is her refusal "in character"? Is it in character with her later flight with Staunton? Interpret, in terms of consistency of her character, her words at this point, when Staunton urges her to flee, on the invasion of the Tolbooth: "Better tyne life, since tint is gude fame." How does the complex notion of law, as suggested above, bear on the figure of Jeanie Deans?

3. In Chapter 13, is the "law" (in the persons and deportment of the magistrates) presented sympathetically or unsympathetically? In becoming an instrument of the law, does the ex-outlaw Ratcliffe become a pleasanter figure to us, or the reverse? In Chapter 17, Ratcliffe flouts the law in order to warn Robertson: here, as "outlaw," is Ratcliffe a more or a less sympathetic character than as a tool of the law? Would you say that these matters put us, as readers, on the side of the law, or on the side of the outlaw?

4. If Jeanie Deans is presented to us as a sympathetic and even admirable figure because she refuses to break the law of conscience, explain why the book on so many occasions puts us in sympathy with the outlaw. Summarize the attitudes toward law and outlawry so far suggested. Are they consistent and coherent?

5. In the scene of the old laird's death (Chapter 8), we have a good example of Scott's color and energy, his command over certain simple, picturesque forms of psychology and behavior. Why is this scene included in the book? In what way is it connected with, or how does it illuminate, other parts of the book?

6. When Butler meets Robertson on the crags (Chapter 11), and asks him who he is, Robertson answers, "I am the devil!" And later, when Butler turns to go, Robertson speaks in the following mysterious, diabolical accents:

"Do not look after me. I will neither descend through the bowels of these rocks, nor vanish in a flash of fire; and yet the eye that seeks to trace my motions shall have reason to curse it was ever shrouded by eyelid or eyelash. Begone, and look not behind you."

Taking the whole character of Robertson-Staunton into consideration, as he is delineated throughout the book, would you say that he was merely "play-acting" here? If so, why? How would you attempt to justify his tone? Why does he make Muschat's Cairn the place for his

2 See Chapter 7.

meeting with Jeanie—a place where an eerie crime has been committed, a place of "blood and horror"? When he meets her there (Chapter 15) he tells her, in a "hollow" tone, that he is "a wretch predestined to evil here and hereafter." Would you say that, in his choice of the place, and in his describing himself as an evil being, he was using an effective psychological method for influencing Jeanie's attitude, or would you say that he might have influenced her more effectively by a simple and straightforward presentation of the problem, without the demoniacal trappings? If the latter, then why is the diabolism introduced here? For instance, he "thunders" at her like the devil himself.

"I will have no reservation! . . . lawful or unlawful, Christian or heathen, you shall swear to do my hest, and act by my counsel, or— you little know whose wrath you provoke!"

And again.

"There was one accursed deed done at this spot before now; and there shall be another to match it, unless you yield up to my guidance body and soul."

Are words of this kind "in character" with Robertson-Staunton as he is portrayed in the rest of the book? *What kind of person is* Staunton? Referring to Coleridge's criticism of Scott that we have quoted, would you say that Staunton was a fully "imagined" character—that is, a character who, no matter how complex, was a whole and convincing type of imaginary being?

7. Reconsidering the materials referred to in Question 6, in what way would you say that the figure of Robertson-Staunton carried out or contributed to the attitudes toward law and outlawry that are set up in the book? Does the treatment of Staunton illuminate and clarify those attitudes? What, actually, has Robertson-Staunton done in the way of breaking "laws" of one kind or another? What is his worst "crime"? Is it a crime of malice, or of "omission," or of ignorance, or of physical impulse and natural weakness? Does his crime justify his sense of being diabolically evil?

8. In that universe of discourse in which diabolism, or possession by an evil spirit, is meaningful, "evil" is not a generalized thing, for there is no "general evil" but only specific evil—specific kinds of "evil spirits"

representing specific kinds of human attitudes and behavior. If you know Dostoevski's *Crime and Punishment* or Hawthorne's *Scarlet Letter,* what *specific* kind of evil would you say possessed Svidrigaïlov, in the former book, or Roger Chillingworth, in the latter? Is the evil in Staunton (if he is evil) a specific kind of evil? Is Staunton treated by Scott merely as a neurotic who has to whip up his own sense of being wicked? Or is he treated as a seriously wicked and fully punishable person? He is harshly punished, both subjectively and objectively (by his conscience and by what happens to him at the end of the book); is his punishment ethically justified by the whole depiction of his character and by the structure of the book? Using specific illustration from *The Pilgrim's Progress,* make a statement of comparison between Scott's penetration into the nature of evil and that of Bunyan.

9. In Chapter 12, Butler suggests to Davie that he use the legal advice of a certain lawyer who is not a Cameronian, and Davie refuses: Butler suggests, "When you call in a physician, you would not, I suppose, question him on the nature of his religious principles?" and Davie answers,

"Wad I no? . . . But I wad, though; and if he didna satisfy me that he had a right sense of the right-hand and left-hand defections of the day, not a goutte of his physic should gang through my father's son."

How does Davie's attitude, in this and other examples, help to explain Jeanie's refusal to tell a lie? If we call Jeanie's attitude a case of "conditioning," that is, if we "psychoanalyze" Jeanie and explain her to our own satisfaction in the terms of a "case history," would such an explanation be the same thing as an artistic (structural) justification for the fact that her scruple of conscience is used as the pivot for this lengthy book? Has Jeanie an *interesting* conscience? How interesting does a conscience have to be, in order that a book may be pivoted on a moral scruple of the protagonist? Could you imagine an interesting and valuable novel pivoted on Davie's own attitude toward lawyers or physicians? Is Jeanie's scruple about the lie morally more profound than Davie's scruple about using non-Cameronian legal advice?

10. Suppose, on the other hand, that we explained Jeanie's action, in refusing to save Effie's life, by an unconscious jealousy of her pretty

younger sister, the daughter of another mother.[3] (A modern novelist, handling this situation "psychoanalytically," might exploit such an unconscious motivation.) Would we thereby supply a structural justification for Scott's pivotal use of Jeanie's refusal to lie? Or would we be imposing on the book something from *outside* the book itself, something not actually *in* the book as a functioning structural factor?

11. In the episode, Chapter 17, in which Madge and Ratcliffe lead the search party of the law, how credible as a character do you find Madge? Thinking comparatively of Shakespeare's mad people (Ophelia, for instance), would you say that the mad Madge carried the same or an inferior credibility? One finds in such a scene Scott's interest in reviving ballads and folk songs; would you say that he uses Madge's songs *imaginatively* (in Coleridge's sense) for the creation of convincing character and convincing human relations, as Shakespeare does in the use of similar material in Ophelia's mad scene? Or would you say that the folk material seems to be used somewhat for its own sake and for the sake of a colorful plot device, and that it does not make a true synthesis of character in Madge? How credible is Ratcliffe in this scene? If you find him more credible than Madge, more "real" in the sense of imagined character, where would you say the difference lay?

12. Evaluate the scene, Chapter 20, between Effie, Jeanie, and Ratcliffe, in the jail. Whereas in treating Madge Wildfire, Scott overtly employs folk material (snatches of ballads, and so forth), in this scene in the Tolbooth he draws from emotional and dramatic resources that are the same as those from which the ballads and folk songs draw (the natural lyricism and metaphoricalness of passionate peasant speech, the pathos and fatality of simple, brutal emotional situations), but he does so only implicitly, rather than explicitly as in the Madge Wildfire scenes. Do you find the method more successful in creating an imaginative reality? For instance, when Effie cries out,

> "And what am I but a poor wasted, wan-thriven tree, dug up by the roots, and flung out to waste in the highway, that man and beast may tread it under foot? I thought o' the bonny bit thorn that our father rooted out o' the yard last May, when it had a' the flush o' blossoms on it; and then it lay in the court till the beasts had trod them a' to pieces wi' their feet. I little thought, when I was wae for the bit silly green bush and its flowers, that I was to gang the same gate mysell."

[3] A possibility pointed out by V. S. Pritchett.

or in the following bit of dialogue between the two girls,

"And he wanted you to say something to yon folks, that wad save my young life?"

"He wanted," answered Jeanie, "that I suld be man-sworn."

"And you tauld him," said Effie, "that ye wadna hear o' coming between me and the death that I am to die, and me no aughteen year auld yet?"

or when Effie speaks of the nightmare visions that beset her broken spirit, visions of

"a high, black gibbet, and me standing up, and such seas of faces all looking up at poor Effie Deans . . . And then they stretch out their faces, and make mouths, and girn at me . . ."

—in such passages do you find true imaginative power? If you do find real passion of the imagination here and a convincing reality in the rhythms of Effie's distressed speech—that is, if you find Scott successful in this particular scene—would you say that there was consistency or inconsistency in the fact that he manages to move the reader *for* Effie while at the same time he attempts to make Jeanie's scrupulosity (*against* saving Effie) a moral norm for our admiration?

13. Evaluate now the trial scene, Chapter 23; in this scene occurs the moment on which the whole novel hangs—the moment when the oath of truth is administered. When Jeanie is called as witness,

the poor prisoner instantly started up, and stretched herself half-way over the bar, towards the side at which her sister was to enter. And when, slowly following the officer, the witness advanced to the foot of the table, Effie, with the whole expression of her countenance altered, from that of confused shame and dismay, to an eager, imploring, and almost ecstatic earnestness of entreaty, with outstretched hands, hair streaming back, eyes raised eagerly to her sister's face, and glistening through tears, exclaimed, in a tone which went through the heart of all who heard her—"O Jeanie, Jeanie, save me, save me!"

The oath is then administered.

"The truth to tell, and no truth to conceal, as far as she knew or should be asked, . . . in the name of God, and as the witness should

365

answer to God at the great day of judgment"; an awful adjuration, which seldom fails to make impression even on the most hardened characters, and to strike with fear even the most upright. Jeanie, educated in deep and devout reverence for the name and attributes of the Deity, was, by the solemnity of a direct appeal to his person and justice, awed, but at the same time elevated above all considerations, save those which she could, with a clear conscience, call HIM to witness.

She gives her negative testimony, and

A deep groan passed through the Court. It was echoed by one deeper and more agonised from the unfortunate father. The hope, to which unconsciously, and in spite of himself, he had still secretly clung, had now dissolved, and the venerable old man fell forward senseless on the floor of the Courthouse, with his head at the foot of his terrified daughter. The unfortunate prisoner, with impotent passion, strove with the guards, betwixt whom she was placed. "Let me gang to my father!—I *will* gang to him—I *will* gang to him—he is dead—he is killed—I hae killed him!"—she repeated in frenzied tones of grief, which those who heard them did not speedily forget.

And now Jeanie's reaction to her father's collapse.

Even in this moment of agony and general confusion, Jeanie did not lose that superiority, which a deep and firm mind assures to its possessor, under the most trying circumstances.

"He is my father—he is our father," she mildly repeated to those who endeavoured to separate them, as she stooped,—shaded aside his grey hairs, and began assiduously to chafe his temples.

Does the scene, as it is handled in these passages, convince you of the moral "superiority" of Jeanie, the superiority of a morally "deep" mind? Does the handling of this scene seem to you psychologically and morally consistent with Effie's long punishment and Jeanie's happy rewards?

14. In Chapter 25, Jeanie tells Effie of her decision to go to London. The relevant passage is the following one:

"My sister shall come out in the face of the sun," said Jeanie; "I will go to London, and beg pardon from the king and queen. If they pardoned Porteous, they may pardon her; if a sister asks a sister's life on her bended knees, they *will* pardon her—they *shall* pardon her—and they will win a thousand hearts by it."

Effie listened in bewildered astonishment, and so earnest was her sister's enthusiastic assurance, that she almost involuntarily caught a gleam of hope; but it instantly faded away.

"Ah, Jeanie! the king and queen live in London, a thousand miles from this—far ayont the saut sea; I'll be gane before ye win there!"

Jeanie assures her that it is not so far, and then says farewell,

"Fare ye weel! Unless I die by the road, I will see the king's face that gies grace."

Look up the ballad of "Johnnie Armstrong," where this same motif occurs and even the same phrase as that last quoted above. How would you evaluate comparatively the imaginative truth conveyed by the ballad and that carried by Scott's scene? In view of other scenes we have examined, do you find Jeanie's motivation as purely selfless and heroic as it is offered to us by the text? Is there anything in the quoted passage that suggests that Jeanie might be motivated by an unconscious desire for the glory of wringing a pardon from the king and queen, subduing majesty itself by "her bended knees"? Does Scott *use* such a possibility in the structure of his book?

15. What makes the scene at Dumbiedikes' house, Chapter 26, "good Scott"? Would you say that the scene is "local color" for its own sake, or that it is functionally integrated with the rest of the book and structurally significant in it?

16. What is Meg Murdockson's purpose in capturing Jeanie (Chapters 29 and 30)? Does this motivation seem to you psychologically consistent with the fact that Meg herself had caused her daughter's insanity by destroying Madge's baby?

17. In Chapter 33, George Staunton reads to Jeanie the narrative of his life. Does this narrative have an integral and necessary relation with the total action of the book? Why does he have his life history prepared in manuscript? Is his engaging in this literary endeavor psychologically justified to your satisfaction? His explanation for his tendencies to vice is that he drew them in with the milk of his nurse (Meg Mur-

dockson), and he speaks of himself as therefore having been "fated" to viciousness. Does this seem to you an absurd or a valid explanation? Jeanie tells George that Effie was right to remain in jail when offered her freedom. Jeanie knows quite well by this time that Effie is innocent (except of sexuality). How, therefore, would you account for Jeanie's moral reasoning here?

18. Evaluate the scene of Madge Wildfire's death, at the end of Chapter 40. Does the use of the folk song and ballad material here seem to you imaginatively justified? Do Madge's lyrical articulateness and coherence seem appropriate in a woman dying of pneumonia and "not expected to live above an hour or two"? The scene of Clarissa Harlowe's death is grotesque and theatrical: why, then, is it any more justifiable, in terms of its integrity in the total aesthetic structure, than the present death scene?

19. In Chapter 48, in Effie's letter to Jeanie, the contrast between the two women is drawn thus:

> "You [Jeanie] live happy in the esteem and love of all who know you, and I drag on the life of a miserable impostor, indebted for the marks of regard I receive to a tissue of deceit and lies, which the slightest accident may unravel . . . you, the pure, the virtuous, the heroine of unstained faith, unblemished purity, what can you have to fear from the world or its proudest minions?"

Effie then goes on to speak of her own "guilt," and of the tortures she experiences from constant apprehension that she may be "discovered" and "branded." Can you suggest any concrete content for Effie's sense of guilt? Clarissa Harlowe's reaction after the rape would seem to be far more fantastically exaggerated than Effie's response to her situation; can you explain, in terms of total structure, why Clarissa's agony of mind is nevertheless convincing to the imagination, while Effie's is not? If you know Tolstoi's *Anna Karenina,* where an implicit contrast is drawn between Anna as the adulterous and unhappy woman and Kitty Levin as the simply virtuous and happy wife (a contrast that, in a general and schematic fashion, is somewhat similar to the one Scott draws between Effie and Jeanie), can you offer any suggestion as to why Tolstoi is convincing and Scott is not? Would you say that Scott is exploiting any "stock responses" here? Comparing the early and the later depictions of Effie, at eighteen and then as a mature woman, which depiction would you say carried the more authenticity for the imagination? Try to account for the difference in validity between the earlier and the later portraits of Effie.

20. Why does George Staunton wear a hair shirt (see Chapter 52)? Would you say that his wearing a hair shirt was psychologically justified by the whole presentation of this character? Note that he has become a Roman Catholic. Taking Scott's whole presentation of George into consideration—his sense of diabolical evil in himself, his feeling that he is damned, and the bad end that he actually comes to—would you say that, by making him turn Roman Catholic, Scott implies that the Catholic church is an institution for normal minds, a spiritually healthy institution, or that he implies the opposite? What "stock response" would you say Scott was exploiting in having George turn Catholic? (For an answer here, you would have to find out something about religious attitudes in Scott's time and milieu.) Lovelace, in *Clarissa Harlowe*, is a far more "mythological" type than is George Staunton; why, nevertheless, is he more convincing than George?

21. Why does Jeanie set the Whistler free (Chapter 52)? Is this action consistent with her refusal to tell a lie to set her sister free? Is it consistent with her conviction that Effie was right to remain in jail?

22. Scott states, at the very end of the book, what he sees as the moral meaning of the tale,

> . . . that guilt, though it may attain temporal splendour, can never confer real happiness; that the evil consequences of our crimes long survive their commission, and, like the ghosts of the murdered, for ever haunt the steps of the malefactor; and that the paths of virtue, though seldom those of worldly greatness, are always those of pleasantness and peace.

Whether or not these statements are "true" in any absolute sense is a question that does not concern us here; what we are concerned with is their validity in the context of the book. Our only criteria of their validity must be the wholeness and coherence of the world created in the book, the world from which Scott draws his moral. Judging by the soundness of that world, how sound would you say the moral was?

Great Expectations

1. The second and third paragraphs of the opening chapter give Pip's family background and the physical setting of marshes and sea, as the child first experiences awareness of these. Do his family circumstances suggest that Pip "belongs" or that he is an "alien," a disconnected fragment, in human society? In the "dark flat wilderness" beyond the churchyard, the "low leaden line" of the river, and the "savage lair" of the sea, are the connotations those of emotional security and integration for the child, or are they the reverse? Note that certain important elements in the physical setting are the gibbet and the hulks, whose guns sound recurrently; later, Newgate prison becomes important as setting; and convicts appear again and again in the story. What is the significance of this particular symbolical configuration?

2. Considering that Pumblechook, who seems to be the great human denominator of acquisitiveness and egotism and brutality in this world (the universal human "average"), takes upon himself the role of "father" toward Pip, and that Pumblechook is a corn chandler, a dealer in seeds, can you suggest any significance in Pip's name? Refer to the parable of the seeds in St. Luke 8:5–8: does it seem to have any bearing on Pip's childhood? on Magwitch's? In this connection, what is implied by Wemmick's metaphor for Newgate, a "greenhouse" (Chapter 32)?

3. At the end of Chapter 4, when Pip breaks in terror from the table and runs head foremost into the soldiers holding out a pair of handcuffs to him, the abrupt incongruity is comic. But psychologically considered, is this a real incongruity and "coincidence"? Similarly, earlier, when the child is quietly ruminating on the "identity of things," and Magwitch suddenly appears, is this comically abrupt meeting really "incongruous" and "coincidental," or does it imply a deeper congruity, causality, and fitness? Is there any symbolic appropriateness in the fact that Magwitch appears "from among the graves"?

4. In Chapter 4, Pip speaks of having been brought up to think that he had outraged the Law in some way.

I think my sister must have had some general idea that I was a young offender whom an Accoucheur Policeman had taken up (on my birthday) and delivered over to her, to be dealt with according to the outraged majesty of the law. I was always treated as if I had insisted on being born in opposition to the dictates of reason, religion, and morality . . .

And when he is taken to the Town Hall to be bound apprentice (Chapter 13), Pumblechook pushes him over

exactly as if I had that moment picked a pocket or fired a rick; indeed, it was the general impression in Court that I had been taken redhanded.

Explain this pedagogical attitude on the part of Mrs. Joe, Pumblechook, and others. What aspect of the theme of guilt and alienation appears here? In Pip's stealing of "wittles" for the convict, what other aspect of the theme of guilt appears, or would you say that this incident has no significance for the guilt theme? What aspect of the same theme do you find in the following reflections of Pip (Chapter 6)?

My state of mind regarding the pilfering from which I had been so unexpectedly exonerated, did not impel me to frank disclosure . . . It was much on my mind (particularly when I first saw him looking about for his file) that I ought to tell Joe the whole truth. Yet I did not, and for the reason that I mistrusted that if I did, he would think me worse than I was . . . In a word, I was too cowardly to do what I knew to be right, as I had been too cowardly to avoid doing what I knew to be wrong. I had had no intercourse with the world at that time, and I imitated none of its many inhabitants who act in this manner. Quite an untaught genius, I made the discovery of the line of action for myself.

Out of what impulse arise Pip's wonderful lies to Mrs. Joe and Pumblechook about his visit to Miss Havisham's (beginning of Chapter 9)? In Chapter 8, does Estella's persecution of Pip arise from the same impulse and is it of the same quality as adult brutality, or does it differ? What do the visit to Miss Havisham's, and Estella's childish persecution of him, have to do with the development of guilt attitudes in Pip?

5. What significance has the following configuration (in Chapter 8) and

371

the various elements within it: the absolute arrest and decay of everything at Miss Havisham's house? the constant use of artificial lighting within it? ("I have often thought since, that she must have looked as if the admission of the natural light of day would have struck her to dust . . .") the fact that the house is called Satis? the fact that it is on the site of an abandoned brewery, near the marshes, and within sound of the guns of the hulks? the name of the card-game which the children "play"? What is the connection between this particular symbolic configuration (arrest, decay, artificial light—lighting up jewels—the house Satis, the abandoned brewery, the marshes, the hulks, the card game) and the prison-convict configuration spoken of in Question 1? Are Miss Havisham's impulses fundamentally different from those of Mrs. Joe and Pumblechook? In what way do these two symbolic configurations suggest a connection between public and private guilt?

6. Why does Orlick attack Mrs. Joe (Chapter 15), rather than Pip or Joe himself? Would you say that the sudden violent unreasonableness of this attack was a flaw in the plot of the book, or, if you find it consistent with the rest, how would you justify the episode? Comparing Orlick's sudden violence with Meg Murdockson's violence against Jeanie Deans, which of the two do you find most unreasonable, and which do you find most justifiable structurally? Explain, psychologically, Mrs. Joe's pantomimic propitiation of Orlick, at the end of Chapter 16. In terms of the coherence of human relationships and the emotional integration of individuals with their human surroundings (as against the alienation, "disconnectedness," and irresponsibility that we see, for instance, in Miss Havisham's way of life), would you say that Mrs. Joe, when she has become an imbecile, is a more or a less *coherent* person than when she had her wits? If Orlick himself represents the incoherence of irresponsible violence, how does Orlick's madness differ from Joe's simple-mindedness and Mrs. Joe's imbecility? What appropriateness is there in the fact that Orlick later becomes Miss Havisham's gatekeeper?

7. In the organization of his plot, how does Dickens use the common folk-tale pattern of a "fairy wishing"? In the examples of this pattern that you know in folk literature, do you find any suggestion of either wrong-doing or menace such as we find in Dickens' treatment of the pattern? How does Pip's conversation with Biddy, in Chapter 17, prepare morally for the appearance of Jaggers in the next chapter? Attempt to ex-

plain Jaggers' part in the plot, either as an interested or a disinterested party to events. One of Jaggers' "signatures" is his constant washing of his hands: does this seem to be an arbitrary attribute, or does it actually "signify" anything? Explain the fact that Pip is allowed to think of Miss Havisham as his "fairy godmother." What are the psychological and ethical connotations of the following image of Miss Havisham (near the end of Chapter 19, where Pip takes leave of her to go to London and to his great destiny)?

. . . and so I left my fairy godmother, with both her hands on her crutch stick, standing in the midst of the dimly lighted room beside the rotten bride-cake that was hidden in cobwebs.

How, in Magwitch's later return as Provis and Pip's horrified recognition that his mysterious benefactor is a criminal, does Dickens manipulate the common fairy tale pattern of which we have spoken? Why the change to the name Provis?

8. In the following passage (Chapter 20), where Pip is introduced into Mr. Jaggers' London office, what psychological suggestions, consistent with the theme of the novel, do you find in the animistic treatment of physical setting?

Mr. Jaggers's room was lighted by a skylight only, and was a most dismal place; the skylight, eccentrically patched like a broken head, and the distorted adjoining houses looking as if they had twisted themselves to peep down at me through it.

What *thematic* significance has the following?

I called to mind that the clerk had the same air of knowing something to everybody's disadvantage, as his master had. I wondered how many other clerks there were up-stairs, and whether they all claimed to have the same detrimental mastery of their fellow-creatures.

In view of the rigors of Wemmick's professional status, what consistent use would you say Dickens made of the device of the "signature" in his description of Wemmick's "post-office of a mouth" with its "mechanical appearance of smiling"?

9. Waiting for Jaggers, Pip wanders about the environs (Chapter 20).

So, I came into Smithfield; and the shameful place, being all asmear with filth and fat and blood and foam, seemed to stick to me. So I rubbed it off with all possible speed by turning into a street where I saw the great black dome of Saint Paul's bulging at me from behind a grim stone building which a bystander said was Newgate Prison . . .

The bystander offers to act as guide.

. . . he was so good as to take me into a yard and show me where the gallows was kept, and also where people were publicly whipped, and then he showed me the Debtors' Door, out of which culprits came to be hanged . . .

Considering such a passage out of context of the book, one might suspect that Dickens was piling up menacing perspectives quite arbitrarily here; but how does the general context that we have been studying justify the use of these particular scenes as Pip's induction into his great expectations?

10. In the early scene (Chapter 8) where Pip sees Estella walking the casks in the old brewery, she seems to

pass among the extinguished fires, and ascend some light iron stairs, and go out by a gallery high overhead, as if she were going into the sky.

In view of Estella's significance in Pip's great expectations, what appropriateness has this vision? You should be aware that the present "happy ending" of the book was not the one Dickens first wrote for it, but was unfortunately used by him on the suggestion of Lord Lytton as more befitting popular taste. He had planned that Estella should simply go out of Pip's life. Why is the original ending more appropriate?

11. There is apparent arbitrariness (an apparently arbitrary manipulation of the materials, for "atmospheric" effects, that does not seem necessitated causally by the earlier steps of the plot, as such) in the phantom of Miss Havisham hanging by the neck while Estella walks the casks (Chapter 8), and on other occasions, as at the end of Chapter 32, when

the "proud and refined" Estella is placed in emotional relation with the contaminate dust of Newgate. Do you find in the latter passage, quoted below, any *psychological* means by which Dickens justifies the association between Estella and Newgate?

I consumed the whole time in thinking how strange it was that I should be encompassed by all this taint of prison and crime; that, in my childhood out on our lonely marshes on a winter evening I should have first encountered it; that, it should have reappeared on two occasions, starting out like a stain that was faded, but not gone; that, it should in this new way pervade my fortune and advancement. While my mind was thus engaged, I thought of the beautiful young Estella, proud and refined, coming towards me, and I thought with absolute abhorrence of the contrast between the jail and her . . . I beat the prison dust off my feet as I sauntered to and fro, and I shook it out of my dress, and I exhaled its air from my lungs. So contaminated did I feel, remembering who was coming, that the coach came quickly after all, and I was not yet free from the soiling consciousness . . . when I saw her face at the coach window and her hand waving at me.

What *was* the nameless shadow which again in that one instant had passed?

In Chapter 28, when Pip, having been invited to see Estella at Miss Havisham's, takes the coach for the village, where he plans to stay at the Blue Boar instead of going to Joe's, he encounters two convicts on the coach, and the episode is handled in much the same way as the one spoken of above.

I could not have said what I was afraid of, for my fear was altogether undefined and vague, but there was great fear upon me. As I walked on to the hotel, I felt that a dread, much exceeding the mere apprehension of a painful or disagreeable recognition, made me tremble. I am confident that it took no distinctness of shape, and that it was the revival for a few minutes of the terror of childhood.

Here, do you find that Dickens is able to justify *psychologically* Pip's sense of dread, or do you feel that he is indulging unjustifiably in the use of coincidence (the coincidental appearance of the convicts on the

375

coach) and that he is arbitrarily manipulating his materials to extract "symbolic" meaning from them?

12. In the following two passages, Pip finds an inexplicably meaningful resemblance, first (Chapter 29) between Miss Havisham and Estella, and second (Chapter 48) between Estella and Jaggers' housekeeper.

> What *was* it that was borne in upon my mind when she stood still and looked attentively at me? Anything that I had seen in Miss Havisham? . . . In some of her looks and gestures there was that tinge of resemblance to Miss Havisham which may often be noticed to have been acquired by children, from grown persons with whom they have been much associated and secluded, and which, when childhood is passed, will produce a remarkable occasional likeness of expression between faces that are otherwise quite different. And yet I could not trace this to Miss Havisham. I looked again, and though she was still looking at me, the suggestion was gone . . .
>
> In another moment we were in the brewery so long disused, and she pointed to the high gallery where I had seen her going out on that same first day, and told me she remembered to have been up there, and to have seen me standing scared below. As my eyes followed her white hand, again the same dim suggestion that I could not possibly grasp, crossed me. My involuntary start occasioned her to lay her hand upon my arm. Instantly the ghost passed once more and was gone.

> I looked again at those hands and eyes of the housekeeper, and thought of the inexplicable feeling that had come over me when I last walked—not alone—in the ruined garden, and through the deserted brewery. I thought how the same feeling had come back when I saw a face looking at me, and a hand waving to me, from a stage-coach window; and how it had come back again and had flashed about me like lightning, when I had passed in a carriage—not alone—through a sudden glare of light in a dark street. I thought how one link of association had helped that identification in the theatre, and how such a link, wanting before, had been riveted for me now, when I had passed by a chance swift from Estella's name to the fingers with their knitting action, and the attentive eyes. And I felt absolutely certain that this woman was Estella's mother.

What, in each case, is the *psychological* justification for these obscure impressions of resemblance? What is the *moral* link between Estella

376

and Miss Havisham, such as would imply that kind of "resemblance" which would lie in a complementary relationship between them? Since Estella "resembles" both Miss Havisham and the murderess who is Jaggers' housekeeper, what *moral* link would you say exists between Miss Havisham and the murderess? Do you think that Dickens' frequent insistence on Pip's vague impressions of this kind is an arbitrary exploitation of "atmosphere," or do you think that it is structurally justified in the book? Is there anything in the basic fairy tale model, the cornerstone of structure here, that gives imaginative justification to Pip's constant duality of vision, which leads him always to associate some namelessly dreadful shadow with Estella?

13. The scene of Magwitch's return as Provis (Chapter 39) provides the major turning point of the book. Aristotle, in the *Poetics*, suggests that the turning point of a dramatic action is more effective when it coincides with a "recognition" or "discovery." In what way does this particular reversal scene automatically "discover" to Pip the meaning of his recurrent sense of a prison taint in his life? the meaning of the various appearances of convict emissaries on coaches, in inns, and so forth? the meaning of his association with the criminal lawyer Jaggers? the meaning of his past relations with Miss Havisham? the meaning of his actions toward Joe? In what way do all these "recognitions" or "discoveries" provide Pip with insight into the nature and fatality of his "great expectations"?

14. Storms frequently are used by novelists as "atmosphere" for psychological crises (and the connection between actual atmospheric disturbances and human crisis is by no means an arbitrary or unnatural one, for uneasy weather sometimes exacerbates human feelings). Does the storm on the night of Magwitch's reappearance seem to you to be structurally justified? In what way would you say that the handling of the whole story warrants the excessive superstitiousness in the following passage (Chapter 39)?

In every rage of wind and rush of rain, I heard pursuers. Twice, I could have sworn there was a knocking and whispering at the outer door. With these fears upon me, I began either to imagine or recall that I had had mysterious warnings of this man's approach. That, for weeks gone by, I had passed faces in the streets which I had thought like his. That, these likenesses had grown more numerous, as he, coming over the sea, had drawn nearer. That, his wicked spirit had somehow sent these messengers to mine, and that now on this stormy night he was as good as his word, and with me.

Explain, both at the *plot level* and at the *symbolic level,* Orlick's presence on the stairway on this night. What is Pip's first emotional reaction to Magwitch? In the spiritual framework of the book, how is this reaction justifiably associated with the storm and with the mysteriously menacing background figure of Orlick?

15. The convict can now boast of "owning" a "brought-up London gentleman" with a ruby on his finger and foreign language books in his library. In Chapter 40, in the following passage,

> The imaginary student pursued by the misshapen creature he had impiously made, was not more wretched than I, pursued by the creature who had made me, and recoiling from him with a stronger repulsion, the more he admired me and the fonder he was of me.

Pip draws an ambiguous analogy between the story of Frankenstein and his own situation (ambiguous because, though Magwitch is thought of in this analogy as the monster who has created a man, there is a more subtle sense in which Pip has created the monster who now terrifies him). Could you define what might be said to be the "impiousness" of Magwitch in creating his "London gentleman"? Have his benefactions to Pip been unadulterated by egoism? Have they been wholly different, in spiritual quality, from Miss Havisham's "benefactions" or Mrs. Joe's or Pumblechook's?

16. In Chapter 42, Magwitch recounts his early history. In what way does this history resemble Pip's? In the parallelism between Pip and Magwitch, what new and "universal" meaning is implicitly given to the symbolic "convict" figure that has haunted the book—the figure who, in the first chapter, is described as

> A man who had been soaked in water, and smothered in mud, and lamed by stones, and cut by flints, and stung by nettles, and torn by briars . . .

and who, in Chapter 40, is described as revealing in all his actions the influences of "his branded life among men" and his "consciousness that he was dodging and hiding now," so that there is written upon him

in these ways and a thousand other small nameless instances arising every minute in the day . . . Prisoner, Felon, Bondsman, plain as plain could be.

How "innocent" and how "guilty" is Magwitch? How "innocent" and how "guilty" is Pip?

17. What psychological change (see Chapter 46) comes over Magwitch during the period in which Pip undertakes to protect the convict? What accounts for this change? What radical change (see Chapter 54) takes place in Pip's attitude toward Magwitch when the latter is dying in prison? Notice that Pip does no particular penance and makes no particular retribution to Joe for his guilt toward the latter, but that Joe typically without "expectations" nurses Pip in his illness. In what way, then, does Pip really "atone"? Remembering that Mrs. Joe, too, did no particular penance and made no particular retribution to either Joe or Pip, in what way, would you say, does Pip's highly indirect "atonement" resemble that of Mrs. Joe when she propitiates Orlick? In what way does Joe himself symbolize the changes that take place in Pip and Magwitch, and the new relationship between the boy and the convict?

18. Consider this verse from St. John (12:24): "Except a corn of wheat fall into the ground and die, it abideth alone: but if it die, it bringeth forth much fruit." Does the verse (again about "seeds") have any significance for the final developments in Pip and Magwitch? Note that the whole story begins at the Christmas season: does this fact seem to you to have any meaning?

19. The plot of *Great Expectations*, considered merely as plot and without reference to other structural elements, is quite as full of major coincidences and forced intrigue as the plot of *The Heart of Mid-Lothian* —coincidences and intrigue that are, indeed, a good deal more fantastic. But a "plot" does not stand or fall by itself, but only by its integralness to, or failure to integrate with, the whole structure of the novel. Give as many reasons as you can adduce for the fact that the fantastic plot of *Great Expectations* is an integral element of structure, and convincing to the imagination, while that of *The Heart of Mid-Lothian* is not.

Vanity Fair

1. How do the incidents at the end of Chapter 1, when the girls leave Miss Pinkerton's academy, help to illuminate Becky's later social attitudes? In Chapter 2 her background is sketched. Why does Thackeray make her father an artist and her mother an opera-girl? What, in the milieu at Miss Pinkerton's, develops in Becky the talent for dissembling—that talent which serves her so magnificently later on? At the same time, she is shown as rigorously forthright and honest in her responses (as in her adieu to Miss Pinkerton and her treatment of the dictionary): how do these two antagonistic qualities—hypocrisy and honesty—manage to combine credibly in Becky's temperament? In what sense does Thackeray have and communicate an ambivalent attitude toward Becky, and why does this ambivalence contribute to a greater credibility in Becky than in Amelia, toward whom his attitude is quite unambivalent?

2. Is there any suggestion of symbolic meaning in the "green silk purse" which Becky knits at the Sedleys'? and in this picture of her tête-à-tête with Jos at the end of Chapter 4?

   . . . his arms stretched out before her in an imploring attitude, and his hands bound in a web of green silk, which she was unwinding.

   In what qualities do both George and Jos show themselves as appropriate scions of their class? and Rawdon, of his class? Becky's first near-success as a freewheeling sexual aggressor is with Jos, and the portrait of Jos (Chapters 3 and 4) is dominated by his loneliness and liver complaint; at the very end of the book, she is again with Jos, and now Jos is taking other pills—poison—and suffering from another disease—murder. Meanwhile Becky has reached the peak of her social success with another sick man, Lord Steyne, who has insanity in his blood. What significance is there in the fact that Becky, so perfectly healthy, is most deeply involved with sick men? Where else, specifically, do you find sickness of one kind or another in this world? Is there a sense in which Jos's loneliness is itself as organic a disease as his liver complaint and as symbolic as his gluttony?

3. This is a civilization in which money relationships are the fundamental governing relationships between people; but in a sophisticated society money relationships are almost always veiled by fantasies that emphasize other kinds of value. In the following (Chapter 6), George expresses his disapproval of an alliance between Jos and Becky: how would you describe his particular fantasy of values and disvalues? Does it differ essentially from Miss Pinkerton's?

"Hang it, the family's low enough already, without her. A governess is all very well, but I'd rather have a lady for my sister-in-law. I'm a liberal man; but I've proper pride, and know my station: let her know hers."

On the morning after Vauxhall (the same chapter), Becky senses that George is trying to spoil her chances with Jos, and she

began to have a feeling of distrust and hatred towards this young officer, which he was quite unconscious of having inspired.

Do George's attitude here and Becky's intuition of his attitude have any causal bearing on her later affair with George in Brussels?

4. In the incident in Chapter 7, when the groom refuses to handle Becky's trunks, and leaves her with this parting question—

"I hope you've forgot nothink? Miss 'melia's gownds—have you got them—as the lady's-maid was to have 'ad?"

—do you find the same fantasies of value, and the same ethos in the groom as in Miss Pinkerton, for instance, and as in George Osborne? What is the implicit psychological effect of incidents such as this on Becky? In what way do such incidents explain her predatory activities later? The servants at the Sedleys' say (Chapter 6) that Becky snoops in drawers. Snooping in drawers is a form of activity that ought to make a heroine very unpleasant to us (later, we find Miss Horrocks acutely unpleasant as she snoops in drawers while Sir Pitt is dying). How does the ambivalent presentation of Becky account for the fact that this trait does not make her repulsive, but, rather, that we find it not only humanly credible and characteristic, but even sympathetic?

5. In what way does Sir Pitt's attitude toward his wife, the ironmonger's daughter (Chapters 8 and 9), exhibit the same ethos that we have seen in Miss Pinkerton, in George Osborne, and in the Sedley groom? Thackeray picks the detail of Lady Crawley's "enormous interminable piece of knitting" as the image that chiefly characterizes her: why is it that the knitting is able to signify so much of Lady Crawley's spiritual state and her relations with her household? We see such people as Mr. Osborne acquiring more and more power in the city; on the other hand, Sir Pitt, a member of the baronetage, gets drunk nightly with his butler, and spends his cunning on foolish, disreputable litigation, while his estate falls to pieces: in what way do these contrasts represent social developments in general and the general economy of public life? Is the public life healthy?

6. The Bute Crawleys are described in Chapter 11. Is the Reverend Bute Crawley a responsible member of the body politic? a responsible officer of his spiritual calling? What, in terms of social generalization, has happened to the baronetage, and how is this phenomenon related to its ethos? In the relation of the two brothers (Sir Pitt and the Reverend Bute Crawley) to their sister, old Miss Crawley, do you find the acquisitive ethos dressed up in dignified fantasies (as it is with George Osborne or with Miss Pinkerton), or do you find it quite unveiled? In the following conversation (Chapter 11) between the rector and his wife, concerning Miss Crawley's gustatory habits, how does the concern for Miss Crawley's health reflect the typical ethos of this family?

> "I think she's going," said the Rector's wife. "She was very red in the face when we left dinner. I was obliged to unlace her."
>
> "She drank seven glasses of champagne," said the reverend gentleman, in a low voice; "and filthy champagne it is, too, that my brother poisons us with—but you women never know what's what."
>
> "We know nothing," said Mrs. Bute Crawley.
>
> "She drank cherry-brandy after dinner," continued his Reverence, "and took curaçoa with her coffee. *I* wouldn't take a glass for a five-pound note; it kills me with heartburn. She can't stand it, Mrs. Crawley—she must go—flesh and blood won't bear it! and I lay five to two, Matilda drops in a year."

7. The servants report to Mrs. Bute in Chapter 11 that the new governess (Becky)

had "come round" everybody—wrote Sir Pitt's letters, did his business, managed his accounts—had the upper hand of the whole house, my lady, Mr. Crawley, the girls and all; at which Mrs. Crawley declared she was an artful hussy, and had some dreadful designs in view.

Are Becky's activities different in intention from those of Mrs. Bute? What is the responsive ethical chord in Mrs. Bute that explains her intuition of "dreadful designs" on Becky's part? Why has Becky more *symbolic* significance than Mrs. Bute herself, though their motivations are similar?

8. Old Miss Crawley is characterized (Chapter 10) as

a dreadful Radical for those days . . . She read Voltaire, and had Rousseau by heart; talked very lightly about divorce, and most energetically of the rights of women. She had pictures of Mr. Fox in every room in the house.

How do the names of Voltaire, Rousseau, and Fox contribute to the irony of the following passage (Chapter 11)?

"What is birth, my dear?" she would say to Rebecca. "Look at my brother Pitt . . . look at poor Bute at the parsonage;—is any one of them equal to you in intelligence or breeding? . . . You, my love, are a little paragon—positively a little jewel—you have more brains than half the shire—if merit had its reward, you ought to be a duchess —no, there ought to be no duchesses at all—but you ought to have no superior, and I consider you, my love, as my equal in every respect; and—will you put some coals on the fire, my dear; and will you pick this dress of mine, and alter it, you who can do it so well?"

In the same context she tells Becky,

"I adore all imprudent matches. What I like best is for a nobleman to marry a miller's daughter . . . I wish some great man would run away with *you*, my dear."

In view of these sentiments, explain Miss Crawley's reaction (Chapter 16) to Becky's clandestine marriage with Rawdon. Is Miss Crawley ethically superior to the rest of this civilization? How, in a word, would you describe the particular fantasies which she has formulated for social relationships? When she is dying (end of Chapter 25) we see her in a momentary illumination of the motives of everyone around her.

". . . I won't be a slave in my own house—and I won't be starved and choked with poison. They all want to kill me—all—all"—and with this the lonely old woman burst into a scream of hysterical tears.

Is the ethos that she senses in others quite unrelated to her own? Is there any common significance between Miss Crawley's loneliness and that of Jos Sedley?

9. Does the portrait of Mr. Osborne, in Chapter 13—his gloom and surliness, his face "puffy, solemn, and yellow at the best of times"—suggest that Mr. Osborne is in a state of either spiritual or physical health? What is the relationship, generally, between spiritual and physical health in this book? In the conversation between father and son in Chapter 13, regarding George's gambling debts contracted with certain young "bloods" of the nobility, Mr. Osborne says,

"You shan't want, sir—the British merchant's son shan't want, sir. My guineas are as good as theirs, George, my boy; and I don't grudge 'em. Call on Mr. Chopper as you go through the City to-morrow; he'll have something for you. I don't grudge money when I know you're in good society, because I know that good society can never go wrong. There's no pride in me. I was a humbly born man—but you have had advantages. Make a good use of 'em. Mix with the young nobility. There's many of 'em who can't spend a dollar to your guinea, my boy."

From these remarks, what would you say was the particular fantasy of human values which Mr. Osborne has created out of the cash relationships that govern this society? When he tells George to "call on Mr. Chopper" (his banker), in what sense is this a kind of bribery of George —a bribe intended to influence George in what way? Later (Chapter 24), when he disinherits George, he erases his name and birth date from the family Bible, where the record had been written on a sheet next to a frontispiece of Abraham sacrificing Isaac. What ironic inflections does Thackeray get out of this detail? (Refer to the Old Testament story, Genesis 22:1–13.)

10. Chapter 14 illuminates another father-son relationship—that between

Sir Pitt and Rawdon, each waiting for Miss Crawley to die (meanwhile the mother, Lady Crawley, is dying untended), each watching the other's movements ghoulishly as Becky keeps both in suspense as to where her favor will land. Explain the fact that, though Sir Pitt is amused (Chapter 15) when Becky confesses a secret marriage, he becomes a "frenzied old man, wild with hatred and insane with baffled desire" when she tells him that her husband is his son (Chapter 16). Define both the differences and the common moral elements among these three father-son relationships: that between Sir Pitt and Rawdon, that between Mr. Osborne and George, and that implied by Mr. Sedley's exercise of parental responsibility when (Chapter 46) he tampers with the household funds and sells Jos's remittances for experimentation in the stock market.

11. Of Becky's tendance on Miss Crawley's sickbed, we are told (Chapter 14),

She passed as weary a fortnight as ever mortal spent in Miss Crawley's sick-room; but her little nerves seemed to be of iron, as she was quite unshaken by the duty and the tedium of the sick-chamber.

In what sense is this a "moral" characterization? Does it in any way prepare the reader for her final disposal of Jos at the end of the book? We are told that Becky really likes Amelia; explain her cruelty to Amelia with regard to George. If Becky has her eye on the main chance, why does she bother about George at all? Becky has been schooled, in a very severe school of experience, to take money more seriously than anything else; what is it in her character, then, that makes her "burst out laughing" when Miss Crawley cuts herself and Rawdon off with twelve pounds (end of Chapter 25)? What is it in her character that makes her "like the life" of penniless, vagabond Bohemia (see Chapter 65)?

12. What is your own judgment as to the architectural integration of the two plots—the one woven about Becky and the other about Amelia? Is the following a satisfactory structural rationale for the juxtaposition of the Amelia-plot with the Becky-plot: Amelia shows us what a good woman does with her life and gets out of it, in contrast with what Becky, a bad woman, does with her life and gets out of it? According to such a rationale, the significance of the book would be what is called the "doctrine of deserts," which we have previously seen in *The Heart*

of Mid-Lothian, where the "wicked" are punished and the "good" are rewarded. If you do not agree that this is the chief meaning of the book, then what would you say was its meaning?

13. Note Thackeray's epithets for Amelia: "the weeping, trembling young bride," "this little heart," her "pretty little hand," her "sweet, pretty little foot," "her little head," "tender little parasite," and (Chapter 38):

> Her sensibilities were so weak and tremulous that perhaps they ought not to be talked about in a book . . . all men who came near her loved her . . . it was her weakness which was her principal charm—a kind of sweet submission and softness, which seemed to appeal to each man for his sympathy and protection.

(Incidentally, there was no irony in Thackeray's *intentions* with regard to Amelia: he seems to have modeled her on a woman with whom he was in love and whom he admired without reserve.) What, judging from the portrait of Amelia, is Thackeray's ideal of womanhood? Is his ideal of womanhood aesthetically validated by the structure of the book? Does it play an organically necessary structural part? To what degree does the aesthetic structure of a work affect the persuasiveness that an author's personal ideals, if expressed in the work, have for the reader? Waiving the matter of Thackeray's personal sentiments and ideals, would you say that what the book itself (not the author) does is to present and document an ideal way of life, or to present a world that is anything but ideal? If it does the latter, is the book then an "immoral" book?

14. In the Brussels episode, we have a new national background. This background is presented largely through the reactions of Brussels citizens to the news from the front (Chapter 31): the reports always distorted by Belgian sympathy with Napoleon, and by antagonism against the snobbish and brutally conceited English (who are the only real "invaders"); but most concretely and immediately we are presented with this social background through Isidore, Jos's valet. As the Belgian citizenry calculates probable loss and gain, so does Isidore (Chapter 31).

> As he helped Jos through his toilsome and complicated daily toilette, this faithful servant would calculate what he should do with the very articles with which he was decorating his master's person . . .

And, as reports of English defeat come in,

> So Jos's man was marking his victim down, as you see one of Mr. Paynter's assistants in Leadenhall Street ornament an unconscious turtle with a placard on which is written, 'Soup tomorrow.'

Is the Belgian national moral environment, symbolized by Isidore's responses, fundamentally different from the moral environments that we have observed so far in the English scenes? Thackeray calls the Belgians a "nation of shopkeepers": in what sense are the English, as they have been represented in the book, also a "nation of shopkeepers"?

15. In Chapter 30, immediately after Rawdon's departure for the front, Becky coolly calculates her possessions and prospects. What earlier heroine of fiction does she remind you of? In Chapter 32, where she sews up her money in her clothes, we are told that she was

> ready for any event—to fly if she thought fit, or to stay and welcome the conqueror, were he Englishman or Frenchman.

Why is it that all the previous scenes, in England and Belgium, prevent us from being repelled by Becky's lack of loyalties here? Why is her attitude more admirable, in a sense, than that of Jos or of Lady Bareacres, for instance?

16. In the anguished rush from Belgium, the profitable buying and selling of commodities, the calculation of personal material benefit at no matter what destruction to others, is seen quite nakedly as the dynamics of life. Against the background of this nakedly exposed motivation, explain the peculiar horror of the scene (Chapter 32) in which Jos asks Isidore to shave him and Isidore thinks for a moment that Jos wants his throat cut. Consult the scene (in the same chapter) where Jos bargains with Becky for the horses: why is it that this scene strikes one as containing such profound demoralization and spiritual corruption that even Becky's murder of Jos for his insurance, at the end of the book, doesn't seem nearly so vicious?

17. Note that after Waterloo there is a great break in the design of the action and a time lapse of several years; definitive crises and reversals have occurred for the plot patterns so far; George is dead, Miss Crawley is dead and her fortune has been disposed of, Amelia has a child, Becky

and Rawdon are now on their own; a new series of plot relations is starting, new characters are to be introduced (the Southdown-Sheepshanks group, the Steyne group, Raggles, Briggs, etc.). Is there any relaxation of the dramatic energy of the novel because of the lapse and change? Why is it that the structure of the novel, so far, demands this broadening out of the time span and of the social perspective?

18. In what sense is young Sir Pitt—like Rawdon and George and Jos, but with a difference of inflection—a fitting scion of his class and an appropriate son of his father? Do his alliance (Chapter 33) with the Countess Southdown and Lady Jane, and his new attitude toward his aunt, Miss Crawley (though he had "held off all his life from cultivating Miss Crawley's friendship," lately he has begun to take "every becoming means" to "save her soul"), represent an ethical outlook similar to or different from the general ethos of the *Vanity Fair* world? In the Countess Southdown ("A mature spinster, and having but faint ideas of marriage, her love for the blacks occupied almost all her feelings"), what aspect is given to the humanitarian impulse?

19. In what sense is Becky's and Rawdon's mode of life on Curzon Street (see Chapter 37) symbolic of the general way of life represented in this book? Explain the attitude of Rebecca's servants and tradesmen as suggested here (Chapter 44):

I shame to say, she would not have got credit had they not believed her to be guilty. It was the sight of the Marquis of Steyne's carriage-lamps at her door, contemplated by Raggles, burning in the blackness of midnight, "that kep' him up," as he afterwards said . . .

Why is Becky hated by women, and why are her personal relationships almost wholly with men (cf. Chapter 35: "She had all the men on her side. She fought the women with indomitable courage . . .")? What is the function of the "moral sheep-dog," Briggs? Explain Becky's attitude toward her child: he "bored her"; "the mother's dislike increased to hatred . . ." (Chapter 54). What is the peculiar force of this image: the child is greatly impressed with the "wondrous bronze hand on the dressing-table, glistening all over with a hundred rings . . ." (Chapter 37)?

20. While staying at Queens Crawley (Chapter 41), Becky ruminates: "I think I could be a good woman if I had five thousand a year." Interpret

the word "good" here. How persuasive is the statement, in terms both of Becky's temperament and the whole structure of her world? It is said (Chapter 48) that "to be thought a respectable woman was Becky's aim in life"; and she accomplishes this by her presentation at court (in stolen lace and the pearls of an adulteress): how does this incident characterize the ethos of her world? What is the irony (in the same statement) in the phrase "to be thought" and in the word "respectable"? Much later, in her sojourn abroad as a "boarding-house queen," we are told (Chapter 54) that "her taste for disrespectability grew more and more remarkable" and "she became a perfect Bohemian ere long." What is the congruence, if any, between these opposed tastes for "respectability" and "disrespectability"? What, in the general nature of Becky's world, makes it possible that these two apparently opposite tastes could inhabit congenially the same person's psychology?

21. Define the symbolic value of Lord Steyne in the society depicted in the book—his symbolic value, for instance, as one of the "fathers." Elucidate the combined implications of his *petits appartements,* led to by a back door, one of them "fitted up all in ivory and white satin, another in ebony and black velvet" (Chapter 47), and his own description of his private life, when he tells Becky,

> "I daren't sleep in what they call my bedroom. The bed is like the baldaquin of St. Peter's, and the pictures frighten me. I have a little brass bed in a dressing-room; and a little hair mattress like an anchorite. I am an anchorite."

We are told that, for the "dark presentiment" (of insanity) that haunts him, he "knew of a remedy by which he could balk his enemy" (Chapter 48). What remedy?

22. In Chapter 59, Jos's return to London is described: his waistcoats, his splendid entertainments, his alarm under the glances of women—

> . . . it was chiefly from a dread lest they should make love to him that he avoided them, being averse to marriage altogether . . .

—his "native," his chests of mangoes, chutney, and curry powders, his "shawls for presents to people whom he didn't know as yet," and a typical day's food and drink—

. . . when he drove into town he was as full of wine, beer, meat, pickles, cherry-brandy, and tobacco as the steward's cabin of a steam-packet.

In terms of these details, redefine Jos's symbolic relationship with the world of this book.

23. In the last chapter, when Becky tells Amelia of George's infidelity—

"He never cared for you. He used to sneer about you to me, time after time; and made love to me the week after he married you."

—her immediate and obvious motivation is a "good-hearted" one: she wants to free Amelia from her obsession with George's image so that Amelia can find happiness with Dobbin; but beside this motivation, do you find any other—a motivation that is not "good-hearted" at all, but that is deeply consistent with Becky's past associations with Amelia?

24. Has there been any implicit preparation, in the development of Becky's character previously in the book, for her final shocking disposal of Jos? Is Becky, as a murderess, a moral anomaly in her world? The psychologist Karl Menninger, in *Man against Himself*, discriminates what he calls "acute suicide" and "chronic suicide"; perhaps we might also speak of "acute murder" and "chronic murder." In what sense is Becky's murder of Jos merely the "acute" form of an activity that is otherwise "chronic" throughout the world of *Vanity Fair*?

Wuthering Heights

1. A novelist can make any weather he chooses. What is the symbolic appropriateness of the atmospheric tumult signified by the adjective "wuthering"? One can imagine some rearrangement of plot which would have forced Lockwood to stay overnight at the Heights in calm weather; he might have sprained an ankle, for instance; but why would calm weather conditions have been deeply inconsistent with what happens during his overnight stay (see Chapter 3)?

2. There are only two animals in the story that have plot significance, namely, the pony over which Hindley and Heathcliff quarrel, and the bulldog at the Lintons'. For any plot need, all the other animals could have been left out. Why, then, is the Heights overrun with fierce dogs? (Note the names "Wolf" and "Gnasher," and that not only is Lockwood twice attacked by them, but "other dogs haunted other recesses.") What is the effect of such a notation as this (Chapter 2)?

> "Ah, your favourites are among these?" I continued, turning to an obscure cushion full of something like cats . . . Unluckily, it was a heap of dead rabbits.

The student may be interested in listing some of the metaphors involving references to animals throughout the book, and in differentiating and defining the variously expressive values of these metaphors in terms of the total context.

3. Already, as Lockwood finds noted in Catherine's diary (Chapter 3), Hindley was a domestic tyrant even before the death of his wife (" 'You forget you have a master here,' says the tyrant. 'I'll demolish the first who puts me out of temper!' "); and the novel itself starts with a picture of Heathcliff's uncontrolled tyranny. Can you find any *common ground* of expressiveness, that is, any connection at the symbolic level, between (a) the multiplied occasions of male tyranny, (b) the multiplied animal images, and (c) the violent storm, with which three figurations the book sets its tone?

4. In Chapter 1, a love affair of Lockwood's is briefly sketched; what contrast does it serve? Does that part of Lockwood's dream (Chapter 3) which concerns Jabes Branderham's sermon on 490 different sins ("odd transgressions that I never imagined previously") seem to have any functional significance? or the fact that the sermon is delivered in a chapel near a swamp "whose peaty moisture is said to answer all the purposes of embalming on the few corpses deposited there" (note that, in Chapter 16, it is said that Catherine's grave is almost buried under peat mold)? Suggest reasons, either "psychological" or symbolical or both, for the fact that Catherine appears in the dream as a child ("I've been a waif for twenty years!") rather than as an adult.

5. What difference, if any, would it have made to the story if Mr. Earnshaw had found the child Heathcliff in an orphan asylum, with an

implied ordinary parentage of some kind? How far can you go in interpreting Heathcliff as a victim of social neglect and oppression? In Chapter 7, where Catherine returns from the Lintons' and Heathcliff asks Nelly to "make him decent," he says, comparing himself with Edgar,

"I wish I had light hair and a fair skin, and was dressed and behaved as well, and had a chance of being as rich as he will be!"

What distortion of the symbolic construction of the story, and particularly of the "two children" figure, does Heathcliff's wish suggest? How is that distortion carried out in his son? What oblique significance (at the mythopoeic, archetypal level) is there in Nelly's remarks,

"You're fit for a prince in disguise . . . Were I in your place, I would frame high notions of my birth . . ."?

In view of the metamorphosis always potential in the "two children" figure, whereby the "dark" child might be made "golden," how psychologically damaging for Heathcliff's destiny is Hindley's brutality to him (in Chapter 7) and Edgar Linton's remark that his hair is like a "colt's mane" over his eyes, just after Nelly has "made him decent" for play with the other children?

6. Explain Heathcliff's delight in Hindley's degeneration, in Chapters 8 and 9. In a "realistic" novel of manners, the emotional extravagances described in Chapter 9 would no doubt strike the reader as false and crudely melodramatic (Hindley's "I want to kill some of you; I shall have no rest till I do!"; his forcing the carving knife between Nelly's teeth; his paternal piety toward his son—"As sure as I'm living, I'll break the brat's neck"; Heathcliff's impulse to smash Hareton's skull on the steps after he has accidentally rescued the child; Hindley's drinking to the damnation of his own soul). Explain why the context of this book provides for a "temporary suspension of disbelief" and validates such extravagances for the imagination.

7. We are told (Chapter 8) that Edgar Linton "wanted spirit in general"; and you will note that there are really only two extreme types of men in the book—the excessively violent man, like Hindley and Heathcliff,

and the epicene, milquetoast type, like Edgar Linton (and Lockwood). What does this fact suggest as to the conception of *virility* that the book holds? With which of the schismatic impulses that split the world of *Wuthering Heights* (the impulse toward civilized limitation and control, and the impulse toward limitless excess) does this conception of virility associate itself?

8. Interpret whatever implications you find in Catherine's dream of being thrown out of heaven (Chapter 9).

> ". . . heaven did not seem to be my home; and I broke my heart with weeping to come back to earth; and the angels were so angry that they flung me out into the middle of the heath on the top of Wuthering Heights; where I woke sobbing for joy . . ."

Do you find any implicit connection between her statement: "I've no more business to marry Edgar Linton than I have to be in heaven," and Heathcliff's description of the Lintons' drawing room (Chapter 6) which looked like "heaven" to the two children peering through the window? Interpret in terms of the mythological construction of the book what she says to Nelly about her feeling toward Heathcliff (Chapter 9).

> "If all else perished, and *he* remained, *I* should still continue to be; and if all else remained, and he were annihilated, the universe would turn to a mighty stranger: I should not seem a part of it."

In what sense is the following statement (in the same context)

> "I've dreamt in my life dreams that have . . . gone through and through me, like wine through water, and altered the colour of my mind . . ."

a succinct, though oblique, expression of the significance of this strange novel, and at the same time an expression of the part played by myth in human psychology?

9. Since, as we have said, a novelist can make any weather he chooses, why is there an unusually furious storm on the night when Catherine makes her decision to marry Edgar and Heathcliff disappears (Chapter 9)?

What ironic contribution to the sense of cross-purposes between rational and irrational motivations, theological and mythological determinations, is made by the following passage (Chapter 9)?

We thought a bolt had fallen in the middle of us; and Joseph swung on to his knees beseeching the Lord to remember the patriarchs Noah and Lot, and, as in former times, spare the righteous, though He smote the ungodly. I felt some sentiment that it must be a judgment on us also.

What in general would you say was contributed to the book by the continuous note of Joseph's Calvinistic piety? Would you explain Catherine's serious illness here by "natural" causes (her exposure to the storm on the night of Heathcliff's disappearance), or as neuroticism, or otherwise?

10. What is Heathcliff's motivation in returning (Chapter 10)? Viable conceptions of "sin" and "guilt" demand an at least implicit context of ethical values, and in one way or another produce (in a novel) illumination as to the ethical values that have been transgressed (in order to secure the point, the student may want to illustrate this briefly from the novels so far read). Would you say that the context of the present novel suggests the moral judgment of "guilty" upon Heathcliff's treatment of Hindley after his return? (Note, in Chapter 10, that Catherine says Hindley "can't be made morally worse than he is," and Joseph says that Hindley "gallops down t' broad road" while Heathcliff "flees afore to oppen t' pikes.")

11. What is Heathcliff's motivation in marrying Isabella? Consider the following references: Isabella is said (Chapter 10) to be "infantile" in manners, and to have taken "a sudden and irresistible attraction" toward Heathcliff; Catherine warns her that he is "an unreclaimed creature . . . an arid wilderness of furze and whinstone" and "a fierce, pitiless, wolfish man," who would crush her "like a sparrow's egg"; when Heathcliff first becomes aware of her infatuation, he stares at her "as one might do at a strange repulsive animal: a centipede . . ." and quite openly expresses his willingness to wrench her fingernails off her fingers; and (in Chapter 14) he comments to Nelly on Isabella's

"senseless incapability of discerning that I was in earnest when I gave her my opinion of her infatuation and herself . . . I never told her

394

a lie about it. She cannot accuse me of showing one bit of deceitful softness. The first thing she saw me do, on coming out of the Grange, was to hang up her little dog . . . But no brutality disgusted her: I suppose she has an innate admiration of it . . ."

In view of these references, would you say that the appalling brutality of his treatment of Isabella suggests the moral judgment of "guilty" upon him? What effect, in interpreting motivations here, have the specific images, metaphors, and comparisons in the passages quoted above? If one does not judge Heathcliff's action in terms of moral "evil," what significance or "meaning" can it possibly have? Does the conception of virility suggested in Question 7 illuminate "meaning" here?

12. In the scene in Chapter 10 between Heathcliff, Catherine, and Edgar, where Edgar is described as appearing "quite slender and youth-like" beside the strongly masculine figure of Heathcliff, and where he is rather peevishly reluctant to allow Catherine to welcome the guest; and in Chapter 11, where Edgar tries to have Heathcliff thrown out of the house by the servants, where are the reader's sympathies, and why? Granting the extraordinary egotism and sadism shown by both Heathcliff and Catherine to Edgar, what effect on our judgment of personalities and motivations have Heathcliff's epithets for Edgar— "this lamb of yours," and "the milk-blooded coward," and "the slavering, shivering thing you preferred to me!"—and Catherine's own expression of attitude toward her husband—"Your type is not a lamb, it's a suckling leveret," and "Heathcliff would as soon lift a finger at you as a king would march his army against a colony of mice"? Attempt to generalize more completely at this point the expressive value of the exceedingly numerous animal images of various kinds.

13. Since it is clear that, at the beginning (Chapter 11), Catherine develops her dangerous hysteria as a weapon with which to threaten Edgar into letting her have her own way in regard to Heathcliff, and then as a weapon of revenge ("If I cannot keep Heathcliff for my friend—if Edgar will be mean and jealous, I'll try to break their hearts by breaking my own"), why do we not look upon her performance with the contempt one would have for a purely egotistical, self-indulgent neurasthenic? If we should explain Catherine's psychology as "merely" that

of a neurotic, do you think she would have the stature for the imagination, the "universality," that she does?

14. Analyze carefully the scene of her illness in Chapter 12. What, at the symbolic level of reading, is the implication of Catherine's saying to Nelly, "I thought, though everybody hated and despised each other, they could not avoid loving me," and of the feeling of everyone, including the doctor, that her passions should be indulged and that she should not be "crossed"? What is the symbolic expressiveness of her "childish diversion" in pulling the feathers from the pillow; of Nelly's "Give over that baby-work!"; and of Catherine's reduction to a "wailing child" after Nelly has opened the window? In view of the earlier potentialities of Catherine's destiny (as the golden child in the mythopoeic "two children" figure), how would you interpret her hallucination of seeing *someone else's* face in the black press (the mirror), and her horror in realizing that it is *her own?* In her exclamation,

> "Myself!" she gasped, "and the clock is striking twelve! It's true, then! that's dreadful!"

what is "true" and "dreadful," and why does the clock strike twelve? Interpret, at the symbolical level, her illusion of being "enclosed in the oak-panelled bed at home" (note that her coffin also has a *panel* which Heathcliff bribes the sexton to remove); her comment,

> "and my heart ached with some great grief which, just waking, I could not recollect,"

and her feeling that for the past seven years she has been "an exile, and outcast." Is there any connection between this latter remark and her dream (Chapter 9) of being thrown out of heaven? When Nelly refuses to open the window a second time, saying, "I won't give you your death of cold," and Catherine answers, "You won't give me a chance of life, you mean," what ambiguity is there in the words "death" and "life"?

15. What expressive value, in connection with Catherine's ruined health and death longing, has the description of mild early spring weather at the beginning of Chapter 13 and Chapter 15? We have referred frequently to the *amorality* of Catherine and Heathcliff, and to the difficulty of framing a moral judgment upon their actions. In what way, then, does the terrible scene of recrimination of Chapter 15 contain a

moral assertion that is central to the book? [1] See the passage in which Heathcliff says,

> "*Why* did you despise me? *Why* did you betray your own heart, Cathy? . . . You deserve this. You have killed yourself. Yes, you may kiss me, and cry; and wring out my kisses and tears: they'll blight you—they'll damn you. You loved me—then what *right* had you to leave me? What right—answer me—for the poor fancy you felt for Linton? Because misery and degradation, and death, and nothing that God or Satan could inflict would have parted us, *you,* of your own will, did it. I have not broken your heart—*you* have broken it: and in breaking it, you have broken mine . . ."
>
> "Let me alone. Let me alone," sobbed Catherine. "If I have done wrong, I'm dying for it."

16. Nelly says of this last meeting of the two that it "made a strange and fearful picture," and that she did not feel as if she were "in the company of a creature of her own species"—with Catherine tearing out Heathcliff's hair by the handful, and Heathcliff foaming "like a mad dog." In what way does the general symbolic construction of the book validate the psychology of the scene, despite its excesses? How does it justify Heathcliff's un*lover*like expression of grief in the following outburst (Chapter 16)?

> "May she wake in torment! . . . Catherine Earnshaw, may you not rest as long as I am living! . . ."
>
> He dashed his head against the knotted trunk; and . . . howled, not like a man, but like a savage beast . . .

17. How would you evaluate aesthetically the violence piled upon violence in Chapter 17, as an excess totally out of proportion to motivating causes or as contexturally justified—Heathcliff's slitting up Hindley's arm and then trampling him on the floor, his throwing a knife at Isabella's head, her throwing another knife at him, while Hareton "was hanging a litter of puppies from a chair-back"? Would you be able to suggest any connection between this mounting insanity and the deaths

[1] Richard Chase's essay "The Brontës, or Myth Domesticated," in *Forms of Modern Fiction* (Minneapolis: University of Minnesota Press, 1948), emphasizes this important dramatic point.

that have now begun to multiply in the book (Catherine's, Hindley's, Isabella's, and shortly Edgar Linton's and young Linton's)?

18. What is the motivation of Heathcliff's treatment of Hareton (see Chapter 21)? What explains the sympathy between the two, despite Heathcliff's robbery and brutalization of the boy?

19. What is the symbolic expressiveness of the description of Penistone Crags at the beginning of Chapter 18—their goldenness (they are "bright long after it is evening"), Nelly's explanation that they are "bare masses of stone," where the frost comes early in winter and where snow remains in black hollows deep into the summer? In what way is the treatment of landscape and weather in this second section of the book—spring and summer days, blue sky, bright sun, larks singing, bees humming, heather scent in the air—associated with the new character groupings?

20. What is Heathcliff's motivation in demanding charge of his son, though he despises him? What is his motivation in planning the marriage of Cathy and Linton? Heathcliff's sadistic treatment of Linton would apparently offer a real occasion for moral condemnation. What specifically in the characterization of Linton, and generally in the structure of the book as a whole, makes such a judgment inappropriate or irrelevant?

21. What are the specific inflections of the "two children" figure in Cathy's treatment of Hareton at this point (she mocks his effort to learn his letters and cuts him with her whip when he attempts to apologize for rudeness), and in her attitude toward Linton ("Pretty Linton! I wish you were my brother"; ". . . she commenced stroking his curls, and kissing his cheek, and offering him tea in her saucer, like a baby"; and

"I'm certain Linton would recover quickly if he had me to look after him . . . And he'll soon do as I direct him, with some slight coaxing. He's a pretty little darling when he's good. I'd make such a pet of him, if he were mine.")?

In what way does the eventual evolution of the "two children" figure (Cathy's relationship with Hareton as described in Chapter 32) still preserve something of the psychology of the Cathy-Linton relationship? What radical change, however, does the final version of the figure (Cathy and Hareton) show in comparison with the first version (Catherine and Heathcliff)?

22. Considering Heathcliff as "the father," how would you associate him with the figures of "the father" that we have seen in our studies of Dickens and Thackeray? In what relationship, as "father," does Heathcliff stand to "the law"—as instanced in his demanding charge of his son, in his taking over Thrushcross Grange after Edgar's death and forcibly removing Cathy to the Heights, in his bribing the lawyer so that Edgar is prevented from changing his will, and in his immuring of Cathy while her father is dying and thus insuring her marriage to Linton (while Nelly impotently threatens him with the judgment of the law upon this "unlawful" act)? What version of "the father" do you find in the incident in Chapter 27 where Heathcliff slaps Cathy ferociously and says,

"I know how to chastise children, you see . . . I shall be your father, to-morrow—all the father you'll have in a few days . . ."?

Placing against this version of "the father" the picture of *the son* that we have in the scene on the heath (Chapter 27) where Linton drags himself along the ground and Cathy says, "Don't degrade yourself into an abject reptile—don't!", would you say there was any significant connection between the conception of "the father" here and the conception of virility as suggested in Question 7? When Heathcliff expresses his paternal feeling (Chapter 27) toward Linton and Cathy in the statement

"Had I been born where laws are less strict and tastes less dainty, I should treat myself to a slow vivisection of those two, as an evening's entertainment."

would you say that the sentiment was an outrage to psychology as well as an aesthetic outrage of melodrama, or that it was an expression of a pathological personality, or would you find it justifiable aesthetically? How does the statement associate itself with the multitude of animal images and metaphors in the book?

23. When Heathcliff tells Nelly, in Chapter 29, of having the sides of the coffins struck loose so that his and Catherine's corpses will blend, and describes to her what he had done on the night of Catherine's burial, Nelly says, "And if she had been dissolved into earth, or worse, what would you have dreamt of then?" and Heathcliff replies, "Of dissolv-

399

ing with her, and being more happy still!" What connection do you make between Heathcliff's necrophilism, as expressed here, and Catherine's statement, in Chapter 25, "I'm tired of being enclosed here. I'm wearying to escape into that glorious world, and to be always there: not seeing it dimly through tears, and yearning for it through the walls of an aching heart; but really with it, and in it"? In conjunction with Heathcliff's necrophilism, what significance do you find in Cathy's long lonely struggle with death in Chapter 30 (she says to Zillah: "You have left me so long to struggle against death alone, that I feel and see only death! I feel like death!")? Try to define the place and meaning of the theme of death in this novel. How would you express its connection with the theme of childhood?

24. Heathcliff is still a fairly young man and in good health, but what signs are there in Chapter 33 of a flagging of his energies and of the action of the "death wish"? How would you explain his manic aspect in Chapter 34? He looks "almost bright and cheerful . . . *very much* excited, and wild and glad," after a nightwalking, with "a strange, joyful glitter" in his eyes, and Nelly speaks later of

the same unnatural—it was unnatural—appearance of joy under his black brows; the same bloodless hue, and his teeth visible, now and then, in a kind of smile; his frame shivering, not as one shivers with chill or weakness, but as a tight-stretched cord vibrates—a strong thrilling, rather than trembling . .

What does he mean by "hardly three feet" in the following?

"Last night I was on the threshold of hell. To-day, I am within sight of my heaven. I have my eyes on it: hardly three feet to sever me!"

What special interpretations has the word "heaven" gone through in the book?

25. Chapter 34 starts with April weather, "sweet and warm," green grass, sun, apple trees in bloom; why, then, is there a hard storm on the night of Heathcliff's death? A peasant says he has seen Catherine and Heathcliff "on every rainy night" since Heathcliff's death; and Nelly, on a "dark evening, threatening thunder," meets a little boy who has seen them: why the accompaniment of darkness and rain? Is this mere arbitrary "ghostly" atmosphere?

26. One might imagine that, later (that is, as the book projects his future), Hareton would strike the mean of "normal" manhood, as contrasted with the extreme types that the book presents; but the book isn't structurally interested in pursuing him so far—that is, it doesn't seem to be interested in presenting any psychologically and ethically approved "norm" of the social male—and we are left with Hareton as still a child, culturally speaking, and Cathy's docile pupil, exchanging kisses for lessons. Referring to Question 7, what would you say that the comparison of male types there suggests as a reason, at the symbolic level, for the fact that Hareton alone mourns Heathcliff's death (Chapter 34)?

". . . poor Hareton, *the most wronged*, was the only one who really suffered much. He sat by the corpse all night, weeping in bitter earnest. He pressed its hand, and kissed the sarcastic savage face that every one else shrank from contemplating . . ."

Has the word "wronged" an ambiguous meaning here?

27. The convention of narration ("point of view") in this novel necessitates an obviously crude involvement whereby Lockwood quotes Nelly who quotes Heathcliff who quotes Catherine, or Lockwood quotes Nelly who quotes Isabella who quotes Joseph, or Lockwood quotes Nelly who quotes Zillah who quotes Cathy, and so forth. To what extent, on first reading, are you aware of this quite awkward manipulation of the fictional illusion? What difference would it have made to the story if Emily Brontë had tried to write it as omniscient author? If you think that the novel could not, with successful technique, have been written by an "omniscient author," what would be your reasons?

Adam Bede

1. Frame an evaluative comparison between the convention of narration ("point of view") adopted in this book, that in *Vanity Fair,* and that in *Wuthering Heights.* What specific damage does the chosen conven-

tion of narration do to the fictional illusion in the following passage (Chapter 5) where the rector is introduced? The author says,

> Let me take you into that dining-room, and show you the Reverend Adolphus Irwine . . . We will enter very softly, and stand still in the open doorway, without awaking the glossy brown setter who is stretched across the hearth . . .

What specific damage to illusion is offered by the following (from Chapter 6), from the beginning of the description of Hall Farm?

> Yes, the house must be inhabited, and we will see by whom; for imagination is a licensed trespasser: it has no fear of dogs, but may climb over walls and peep in at windows with impunity. Put your face to one of the glass panes in the right-hand window: what do you see? . . .

Do you feel that the convention of the "omniscient author" is actually not the right one for this book, or do you feel that it is the only adequate one for the materials, but that George Eliot has allowed it too much license? Glance over the first four or five pages of Chapter 15, where Hetty is indulging her fantasy before the mirror: point out specific places where the "omniscient" point of view allows the author to load the dice against Hetty in such a way that we become uncomfortably conscious that we are not being given the opportunity to make up our own minds but are having a *parti pris* forced on us. Do you think that these awkwardnesses that are indulged by the chosen convention of narration are serious defects in the structure of the book, or that they are compensated by a generally vivid and convincing "illusion of life"?

2. One critic says of George Eliot that

> she seeks, in her morality, the positive foundations of natural law, a kind of Fate whose measures are as fundamental as the changes of the seasons in nature.[1]

He compares her then with Hardy.

[1] V. S. Pritchett, *The Living Novel* (New York: Reynal & Hitchcock, 1947), p. 98.

Hardy alone is her nearest parallel, but he differed from her in conceiving a fate outside the will of man and indifferent to him.[2]

To clarify this comparison, we might substitute for the word "positive" (in the phrase "the positive foundations of natural law") the words "definite" and "concrete," but especially the word "knowable," for thus we more clearly discriminate the boundaries of George Eliot's conception from any conception of "natural law" that places it outside the will of man and in the "unknowable." Tentatively accepting these terms for what value they may have for us in our attempt to define the world of *Adam Bede,* let us look at an episode rather far along in the book, toward the end of Chapter 16, where Arthur, having gone to Mr. Irwine to confess his ambiguous situation with Hetty, finds himself at the critical moment unable to say anything about it. His psychology is analyzed thus:

Was there a motive at work under this strange reluctance of Arthur's which had a sort of backstairs influence, not admitted to himself? Our mental business is carried on much in the same way as the business of the State: a great deal of hard work is done by agents who are not acknowledged. In a piece of machinery, too, I believe there is often a small unnoticeable wheel which has a great deal to do with the motion of the large obvious ones. Possibly there was some such unrecognised agent secretly busy in Arthur's mind at this moment—possibly it was the fear lest he might hereafter find the fact of having made a confession to the Rector a serious annoyance, in case he should *not* be able quite to carry out his good resolutions? I dare not assert that it was not so. The human soul is a very complex thing.

As events develop, what significance has this incident? What relationship would you say it had to the "natural law" or "fate" whose origin and germination lie in individual moral will?

3. Again, before returning to earlier matters, let us speak of the conversation between Adam and Arthur (Chapter 28) that takes place after they fight in the grove. Adam apologizes, believing that he has judged Arthur too harshly and that perhaps the implications of what he has seen taking place between Arthur and Hetty are not as serious and condemnable as he had supposed. But as for Arthur,

[2] *Ibid.,* p. 96.

The native impulse to give truth in return for truth, to meet trust with frank confession, must be suppressed, and duty was become a question of tactics. His deed was reacting upon him—was already governing him tyrannously, and forcing him into a course that jarred with his habitual feelings. The only aim that seemed admissible to him now was to deceive Adam to the utmost: to make Adam think better of him than he deserved. And when he heard the words of honest retractation . . . he was obliged to rejoice in the remains of ignorant confidence it implied. He did not answer immediately, for he had to be judicious, and not truthful.

What does the passage imply as to "the positive foundations of natural law"? In what sense is "fate" working in Arthur at the moment? Is it a "fate" outside his will or in the control of his will? It is said here that "duty was become a question of tactics"; what has occurred to make duty a question of tactics at this time?

4. Referring back to the passage quoted in Question 2, where submerged motives are suggested for Arthur's unwillingness to make his confession to Mr. Irwine, would you say that Arthur was then a quite helpless victim of his own "subconscious" and therefore not truly a knowing and responsible moral agent? If so, and if events since that time have in some degree been the result of his inability to make the confession, how can he be called a responsible moral agent when he decides to lie to Adam as to the extent of his affair with Hetty? Judging from Arthur's situation in our view of it so far, would you say that we had in the book a "tragedy of circumstance," where individuals are caught in circumstances beyond their control, or a "tragedy of character," where the tragedy evolves out of, is created by, personal character?

5. Turning back now to the earlier chapters, in what sense would you say that we find the "positive foundations of natural law" implied in the more simply descriptive passages—those parts of Chapters 6 and 7 that describe Hall Farm and the dairy, the description in Chapter 14 of the Poyser household of an evening, Chapter 18 describing the Poysers on their way to church and the funeral of Thias Bede, and Chapter 21 describing Bartle Massy?

6. Given the fact that the view of life which this book offers is a *moral* view, what justification would you suggest for George Eliot's confining that view largely to the lives of simple people, unassuming people, poor people, people without any very complex sensibility or unusual

moral capacity? Do you find that the bits describing Lisbeth Bede— for instance, her tireless complaints and her reaction to Dinah's visit in Chapter 10, or her superstitious feeling that the burial service is "doing her husband good" (Chapter 18), or the scene in Chapter 51 where she sits watching Adam reading his Bible—have any significance for the moral foundations of "natural law" as this book explores those foundations?

7. What justification would you suggest for the fact that the chief tragic character in the book (the person chiefly to suffer the effects of "natural law") is Hetty, a morally and intellectually mediocre person? How much value does the book implicitly place on however simple or ignorant or mediocre a human life?

8. Dinah Morris and Mr. Irwine are representatives of the religious calling, and our next four questions will refer to the structural significance of these two characters. In the chapter on "The Preaching" (Chapter 2), what are the specific effects of Dinah's sermon, for instance on Wiry Ben, Sandy Jim, and Bessy Cranage? Does the effect of the sermon seem on the whole profound or incidental? Would you say that Dinah's place in the book generally is significant of the importance of the specifically *religious* attitude in laying the foundations of morality? Why is Dinah more effective among the urban proletariat of Stonyshire than among the peasants and yeoman class of the softer Loamshire country? We are made aware, in Chapter 2, of the neighborhood of the "grim outskirts" of Stonyshire, and again in Chapters 35, 36, and 37, when Hetty makes her "journey in despair." Is there a sense in which that stony country, where people are in special need of the word of the spirit, has a symbolical reflection in the tragic situation of Hetty, who belongs to the soft country?

9. As contrasted with Dinah's evangelical fervor and active earnestness of faith, Mr. Irwine, representing the Established Church, is lax in his divinity, with "no enthusiasm, no self-scourging sense of duty," and content to do the nominal duties of a clergyman without "fussing about trifles" such as Bessy Cranage's earrings or Will Maskery's tippling. Is Mr. Irwine treated sympathetically or unsympathetically? Why? Do you find any indication in Chapter 16, where Arthur comes to confess to him and then changes his mind, that Mr. Irwine's lack of spiritual intensity has anything to do with Arthur's failure—for instance, in the following?

> If there had been anything special on Arthur's mind . . . it was clear he was not inclined to enter into details, and Mr. Irwine was too delicate to imply even a friendly curiosity. He perceived a change of subject would be welcome, and said, . . .

What are the indications in Chapter 39 that Mr. Irwine perceives a fault in himself in this case? Glancing again at Chapter 16, where the rector is seen at breakfast in his study as Arthur enters, would you say that there was anything in the comfort and grace of the setting itself such as to inhibit exposure of those lonelier and stonier parts of the soul which are causing Arthur anxiety? In this "realistic" novel, are Stonyshire and Loamshire only physical places located by a map?

10. Compare now with Arthur's unsuccessful attempt to confess, the scene of Dinah's appeal for Hetty's confidence, in Chapter 15. Dinah's approach is direct and unequivocal, whereas Mr. Irwine "was too delicate to imply even a friendly curiosity"; and yet Dinah is quite as ineffectual with Hetty as Mr. Irwine is with Arthur. In the tragedy of the book, which is the more responsible moral agent, Hetty or Arthur? Which then is the more important failure of the spiritual adviser, Dinah's failure or Mr. Irwine's?

11. Consider now the scene between Hetty and Dinah in the prison (Chapter 45). Dinah cannot save Hetty from the hangman, and Hetty is not a character who is capable of spiritual "illumination" or "revelation." But what actual spiritual efficacy does Dinah have in this scene? In what sense, however meager, is she able to relieve Hetty's situation? On the whole, would you say that the comparisons made in the last few questions (8, 9, 10, and 11) indicated that the view of life contained in this book had at its center the convictions of a specifically religious, supernaturalistic attitude? In the vision of life that the book presents, what place, positive or negative, would you say religion occupied in relation to morality and to the "foundations of natural law"?

12. The plot of *Adam Bede* confessedly owes something to that of *The Heart of Mid-Lothian*. In our discussion of *The Heart of Mid-Lothian*, we suggested that the "sin" for which Effie and George were so exhaustively punished was sexual indulgence outside of marriage. The same motif is paralleled in *Adam Bede;* but would you say that the emphasis in this book is actually and narrowly on the "sin" of sexual indulgence, or would you say that Hetty's and Arthur's transgression had a wider

meaning? If a wider meaning, what? What has the difference in social class between Arthur and Hetty to do with it? What has the patient and massive building up of the community life, in all its humble routines, to do with the wider meaning of Hetty's and Arthur's transgression? What implications as to a wider meaning has the necessary secrecy of the affair? On how many lives, altogether, does the affair rebound? How much destruction does it involve?

13. Victorian novelists, before Hardy, tend to be extremely reticent about sex, often ridiculously so, and George Eliot has been criticized for the same overdelicacy in *Adam Bede:* it has been said, for instance, that the pink silk scarf that Arthur stuffs into the wastebasket in Chapter 28 is the only concrete evidence that is given of the sexual relationship between Arthur and Hetty. Consider, however, the significance of the earrings: how is the motif of the earrings adumbrated at the end of Dinah's sermon in Chapter 2? In what way is the same motif picked up again in Chapter 15? What extension of significance does it receive in Chapter 22 when Hetty is preparing for the ball? Do you think that the symbolism of the earrings is a quite sufficient suggestion of Hetty's relationship with Arthur, or do you feel that the handling of this relationship suffers from Victorian overreticence? How would you defend the statement that the total structure of the book not only makes is unnecessary that the sexual nature of the relationship should be explicated more fully, but that if it had been further explicated the wider and tragic meaning of Hetty's and Arthur's disruption of patiently evolved values would have been blurred or lost?

14. In all tragedy, the suffering of the tragic character is out of proportion to his deed; this disproportion is of the essence of the tragic feeling and the tragic view. So, also, poor Hetty's punishment is out of proportion to her deed. Nevertheless, tragedy gives us the feeling of the inevitability of this disproportion, its naturalness in the frame of things. Why is it that we feel Hetty's punishment to be, in this way, an operation of natural law, whereas we felt the unnaturalness, gratuitousness, and arbitrariness of the punishment Scott inflicted on Effie Deans and George Staunton?

15. Given the dominant dramatic contrast in the book, on which its chief significance rests—on the one hand, the disciplined and unassuming community life, with its humble graciousness and its secure place for the weaker souls as well as its gratifications for the stronger ones, and

on the other hand, the momentary frivolity represented in Arthur's and Hetty's relationship, with its vast and irreparable destructiveness —suggest a reason for the fact that Chapter 14, describing the homely life in the Poyser household, is placed between the chapter describing Arthur's first meeting with Hetty in the wood (Chapter 13) and a chapter describing Hetty's midnight ritual of self-admiration (Chapter 15). How would you account structurally for the juxtaposition of Chapters 16 and 17, the one having to do with Arthur's failure to confess to Mr. Irwine, the other having to do with Thias Bede's funeral, and both having the common element of spiritual need though the one deals with literate and sophisticated people while the other deals with unsophisticated and illiterate people? Suggest a structural reason for the very lengthy development, through Chapters 22, 23, and 24, of the celebrations for Arthur's birthday, the birthday speeches, the promotion of Adam, Arthur's pleasure in the respect of his tenants, the various expressions of the general hope and trust.

16. By her monumental building up of the community life, detail by detail, George Eliot gives us a whole view: judging from the following two passages, how much or what specific parts of the whole—that is, speaking not of events as such (or "plot") but of moral significance—does Arthur leave out from his own measurement of things? For instance, when he says to himself, after the fight in the grove (Chapter 29),

> It was an unfortunate business altogether, but there was no use in making it worse than it was, by imaginary exaggerations and forebodings of evil that might never come . . . Hetty might have had the trouble in some other way if not in this. And perhaps hereafter he might be able to do a great deal for her, and make up to her for all the tears . . . She would owe the advantage of his care for her in future years to the sorrow she had incurred now. *So* good comes out of evil.

And again, his thoughts on his return (Chapter 54),

> Nay, he would do a great deal more for Adam than he should otherwise have done, when he came into the estate; Hetty's husband had a special claim on him—Hetty herself should feel that any pain she had suffered through Arthur in the past, was compensated to her a

hundredfold. For really she could not have felt much, since she had so soon made up her mind to marry Adam.

Consider now the following passage, from Chapter 58. It is the day after Hetty's reprieve from the gallows, and Arthur and Adam again talk in the wood. Arthur says that no one else's life should be disturbed, for he is going to take all punishment on himself, by voluntary exile into the army, thus giving up his own "most cherished hopes." But in Arthur's words

Adam thought he perceived . . . that notion of compensation for irretrievable wrong, that self-soothing attempt to make evil bear the same fruits as good, which most of all roused his indignation . . .

and he says, "There's a sort of damage, sir, that can't be made up for." How much of the significance of the book is contained in these last statements? Would you say that, as the denouement is handled, with Hetty's reprieve, her transportation to America and death there, Arthur's years of exile and ill-health, and the marriage of Dinah and Adam, there is nevertheless an effort at the end of the book to commensurate the good and the evil? Does the book's "happy ending" leave you with the sense that Hetty's suffering has been "paid for"? Or does it leave you with a sense of structural mismanagement?

The Egoist

1. In his "Prelude," Meredith says that the "realistic method," with its "conscientious transcription of all the visible" and its "repetition of all the audible," tends to "obscure the glass it holds to mankind, rendering us inexact in the recognition of our individual countenances." Why should the "realistic method" (as Meredith conceives the realistic method) obscure our "recognition of our individual countenances"? Running over in your mind the various possible interpretations of the word "realism" which our studies may have suggested to you, would

you say that Meredith is pleading for an *unrealistic* representation of mankind or that he is pleading for a realism of a special kind? What kind? What "real" elements in the nature of man does he want to see selected for representation? What other elements does he believe should be minimized in the representation, and why? When he says,

Being a spirit [Comedy] hunts the spirit in men: vision and ardor constitute his merit; he has not a thought of persuading you to believe in him . . .

he surely does not mean by the last clause that comedy is either trifling or false, but what, then, does he mean?

2. We shall quote here two passages from Ramon Fernandez' essay on Meredith, for later reference in these questions.

To live, for Meredith, is first to affirm oneself absolutely, but it is also and essentially to be estimated, judged, and situated . . . Hence the importance of the "Comic Spirit" in [his] work. It may be said that a man is comic in so far as he does not perceive his place in the human hierarchy, believes he is the centre of the world . . .[1]

[Meredith] made intelligibility the condition of the full blooming of the vital instinct . . . [He] convinces us that the exercise of intelligence is indispensable, not only for the full comprehension, but also for the perfect *realization* of life, that one lives more intensely and better in proportion to one's being more lucid . . . [Thought] must be made to participate as a necessary agent in the creation of life.[2]

In what way is the subject matter of *The Egoist* particularly suitable for treatment under the aspects suggested by these passages? Generally, where do you find in the book the need for absolute self-affirmation as a condition of life? Where do you find the need for estimation, judgment, situation? Where do you find the necessity of thought as an agent in the creation of life? Would you be able to apply the same passages to Jane Austen's *Pride and Prejudice?*

3. How does Willoughby sin against the Comic Spirit in Chapter 1, when he cuts Lieutenant Patterne and says, "I'll send him a check"? Can you apply either of the passages from Fernandez to this incident? With re-

1 In *Messages* (New York: Harcourt, Brace & Company, Inc., 1927), pp. 163–164.
2 *Ibid.*, pp. 165–167.

spect to Willoughby's relationship with Constantia Durham (see Chapter 3), do you find any suggestion of the *suicidal* effect of this incident? Since the book has largely to do with Willoughby's relationship with Clara, why is the situation with Constantia in the book at all? It is said in Chapter 3 (with regard to Constantia's flight with Captain Oxford) that Willoughby was "quaintly incapable of a jealousy of individuals . . . His enemy was the world, the mass . . ." How does this idiosyncrasy of Willoughby's show him, *in the terms given by Fernandez,* as a comic character? How is it suicidal in this particular instance?

4. In what way is the following passage, from Chapter 3, typical of Meredith's prose manner?

> Rumor went the round that he intended to give Laetitia to Vernon for good, when he could decide to take Miss Durham to himself; his generosity was famous; but that decision, though the rope was in the form of a knot, seemed reluctant for the conclusive close haul; it preferred the state of slackness . . .

And the following, from Chapter 4, when he meets Laetitia after his return from America?

> The anxious question permitted him to read deeply in her eyes. He found the man he sought there, squeezed him passionately . . .

And the following?

> . . . she quietly gave a wrench to the neck of the young hope in her breast.

5. In Willoughby's identification, in Chapter 5, of Clara with the "essentially feminine"—

> . . . his original conclusion that she was essentially feminine, in other words, a parasite and a chalice, Clara's conduct confirmed from day to day. He began to instruct her in the knowledge of himself without reserve, and she, as she grew less timid with him, became more reflective.

—how does he sin against the Comic Spirit? against the necessity of self-affirmation? against the exercise of intelligence as an agent in the creation of life? It is said here that, the more he "instructed" her in himself, the more "reflective" Clara became: in what way is this a hint of the working of the Comic Spirit, and a hint also of Willoughby's suicidal tendency? Willoughby fancies himself as a thinker: what does he think of other people's thinking? Interpret his sin against the Comic Spirit in the following (Chapter 14):

He was of a vast embrace; and do not exclaim, in covetousness—for well he knew that even under Moslem law he could not have them all —but as the enamored custodian of the sex's purity, that blushes at such big spots as lovers and husbands; and it was unbearable to see it sacrificed for others. Without their purity what are they?—what are fruiterer's plums?—unsalable. Oh, for the bloom on them!

6. In Chapter 6, and again in Chapter 7, Willoughby expresses his dislike of poetry. Poetry, he says, is an artifice and a profession; he stands for "sincerity." And in Chapter 31 he tells Laetitia,

"I feel too intensely for poetry. By the nature of it, poetry can not be sincere. I will have sincerity."

Interpret Willoughby's cult of sincerity. Why are poetry and sincerity, in this sense, irreconcilable? In Chapters 6 and 7 he prescribes a "practicable poetry" for Clara: what is it? What has "the world" to do with this poetry? In Chapter 8 Clara consults Vernon on "the world": how do Vernon and Willoughby differ in their attitudes toward the world? Near the beginning of Chapter 6, mention is made of Clara's egoism.

She would not burn the world for him; she would not, though a purer poetry is little imaginable, reduce herself to ashes, or incense, or essence, in honor of him, and so, by love's transmutation, literally be the man she was to marry. She preferred to be herself, with the egoism of women. She said it; she said: "I must be myself to be of any value to you, Willoughby."

What is the difference between Clara's egoism and Willoughby's egoism?

7. As explicated in Chapter 9, what is his attitude toward Crossjay's education and future? How is it consistent with his attitude toward Vernon and Vernon's scholarship, as shown in Chapter 10? How is it

consistent with his plans for Vernon and Laetitia? Explain his need for keeping Vernon and Laetitia around. How do his attitudes toward Clara, Crossjay, Vernon, and Laetitia severally illustrate the description of egoistic felicity at the beginning of Chapter 14: "Possession without obligation to the object possessed"?

8. Aside from his place in the plot, what symbolic value would you say the child Crossjay had—for instance as we see him racing with Clara in Chapter 12? In the same chapter, Clara makes a preliminary effort to get help from Vernon, but he refuses to give her any help. Referring back to the second quotation from Fernandez in Question 2, why, would you say, does Vernon refuse to help her?

9. In Chapter 13, she starts an active campaign for freedom by trying to convince Willoughby that it is Laetitia he should marry because of the latter's "unbounded devotion" to him; what interpretation does he put upon her reference to Laetitia's love, and how does he use that interpretation as a means of frustrating her effort toward freedom (see also Chapter 15)? At the beginning of Chapter 21, we are told that she is appalled at the "false course she had taken through sophistical cowardice"; why, would you say, are trials and errors of this kind necessary to a full picture of Clara's development? In the following passage from Chapter 15,

> "You can not be released. We are united. Recognize it; united. There is no possibility of releasing a wife!"
> "Not if she ran—"
> This was too direct to be histrionically misunderstood. He had driven her to the extremity of more distinctly imagining the circumstance she had cited . . .

where do you find the note of the egoist's suicidal tendency, and how is it associated with the activation of imaginative thought in Clara? When she says, "Not if she ran—" do you find a resonance of the scene with the child in Chapter 12? How does "Not if she ran—" adumbrate a later crisis in the story, and how does the awakening of Clara's imagination at this point lay grounds for the later event?

10. When Clara tells Willoughby, in Chapter 13,

> "I can not idolize. I see faults; I see them daily . . . Your pride would not bear them spoken of, least of all by your wife."

what aspect of the final denouement between Willoughby and Laetitia (in Chapter 49) are adumbrated? In Chapter 16, where Clara talks with Laetitia and, in an effort to show Laetitia why it is she who is the most suitable wife for Willoughby, says,

> ". . . men who are Egoists have *good* women for their victims; women on whose devoted constancy they feed; they drink it like blood . . ."

why does Laetitia say that Clara has a "dreadful power" to express ideas? What is the actual effect of the conversation upon Laetitia, and how does this effect contribute one more impulse to Willoughby's destruction?

11. What is the significance of the breaking of the porcelain vase in Chapter 17? Does it seem to you that this symbol has a quite spontaneous and integral, or a somewhat arbitrary association with the context? Consider the description of the double-blossom wild-cherry tree at the end of Chapter 11; seeing Vernon asleep under the tree, Clara has the impression that "he must be good": does it seem to you that the description of the tree—excellent in itself—has an integral symbolic relation to total context or that the relation is to some extent arbitrary and superimposed? Now consider the description in Chapter 18, of Clara as a silver birch and then as a yacht: do you find the description in any degree overdeveloped for its own sake and at the expense of integral function? Decide the same question with regard to the description of the rain in Chapter 26.

12. Now let us reconsider some of the same passages (Chapters 18 and 26) from another point of view. We shall quote them below for immediate reference.

> . . . she wore a dress cunning to embrace the shape and flutter loose about it, in the spirit of a summer's day . . . See the silver birch in a breeze; here it swells, there it scatters, and it is puffed to a round, and it streams like a pennon, and now gives the glimpse and shine of the white stem's line within, now hurries over it, denying that it was visible, with a chatter along the sweeping folds . . . These hues of red rose and pale green ruffled and pouted in the billowy white of the dress ballooning and valleying softly, like a yacht before the sail bends low; but she walked not like one blown against; resembling

rather the day of the south-west driving the clouds, gallantly firm in commotion . . .

South-western rain-clouds, too, are never long sullen: they infold and will have the earth in a good strong glut of the kissing overflow; then, as a hawk with feathers on his beak of the bird in his claw lifts head, they rise and take veiled feature in long climbing watery lines: at any moment they may break the veil and show soft upper cloud, show sun on it, show sky, green near the verge they spring from, of the green of grass in early dew . . . it may mean fair smiling for awhile, or be the lightest interlude; but the water lines, and the drifting, the chasing, the upsoaring, all in a shadowy fingering of form, and the animation of the leaves of the trees pointing them on, the bending of the tree-tops, the snapping of branches, and the hurrahings of the stubborn hedge at wrestle with the flaws, yielding but a leaf at most, and that on a fling, make a glory of contest and wildness . . .

If you should be asked to fix on some one single quality that chiefly is evoked by both passages, what quality would you say it was? In what specific kinds of words is that quality made most evident? in what specific images? in what strong idiosyncrasy of the syntax? With what aspect of Meredith's "view of life," as represented in *The Egoist* as a whole, is this quality most closely associated?

13. In Chapter 28, as she returns from the station, it is said that Clara finds her own motivations incomprehensible, and yet

She had acted of her free will; that she could say. Vernon had not induced her to remain; assuredly her present companion had not; and her whole heart was for flight; yet she was driving back to the Hall . . .

What reason would you give for her decision to return? In the following statement, what suggestion do you find of Meredith's view of the processes by which the civilized individual is developed?

She could have accused Vernon of a treacherous cunning for imposing it on her free will to decide her fate.

14. Explain the fact that Willoughby is jealous of De Craye but not of Vernon. Noting that he was "quaintly incapable of a jealousy of in-

dividuals," his enemy being "the world, the mass," what is there in the personality of De Craye that represents, to his jealous eye, "the world," and what is there in the personality of Vernon that blinds him to his real, his individual, rival? Explain Willoughby's thirst for Clara's misery (Chapter 29).

> . . . he had an infinite thirst for her misery, that he might ease his heart of charitable love . . . An illness, fever, fire, runaway horses, personal disfigurement, a laming, were sufficient. And then . . . to lead the limping thing to the altar, if she insisted.

In what way is such a sentence as the following typical of Meredith's prose manner? "It was his burning wish to strain her in his arms to a flatness provoking his compassion."

15. With the whole house, down to the maid Barclay, in conspiracy against him, why is he unable to confide in anyone, least of all in Vernon? In what way is the position he has got himself into—the position of being able to have no confidant of his agony—significant of his sins against "the spirit born of our united social intelligence . . . the comic spirit"? How is it significant of his failure, as Fernandez puts it, to allow himself to "be estimated, judged, and situated"?

16. Explain his need for *pathos* with Laetitia (Chapter 31): why, as the character of the egoist is described, should his need be, not to confide, but to be pathetic? In the following piece of dialogue with Laetitia,

> "I do not forgive; I am at heart serious and I can not forgive—there is no possible reconciliation, there can be only an ostensible truce, between the two hostile powers dividing this world."
> She glanced at him quickly.
> "Good and evil!" he said.

how does he sin against the Comic Spirit? What makes his metaphysics here ridiculous? At the end of this interview, Laetitia weeps; how does Willoughby interpret her weeping? And how does it actually signify a miscarriage of his pathos?

17. In Chapter 38, when he has definitely decided to cast Clara off and to take Laetitia, why does he start his program by telling Clara of Vernon's previous marriage? In the scene of his proposal to Laetitia (Chapter 40), he tells her,

"To love like Laetitia Dale, was a current phrase. You were an example, a light to women; no one was your match for devotion. You were a precious cameo, still gazing. And I was the object. You loved me. You loved me, you belonged to me, you were mine, my possession, my jewel . . ."

and she answers: "Do you insist on shaming me through and through, Sir Willoughby?" What, in Laetitia's response, reverberates the conversation with Clara which we referred to in Question 10? What enlightenment, as to her own position, had Laetitia received then? How, in Laetitia's case, does the excitement of stirred intelligence (her sight of herself "estimated, judged, and situated") reflect Meredith's general view of the creative processes of life, and how does it mark the suicidal path of the egoist himself? In what devious ways are Mrs. Mountstuart and the other ladies of the county added to Willoughby's secret scorners and despoilers?

18. What ironic miscarriage of intent is there in Willoughby's generosity in handing Clara and Vernon over to each other? Why does he, in Chapter 47, encourage De Craye's illusion that he is to be the happy man? Why does he exult in toppling over that illusion in the final chapter? In what way does the scene in Chapter 49, where Laetitia wins her concessions in the presence of the aunts, provide the perfect and inevitable denouement?

19. If we were to seek in modern history a supreme "egoist" in whom we could see Willoughby's characteristics exemplified with all the emphasis of psychological and moral and social seriousness of effect, we might find that figure in Hitler. From a certain point of view, Hitler was a "comic" figure (providing subject matter, for instance, for one of Chaplin's films). He sinned against the Comic Spirit quite in Meredith's sense—by "failing to perceive his place in the human hierarchy," by attempting to suppress intelligence in others, by denying the function of thought in human creativity and well-being. But Hitler's success, during his flourishing period, was due to the *response* he found in the souls of millions of others—and not only in the German people but also in other peoples,—who were little "Hitlers" in some part of their beings, however submerged, and needing only Hitler's call to bring forth into action that submerged quality. We have said several times that "comedy is serious"—meaning the kind of comedy that appeals to stable and permanent elements in our intelli-

gence and our morality. The case of Hitler—considered as a comic figure of the "egoist" in Meredith's sense—illustrates that seriousness. But the seriousness of the "case of Hitler" lay in the response which this personality evoked in the souls of others. Do you find in Willoughby's case—murderously destructive as Willoughby's potential is in his confined field of action—any real identity between Willoughby and other characters in the novel? Is there, in the over-all psychology of any of the other characters, a tangible "Willoughby"? Is he an *inner* spiritual threat to the others—something to which they themselves give birth—or is he only an external monster like the dragons and giants of fairy tales? Would you say, finally, that Meredith's *The Egoist* is a novel with mature and serious insights into the human condition?

Tess of the D'Urbervilles

1. If you reduce this novel to its rudimentary plot elements, what traditional popular story formula does it exhibit? One way that Hardy makes this simple popular story stuff a strength rather than a weakness is to stitch into it other traditional motifs of folk literature, that enrich the texture of the tale, and that tend to give it the deep-lying authority of our own almost unconscious backgrounds of fairy tale and legend heard in childhood. For instance, how is the folk-motif of the "highborn heroine in disguise" (found in many fairy tales and romances) illustrated early in the book? What special use does Hardy make of it for his psychological and spiritual characterization of Tess herself? Note that when the parson and John Durbeyfield speak of the grand lineage, it is in terms of vaults, coffins, and the dead (John: "There's not a man in the county of Wessex that's got grander and nobler skellingtons in his family than I." And: "I've got a great family vault at Kingsbere, and knighted forefathers in lead coffins there!"). Is there, in this kind of reference, any connotation for the way in which the motif of the "highborn heroine in disguise" is carried out

in the book? What tie-up does it have with the refuge which the Durbeyfield family finds in Chapter 52?

2. Define specifically the symbolic reverberations in the fact that Clare first sees Tess at a celebration of an ancient fertility rite that has lost its meaning. Though we see the "folk" in a process of transition, when much has been forgotten and insecurity has increased, nevertheless the folk background of ancient mores and patterns of thought and behavior is deeply inlaid in the book: against this background, what specific thematic significance has the description of Clare in Chapter 2 (he is "of a superior class"; there is something "uncribbed, uncabined" in his aspect; he appears to be a "desultory, tentative student of something and everything"; etc.)? In what way would you say that his impulse to indulge in the folk dancing was of the same quality as his later impulse to marry a girl of the "people"?

3. If we should say that one of Hardy's themes is modern deracination (in all the multifold economic, social, and spiritual meanings of the word, and what it implies as to sterility and disintegration), how is this theme suggested in Chapter 5 with the presentation of the Stoke-D'Urbervilles, their name and the kind of estate they run, and in Chapter 9 with the description of Mrs. Stoke-D'Urberville and the duties she sets Tess? Toward the end of Chapter 5, Hardy makes a direct forecast of the fact that Alec is going to be the villain of the piece: is this a flaw in Hardy's particular storytelling art? The outright verbal forecast is immediately followed, at the beginning of Chapter 6, with an "omen"—the thorn that pricks Tess's chin: since the omen is just as directly predictive as the forecast, how would you support the statement that devices of surprise and "suspense," by which an author keeps the reader in uncertainty as to what is to come, are irrelevant and unsympathetic to Hardy's kind of art?

4. What simple popular symbolism is there in the fact that Tess returns from her first interview with Alec loaded with roses (Chapter 6)— "roses at her breast; roses in her hat; roses and strawberries in her basket to the brim"? By what means, in Chapter 11, has Hardy managed the seduction so that, while he leaves the impression that Tess is an innocent victim, he succeeds also in suggesting a certain acquiescence on her part? Why is the double impression—of innocence and guilt—necessary, in view of Tess's character? Why does it give greater

depth to the scene and to its consequences than if he had treated the seduction as a rape?

5. Make an evaluative comparison between Hardy's writing in the last page of Chapter 5, where he speaks of the mischances and catastrophes of destiny, and in the last paragraph of Chapter 10, where he describes the village women as they stagger through the moonlight with opalized haloes around their heads: noting that the latter passage, like so many others that seem purely naturalistically descriptive, is still impregnated with Hardy's governing vision (here particularly his vision of the harmonious relationship between the "folk" and nature, as contrasted with the disharmony created by uprooted individuals), which of the two passages would you say was the more integral to total structure, which the more "external"? Explain precisely the reason for the observed difference.

6. What is Joan Durbeyfield's reaction (end of Chapter 12) to Tess's situation? What essential difference of attitude is shown here between Tess and her mother, and what, in general thematic terms, is the significance of the difference? How do Joan's words at the very end of Chapter 12 signify the quality of temperament which Tess—to her own doom—has lost? What is the attitude of the fieldworkers (Chapter 14) toward Tess's predicament as an unwed mother? How does it differ from Tess's attitude toward herself (see the end of Chapter 13)? Do you find implicit in the latter passage one structural reason for Hardy's extensive use of earthy settings and nature description? What similar reason is there, with reference particularly to Tess's situation at this point in the story, for his presentation of the folk attitudes toward the accidents of procreation?

7. In Chapter 12, when Tess is returning home to Blackmoor Vale, she encounters a sign painter who is painting accusatory religious texts to which Tess reacts with horror, feeling them pointed at herself. What, generally in the book, is the relationship of evangelical dogma to the conflict that is thematically central? The sign painter happens to have been converted by Clare's father, a coincidence that is later repeated in Alec's conversion: does this particular coincidence seem to you justified in the way that, say, the coincidence bringing on the death of Prince is justified, or does it seem an arbitrary and gratuitous piece of mechanics on Hardy's part? Evaluate the episode of the baptism and burial of the child Sorrow in Chapter 14, attempting to

imagine what difference it would have made to the full projection of Hardy's vision in the book as a whole if the baby's death had been treated much less conspicuously and without this dramatic extension of pathos.

8. Albert Guerard, in his book on Hardy, points out the danger Hardy faced in giving to the section called "The Rally" the setting of a dairy: "The idyll of Talbothays, which is certainly beyond praise, especially required tact," he says,

> For the over-all intention could hardly have been a balder one: to blend Tess's recovery of calm and the resurgence of her "unexpended youth" with an environment which suggests more than any other both fertility and a changeless placidity—that of a great dairy. It is no exaggeration to say that Tess might have become, when subjected to such symbolism, a figure of bovine rather than natural simplicity.[1]

What means does Hardy use, in the last two paragraphs of Chapter 17, when we first see the great-uddered cows and the milkers at their work, to give the setting immediate dignity and perspective, so that the danger Mr. Guerard points out—the danger of a bovine bathos—is instantly transcended?

9. Consider also the description of the water birds and the cows in the sixth and fifth paragraphs from the end of Chapter 20, beginning: "At these non-human hours . . ." There is nothing in this description that is not of the quality of a simple naturalism, but how does it manage nonetheless to reflect in every detail the depth and austerity and passion of the larger vision governing the book? Again, in the last paragraph of Chapter 27—

> All the girls drew onward to the spot where the cows were grazing in the farther mead, the bevy advancing with the bold grace of wild animals—the reckless unchastened motion of women accustomed to unlimited space—in which they abandoned themselves to the air as a swimmer to the wave.

—how would you define the means by which the simplest bit of rural naturalism is given the perspective and the dignity of the larger vi-

[1] *Thomas Hardy, The Novels and Stories* (Cambridge: Harvard University Press, 1949), p. 80.

sion? In what sense does this single inconspicuous sentence express Tess's emotional situation during the summer at Talbothays?

10. In the Talbothays section, how does Hardy use the changes of the seasons for purposes of symbolic atmosphere? Select for illustration a few specific correlations between atmosphere and incident. Would you say that setting and atmosphere are described at any time at the expense of the foreground action, or would you say that action and atmosphere are integrated ("internally," *necessarily* related to each other) in such a way that they are not separable? For the sake of a further generalization as to the use of setting, attempt to make a statement of comparison, in this respect, between the world of *Pride and Prejudice* and that of *Tess of the D'Urbervilles:* why does the view of life in the one book require only the barest abstract sketch of physical setting and atmosphere, and the view of life in the other require an extremely rich and full qualification of setting?

11. Define the function and effect of Dairyman Crick's stories: what significance for the "folk" psychology and for Tess's own peculiar situation and sensitivity has the fact that these stories usually turn on a trick—the trick William Dewy played on the bull (Chapter 17), the trick the widow played on Jack Dollop (Chapter 29)—and that one of them, the one in which Jack Dollop is "churned" (Chapter 21), contains a roughly forthright and humorous attitude toward seduction? Is this particular folk material gratuitous (presented for its own sake as "documentation" of the background) and external to the foreground action, or is it internally related and integral to the foreground action? What is the attitude of the other milkmaids, Retty and Izz and Marian, toward their hopeless passion for Angel Clare (see Chapter 23)? What, in the folk psychology, gives them their resignation and dignity, even as lovelorn lasses? Do the figures of these girls seem essential to the full texture of the story, or inessential, and why?

12. Define, as precisely as you can, Angel Clare's temperament and intellectual attitudes. What naïvely bold ironic contrast does Hardy achieve by placing a person such as Angel in a setting such as Talbothays? In what way does this contrast articulate the central theme and central conflict in the book?

13. Tess makes several conscientious but ineffectual attempts, "as an honorable woman," to evade or refuse Clare's advances when she realizes that he is in love with her: in what way is the quality of the life

at Talbothays itself unsympathetic to her sense of what is "honorable"? Tess's attitudes, the rhythms of the dairy work, and the aspects of the landscapes are all bound up together: to what degree would you say that these correlations—between background and foreground, between setting and psychology—were "natural" or "symbolic" or both?

14. In Chapter 30, what frustrates Tess's attempt to tell Clare of her sinful past? What is Joan Durbeyfield's attitude toward her daughter's problem at this time, as expressed in the letter in Chapter 31, and what radical difference is there between mother and daughter on the subject? What pressure is put upon Tess by the kindness and weary fatalism of Retty and Marian and Izz, when they learn of her betrothal (see the end of Chapter 31)? And in what way is her sense of treachery (see the same passage) an inflection of the chief thematic conflict in the book?

15. Note that there begins at this time an acute accumulation of quite minor coincidences, some of them having the significance of "omens" although none of them are actually unnatural, and many of them having no direct bearing on the main action. One calling of the banns is missed, and this is "unlucky"; a man from Trantridge, who apparently knows of Tess's former life, appears at the inn where Tess and Clare are staying and Clare strikes him for a suspected insult (Chapter 33); the cock crows three times in the afternoon on the day of the marriage—suggesting either betrayal or a change in the weather (the weather does change); and so forth. How much of the "omen" significance of these matters do you think can be explained by Tess's growing acuteness of anxiety, leading her to place interpretations upon things she might not otherwise have noticed? How justifiable do you think would be the suggestion that her increasing disturbance of conscience also accounts for the resurrection in her of folk superstitiousness, such as leads her to think of the ballad of the mystic robe (Chapter 32) and to revert several times (Chapters 30 and 31) to the "ill-omen" of Clare's not dancing with her on the May-green?

16. The mislaid letter (Chapter 33) is almost always pointed to as a major instance of Hardy's overworking of coincidence. Is there actually anything unusual in the fact that a letter, pushed under a door, goes under the carpet? Does the circumstance of the mislaid letter have any really determinative influence on the plot—in any way as determinative, for instance, as the psychology of the protagonists? (If the plot were ac-

tually pivoted on this coincidence, we would certainly feel that it constituted a major weakness.) In what way does the mounting of minor coincidences spoken of in Question 15—all largely associable with Tess's own disturbed state of mind and exacerbated sensitivity, yet nevertheless creating a special atmosphere—influence our attitude toward the mislaying of the letter? So far as the "omen" of the cock's crowing is concerned, does it apply any more or any less, with as much or as little relevance, to Tess's situation as it does to Retty's attempted suicide? (The handy man Jonathan, for instance, thinks the omen referred to the suicide.) In what way do Retty's suicide and Marian's drunken binge influence Tess's confession (Chapter 34)? As seen at this point, does the tragic fatality that hangs over Tess appear to be some predetermined—supernaturally determined—doom, or a natural function of the given circumstances and the characters of the persons involved in those circumstances? If the latter appears to you to be the case, how would you justify structurally Hardy's wide use of supernaturalistic suggestion?

17. Given Clare's liberal ideas, explain his reaction to Tess's confession. Clare has renounced "dogma" in religion and in social behavior: what dogma and what intellectual inconsistency do you find in his remark, in Chapter 35, to Tess (who has just told him what her mother had said—that there had been other cases of the kind, where the husband had forgiven the wife)?

> "Don't, Tess, don't argue. Different societies, different manners. You seem like an unappreciative peasant woman, who has never been initiated into the proportions of things."

What double dogma do you find in the following:

> "I cannot help associating your decline as a family with this other fact—of your want of firmness. Decrepit families imply decrepit wills, decrepit conduct. God, why did you give me a handle for despising you more by informing me of your descent! Here was I thinking you a new-sprung child of Nature; there were you, the exhausted seed of an effete aristocracy!"

What play of irony is there between the phrases, "an *unappreciative* peasant woman," and "a new-sprung child of Nature"? What speculative connection would you make between Clare's comparative lack of virility (it is on his natural virility that Tess is banking, for her salvation, during the three days they spend together at the lodge, after her confession), his "self-mastery," and his advanced and liberal intellectualism? Does Hardy investigate this connection, or does he leave it implicit? In what sense can it be said that Clare is as much Tess's violator—and a violator of life—as Alec? In what way is Clare's rejection of Tess an inflection of the theme of deracination?

18. Evaluate the episode of Clare's sleepwalking (Chapter 37): the psychology of repression that this episode contains is sound enough; how sound or convincing do you think the handling of the episode itself? How does the episode in Chapter 40, when he offers to take Izz to Brazil with him, then retracts the offer, accent Hardy's judgment of Clare?

19. We have spoken, in Question 1, of Hardy's use of folk-tale motifs as a kind of "stitch-rhythm" in *Tess,* enriching and solidifying the simple popular contour of Tess's story with correlative traditions. How is the motif of the "Patient Griselda" illustrated in Tess's life after Clare leaves her? (Having read *Clarissa Harlowe,* you may recall the same motif there—after Richardson's peculiar manner. The ancient and perennial popularity of Patient Griselda seems to have an obvious explanation in masculine psychology.) In the episode at the end of Chapter 41, where Tess finds the wounded and dying pheasants, do you feel that naturalism is sacrificed to symbolism, or do you feel that the "natural" and the "symbolic" aspects of the episode are integrated? Compare this episode with that of the ratcatching in Chapter 48: what is the common symbolic value? which of the two episodes do you feel has the greatest natural integrity? Toward the beginning of Chapter 42, it is said: "Thus Tess walks on; a figure which is part of the landscape." In what extensive sense is Tess, in this last section of the book, and in the book as a whole, "part of the landscape"?

20. In considering the motivation of Tess's final return to Alec, what effect on her has Marian's revelation of Clare's offer to Izz Huett (Chapter 43)? What effect has the fiasco of her visit to the vicarage (Chapter 44)? Evaluate the structural integrity of her meeting with Mercy Chant and Angel's brothers, and their treatment of the boots (Chap-

ter 44), and the immediately following coincidence of her passing the barn where Alec is preaching.

21. Explain Alec's conversion, in terms of his character as we have previously known it. Does the conversion (see Chapter 45) seem to you to be psychologically accountable or not? What relation has his conversion to the theme of deracination? Explain why Alec is obsessed with the desire to convert Tess. Evaluate the episode, Chapter 46, in which Tess unwittingly destroys Alec's faith by retailing to him Angel's liberal doctrines: in view of the fact that Tess's mere natural appeal to Alec's sensuality is itself obviously sufficient to "tempt" him and to upset his perversely founded "faith," does this episode seem to you convincing, or does Hardy appear here to be manipulating irony arbitrarily and mechanically?

22. In the scene of the wheat threshing, Chapter 47, what significance is there in the association of the newfangled, scarlet-colored threshing machine, the smokestack, the heap of coals, the itinerant engineer (who is "in the agricultural world, but not of it," who speaks "in a strange northern accent . . . hardly perceiving the scenes around him, and caring for them not at all," with the strap connecting his engine to the thresher "the sole tie-line between agriculture and him"), with Alec's sudden appearance in a new converted aspect—from preacher back to flashy, flippant sensualist—and with the general theme of deracination? What symbolic correlation is there between the threshing machine (Tess is the only one who has to work on top of the throbbing, shaking mechanism) and her anguish and doom?

23. If we say that Angel Clare's exploitation and violation of Tess suggest a judgment against intellectual and moral abstractions as functions of human impotence—of inability to live—in what sense could one say that Alec simply carries out in another key (the sensual) the symbolic impotence of Angel Clare?

24. Refer back to Question 20, where we have spoken of cumulative motivation for Tess's final return to Alec. You will notice that Hardy does not describe her return to him, but leaves it for inference between Chapters 52 and 53. Evaluate, as additional motivational pressures, Alec's reiterated offers to maintain the Durbeyfield family, Tess's lack of word from Angel in reply to her desperate letters, John Durbeyfield's death and the end of the householding lease, the enforced migration of the family, and the refusal of lodgings (Chapter 52): does the

motivation seem to you adequate? Note, toward the beginning of Chapter 51, the economic backgrounds for the migration of the cottagers on Old Lady Day: what is the historical economic correlation between this background and the threshing scene in Chapter 47?

25. Mrs. Brooks is given adequate description at the beginning of Chapter 56: it might be improbable that the blood from a stabbing wound would soak through a ceiling, but Mrs. Brooks *does* see it: what is the effect, on the reader's acceptance of this improbability, of giving us an unimaginative observer like Mrs. Brooks? Is Hardy's device here successful or not? [2]

26. Do you feel that Tess's primitive act of retributive murder is sufficiently founded in her backgrounds and psychology and the pressures upon her that have been given? What support does Hardy's constant use of folk-tale motifs and folklore give the imaginative credibility of this final act? Considering the character of the universal conflict in which Tess is caught, what is the significance of her reversion to the primitive act?

27. Formulate the symbolism of the scene at Stonehenge. How does this scene reassert, in sum, the significance of the whole mass of earth symbolism and folk symbolism in the book? What is the relation of the scene to the central thematic conflict?

28. As we have seen, there are a number of occasions in this book where Hardy's ironies of incident seem arbitrary and gratuitous—rather as if he were intoxicated and reeling with the rich ironic possibilities thrown up by his subject matter. Make a definitive evaluative statement of the conviction of integrity—or lack of such conviction— carried by the book as a whole, and of the relationship of the book's richness of texture to its simplicity of "plot."

[2] Albert Guerard draws attention to Hardy's cunning in this matter, in his Introduction to the edition of *Tess* in *Harper's Modern Classics* (New York: Harper & Brothers, 1950).

The Portrait of a Lady

1. The story starts with an immediate staging of its germinal dramatic idea, the entrance of an American into Europe. Clearly, this is a dramatic idea only insofar as the American protagonist and the European setting have each a special character such as to produce drama by their confrontation. In the first scene on the lawn of the Touchett home, do you find any notes in the physical setting and atmosphere that suggest what Europe has to offer Isabel? In the first few chapters, and particularly in Chapter 6, what are the special characteristics that Isabel herself exhibits, and why is it that these suggest that her experience of Europe will be a significant spiritual adventure? Why are her fondness for her "liberty" and her "respect for her own motives" emphasized?

2. In terms of the Jamesian mythology, Henrietta Stackpole is, like Isabel, a representative American product; but, as Henrietta is presented in Chapter 10, what is the functional contrast between Isabel and Henrietta? At the end of this chapter, Isabel says,

> "I like the great country stretching away beyond the rivers and across the prairies, blooming and smiling and spreading till it stops at the green Pacific! A strong, sweet, fresh odour seems to rise from it, and Henrietta . . . has something of that odour in her garments."

And Ralph adds, "[Henrietta] does smell of the future—it almost knocks you down!" In what degree would you say that Isabel's statement here conveys a serious Jamesian idealism as to what "America" means as it is represented through the Henrietta type, and in what degree would you say that Ralph's remark conveys either cynicism as to this idealism or a necessary qualification of it? Isabel says (still at the end of Chapter 10),

> "I like people to be totally different from Henrietta—in the style of Lord Warburton's sisters for instance. So long as I look at the Misses

Molyneux they seem to me to answer a kind of ideal. Then Henrietta presents herself, and I'm straightway convinced by *her;* not so much in respect to herself as in respect to what masses behind her."

What is it that "masses behind" Henrietta? What, in the story as a whole, does the "civilized" consciousness seem to owe to what James conceives (and illustrates in Henrietta and Mrs. Touchett as well as in Isabel) as the characteristic American contribution?

3. In Chapter 3, when her aunt suggests that the old house in Albany be pulled down and a row of shops set up for rent, what does Isabel's response indicate as to what her European experience will be likely to mean to her? In this chapter it is said that Mrs. Touchett "had a face with a good deal of rather violent point," and in Chapter 31 she is said to be "as honest as a pair of compasses" (a "pointed" instrument); but then immediately we are told that

there seemed something so dreary in the condition of a person whose nature had, as it were, so little surface—offered so limited a face to the accretions of human contact . . . Her offered, her passive extent . . . was about that of a knife-edge.

Compare these descriptions of Mrs. Touchett with what is said of Madame Merle: who is a "smooth woman," "round and replete" (Chapter 18); whose "angles" had been "too much rubbed away," so that she "had become too flexible, too useful, was too ripe and too final," existing "only in her relations, direct or indirect, with her fellow mortals" (Chapter 19). Among these contrasting figures of "points," "edges," "angles," and "surfaces," "smoothness," "flexibility," as they are used to characterize Mrs. Touchett and Madame Merle, what chief significance is conveyed as to personality values and disvalues? Since Isabel's actual development is a development of an increased sense of "relations with her fellow mortals," why is a criticism of Madame Merle implied by this phrase? In Chapter 6, Isabel herself is said to have a good deal of expressive "point" in her personality, and Mr. Touchett is reminded by her of his wife in her youth; why, then, are we given to understand that Mrs. Touchett's "pointedness," her lack of "passive extent," of "surface," is pitiable?

4. You will note that though the book, on its simplest plan, is about the experience of an American girl in Europe, actually Lord Warburton

and his sisters are the only "real" Europeans among the characters, that Madame Merle and Osmond are both Americans Europeanized, and that Ralph as well is a Europeanized American. We want to be able to define the meaning of James's discriminations among these types. A good deal of Chapter 4 is given to Ralph: judging from the presentation there, what reason would you give for James's making Ralph a Europeanized American rather than a European or an American? How does he differ from "Americans" like Henrietta and Caspar Goodwood, from "Europeans" like Lord Warburton, and from other Europeanized Americans like Madame Merle and Osmond? In what way do the two following statements about Ralph project something of the values explored by the book as a whole? "With the prospect of losing them the simplest use of his faculties became an exquisite pleasure; it seemed to him the joys of contemplation had never been sounded." And: "the imagination of loving—as distinguished from that of being loved—had still a place in his reduced sketch. He had only forbidden himself the riot of expression." Yet it is said of Ralph (again in Chapter 4) that

his outward conformity to the manners that surrounded him was none the less the mask of a mind that greatly enjoyed its independence . . . which, naturally inclined to adventure and irony, indulged in a boundless liberty of appreciation.

In what way does the statement contain aspects that are both "European" and "American" (in James's European-American construct), and in what way does it define an ideal of the civilized consciousness? What, when all of these discriminations have been considered, would you say was the reason for James's making Ralph a man who is dying of a fatal disease?

5. The description of Ralph conveys strongly the idea of certain renunciations. Toward the end of Chapter 8, Lord Warburton's political radicalism is discussed, and Isabel sighs, "Ah, he couldn't be a martyr even if he wished!" In rejecting Lord Warburton, Isabel renounces certain values that Europe (as conceived here) might have for her: what has his inability to be a "martyr" to do with her rejection of him? What bearing has it on her "prejudice in favour of a free exploration of life"? In what way, later, does Osmond's personality—as it first appears to Isabel (Chapter 24)—seem to combine the values suggested

by voluntary renunciation and "free exploration of life"? Explain the paradox contained in this combination of "renunciation" and "exploration" as James uses the paradox in this book.

6. In the first few chapters, Isabel rejects the marital offers of both Lord Warburton and Caspar Goodwood: what, in terms of James's "international theme," would you give as a structural reason for his having Isabel reject both offers? What strong contrast is offered by the characterizations of the two men? What has the "ghost" (end of Chapter 5) to do with Isabel's rejection of both suitors? With what significance does the ghost reappear at the end of the book (Chapter 55)?

7. In Chapter 18, two important dramatic inceptions occur: the introduction of Madame Merle, and Ralph's conversation with his father about the inheritance. What would you say was the structural justification for bringing these two events together in a short chapter? Ralph says to his father that he would like to make Isabel rich, and that he calls people "rich" when "they're able to meet the requirements of their imagination." He adds, "Isabel has a great deal of imagination," and Mr. Touchett comments, "So have you, my son." At the end of the chapter, when Mr. Touchett says, "I don't see what good you're to get of it" (of sharing his inheritance with Isabel), Ralph answers, "I shall get just the good I said a few moments ago I wished to put into Isabel's reach—that of having met the requirements of my imagination." What place, in James's total scheme of values, does "imagination" have, and as the value of "imagination" is explored, what ambiguity lies in it? For instance, in Ralph's case, does the satisfaction of imagination ultimately imply any guilt? Or, in the following passage, from Chapter 49, when Madame Merle accuses Isabel of having prevented Pansy's marriage to Warburton, and says,

> "I had set my heart on that marriage; the idea did what so few things do—it satisfied the imagination."
> [Isabel replies] "Your imagination, yes. But not that of the persons concerned."

what difference lies between Madame Merle's and Ralph's use of almost identical phrases? The acquisitive motive is certainly dramatically important in the novel: what aspect does the acquisitive motive wear in Ralph's case (for example, in his disposal of his inheritance), in the case of Madame Merle and Osmond, and in Isabel's own case (as in her own disposal of her money)? Why does James find it necessary that Isabel should come into a fortune?

8. What does Madame Merle mean (Chapter 19) when she says to Isabel, "I was born before the French Revolution . . . *je viens de loin;* I belong to the old, old world . . ."? Explain her statement in conjunction with the fact that she does not *literally* belong to the "old world" but is an American abroad. Why has James made her a Europeanized American rather than a European? While Osmond is associated, with a good deal of symbolic inference, with certain *houses* —his house in Florence, and later his Roman palace, each of which says certain complete things about him—one thinks of Madame Merle as always going in and out of other people's houses, having no fixed place (even her apartment in Florence is pretty incidental to her way of life): why this difference? Is there any point in the fact that she was born in the Brooklyn navy yard? She tells Isabel,

"When you've lived as long as I you'll see that every human being has his shell and that you must take the shell into account. By the shell I mean the whole envelope of circumstances. There's no such thing as an isolated man or woman; we're each of us made up of some cluster of appurtenances. What shall we call our 'self'? Where does it begin? where does it end? It overflows into everything that belongs to us . . . I've a great respect for *things!*"

Are these statements in contradiction, or not in contradiction with her extreme mobility, her lack of identification with any one place and any one set of circumstances? In what way does this very important passage relate to James's particular structure of symbols or "objective correlatives" in this book—his use of images for the eye, art objects, houses, and so on? Does Isabel's total experience tend to demonstrate wisdom or unwisdom in what Madame Merle says about the "self" as an "envelope of circumstances," and in the statement that "There's no such thing as an isolated man or woman"? If you feel that Madame Merle's words do articulate much of the meaning that experience will have for Isabel, account for the fact that Madame Merle herself is shown to be morally corrupt. What irony is there in her last statement here, "I've a great respect for *things*"? In Chapter 36, in the interview between Madame Merle and Rosier, who are both "collectors," Madame Merle says she "hates" her things, and Rosier exclaims, "I love my things." In view of the fact that Rosier later sells most of his collection in the frail hope that, with the money, Osmond will approve him as a husband for Pansy, interpret the full ambiguity of human relations with *things* as these passages suggest such ambiguity.

9. In what sense is Chapter 20 a major turning point in the book? Why is the revelation of Isabel's inheritance given through Madame Merle's consciousness (or "point of view") rather than, say, through Isabel's own? When we are told that Madame Merle was "irritated with a sense of exclusion" at this point, because she had "desires that had never been satisfied," is it implied that she is merely money greedy? What subtle failure of "good taste," on Madame Merle's part, occurs in her short conversation with Mrs. Touchett here, and in what sense is a failure of "taste" in this case symptomatic of moral insensibility? What indication is there that Madame Merle places a certain interpretation on Ralph's sudden departure? Considering the fact that James (like Jane Austen) places high value on intelligence, and that this scene is an example of the functioning of Madame Merle's very keen intelligence, define the relationship of intelligence to what we have called the "civilized consciousness" (as we have used this term to summarize James's ideal values).

10. Consider the following descriptions of Osmond. He has an "extremely modelled and composed face"; his features are "overdrawn, retouched"; he is "as fine as one of the drawings in the long gallery above the bridge of the Uffizi"; and finally, "he suggested, fine gold coin as he was, no stamp nor emblem of the common mintage . . . he was the elegant complicated medal struck off for a special occasion." How, specifically, do these descriptive figures used for Osmond relate to James's general style of imagery in this book, and how do they serve to establish Osmond's personality and character? What is the irony of the image of the "fine gold coin"? Note the obliquity of the conversation between Madame Merle and Osmond in Chapter 22:

In the manner and tone of these two persons . . . was something indirect and circumspect, as if they had approached each other obliquely and addressed each other by implication . . . The point to be made is, however, that at a certain moment the element between

433

them, whatever it was, always levelled itself and left them more closely face to face than either ever was with any one else.

What contrast is offered by their manner with each other and the manners, say, of Mrs. Touchett, Henrietta, and Caspar Goodwood, and what significance would you say there was in the contrast? When Osmond asks Madame Merle about Isabel,

"Is she beautiful, clever, rich, splendid, universally intelligent and unprecedentedly virtuous? It's only on those conditions that I care to make her acquaintance . . ."

explain his emphasis on "virtue."

11. In Chapter 24, where Osmond shows Isabel his collection of treasures, she gains her first deep impression of him. As the occasion is handled, what special interpretation does it give to Madame Merle's earlier statement that a human being is an "envelope of circumstances," a "cluster of appurtenances" (see Question 8)? Consider the conversation, toward the end of Chapter 24, between Osmond and Isabel: what specifically would you point to in Osmond's remarks about himself that explains Isabel's attraction toward him? In view of those remarks, what irony is there in his suddenly taking her—a stranger—so much into his confidence?

12. In Chapter 27 the scene shifts to Rome and remains there throughout most of the rest of the book. Using, perhaps, this passage (from Chapter 28) as a point of reference,

They shook hands [Warburton and Isabel], and he left her alone in the glorious room, among the shining antique marbles. She sat down in the centre of the circle of these presences, regarding them vaguely, resting her eyes on their beautiful blank faces; listening, as it were, to their eternal silence. It is impossible, in Rome at least, to look long at a great company of Greek sculptures without feeling the effect of their noble quietude . . . The golden sunshine mingles with them, the deep stillness of the past, so vivid yet, . . . seems to throw a solemn spell upon them . . . Isabel sat there a long time, under the charm of their motionless grace, wondering to what, of their experience, their absent eyes were open, and how, to our ears, their alien lips would sound . . .

what reason would you give for James's setting the rest of the book in Rome—a reason that would indicate what it is that Rome symbolizes in Isabel's quest of "life"? Osmond comes into the room in the Capitoline gallery just as Warburton leaves: what accounts for his decision, at this moment, to ask Isabel to become his wife? At the beginning of Chapter 29, what explanation is given of Osmond's notion as to how he can "use" Isabel? If, in James's system of values, a sense of one's relationship with the past is an important element in the civilized consciousness, how, at this point, would you differentiate Osmond's sense of the past, the sense of the past as it is symbolically realized in Lord Warburton's person, and Isabel's still innocent but imaginative sense of the past?

13. Why, at the very end of Chapter 32, when she has again rejected Caspar Goodwood, does Isabel burst into tears? In Chapter 33, Ralph has a revelation (when he learns of Isabel's engagement to Osmond): he "was shocked and humiliated; his calculations had been false and the person in the world in whom he was most interested was lost." Since Ralph, among the important characters in the book, has the most civilized consciousness, what significance would you attach to the fact that he has, in a sense, become guilty (for Isabel's inevitable suffering) precisely through a generous act (giving her money)? Has Ralph's revelation of his full part in Isabel's destiny anything to do with the "ghost" (of Chapter 5)? Is there any sense in which Isabel herself becomes guilty? How would you apply, in these instances, a maxim of a modern German writer: *Schuldig müssen wir werden wenn wir waxen wollen* (guilty must we become if we would grow)?

14. In Chapter 34, Ralph tries to warn Isabel away from Osmond. He says that, whereas "one ought to feel one's relations to things—to others," this is exactly what Osmond is incapable of feeling. Explain the fact that, while Ralph's words here, about one's relations to things and to others, are a close parallel of what Madame Merle has told Isabel about the relations of "self" and "circumstances" (see Question 8), and of what was said of Madame Merle herself in Chapter 19, that "she existed only in her relations, direct or indirect, with her fellow mortals," Ralph's and Madame Merle's perceptions of what is meant by a person's relations with the world are radically different. How, in Chapter 34, does Isabel explain her decision with regard to Osmond, and how does Ralph interpret her explanation? In what way

does the conversation in this chapter prevent any later understanding between Ralph and Isabel, until his death?

15. We learn first of Isabel's relations with her husband in the scene between Rosier and Madame Merle in Chapter 36. Suggest a structural reason for James's revealing these relations indirectly, through Madame Merle and Rosier, rather than directly from Isabel's own point of view. What is Madame Merle's "game" in the scene with Rosier? At the end of this chapter the Roman dwelling of the Osmonds is described: what symbolic significance has the *house* here? In what way—complicating the relations between how many people—does the question of Pansy's destiny provide the primary motivation for most of the drama of this latter part of the book?

16. The episode, Chapter 42, in which Isabel inwardly takes stock of her situation, is singular of its kind in the book—singular, that is, technically, in comparison with James's devices of scene and narration and summary elsewhere through the novel: in what way does the technique here differ from the technique elsewhere? If you know what is called the technique of the "stream of consciousness," for instance in the work of James Joyce or of Virginia Woolf, would you say that the term "stream of consciousness" applied here, and if not, how would you differentiate the technique of this chapter from that of the "stream of consciousness"? In what sense can this be called a "recognition scene"? There is a very slight and delicate "recognition scene" of another kind, in Chapter 40, where Isabel suddenly catches sight of Madame Merle and Osmond together: what faintest of tokens are offered there for "recognition," and how much or how little does Isabel "recognize"? What has that most meager of "recognitions" in Chapter 40 to do, in terms of motivation, with Isabel's solitary probing of situation in Chapter 42? Early in her reflections in this chapter, it is said that there was no "crime" of which she could accuse Osmond; all she has to accuse him of is of hating her—"and the miserable part of it was precisely that it was not a crime, for against a crime she might have found redress." Is Osmond a "villain" in the traditional sense (a "villain" like Alec D'Urberville in *Tess,* for instance)? Why, nevertheless, *at this point,* does Isabel think of him as "evil"? How does she analyze her own motivation in marrying him? As she sees it now, what part has her money played in her motivation and her destiny? What reason does she see for Osmond's hatred of

her? It is said that "they attached such different ideas, such different associations and desires, to the same formulas": define these differences with regard to "the conventional," "the traditional," the "aristocratic life." Explain Osmond's hatred of Ralph: what, in terms of character, do Ralph and Isabel share in common, that Osmond hates? How does the depiction of Osmond, given here through Isabel's eyes, explain his education of Pansy?

17. In the mounting series of recognitions in this part of the book, an important one but one that is least stressed occurs toward the end of Chapter 43, between Isabel and Lord Warburton: "She met his eyes, and for a moment they looked straight at each other . . . she saw in his expression the gleam of an idea . . . It showed a suspicion, not a hope, but such as it was it told her what she wanted to know." What precisely is it that Isabel recognizes here, how important is the recognition in determining her actions with regard to Pansy, Warburton, and Osmond, and how has James contrived to pack so much dramatic significance into a single glance?

18. In the scene of recrimination between Osmond and Isabel in Chapter 46, what "deep game" does Osmond accuse Isabel of playing? In what sense does this scene deepen Isabel's "recognition" of her husband? With what modulations do acquisitive and utilitarian motives operate here, and how do they define moral differences between Osmond and Isabel?

19. In Chapter 49, three different recognitions take place. The first occurs between Isabel and Madame Merle: what is "recognized," by what means is the recognition contrived dramatically, and why should it affect Isabel with horror? Isabel shortly later asks herself what "gain," what "profit," Madame Merle may have looked for in Pansy's marriage to Warburton: explain Madame Merle's motivation on this point. We have observed that a sense of tradition, of the past, is important in James's depiction of the civilized consciousness: what modulation of meaning is given to the sense of the past in the passage following Isabel's conversation with Madame Merle in this chapter, when she takes her sorrow into Rome? In this part of the chapter, Isabel asks herself whether "the great historical epithet of wicked" can be applied to Madame Merle: can it? Here also, during Isabel's solitary drive, occurs the second recognition in the chapter, a recognition of Osmond's motivation: what is it? how does it extend her knowledge of Osmond

beyond that shown in her reflections in Chapter 42? and can the "great historical epithet of wicked" be applied to it? The third recognition in this chapter occurs between Madame Merle and Osmond. In the scene between them, what does Madame Merle "recognize"? In what sense does her recognition show her as having a consciousness more subtle and various than Osmond's? At the beginning of this passage, when Osmond says to her, "I should like to know what's the matter with you," she answers, "The matter is that I would give my right hand to be able to weep, and that I can't!" Consider this remark in conjunction with the passage in Chapter 54, where Isabel feels pity for Mrs. Touchett's inexpressiveness: what, would you say, in James's spiritual cosmography, is—in the most comprehensive sense—"hell," the native domain of evil and the realm of punishment? In this scene between Merle and Osmond, the latter says that he had really asked very little of Isabel—he had asked only "that she should adore me." Compare this remark with Ralph's very last words, as he is dying, to Isabel (see the last sentences of Chapter 54): what does the comparison elicit in the way of a value judgment on types of human relations? In the scene between Merle and Osmond, what is the function of the porcelain cup? So far we have been noticing largely the effect of Europe upon the American; in this scene is there any indication of a reverse or reciprocal effect?

20. Chapter 51 contains two major recognition scenes, which together constitute the major crisis or "reversal" of the book: in each case—the scene in Osmond's study, and the scene between Isabel and the Countess —what is "recognized," and in what sense do these recognitions provide what Aristotle calls the "reversal" of action? In the first scene, between Isabel and Osmond, what two instincts, what two ideals, are at clash? How has the novel, in its long growth, made it inevitable that they clash? Previously (in Chapter 42) it has been said that Isabel and Osmond "attached different ideas, different associations and desires, to the same formulas": how is this illustrated in Osmond's statement, "I think we should accept the consequences of our actions, and what I value most in life is the honour of a thing!"? Osmond is not a hypocrite; as Isabel realizes, he is "sincere"; how does his "sincerity" complicate the morality of the situation? What is the motivation of the Countess Gemini in revealing to Isabel the past circumstances between Merle and Osmond? In what the Countess reveals, Henrietta Stackpole

would see adultery as the shocking evil; is this the evil that Isabel recognizes? And if not, what is the nature of the evil that she recognizes in what the Countess tells her? Why, as you have experienced analytically the structure of a Jamesian masterpiece and of the Jamesian universe of interests and values, would you say that the "recognition scene" should inevitably be the chief focus and source of dramatic emotion in James's work?

21. In Chapter 52 are two further recognitions—one occurring before Isabel goes up to see Pansy, and one afterward. The first takes place in Madame Merle, and it is wordless but "the discovery was tremendous": what is it that Madame Merle understands at this moment, and how does James manage to pack it with significance although he does not represent it by direct discourse between the two women? The convent offers another architectural metaphor: why does the convent have such a depressing effect upon Isabel? What is the decisive effect, on Isabel, of her interview with Pansy? It is said that they embrace "like two sisters": in what sense are they "sisters"? What, at the end of this chapter, in the final scene between Isabel and Madame Merle, is "recognized," and why is this a singularly important recognition? What motivates Madame Merle in the revelation that she makes to Isabel?

22. In what sense is Isabel's last meeting with Ralph (Chapter 54) another recognition scene? What is "recognized"? How important is this recognition for the whole complex of value significance in the book? Isabel's last word to Ralph is the cry, "Oh my brother!" Interpret this cry in all its complexity of meanings acquired from the book as a whole. In Chapter 55, Isabel sees the ghost, and it is, at the immediate level of significance, her own intimation of Ralph's death; what else is the "ghost"? Suggest a reason for the fact that the final scene is a scene with Caspar Goodwood. Why is it that Caspar acts here as a catalyst of Isabel's moral destiny ("She had not known where to turn; but she knew now. There was a very straight path.")?

23. Do you find that James's mode of thought has any relevance to current social problems, problems regarding the state of civilization and the individual's relationship to the social past, the social present, and the social future?

Lord Jim

1. The first paragraph briefly presents Jim as he appears physically to others: in what way do the few details of appearance given here project the personality that we come to know later? At the end of the third paragraph, with the reference to the name the Malays gave Jim in the final phase of his career, Conrad's typical manipulation of time sequences is suggested in advance (that is, it is obvious that Conrad is going to handle his material cross-chronologically). Aside from the naturalness of the circumstance that the Malays should give their white protector the name "Lord Jim," do you find any symbolic significance in the name—that is, symbolic of Jim's meaning for the reader?

2. Conrad now turns to Jim's early background. On the training ship Jim was known to be "very smart aloft," and "his station was in the fore-top" where he "looked down" on the others and off into "the hazy splendour of the sea in the distance": do these details seem to you significant? In what way does the incident of the storm and the manning of the cutter (end of Chapter 1) set Jim's "pattern"? Does the shape of this incident (interpreted in the light of the rest of Jim's career) seem to be a shape determined by external and accidental circumstances, or does it seem to be determined by Jim's character?

3. In the second paragraph of Chapter 2, Conrad speaks of an appearance of "sinister violence of intention," "a purpose of malice," in the natural elements. Making an attempt to appraise (through your knowledge of the rest of the book) Conrad's attitude with regard to external nature—the "nature" of wind and sea—would you say that he tends to anthropomorphize nature, actually to ascribe "intention" and "purpose" to it, a "soul" of some kind? Or is his emphasis rather on the mysteries of purely human intention and purpose in a soulless, fathomless universe? Do you think that the incident given in the third paragraph of this chapter—the storm and Jim's disablement —has any significance for Jim's psychological "pattern" that we have

begun to see evolve in Chapter 1? Can you explain Jim's sudden decision to ship on the *Patna?*

4. Presumably Conrad could have given the *Patna* other kinds of cargo than eight hundred Moslems, but he chose to make the ship a "pilgrim ship," filled with "the unconscious pilgrims of an exacting belief," a ship with an "errand of faith." What reason or reasons would you suggest for Conrad's special choice of cargo for the *Patna?* In the last few paragraphs of Chapter 2, do you find any note of symbolic identification between Jim and the ship? Suggest a reason for this kind of notation: the wake which the steamer leaves is "like the phantom of a track drawn upon a lifeless sea by the phantom of a steamer." This sentence, and the one following it (the first sentence of the last paragraph of the chapter) hold echoes of Coleridge's *Rime of the Ancient Mariner* (compare: "All in a hot and copper sky, / The bloody sun, at noon, / Right up above the mast did stand, / No bigger than the moon . . . ," and so forth). Do you find any deeper resemblance between Coleridge's poem and *Lord Jim?*

5. The third chapter is magnificently constructed. Analyze the chief elements provided by this chapter, their function within the total structure of the book, and the dramatic unity of the chapter itself. Define Conrad's descriptive technique in the third paragraph of this chapter. What is the effect of the accumulation of apparently uncoordinated physical details? Suggest a reason for introducing (in the fourth paragraph) the following details, explaining their irony and their relation to the theme of the book:

> The sheet of paper portraying the depths of the sea presented a shiny surface under the light of a bull's-eye lamp lashed to a stanchion, a surface as level and smooth as the glimmering surface of the waters. Parallel rulers with a pair of dividers reposed on it; the ship's position at last noon was marked with a small black cross, and the straight pencil-line drawn firmly as far as Perim figured the course of the ship—the path of souls towards the holy place, the promise of salvation . . .

and the final line of the paragraph:

> When he happened to glance back he saw the white streak of the wake drawn as straight by the ship's keel upon the sea as the black line drawn by the pencil upon the chart.

441

Why are the three members of "the *Patna* gang" described rather fully here? Do you find any particular significance in the emphasis on the extreme obesity of the skipper and the almost skeletal leanness of the chief engineer, his crony? Since the author's choice of detail is limited only by its function in the large unity of the book, why would you say Conrad chose to present the second engineer in the particular way he does, drunk and boasting of his courage, "a shadowy figure with flexible legs"? Noting that the skipper is in pajamas and "only half awake," that the chief engineer is asleep with a bottle under his pillow, and the second drunk, would you say that these facts formed a symbolically meaningful configuration with Jim's response to their presence as described in the following?

The quality of these men did not matter; he rubbed shoulders with them, but they could not touch him; he shared the air they breathed, but he was different . . . Would the skipper go for the engineer? . . . The life was easy and he was too sure of himself—too sure of himself to . . . The line dividing his meditation from a surreptitious doze on his feet was thinner than a thread in a spider's web.

Referring back to Question 3, regarding Conrad's attitude toward external nature, and comparing the treatment of the *Patna*'s accident in the last paragraph of Chapter 3, would you say that this crisis suggested an "intention," a "purpose" in nature, a kind of daemonic soul-stuff conniving to bring about Jim's disaster, or would you define Conrad's treatment of natural forces and "accidents," in relation to men, in a different way?

6. In the fourth chapter, having to do with the formal inquiry, Jim's dilemma is presented in terms of his desperate feeling of the inadequacy of "facts" to explain what had happened: "They wanted facts. Facts! They demanded facts from him, as if facts could explain anything!" In the context of the book as a whole, would you say that Conrad's attitude toward Jim's dilemma here was an attitude *depreciating* the meaningfulness of "facts"? Consider the following:

The facts those men were so eager to know had been visible, tangible, open to the senses, occupying their place in space and time . . . they made a whole that had features, shades of expression, a complicated aspect that could be remembered by the eye, and something else besides, something invisible, a directing spirit of perdition that dwelt within, like a malevolent soul in a detestable body.

This seems to imply a magical notion of the universe, something like Hardy's; but, read in the light of the whole book, what would you say was the "something else besides, something invisible, a directing spirit . . . that dwelt within"? Could you define what is really a very great difference between Hardy's conception of life and Conrad's?

7. In Chapter 4, Marlow appears. Let us ask, at this point, a question raised by Conrad's preface to the book, when he says that the narrative form—specifically the use of Marlow as narrator—has been criticized because "no man could have been expected to talk all that time, and other men to listen so long." The question is one both of narrative *unity* and of *verisimilitude* to the way things happen in "real life." A novelist (like any other artist) is in the very first place aware that art is *not* "life," that it is an "art of illusion": which means that the novelist tries to achieve two apparently contradictory things— he tries to make the work look like "life" (give an illusion of "life"), which is the problem of *verisimilitude;* and at the same time he tries to obey laws of art, which make of the work something very different from life in that they prescribe and demand the singleness, integralness, wholeness that life, being a fluid and unselective continuum, does not apparently have—and this is the problem of *unity.* Conceiving the dual problem, with its contradictory aspects, would you find yourself in agreement with those who have criticized *Lord Jim* on the grounds that Marlow's long oral narrative disturbs the reader's sense of verisimilitude? Would you agree also that the turn, in Chapter 36, from oral narrative to the letter device spoiled the book's unity? Or would you say that the unity of *Lord Jim* exists at a level of perception that is not damaged, or at least not damaged radically and conclusively, by the change of devices of presentation (from omniscience in the first chapters, to the oral monologue, to the letter)? Would you say that the unity of the book at the thematic and moral level solved the problem of "verisimilitude" itself, by the achievement of a *moral* verisimilitude (which may be quite different from naturalistic verisimilitude)? Or would you want to suggest some other approach to the aesthetic problems raised by the book?

443

8. In Chapter 5, Marlow tries to explain his own fascinated interest in Jim, an interest which was stimulated by Jim's mere appearance even before Marlow came to know him. Interpret Marlow's interest in the case. What has Jim's outward typicality to do with it—that is, the fact that Jim "stood there for all the parentage of his kind, for men and women . . . whose very existence is based upon honest faith, and upon the instinct of courage"? What does Marlow mean, do you think, by "the one great secret of the craft" which he says could be put in a simple sentence? Why, in view of this "one great secret," in view of Jim's outward appearance of typifying that attitude, and in view of Jim's actual conduct on the *Patna,* does Marlow find "depths of horror" in Jim's case? In attempting to explain his own fascinated grubbing into the case, Marlow says,

> I see well enough now that I hoped for the impossible—for the laying of what is the most obstinate ghost of man's creation, of the uneasy doubt uprising like a mist, secret and gnawing like a worm, and more chilling than the certitude of death—the doubt of the sovereign power enthroned in a fixed standard of conduct . . . Did I believe in a miracle? And why did I desire it so ardently?

Do these statements seem to you to reflect the ambivalence of Conrad's treatment of Jim?

9. In Chapter 5, when Marlow tells his auditors that he finds scoundrels like the skipper and the chief engineer

> twice as instructive . . . [as] the usual respectable thief of commerce you fellows ask to sit at your table without any real necessity—from habit, from cowardice, from good-nature, from a hundred sneaking and inadequate reasons . . .

a kind of hierarchy of evil is suggested, going from "straight scoundrels" like the skipper up to "respectable" scoundrels with whom we complacently carry on daily business; and this suggests that lines of virtue between men cannot be drawn perfectly clearly. How does the notion of hierarchy here bear on the relativity of Jim's case? When Marlow says that in Jim there was "the least drop of something rare and accursed; the least drop!" and a few lines further says that the skipper "seemed to be swollen to an unnatural size by

444

some awful disease, by the mysterious action of an unknown poison," do these remarks suggest the reason for the characterization of the skipper by emphasis on his grotesque obesity? Do they suggest a reason for Marlow's intense curiosity about the skipper and his crony, even though these two are obviously "straight scoundrels"? In this chapter, while the skipper is characterized by his obesity, the chief engineer is characterized by his delirious visions, and particularly by his fantasy of having wonderful eyesight: only *his* eyes were good enough to see the *Patna* go down. What psychological compulsion is there behind the engineer's fantasies, for instance behind his vision of the sinking of the *Patna*? Is there, in this respect, any psychological relationship between the engineer and Jim (Jim also was convinced that the *Patna* had gone down)? What does Marlow's interview with the engineer contribute toward an understanding of Jim's case—toward "triangulating" it, so to speak, psychologically and morally?

10. In Chapter 6, Brierly acts as a "reflector" of the meaning of Jim's case. To speak of Brierly's suicide at this point puts Marlow a good way ahead of the chronological sequence of the story, and he has to loop back at the end of the chapter. What would you say was the reason for introducing Brierly's reaction to the affair right at this point, immediately following on the picture of the *Patna* gang in Chapter 5? What actual similarity exists between Brierly and Jim? Marlow's intensity of interest in Jim's case might strike one as idiosyncratic, the idiosyncrasy of a man who is perhaps overimaginative, overinclined to subtle doubts, overconcerned with intricacies of psychology; that is, we might suspect, from Marlow's own character, that Jim's case was not really so significant, so "universal," as Marlow seems to think it. How does Brierly—his known character and his shocking response to the affair—help to solidify and justify our appreciation of the importance of Jim's case? Explain why Brierly is so anxious to offer Jim a sum of money so that he will clear out and thus bring the inquiry to an end. Why does Brierly commit suicide?

11. What is the full psychological significance of the "yellow dog" episode at the end of Chapter 6? In this chapter, does Jim's attitude—his anxiety to "explain" (note that he says, "I don't want to excuse myself; but I would like to explain"), his need to differentiate himself entirely from the *Patna* gang, and at the same time his conviction that he can never return home—does his attitude indicate a sense of guilt

or a sense of blamelessness? Does it show "self-knowledge" or not? What explains his anxiety that Marlow "understand"?

12. In Chapter 8, when Marlow says that Jim is talking here, not to Marlow, but to "an invisible personality, an antagonistic and inseparable partner of his existence," what is meant? Why does the discussion seem to represent "a subtle and momentous quarrel as to the true essence of life," and why does Jim appear to Marlow to be "an individual in the forefront of his kind, as if the obscure truth involved were momentous enough to affect mankind's conception of itself"? Why would Marlow's "absolution" which Jim seems to hope for "have been no good to him"? Explain Jim's compulsive laughter at the fact that the first engineer had called him a coward (end of Chapter 8).

13. Why is the burlesque aspect emphasized in the events in Chapter 9 —the "comic business" of trying to get the boat loose, the fact that the third engineer was "fooled into killing himself," the yells to the dead man to jump, and so on? When Jim asks Marlow if he wouldn't jump off the veranda if the house should move a little under his chair, what is the significance of Marlow's saying that he made a rapid estimation of the distance to the bushes? Why is Marlow especially careful here, with regard to Jim's question, not to "be drawn into a fatal admission" about himself "which would have had some bearing on the case," and why does he speak of Jim as "dangerous"? In the light of the whole book, evaluate Jim's attitude as given in the following:

I am forced to believe [Marlow says] he had preserved through it all a strange illusion of passiveness, as though he had not acted but had suffered himself to be handled by the infernal powers who had selected him for the victim of their practical joke.

14. Referring to the beginning of Chapter 10, explain Jim's feeling that not to have seen and heard the *Patna* go down was "somehow the culminating point of an awful misfortune." The other men in the lifeboat keep repeating over and over that the *Patna* had sunk: "it seemed to cause them some sort of satisfaction." Would you differentiate or identify Jim's psychology with theirs? He says that the only thing that kept him from going over the side of the boat (com-

mitting suicide) was the hatred in the other men's voices: explain. Do we have here any suggestion of a new relative evaluation of Jim's behavior, by virtue of the fact that at this point we remember that Brierly *did* commit suicide? What interpretation would you give—in moral terms, which are the only terms that are relevant to Jim's obscure problem—to the fact that he remains standing in the boat for six hours with the tiller in his hand: is it, as Marlow says, "firmness of courage or effort of fear"?

15. Recalling the fact that the men in the boat had said they "hadn't done him any harm," Jim bursts out,

> "No harm! Good God! What more could they have done? Oh, yes, I know very well—I jumped. Certainly. I jumped! I told you I jumped; but I tell you they were too much for any man. It was their doing as plainly as if they had reached up with a boathook and pulled me over."

Interpret these statements as fully as possible in the light of the whole book. Also the following, from Chapter 11:

> [Jim says] "There was not the thickness of a sheet of paper between the right and wrong of this affair . . . Suppose I had not—I mean to say, suppose I had stuck to the ship? Well. How much longer? Say a minute—half a minute. Come. In thirty seconds, as it seemed certain then, I would have been overboard; and do you think I would not have laid hold of the first thing that came in my way—oar, life-buoy, grating—anything? Wouldn't you?"
>
> "And be saved," I interjected.
>
> "I would have meant to be," he retorted. "And that's more than I meant when I" . . . he shivered as if about to swallow some nauseous drug . . . "jumped," he pronounced with a convulsive effort . . .

What value has Marlow's comment here: "It is difficult to see a hair at midnight"? Why does Marlow feel "aggrieved" against Jim for putting the matter this way (in the passage above), as though "he had robbed our common life of the last spark of its glamour"?

16. At the end of Chapter 11, comparing himself with the men who had run away from the trial, Jim says,

"I looked it in the face. I wasn't going to run away . . . I knew the truth, and I would live it down—alone, with myself. I wasn't going to give in to such a beastly unfair thing . . . No! the proper thing was to face it out—alone for myself—wait for another chance—find out . . ."

What psychological and moral intricacies do you find in these statements?

17. In Chapter 12, Jim speaks of hearing shouts for help from the drowning: explain. Why is the story of the French lieutenant introduced just at this point, although Marlow's encounter with the lieutenant occurred long after Jim's trial? Account for these notations: the starred scar from a gunshot on the lieutenant's hand and the stiffness of the three fingers of the hand, the seam of a spear or saber wound on the side of his head. Why the emphasis on the lieutenant's disgust over the lack of wine on the *Patna?* The lieutenant is (in Chapter 13) very calm and tolerant about the fact of cowardice in men; he says, "Man is born a coward . . . It is a difficulty . . . It would be too easy otherwise." His attitude in this matter suggests to Marlow that he takes a "lenient view" of Jim's case, but Marlow is mistaken. Explain the French lieutenant's attitude: why is it that he admits that "there's nothing much to get upset about" in the discovery that one is naturally cowardly, and on the other hand feels that cowardly acts are inexcusable? Why does the lieutenant's attitude make Marlow more discouraged than ever about Jim's case?

18. About the middle of Chapter 13 Marlow returns to his conversation with Jim on the veranda of the hotel, and makes some of the most paradoxical and obscure statements in the book; he says that Jim "had reached the secret sensibility of my egoism," and,

In this transaction, to speak grossly and precisely, I was the irreproachable man; but the subtle intentions of my immorality were defeated by the moral simplicity of the criminal. No doubt he was selfish, too, but his selfishness had a higher origin, a more lofty aim. I discovered that, say what I would, he was eager to go through the ceremony of execution; and I didn't say much, for I felt that in argument his youth would tell against me heavily: he believed where I had already ceased to doubt.

What does Marlow mean? It is Jim's determination to "fight this thing down," his conviction that he is acting the only honorable part in sticking out the inquiry, that disturbs Marlow's sense of moral security and his sense of values: why? And why the special emphasis at this point on the moral complexity of Jim's case, immediately after the section on the French lieutenant?

19. How does Chester interpret (in Chapter 14) Jim's sticking out the inquiry and taking his discharge so seriously? Why the emphasis on Chester's axiom: "You must see things exactly as they are"? In what way does the cannibalistic Robinson reflect light on Chester's axiom (Robinson is one who "sees things as they are") and thus, indirectly, on Jim?

20. Chapter 15 contains a scene in which nothing happens (objectively) and nothing is said: what drama does it nevertheless impart? Marlow thinks,

> To bury him would have been such an easy kindness! It would have been so much in accordance with the wisdom of life, which consists in putting out of sight all the reminders of our folly, of our weakness, of our mortality; all that makes against our efficiency—the memory of our failures, the hints of our undying fears, the bodies of our dead friends.

What contrast does Jim's ordeal offer with this point of view? In Chapter 16, Marlow says, "Still the idea obtrudes itself that he made so much of his disgrace while it is the guilt alone that matters." What psychological possibility, and what possibility of action, do you see for Jim if it had been "the guilt alone that mattered" to him, rather than the disgrace? When the ordeal in the hotel room is over, and Jim says, "Some day one's bound to come upon some sort of chance to get it all back again," what is the implied irony? Interpret this bit of dialogue (end of Chapter 16):

> "Well. I've gone with it to the end, and I don't intend to let any man cast it in my teeth without—without—resenting it." He clenched his fist.
>
> "There's yourself." I said . . .

21. In the two incidents given in Chapter 18 (Jim's first two flights), interpret the apparently fatal inevitability with which the second engineer shows up, and the appearance also of a fatal design in the conversation that takes place at Egstrom and Blake's (particularly in Captain O'Brien's remarks): does it seem to be implied that the universe has some anthropomorphic purpose or intention, in the way the *Patna* affair always catches up with Jim; or is it implied that the reality of "facts" (such as Jim's jump) is such that one's past actions are, in a sense, identical with oneself and inescapable as oneself; or is it implied that only Jim's subjective sense of disgrace is "real" in these instances, while the "facts" of his relation to the *Patna* affair have ceased to determine men's attitudes toward him? Jim tells Marlow, "I preferred to go . . . ; this thing must be buried." Is he acting Brierly's part here—indulging in a kind of continual act of suicide? What irony is there in his notion of "burying the thing"? When, at the end of the chapter, Marlow tells Egstrom that Jim had been mate of the *Patna,* Egstrom says: "And who the devil cares about that?" What irony does this remark add to Jim's situation? At the beginning of Chapter 19, Marlow says, "What I could never make up my mind about was whether his line of conduct amounted to shirking his ghost or to facing himself out." What would you say?

22. Why, in the very complete description of Stein given in Chapter 20, is the full narrative of the ambush given—what does it show about Stein and how does it bear on Jim's case? Why is Stein made an enthusiast for butterflies, rather than, say, for snakes or birds or some other zoological form? Marlow speaks of the bronze butterfly as "an image of something . . . perishable and defying destruction": what? Is there any significance in the fact that Stein captured the butterfly while it was "sitting on a small heap of dirt"? Why is the capture of the butterfly associated with the episode of the ambush (it might have formed a separate episode in Stein's experience)? The passage in this chapter concerning the "destructive element" is a famous one and has yielded itself to various interpretations. How would you interpret it?

23. Suggest a structural reason for the fact that Chapter 21 is given over largely to Marlow's thoughts about going home and about the meaning of "home" (note that the chapter loops a long way ahead of

chronological sequence, and that hence it must—or at least ought to —have a special structural justification for being entered in this place, just at the very beginning of the Patusan episode). Does the meaning of "home" contain for Marlow "truth" or "illusion," and what bearing has the answer to this question on the general meaning of the book?

24. What significance does Jim attach to the silver ring (Chapter 23)? and why is it so important to him? Explain, from every point of view you can bring to it, Jim's enthusiasm for the Patusan project.

25. Why, in Chapter 25, is the incident of the coffee drinking with the Rajah given? At the beginning of his sojourn on Patusan, Jim made two more "jumps"—one over the stockade, and one across the creek: what new interpretation do these "jumps" give to Jim's tendency to "jump"? Is Jim's heroism on Patusan a matter of calculating thought or a matter of instinct? If instinct, how do you explain the original "jump"? Why, in Chapter 27, is the story of the brass pots given? Marlow speaks frequently of the *solitude* of Jim's achievement, its singlehandedness, the strange isolation, even the "captivity" implied by the fact that over the whole island "his word was the one truth of every passing day." Does this solitude seem to you significant of the peculiar psychology of Jim's heroism and truth (for instance, one might speculate on what his psychology would have been if he had not been so alone, with everything dependent solely on himself)? Does it minimize or enhance his achievement?

26. Marlow says, in Chapter 29, that Cornelius "has his place neither in the background nor in the foreground of the story; he is simply seen skulking on its outskirts, enigmatical and unclean . . ." (Nevertheless, Cornelius, let us remember, contributes a definite part to the final action, when he guides Brown's boat—as it were, deceit guiding violence.) This type of epithet is constantly used for Cornelius: "creeping," "slinking," "skulking." If we take Marlow's word for it, that Cornelius has a place neither in the background nor the foreground, but only on the outskirts of the story, why is he in the story? What does he contribute to its symbolic density?

27. In Chapter 28, what is the nature of the paradox that arises when Doramin speaks to Marlow of his apprehension lest the white man go away, and Marlow assures him that Jim will not leave? What is the irony of the following passage, from Chapter 32?

451

[Jim says to Marlow] "Is it not strange . . . that all these people, all these people who would do anything for me, can never be made to understand? Never! . . . It seems hard, somehow. I am stupid, am I not? What more can I want? If you ask them who is brave—who is true—who is just—who is it they would trust with their lives?—they would say, Tuan Jim. And yet they can never know the real, real truth . . ."

What is it that Jim wants, as expressed here? What does he mean by "the real, real truth"? Why, immediately after these words, is Marlow impressed by the darkening of the evening scene?

the irresistible slow work of the night settling silently on all the visible forms, effacing the outlines, burying the shapes deeper and deeper, like a steady fall of impalpable black dust.

In what way do Jim's words here signify his moral isolation?

28. Consider the following passages. Jewel appeals to Marlow:

"You all remember something! You all go back to it. What is it? You tell me! What is this thing? Is it alive?—is it dead? . . . Has it got a face and a voice—this calamity? Will he see it—will he hear it? In his sleep perhaps when he cannot see me—and then arise and go . . . Will it be a sign—a call?"

And Marlow tells her that

From all the multitudes that peopled the vastness of that unknown there would come . . . as long as he lived, neither a call nor a sign for him. Never . . . Never! Never!

In what sense are these passages a preparation for Brown? What value has Jewel's suggestion that it will be "in his sleep" that Jim will see the sign, hear the call?

29. What effectiveness, in Chapter 35, has the appearance of the sea and Marlow's elated response to it? Why is the letter from Jim's father transcribed in Chapter 36, and why in this particular place?

30. Why does Marlow feel a "profound and terrifying logic" (end of Chapter 36) in the last episode of Jim's career? Note how many inflections of the catastrophe have to do with Jim's "truth": his "truth"

in his compact with Brown, which symbolizes for him his "truth" to the ranks of men "out there"; the fact that Dain Waris wanted to direct an attack on the intruders immediately, in Jim's absence (and this would have saved the village), but was prevented from doing so because "he had not Jim's racial prestige and . . . was not the visible, tangible incarnation of unfailing truth and of unfailing victory" like Jim (so that the villagers are really destroyed by their own faith in Jim); and Cornelius' employment of Jim's "truth" as a weapon to undermine him ("If something happened," Cornelius says to Brown, "that they did not believe him any more, where would he be?"—and this is exactly what Cornelius manages to bring about). To Cornelius, Jim is "a fool" and "a child," because of his concept of honor, and to Brown he is, for the same reason, "a sham" and "a fraud" (Brown implies by these epithets that "real men" do not act like Jim). In view of this background to Jim's last acts, how much of the catastrophe— and how much, really, of Jim's whole destiny—would you say was a product of the actual degeneracy of other men, their incapacity for truth, their incapacity even to conceive a moral ideal and moral bond (except as "foolishness," "childishness," lack of "realism," failure to "see things as they are"—in Chester's words)? How does this view of Jim's career affect our previous views of him as an oversensitive and "romantic" character, a captive of his own subjectivity, evasive and in a sense dishonest before his own guilt?

31. Why does Brown "hate Jim at first sight"? Explain the psychological effect on Jim of the dialogue with Brown across the creek (Chapters 41 and 42). Brown and Jim are said to belong to "opposite poles" of a conception of life: what opposite poles? Why is Brown (Chapter 38) called "a blind accomplice of the Dark Powers"? what "dark powers"? Brown's egoism is frequently referred to. Marlow thinks, for instance, during his interview with Brown (Chapter 37), of "how much certain forms of evil are akin to madness, derived from intense egoism." In these last chapters, Jim's egoism is also frequently referred to (" 'For the last time,' she cried, menacingly, 'will you defend yourself?' 'Nothing can touch me,' he said, in a last flicker of superb egoism."—Chapter 45. And in the next to the final paragraph in the book, Marlow speaks of Jim's "exalted egoism.") If both Brown and Jim, then, are driven by "egoism," how can they represent "opposite poles" of a conception of life? Referring back to Question 35, where we suggested that there was a

real (an objective) aspect of Jim's fate that lay in the moral degeneracy of other men, what evaluative decision would you come to with regard to the question as to whether Jim was a blind victim of his own "egoism" or whether he symbolizes a heroic ideal and ethical model? His gesture toward Brown is one of benevolence: he tells Doramin (end of Chapter 42) that "They were evil-doers, but their destiny had been evil, too . . . He believed it would be best to let these whites and their followers go with their lives. It would be a small gift." Is his benevolence a form of egoism (however contradictory the terms)? Does the book as a whole seem to you to condone his benevolence?

32. Interpret these passages in Chapter 45. Tamb' Itam says, "We shall have to fight," and Jim says, "Fight! What for?" "For our lives." "I have no life," Jim answers. The girl also cries, "Will you fight?" and Jim replies, "There is nothing to fight for . . . nothing is lost." "Will you fly?" she cries again. "There is no escape," he says. And this added comment: "There was nothing to fight for. He was going to prove his power in another way and conquer the fatal destiny itself." Does Jim "conquer his destiny" or does it conquer him?

Sons and Lovers

CHAPTER 1. In the description of the Morels before their marriage, what differentiation of character types is made between them, and to what degree are class distinctions important in the characterization of personalities? How much significance seems to be attached to class difference as a factor in spoiling the marriage of the Morels? In the early marital quarrels of the pair, even before the birth of the children, what seems to be the deepest source of conflict?

Does the first incident, concerning the wakes and William's gift to his mother, seem to you to project the theme of the book? In what lies Morel's guilt toward his wife, and in what lies her guilt toward him? What leads her to supplant her husband with her children?

In the description of Morel's morning toilet on the holiday Tuesday when he is going to walk to Nottingham with his friend, how would you define the means by which the man is made vivid and sympathetic in portrayal? In view of the last scene of the chapter, where Morel is drunk and stupid and offensive, what attitude toward the Morels (in terms of sympathies and condemnations) would you say was the final effect of the chapter?

In what sense does the description of the flowers at the end of this chapter deepen and make more precise the meaning of the chapter itself and serve also to project the theme of the book as a whole?

CHAPTER 2. Explain, from the materials here, Morel's alcoholism and progressive brutalization. With the incident at the end of the chapter, when he pretends to leave home and is too craven to do so, would you say that Morel's cravenness marked the man who was incapable of life or the man who needed to and was bound to live no matter how? What significance has the fact that Morel acts his worst during the minister's call on his wife?

In the middle of the chapter, Mrs. Morel takes the baby out into the country and sits down to watch the red sunset over the Derbyshire hills. How would you interpret the gesture of Mrs. Morel as she thrusts the baby up toward the sun? You may have noted the many times in which red color in sun or moon or fire or flowers appears, either in a simple image of a natural phenomenon or in a metaphor. Trying to avoid the limitations of strict allegorical equations, would you be able to interpret any difference or similarity in the significance of red color in the passage cited above, where Mrs. Morel thrusts the baby toward the red sun, and of the blood color in the passage quoted below, which comes toward the end of this chapter, when Morel, drunk, has struck his wife on the temple with the corner of a drawer?

> He was turning drearily away, when he saw a drop of blood fall from the averted wound into the baby's fragile, glistening hair. Fascinated, he watched the heavy dark drop hang in the glistening cloud, and pull down the gossamer. Another drop fell. It would soak through to the baby's scalp. He watched, fascinated, feeling it soak in; then, finally, his manhood broke.

What other associations with redness do you find in the book? (One might note, for instance, that red flowers are associated with girls, blue flowers —scylla and forget-me-nots—with the mother.)

CHAPTER 3. Explain psychologically the bitter passion of Mr. and

Mrs. Morel over the incident of William's tearing of a playmate's collar. In what specific way, in this chapter, does William disassociate himself from his father's way of life, and how is the influence of Mrs. Morel felt in the disassociation? Is Mrs. Morel's psychology with regard to William's girls an abnormal psychology, or is it familiar and "normal"? Would you say that, on the whole, Lawrence's psychological interests in this book were unusual and perverse, or represented a fairly usual psychology of family relationships?

CHAPTER 4. What, in terms of structure, would you say justified the inclusion of the first incident in this chapter, Paul's "sacrifice" of the doll Arabella? In what way does the ash tree, which the children hear shrieking in the wind at night, serve as an expressive image? Given the increasing hatred of the children for their father, how would you justify structurally the sympathetic portrait of Morel as he makes fuses with the children and tells them the story of Taffy the pit donkey? In what way does the incident of Paul's illness further explore the alienation of son from father and his emotional identification with the mother?

How would you define the functional place in the book of Paul's experience when he goes to get his father's pay on Fridays—his shyness and his revulsion? What part is played in this experience by tensions of "class" difference, and what part is played by the innate sensitivity of the boy, or can they be differentiated? Since this novel, like the one by Joyce that we shall read next, is a "portrait of the artist as a young man," would you point to any particular factors in *Sons and Lovers,* so far, that seem to be indicative and determinative of the "artist's" development?

In attempting to define the structure of the book in its deepest determinations and meanings, we might say that the flower image at the end of the first chapter is that chapter's definitive image, and perhaps that the mother's offering of the baby to the sun in the second chapter is that chapter's definitive image. (The third chapter relies more on incident and narrative than on image.) If we should say that the dominant images of the fourth chapter are those of the ash tree and the play in the dark around the lamppost, how would you formulate the function of the latter image —the play around the lamppost, the "great scoop of darkness," the blood-red moon—in terms that are significant both for that part of the narrative which has been covered so far and for the rest of the book?

CHAPTER 5. In what sense does the flesh-pink artificial leg, that figures as the signature of Thomas Jordan's manufacturing establishment, represent an opposite pole of meaning from that of the pit flares that are associated with the father's work, and how is it connected with the values that Mrs. Morel has tried to establish in her sons' minds?

CHAPTER 6. Explain William's attraction to and difficulties about Gypsy in terms that take in as much as possible of the whole book's subject. If a person's death from erysipelas can be said to be "motivated," how would you define the "motivation" of William's death? The pattern of *Sons and Lovers* could, excessively simplified, be reduced to a rhythm of birth, sex, and death—in other words, to the three simplest and most fundamental denominations of animal and human experience. (Note that the book begins with marriage and pregnancy, that the first section—through Chapter 6—describes the emotional growth of the children in an embattled household and ends with the older son's death, that the second section is concerned with Paul's attempts to find sexual definition, and that the novel ends with death.) But though these three things—birth, sex, and death—mark the major rhythm, they are complicated by special involutions of experience, special cultural tensions, which supply the "subject" of the book. Why, in view of Lawrence's "subject," in all its complications, would you say that it was structurally right that he should introduce the apparition of death in the middle point of the book? How much and what kind of value is given to the scene of the bringing in of William's coffin by the fact that it is Morel and the miners who bear this "sorrow on their living flesh"?

CHAPTER 7. Do you find in the passage, early in the chapter, describing the swinging in the barn, that the swinging itself provides an image expressive of the emotional drives with which this chapter ("Lad-and-Girl Love") is concerned and expressive also of the kind of values with which Lawrence is fundamentally occupied? For instance, in this?

> He was swinging through the air, every bit of him swinging, like a bird that swoops for joy of movement . . . Suddenly a swallow came down from the high roof and darted out of the door.
> "I didn't know a bird was watching," he called.
> He swung negligently. She could feel him falling and lifting through the air, as if he were lying on some force.
> "Now I'll die," he said, in a detached, dreamy voice, as though he were the dying motion of the swing . . . Suddenly he put on the brake and jumped out.

457

"I've had a long turn," he said. "But it's a treat of a swing—it's a real treat of a swing!"

Miriam was amused that he took a swing so seriously and felt so warmly over it.

Or in Miriam's fear of the swing? In other Lawrence novels, the arch of a rainbow and the arches of a church form images with which are associated the aspiration toward a selfhood that is in rhythm with natural forces and yet integral in form. The image of the swinging here is also that of an arch, with dynamic movement through it. Freud suggests that children's love for swinging is an early erotic expression. How far would you say that Lawrence realizes all these associations in the very simple and natural childhood incident of the swinging in the barn?

In the scene in the middle of the chapter where Miriam shows Paul her white rosebush in the woods at night, in what way are their different responses significant of the tensions between them? Define the emotional difficulty between Paul and Miriam. How does this chapter develop the mother's striving for possessorship?

CHAPTER 8. Considering the following passage,

> And he, coming home from his walks with Miriam, was wild with torture. He walked biting his lips and with clenched fists, going at a great rate. Then, brought up against a stile, he stood for some minutes, and did not move. There was a great hollow of darkness fronting him, and on the black up-slopes patches of tiny lights, and in the lowest trough of the night, a flare of the pit. It was all weird and dreadful. Why was he torn so, almost bewildered, and unable to move? Why did his mother sit at home and suffer? He knew she suffered badly. But why should she? And why did he hate Miriam . . . at the thought of his mother? If Miriam caused his mother suffering, then he hated her—and he easily hated her. Why did she make him feel as if he were uncertain of himself, insecure, an indefinite thing, as if he had not sufficient sheathing to prevent the night and the space breaking into him?

what would you say is the symbolic value, at this point in the book, of the image of the pit flares in the night? Lawrence has often been misunderstood as advocating *loss of selfhood* by some sort of mystical abandonment of the self in the anonymous energies of nature; in what way does the last sentence in the above passage correct this misunderstanding?

What symbolic expressiveness do you find in the scene in which Paul tussles with Beatrice while the bread burns? Why the use of the dialect in the scene with Beatrice? The first signs of the mother's illness show themselves here: why here, when Paul has let the bread burn, rather than at some other place in the book? What is the particular culmination of emotional pressures that is manifested in the last scene of the chapter, between Paul and his mother and father? And why should this latter scene occur just with the first signs of the mother's illness?

CHAPTER 9. What is the expressive value of the scene at the haystack where Paul tussles with the bull terrier, and why is the use of the dialect fitting here? What suitability does the image of the stallion have, in the scene where Miriam and Clara and Paul are walking in the country? Why is Mrs. Morel not hostile to Clara, while she has been bitterly hostile to Miriam?

Lawrence said in a letter to a friend, "Primarily I am a passionately religious man, and my novels must be written from the depth of my religious experience." How would you interpret this statement in connection with the following passage, where Paul and Miriam are discussing their adolescent attitudes about religion?

> "It's not religious to be religious," he said. "I reckon a crow is religious when it sails across the sky. But it only does it because it feels itself carried to where it's going, not because it thinks it is being eternal."
> But Miriam knew that one should be religious in everything, have God, whatever God might be, present in everything.
> "I don't believe God knows such a lot about Himself," he cried. "God doesn't *know* things. He *is* things. And I'm sure He's not soulful."

CHAPTER 10. In the conversation between mother and son toward the beginning of this chapter, what significance does the mother give to class differences, and what significance does Paul give to them? What is implied when the mother tells Paul she "wants him to be happy," and he answers, "Eh, my dear—say rather you want me to live."

In the scene in which Paul calls on Clara and sees Clara and Mrs. Radford working at their lacemaking, what is the expressive value of the picture of the two women and the heaps of lace? Account for Clara's sense of humiliation.

CHAPTER 11. What, toward the beginning of this chapter, is Paul's interpretation of his strife in love, his inability to make love to Miriam? In what sense does he find his conflict typical of his generation?

Interpret in terms of Lawrence's primary values the following passage:

> [Miriam's] dark eyes, full of love, earnest and searching, made him turn away. Not for an instant would she let him forget . . . he had to torture himself into a sense of his responsibility and hers. Never any relaxing, never any leaving himself to the great hunger and impersonality of passion; he must be brought back to a deliberate, reflective creature . . . she called him back to the littleness, the personal relationship. He could not bear it. "Leave me alone—leave me alone!" he wanted to cry; but she wanted him to look at her with eyes full of love.

Directly after this passage comes the scene of the cherry picking: what is the expository significance here of the redness of the cherries, the gold and crimson of the sunset, and, in the scene in the woods that follows, of the darkness? Considering the following (from the scene in the woods with Miriam), would you say that what was expressed was the "death wish" or something else, an acknowledgment of a vital rhythm that is peculiar to Lawrence's scheme of values?

> To him now, life seemed a shadow, day a white shadow; night, and death, and stillness, and inaction, this seemed like *being*. To be alive, to be urgent and insistent—that was *not-to-be*. The highest of all was to melt out into the darkness and sway there, identified with the great Being . . . "To be rid of our individuality, which is our will, which is our effort—to live effortless, a kind of conscious sleep—that is very beautiful, I think; that is our after-life—our immortality."

Why does the affair with Miriam bring Paul only "the sense of failure and of death"? What part in this failure is played by Miriam's own idiosyncrasies of sensibility, and what part is played by Paul's attachment to his mother?

CHAPTER 12. What is the essential difference of sensibility between Clara and Miriam that makes it easier for Paul to be with Clara? What is the expressive value of the red carnations that Paul buys for Clara, and of the use of the dialect in the passage of the love-making?

How would you define the quality of realization of character and of theme in the scene between Clara, Paul, and Mrs. Radford at the end of this chapter? Mrs. Radford is one of the "common people," like Paul's father: is the portrayal sympathetic or not? What difference of attitude do you find between Mrs. Radford and Mrs. Morel?

CHAPTER 13. It is said of Baxter Dawes: "Paul and he were confirmed enemies, and yet there was between them that peculiar feeling of intimacy, as if they were secretly near to each other." And, after the hostile meeting in the bar, 'Paul had a curious sensation . . . almost of affection, mingled with violent hate, for the man." In what sense would you say that toward Baxter Dawes Paul feels the same ambivalence he feels toward his father?

How is the scene of the love-making of Paul and Clara in the field expressive of Lawrence's positive attitude toward values? Compare this scene with that in the woods where Paul and Miriam make love (Chapter 11): is there any difference in the use of the darkness symbol?

Explain the growing tension and dissatisfaction between Paul and Clara. How much weight seems to be put on the need for separate definition of self—that is, impersonality in the human relationship—and how much weight on the bond between Paul and his mother, who is now very ill? In what sense has the affair between Paul and Clara nevertheless been a gain for Clara?

How does Paul's fight with Baxter Dawes sum up the ambivalence in the relationship between the two men? Note that some of the language in this passage is very similar to that used to describe the love experiences of Paul and Clara, as, for example,

He was pure instinct, without reason or feeling . . . He was quite unconscious, only his body had taken upon itself to kill this other man . . .

and (from the love passage earlier in the chapter),

He became, not a man with a mind, but a great instinct. His hands were like creatures, living; his limbs, his body, were all life and consciousness, subject to no will of his, but living in themselves.

461

How would you interpret psychologically, in terms of the structure of meanings in the book, this similarity of description? We have suggested that Lawrence's imagery has always two main things to do: it has to express both the biological life stream below consciousness and the definitive separateness or "otherness" of natural entities. How does the fight with Baxter Dawes express both of these?

CHAPTER 14.   Account for the growing sympathy between Baxter and Paul while Baxter is in the hospital. Explain Paul's wish for his mother's death (even though her death anguishes him), his efforts to deprive her of nourishment and his giving morphia to her. Interpret the treatment of the image of Mrs. Morel in death as Paul sees her.

> She lay raised on the bed, the sweep of the sheet from the raised feet was like a clean curve of snow, so silent. She lay like a maiden asleep. With his candle in his hand, he bent over her. She lay like a girl asleep and dreaming of her love.

After the mother's death, Morel is maudlinly sentimental and justifies himself with the help of the tavern. Is Morel incapable of feeling any deep response about his wife's death? If we should say that Morel, despite his degradation, possessed the "survival instinct" which his sons do not possess, where in Lawrence's system of values would you place this "survival instinct"? Is there the same thing in Baxter Dawes? Why does Paul give Clara up to Dawes?

CHAPTER 15.   What is signified by Paul's giving Miriam the freesias and scarlet anemones at the end? Define the use of the "darkness" image in the last page, as compared with other uses of "darkness" in the book. When, at the end, Paul turns toward the lights of the town, do you feel that his action is consistent with, or inconsistent with, the emotional structure of his life as it has been represented?

A Portrait of the Artist as a Young Man

1. This novel is not without narrative design; that is, events involving external action do occur in it—like the incident of the pandying in the first chapter, and of Stephen's going to the rector's office. But these events are absorbed into the larger and more constant movement of an "internal action," the action of Stephen's mind and sensibility as he seeks the meaning of things. In what sense does this displacement of emphasis from external action to internal action reflect an extreme development of that "moral isolation" of the protagonist which we have observed with increasing frequency in the later novels we have read?

2. Let us break the first chapter down into three divisions, the first ending with Stephen in the infirmary, the second comprising the episode of the Christmas dinner, the third the episode of the pandying. Having found these divisions in your book, what means would you say Joyce used, if any, to make his transitions between them?

3. To speak now of what we have called the first division of this chapter and the motifs and associative patterns worked up in it, what structural significance do you find in the fact that the first piece of dialogue on the school grounds involves the question of Stephen's name? Why does Nasty Roche's question stir anxiety in Stephen about his father, and how is this anxiety developed in the rest of the chapter? How is the same anxiety developed in the book as a whole? One of the themes of Joyce's *Ulysses* is a son's quest for his "spiritual father": would you say that there is the same theme in the *Portrait*?

4. Referring only to this first division of the chapter, work out carefully, with close textual illustration, the patterns of association between coldness, dampness, sliminess, limpness, whiteness, water sounds in the lavatory, the color of the water in the bath, the smell of the bath, and feelings of repugnance and fear. In what sense can associative patterns of this kind be said to be, for Stephen, an approach to-

ward understanding of the world? What bearing on Stephen's quest for understanding has the bit of dialogue beginning with Wells's question as to whether Stephen kisses his mother before he goes to bed? What bearing on it has Athy's riddle? Two passages from the evening prayers are given. The first is: "O Lord, open our lips / And our mouths shall announce Thy praise . . ." Does this seem to have any connection with a major theme in the book? The second is: "Visit, we beseech Thee, O Lord, this habitation and drive away from it all the snares of the enemy . . ." With what major theme is this passage implicitly connected? In what sense could you speak of the passage about the peasants at Sunday Mass, their "smell of air and rain and turf and corduroy," as an epiphany of a kind? Referring again to this passage, with its vision of the peasant cottage at night, the darkness of the road between the trees, and the woman standing at the half door, with what kind of emotion is the vision associated, and in what way is it connected with one of the major themes of the book?

5. Referring now to the second division of the chapter, describing the Christmas dinner at home, how in general would you define its structural connection with the rest of the novel? What two dominant concerns of Irish life, as Joyce represents that life, appear in the argument between Mr. Casey and Dante? (You should look up some information about Parnell in order to understand this section.) Athletics is another dominant concern of the national life that Joyce depicts: in what way, in the first and third divisions of this chapter, is this national interest symbolized? Do you find it recurrent elsewhere in the book?

6. With reference to the transgression of the boys who are going to be flogged, three different crimes are suggested: what significance has it for Stephen's quest for understanding that the crime is problematic and may be any one of three different things? The sins suggested fall into the three medieval theological categories of (a) sin against one's neighbor (stealing the rector's cash), (b) sin against God (drinking the altar wine), and (c) sin against oneself (the smugging in the square). Which of these later becomes Stephen's own guilt obsession? In Stephen's image of the square where the smugging went on, what has the smell of stale water to do with his confused approach to understanding of what it was the boys had done?

464

7. In what way does the pandying contribute massively to Stephen's understanding of his environment?

8. All through the chapter there have been references to water, to the sound made by drops of water and by water flushed out of a basin, to the smell and the color of the water in the bath, to the slimy water of the ditch where Stephen was pushed; and at the very end of the chapter it is said that the sound of the cricket bats was "like drops of water in a fountain falling softly in the brimming bowl." Since the book as a whole is (as Cranly says of Stephen's mind in the last chapter) "supersaturated" with Roman Catholicism, would you trace any connection between the frequent water images here and the sacrament of baptism? If there is a connection, how would you explain the differences of emotional tone between the various water images?

9. In the first paragraphs of the second chapter, having to do with Uncle Charles, music, athletics, and religion are the thematic notes—as if to set up the span of those traditional Irish concerns into which Stephen is being initiated and with which he is experiencing disenchantment. The image of Uncle Charles humming his favorite songs in the outhouse is a kind of epiphany; and that of Mike Flynn rolling a cigarette is another; and that of Uncle Charles kneeling on his red handkerchief is another—what emotional comment does each of these images make on music, athletics, religion? Note that there follows almost immediately Stephen's fantasy about Mercedes in the country cottage: how would you justify this sequence structurally? And how would you justify structurally the immediately following sequence—the cowyard with its "foul green puddles"? With reference to the paragraph just preceding the first transition (the first set of asterisks), a paragraph concerning Stephen's desire "to meet in the real world the unsubstantial image which his soul so constantly beheld": how is this a prophecy of the final event in the chapter? Note that these first few pages of the chapter have recapitulated the chief elements of Irish life and presented them in an atmosphere of vague sordidness, and have set against that sordidness the dream of Mercedes: in what way does this opposition represent the conflict followed throughout the book?

10. Let us say that the next division of material in this second chapter begins with the removal to Dublin and ends with Mr. Dedalus' ac-

count of his conversation with the rector (at the point of transition to the Whitsuntide play). It is said that the change of fortune which sends the family to Dublin was "reshaping the world" for Stephen "into a vision of squalor and insincerity." How would you justify, in terms of epiphany, the "beautiful Mabel Hunter" episode, and that of the old woman making tea while "a skull appeared suspended in the gloom" of the doorway with something like a monkey under it? Note that there follows an image of Emma (after the children's party) with "cowled head" and standing on some steps with Stephen: how is this image taken up again in the final chapter of the book? What connection is there between this inconclusive episode with the girl and the fact that Stephen begins to write?

11. The next division of material is concerned with Stephen's college experience at Belvedere (ending with the row of asterisks just before the trip to Cork). In terms of the factors of Irish life that have thematic importance, how would you comment on the references to "the smiling face of a priest" and the removal of the Blessed Sacrament to make room for the dumbbells, Indian clubs, gymnasium shoes, and so forth? In what sense is the scene of the inquisition into Stephen's literary "heresy" an extension, on a more mature level, of those passages in the first chapter where Nasty Roche asks Stephen's name, Wells asks him if he kisses his mother, and Athy asks him a riddle? And would you say that the beating administered by Heron, to force a "confiteor," was a kind of duplication, on a more mature level, of the incident of the pandying in the first chapter? Does the motif of the "confiteor" appear significantly anywhere else in the book?

12. Interpret the following (the passage occurs in the context of the Whitsuntide play):

> . . . he saw a likeness between his father's mind and that of this smiling welldressed priest: and he was aware of some desecration of the priest's office or of the vestry itself whose silence was now routed by loud talk and joking and its air pungent with the smells of the gasjets and the grease.

How is this a duplication, on a more mature level, of Stephen's early apprehensive image, in the first chapter, of the stealing of the altar wine? How is it a prophecy of Stephen's final rejection of home, fatherland, and church? Is there any particular point in the fact that Mr.

Dedalus' first name is *Simon?* Interpret whatever symbolism there may be in the last lines before the asterisks, where Stephen is looking up at a morgue and smells the stable smell in the lane and says, "It is a good odour to breathe. It will calm my heart. My heart is quite calm now. I will go back."

13. The next division of material concerns the visit to Cork. Is there any significance in the fact that the father is searching the desks in the anatomy theater for his own initials when Stephen sees the word "Foetus" cut there? In what way is this detail—

It shocked him to find in the outer world a trace of what he had deemed till then a brutish and individual malady of his own mind.

an ironic commentary on the line in the first part of the chapter concerning the fantasy-Mercedes: "He wanted to meet in the real world the unsubstantial image which his soul so constantly beheld"? How does this epiphany (through the word "Foetus") comment on Mr. Dedalus' succeeding remarks?

. . . remember, whatever you do, to mix with gentlemen. When I was a young fellow I tell you I enjoyed myself. I mixed with fine decent fellows . . . we were all gentlemen, Stephen . . . That's the kind of fellows I want you to associate with, fellows of the right kidney.

Feeling cut off from reality by his "monstrous way of life," Stephen repeats to himself,

I Stephen Dedalus. I am walking beside my father whose name is Simon Dedalus. We are in Cork, Ireland. Cork is a city. Our room is in the Victoria Hotel . . .

In what way is this passage a duplication of the notes on the geography flyleaf in the first chapter, and how does it differ in significance? In what sense do the lines from Shelley that close this division repeat the geographical motif, and on what level of significance?

14. How does the disposition of the prize money prophesy Stephen's spiritual dryness at the beginning of Chapter 4? Note that Joyce uses the metaphor of a "breakwater" against a "tide."

>He had tried to build a breakwater of order and elegance against the
>sordid tide of life without him and to dam up, by rules of conduct
>and active interests and new filial relations, the powerful recurrence
>of the tide within him. Useless. From without as from within the
>water had flowed over his barriers: their tides began once more to
>jostle fiercely above the crumbled mole.

What connection would you make between this metaphor and the
water images in the first chapter and the sea in the fourth chapter?
Account for the exalted lyric handling of the encounter with the
whore.

15. How are the first two paragraphs of the third chapter an ironic commentary on the last paragraphs of the preceding chapter? In the paragraph about the equation with its widening tail of starry eyes, how
do you account for the association with the lines from Shelley about
the moon wandering companionless? The equation becomes Stephen's
own soul "going forth to experience, unfolding itself sin by sin": how
does this sequence of associations develop the geographical motif that
started with the notations on the flyleaf of the geography book? The
symbols for the Virgin that Stephen recites to himself are taken from
the Song of Solomon: why is this significant? Do you find any implicit
connection between this passage and the Mercedes-fantasy and the encounter with the whore? You will note that Stephen is most a
theologian when he is deepest in sin. He formulates questions that
(as Lynch says later of his aesthetics) have "the true scholastic stink."
One of these questions is: "If the wine change into vinegar and the
host crumble into corruption after they have been consecrated, is
Jesus Christ still present under their species as God and as man?"
In what sense could one say that Stephen's whole experience with the
church shows the wine changed into vinegar and the host crumbled
into corruption? Referring to Stephen's final talk with Cranly, in
the fifth chapter, would you say that he rejects his religion because
he does not believe in it or because its service has become corrupted?

16. Formulate, with clear textual reference, the divisions of the material
in the section of sermons: that is, with what "last thing" has each
sermon to do? What reason would you suggest for Joyce's representing these sermons in full? What development is given to what we
have called the "geographical motif" in the sermon on doomsday?
What is the specific effect of each sermon on Stephen? When he hears

the rain falling, and thinks, "The water would rise inch by inch, covering the monuments and the mountain tops . . . ," what association would you make between this image and other water images? What is the sin of Lucifer said to be, and how is this motif picked up in the last chapter during Stephen's walk with Cranly? What specific portions of the description of hell and its torments would you point to as absurdly materialistic? Does the materialism of this vision of hell seem to you to have any connection with Stephen's eventual decision not to "serve"? The priest speaks of special torments for each of the senses—eyes, nose, ears, taste, touch: in what sense is this description a development of the sense impressions recorded on the first page of the book; and how is this particular pattern (associated with the five senses) developed still further in Chapter 4, where Stephen attempts to discipline himself spiritually? Why is the portentous mountain of sand given such full and detailed description?

17. Is the vision of the field of thistles an "epiphany," and if so, in what sense? Does the scene in the chapel where Stephen makes his confession suggest any development of his childish impression, in the first chapter, of the "holy smell" of the peasants at Sunday Mass? At the end of this chapter, after taking the Mass, Stephen goes about "in a dream."

> Another life. A life of grace and virtue and happiness! It was true. It was not a dream from which he would wake.

How does this reference to the "dream" reinflect the conflict that we have seen in the book so far?

18. With reference to the beginning of Chapter 4, where Stephen is disciplining himself, interpret the associations between the following passage and Stephen's disposition of his prize money (in Chapter 2) and his vision of his sins in the form of an *equation* (in Chapter 3):

> . . . at times his sense of such immediate repercussion was so lively that he seemed to feel his soul in devotion pressing like fingers the keyboard of a great cash register and to see the amount of his purchase start forth immediately in heaven.

Why, given Stephen's sensibility, is the "august incomprehensibility" of the Trinity more easily acceptable to his mind than God's eternal love? Interpret the association between the following metaphors and the water images that we have considered: it is said that "to merge his life in the common *tide* of other lives was harder for him than any fasting or prayer," and his difficulty is given the name of spiritual *"dryness";* temptation to sin comes to him like waves of a flood

> slowly advancing towards his naked feet . . . Then, almost at the instant of that touch, almost at the verge of sinful consent, he found himself standing far away from the flood upon a dry shore, saved by a sudden act of the will or a sudden ejaculation . . .

In this latter passage, do you find a complex irony that associates itself with the sea scene at the end of this chapter?

19. In the scene between Stephen and the director, his secret musing on the pride of the priestly office is described: how is this impulse toward the priesthood inflected later when Stephen has a revelation of his vocation as artist? The director tells Stephen to pray for enlightenment to his patron saint, the first martyr, Stephen, "who is very powerful with God" (for background refer to Acts, Chapter 7): what significance do you find in Stephen's first name? How does this reference to his name develop and deepen the motif of the *name* which began with Nasty Roche's question, in the first chapter, about Stephen's name? Note that at the end of this chapter, the boys who call to Stephen on the beach give his name a Greek form (Stephanos): suggest a reason for this change in the form of the name.

20. After the discussion with the director, Stephen goes home and confronts "the faint sour stink of rotted cabbages" and other tokens of "the misrule and confusion of *his father's house.*" What reverberations of significance does the last phrase, "his father's house," raise? Is the "father" that is suggested here only Simon Dedalus—or has Stephen known other "fathers" who misrule and confuse their house?

21. On the beach, Stephen sees the reflections of the clouds drifting in the water along with the tangle of seaweed: interpret the expressive value of this mobile image of clouds and water, clouds in water. Does it have any connection with the "geographical motif" that we have followed from the beginning, and what connection has the "geographical motif" itself with Stephen's search for God (who is also a "father")? The girl's thighs are said to be "softhued as ivory": what associative

cluster is contained here? In the fifth chapter, Stephen defines "beauty" as being the "most satisfying relations of the sensible," as against "truth," which is the "most satisfying relations of the intelligible." If we should say that the synthesis at the end of the fourth chapter is a synthesis in terms of "beauty," as defined, in what sense could one say that the fifth chapter develops this synthesis as "truth"?

22. The material of the fifth chapter is derived from Stephen's experience of the university, and the word "university" has been fairly frequently present during the preceding pages. Would you say that there might be here a pun on "universe" and "city"—and if so, what would be the significance of the pun for the whole book? In what sense is there an epiphany in the appearance of the box of pawn tickets with the louse marks on it, and in the alarm clock lying on its side? How would you interpret, in terms of the water symbolism that we have remarked, the passage where Stephen's mother washes him in the bowl?

23. Stephen walks to the university "among heaps of dead language," and his language-consciousness suddenly deteriorates into the absurd rhyme about the yellow ivy whining on the wall, which leads him to the epithets "yellow ivory" and "ivory ivy" and so on; then he thinks of the name for ivory in several different languages: what associative cluster is suggested here by the word "ivory," and what reason would you suggest for the passage of the cluster into French and Spanish and Italian?

24. What is Davin's significance in the book? Why is Stephen drawn particularly to Davin although he has a serflike mind?

25. What is the expressive value of the scene with the dean of studies? There is a network here of oblique associations with the function and meaning of epiphany, in the business about lighting the fire, the reference to Epictetus' lamp, the smell of the molten tallow from the candle butts, the dean's face that is like an "unlit lamp," the quibble about funnel and tundish, the reference to the fact that the dean has in him no "fire" of apostleship, and Stephen's phrasing in the statement that he "can work at present *by the light* of one or two ideas of Aristotle and Aquinas." Attempt to define the relationship of these references to the doctrine of epiphany. (For background, you might look up the fire epiphanies in Acts II: 1–4 and IX: 3–8.)

26. How does Cranly's language ("flaming bloody sugar" etc.) differ significantly from Davin's language, and why is the character of the language of each emphasized? Why is the scene with Davin located on

the playing field and why is Davin's uncle said to be a famous athlete? Interpret this statement, which Stephen makes to Davin: "You talk to me of nationality, language, religion. I shall try to fly by those nets." Later Stephen says to Cranly that his only tools will be silence, exile, and cunning: in what sense is this triad an inversion of the triad through which Davin tries to appeal to him?

27. Analyze term by term Stephen's aesthetics. According to his definitions of the lyrical, epical, and dramatic modes, in what category would you place the *Portrait* itself? In what sense is Stephen's aesthetics also a description of the life experience that the *Portrait* records?

28. What structural justification would you suggest for the fact that, after the discussion of aesthetics, there is the episode of the writing of the villanelle?

29. Stephen is thinking of a lyric of Nash's, and thinking with desire of Emma, when a louse crawls over the nape of his neck: is this an epiphany of a kind? Interpret, with as much depth and complexity of reference as possible to associative patterns throughout the book, the following:

> How could he hit their conscience or how cast his shadow over the imaginations of their daughters, before their squires begat upon them, that they might breed a race less ignoble than their own? And under the deepened dusk he felt the thoughts and desires of the race to which he belonged flitting like bats, across the dark country lanes, under trees by the edges of streams and near the pool mottled bogs. A woman had waited in the doorway as Davin had passed by at night and, offering him a cup of milk, had all but wooed him to her bed: for Davin had the eyes of one who could be secret. But him no woman's eyes had wooed.

30. In his conversation with Cranly, is Stephen's "non serviam" actually a "non credo"? Make an evaluative judgment of Stephen's attitude toward his mother, which he illustrates by speaking of Pascal, who "if I remember rightly, would not suffer his mother to kiss him as he feared the contact of her sex," and which he illustrates also by Christ's attitude toward Mary: would you say that Joyce's portrait of Stephen here is wholly sympathetic or is ironical and objective and has "aesthetic distance"? While we have called this book an "autobiographical novel,"

would you say that Joyce wholly identified himself with Stephen, in sympathy, or not?

31. Make a brief formulation of the total conflict represented in the book, and of each of the five modes under which it appears. Does Joyce's Stephen make any approach to solution of the problems of "moral isolation" and "how to be," and if so, how?